View from the Forum

VIEW FROM THE FORUM

A HISTORY OF ROME TO A.D. 410

●

SECOND EDITION

●

MAURICE KELLY
MA, Dip. Ed. (Sydney), Ph.D. (Laval)
Honorary Fellow and formerly Associate Professor
in the Classics Department of the University of New England,
Armidale, New South Wales

Longman Cheshire

Longman Cheshire Pty Limited
Longman House
Kings Gardens
95 Coventry Street
Melbourne 3205 Australia

Offices in Sydney, Brisbane, Adelaide
and Perth. Associated companies, branches,
and representatives throughout the world.

Copyright © Maurice Kelly
First published 1969
Reprinted 1973, 1974, 1977, 1979, 1982, 1984, 1985
Second edition 1989
Reprinted 1990

Designed by Elizabeth Douglass
Set in 10/12 Plantin
Printed in Malaysia
by Chee Leong Press Sdn. Bhd., Ipoh, Perak Darul Ridzuan

National Library of Australia
Cataloguing-in-Publication data

Kelly, Maurice (Maurice Nugent).
  View from the Forum.

  2nd ed.
  Includes index.
  ISBN 0 582 66356 3.

  1. Rome—History. I. Title.

937

Contents

Acknowledgements

I SHOULD LIKE TO ACKNOWLEDGE the guidance I received from Mr A. Treloar in preparing this, and also the first edition of *View From the Forum*. I am indebted to David Rose of the Armidale College of Advanced Education for the line drawings of the battles. Finally, I am most grateful to Rina Leeuwenburg and Helen Willoughby as editors. Their help has been invaluable.

The publishers wish to thank the following: Badisches Landesmuseum, Karlsrahe, West Germany; The Trustees of the British Museum; Cabinet des Médailles, Bruxelles, Belgium; Galleria Uffizi, Florence, Italy; Pierro Genovesi; Glyptothèque de Munich, West Germany; Museo Civico Archeologico, Bologna, Italy; Museo Nazionale di Villa Gulia, Rome, Italy; Museo Nazionale, Naples, Italy; Ny Carlsberg Glypotek, Copenhagen, Denmark; Soprintendenza Archeologica delle Province di Napoli e Caserta, Italy.

The cover photograph of Bacchus riding a tiger; the centre of a Roman mosaic pavement excavated in Leadenhall Street, London (PS 144225) is reproduced by courtesy of the Trustees of the British Museum.

Illustrations

Introduction

THIS BOOK is intended to serve as a companion volume to my history of Greece, *View from Olympus*, and I have followed the same manner of presentation as in the earlier volume. I have also again consulted the revised syllabus for Ancient History for the H.S.C. in New South Wales. My basic aim, however, has been to produce a text which makes use of recent discoveries and will interest the student of today.

Archaeologists have added greatly to our knowledge of the Romans, both from the sites they have excavated and from the inscriptions they have found, which increase our written record. Both these sources help correct the traditional account, which finally goes back to the writings of the Greeks and Romans themselves.

It is, however, not simply a matter of the information we have at our disposal. With a new age come new attitudes. We are now far more critical of the philosophy of imperialism, of the right of one nation to conquer another and direct its affairs. Hence we look at Rome's imperialism with different eyes.

Yet we need not as a result simply cease to admire the Romans. They were imperialists, and they did commit many crimes in its name, yet they were also an enlightened race. Their will-ingness to extend their citizenship to other peoples in return for service was generally beneficial, and they were able to bring peace and civilisation to the Roman Empire for many centuries. This was no mean achievement.

The Romans had also a great readiness to learn. We are only now, thanks to recent work by archaeologists, becoming aware of the full debt of early Rome to the civilisation of the Etruscans, which raised them from a small agricultural community to a city state. We have always known the debt Rome owed Greece in art, literature and even law, where the Greek gift for systemisation complemented Rome's more pragmatic approach.

In my second edition I have received invaluable assistance from scholars who have written on special topics, and I have listed these books at the end of the each chapter. The scholars of Italy have played an important role, Pallottino for his excellent book on the Etruscans, and Garzetti for his book on Imperial Rome. There have also been a number of books on individual Romans. Here I have found especially useful the series *Classical Lives*, published by Croom Helm, which included the lives of such people as Pompey and Sulla and others. In this century, troubled by so many wars, generals have played

View from the Forum

a significant part and have been of great interest to modern historians. Roman generals were also very interesting men, and sometimes offer a useful comparison to the modern variety.

In the Imperial period we have modified the gloomy view held of so many of Rome's emperors, views which go back to such writers as Tacitus and Suetonius. Archaeology has played an important part in arriving at a more balanced view of these men.

Rome is interesting in that it was so much a race of soldiers, yet it did to a remarkable degree avoid turning into a mere military dictatorship.

The army did have great power, but for the greater part of Rome's history this power was controlled by the government of the day.

I hope that this history will show how an earlier age dealt with problems which confront humanity so often in the course of its development. If it does and if it throws some light on our own problems, then it may be, as the philosopher James once said, a living option, that is a knowledge which still has validity. I hope that is the case.

M.N. Kelly

Chapter 1

Prehistoric Italy

THE BULK OF Roman history falls in a later period than that of Greece. Indeed, when Rome began to be important, Alexander was already dead and his successors were engaged in those unending squabbles which they themselves never resolved. Yet, if we are to examine the origins of Rome and its people, we need to go back to the same point from which we started in the case of Greece, that is, the Bronze Age and the second millennium B.C.

The difference between them is that Greece reached its point of maturity earlier, at a time when Rome was still a small town occupied with purely local conflicts.

First, however, it may be useful to examine the geography of Italy, as geography has just as important a bearing on the history of this country as it had on the history of Greece.

The long peninsula of Italy is defended to the north, but not made inaccessible, by the Alps. It is split lengthwise by the Apennine Range. The area along the east coast is bare of harbours and narrow, but it can be reached from the countries on the other side of the Adriatic.

The plains on the western side of the Apen-

nines are more extensive and better watered than those on the east. Just south of the Alps flows the Po, the largest river of Italy. Further south lie a succession of plains, crossed by short, swift-flowing rivers and made fertile by debris from the volcanic section of the Apennines, which is dominated by Mt Vesuvius. In the west central area is the plain of Latium (Lazio). The western and southern coasts of Italy are also better provided with harbours than those on the east, although Italy cannot compare with Greece in this respect.

The situation then is a curious one. Although Italy and Greece lie side by side, because of their topography they turn their backs on one another. Unlike those of Italy, the main cities of classical Greece were on the eastern side of the country. As a result Greek culture owed much to the Middle East and always had strong links with it.

Earlier historians have not always been aware of the difference between the two countries. This is not surprising. The earliest historians of Rome were Greeks, Polybius for example. Later historians, even where they were Roman, were taught by Greeks. They naturally saw Rome through Greek eyes.

When we began to study the history of Rome in modern times, we were naturally influenced by the ancient historians from whom we derived our material. In addition, the strong cultural influence the Greeks had on the Romans led modern historians to treat the history of the two races as to some extent parallel. This is far from being true.

An interesting comparison for this distortion of viewpoint is found in the history of Australia. We came from England, and our own history has often been presented through English eyes, or by people whose thinking was heavily influenced by the English. Yet the history of our country has strong affinities to that of the USA, both because our origin was somewhat similar and because we are both Pacific powers. This affinity our anglophiliac historians wilfully ignore.

We must not fall into such an error, but when we study the history of the Romans we must examine it in its own terms.

Again, it used to be thought that both Greece and Italy received successive waves of Indo-

European invaders from the north. As we have seen, this is an over-simple view even of early Greek history, and it is much less true for Italy.

The Alps provided a strong bulwark to the north, and our evidence, both archaeological and linguistic, suggests that the movement of peoples

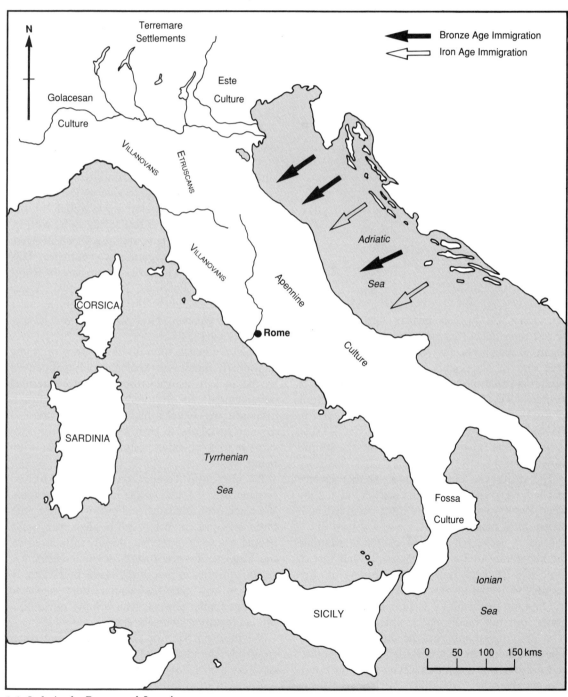

1.1 *Italy in the Bronze and Iron Ages.*

took place over a very long period, beginning as far back as the Neolithic Age, and was in the main over the Adriatic, from East to West.

These invaders do not seem to have come in sufficient numbers to overwhelm the local population, and Italy continued and indeed in many ways still continues in modern times to be a peninsula divided into local areas, each with strong characteristics of its own.

The Bronze Age: Apennine and Terramare Cultures

None the less, on the Italian peninsula there does seem to have been more uniformity of culture during the Bronze Age than afterwards. The population was also much smaller than it was in the Iron Age. There are no written records for this period, and for the most part we rely on graves for our knowledge of the people, which gives us a very incomplete picture.

The people mostly belonged to the Apennine Culture, which took its name from the mountain range that was their home and from which they spread over most of the peninsula. They were agriculturalists, used bronze but still somewhat sparingly, and buried their dead. They manufactured a pot of a special shape, the bi-conical amphora, and the peak of their development occurred in the late Bronze Age, about 1600 B.C.

About 1500 B.C. a new culture appeared in North Italy, known as the Terramare (black-earth) Culture. Our earlier historians attributed great importance to them but we now tend to see them as much more restricted in their influence. We think that they came from the north over the Alps. Unlike the Apennine people they cremated their dead and placed their ashes in urns. They fashioned a characteristic glossy black pottery, they were farmers and kept livestock, including horses. They were more advanced in their use of bronze than the Apennine people, and in areas where they lived close to the Apennine people, they taught them their more sophisticated forms of treatment.

The existence of the Terramare Culture only became known in the nineteenth century, and was associated with the piles of black earth, from

1.2 *A bronze bi-conical urn with helmet lid.*

which our name for the culture derives. The people lived in the rich but marshy area of the River Po, and at first it was thought that they built their settlements on stilts. However, later research has suggested that they raised the level of the land on which they built, and guarded against the onslaught of the Po by means of flood levees, hence the piles of black earth.

Minoan and Mycenaean influence

During this period the Minoan civilisation was at its height. The Minoans, however, confined their activities to Sicily and adjacent islands, although there is evidence that they established a trading base on the mainland, on the site where Tarentum was later built. When the Minoan civilisation collapsed the Mycenaeans followed in their path. Like the Minoans they spread their trade and their culture, but did not attempt to settle permanently in the land to which they came.

A movement of peoples: the Iron Age and the Villanovans

The twelfth century began a period of great change, for which unfortunately our evidence is very fragmentary. With the collapse of the Mycenaean civilisation in this century, the links between Italy and the Aegean were broken. Within Italy, the practice of burying the dead gave way universally to that of cremation.

It was thought earlier that there was an invasion of Italy from the north by an Iron Age people. Such a simple view is now discounted. Movement of people there certainly was, both over the Adriatic and over the Alps from the north, but this was a more drawn out and more sporadic affair than the comparable Dorian invasion of Greece. The very diversity of the peoples of the Italian peninsula bears this out. There was no mass invasion, overwhelming the original inhabitants, but rather a series of smaller incursions, with the invaders tending to fuse with the original inhabitants to produce a new society. A rapid increase in population and prosperity resulted.

The chronology of this period is as disputed as its general development, but it is likely that the ninth century saw the change to the Iron Age. This is associated with the Villanovans of central and north Italy. The origin of this people is hotly argued, and links with the equally controversial question of the Etruscans, which will be discussed in the next chapter. Some think that the Villanovans came from the north, others hold with an origin from over the Adriatic, others again see them as basically the original population of Italy, pushed west by incursions from the east.

The Villanovans take their name from a city excavated at Villanova near Bologna in north Italy. This city was at its height between 900 and 700 B.C. and developed rapidly in power and wealth, a rise based on its working of bronze and iron. The whole area has been called the 'Birmingham of early Italy'. In Bologna itself an urn was found near the Church of San Francesca containing 14 841 objects! The Villanovans cremated their dead, placing their ashes in urns. These were at first bi-conical in shape, but later took the form of a helmet or a hut. Hut urns have been found most commonly in the region of Latium, and they are valuable evidence for the type of dwelling used there at the time.

The evidence of the dialects

In the extreme south of Italy were communities that spoke a language related to Illyrian. That language was the one used on the opposite coast of the Adriatic. On the extreme north coast of Italy in an inaccessible mountain area were the Ligurians, who, as far as we can tell, were the remnants of a pre-Indo-European group.

The languages used in the remainder of Italy fell into two main divisions, both Indo-European. In the east were the Osco-Umbrian tribes. The Oscan dialect originated in the southern highland area, but it spread later to the neighbouring plains of Lucania, Apulia and Campania. North of them were the Umbrian people whose territory extended as far as the fertile valley of the Po.

The western dialects, the Latin family, were used by a group that was originally much less powerful that the Osco-Umbrian and was scattered more widely. These facts would suggest that the western group may have reached Italy first, and then been dispersed by the later arriving Osco-Umbrians. On the other hand, it is not impossible that both groups arrived in a

1.3 *Languages and dialects of Italy.*

succession of waves at different times. In any case the western dialects are found in the region of Latium, in Falerii, a town located in Etruria, in part of Sicily, and among the Veneti, a people who lived in the north-east corner of Italy, near where Venice now is.

Both groups of dialects are related to Celtic, the language spoken by the tribes situated north of Italy, but Umbrian was most strongly influenced in this way.

And what language was spoken by the Villanovans? Again, as we shall see, there is controversy. One school thinks that they spoke Etruscan, the language of the earliest known written records from the area, another asserts that they spoke some form of Indo-European.

The Este and Golacesan Cultures

About 750 B.C. the Este Culture appears in north-east Italy, known by the village where archaeological remains of the culture were discovered. They were an Iron Age people, but are also famous for their bronze work, particularly the very artistic *situlae*, or buckets they produced, filled with realistic scenes from daily life. The most famous is the Certosa *situla*. It shows two lines of soldiers on the top, fantastic animals below, with scenes from daily life between. Recently too a bronze rattle has been found, which was decorated with pictures showing the whole weaving process. These people used the Venetic language, which is related to Latin.

West of them in the Po valley and in north-west Italy was the Golacesan Culture, which was far less homogeneous, and was soon to be swallowed up by the expansion of the Etruscans.

1.4 *The Certosa Situla, found in the Certosa cemetery near Bologna, c. 500 B.C.*

Further reading

J. Reich, *Italy Before Rome*, Elsevier–
Phaidon, Oxford, 1979.
M. Pallottino, *The Etruscans*, Pelican, 1955.

Topics for essays or discussion

1 Give an account of the Indo-European invasion of Italy, comparing it with the same event in Greece.
2 What light does the language distribution in Italy throw on early migrations? Does a comparison with the distribution of dialects in Greece suggest any parallels?
3 What influence did geography have on the distribution of people in primitive Italy?

Chapter 2

The trading nations and Italy

THREE NEW RACES appeared in or near Italy in the eighth century, the Phoenicians, the Greeks and the Etruscans.

In about 750 B.C. the Phoenicians founded a number of settlements along their trade route to the Western Mediterranean.[1] Some of these lay on the southern coast of the island of Sardinia, others along the northern coast of Africa. Of these foundations Carthage in north Africa soon became the most important, eventually outgrowing in wealth and power even the Phoenician mother cities, Tyre and Sidon.

The Phoenicians were of Semitic stock. They had once carried most of the sea-borne trade in the eastern Mediterranean, where their only rivals were the Mycenaean Greeks. In about 750 B.C. they founded Carthage, and, taking Tyre as their model, built it on a peninsula. This meant that while it had access to the sea it was easy to defend from land attack. The drawback was that the position of the town prevented its growth beyond a certain size.

The Phoenicians set up trading posts on the coast of Spain, and their ships even ventured beyond the entrance to the Mediterranean, the Pillars of Hercules as they were called, and explored part of Africa.

The Phoenicians were bold sailors and keen traders. They were not, however, particularly interested in political power. Even when Carthage later dominated the other Phoenician settlements of the central and western Mediterranean, these cities were not bound to it politically, but remained as independent as when they were in Phoenicia's orbit of influence. Moreover the Phoenicians made little attempt to conquer more territory in the countries where they settled. Their towns were essentially trading posts, and many of them were, like Carthage, built on peninsulas or on an island near the coast. They took an interest in the native tribes of the area only when they themselves needed something. These needs were usually food and other supplies for their city, and mercenary soldiers to serve with their armies in the event of war.

The Phoenicians were intensely conservative in their religion. They retained the barbaric custom of sacrificing the eldest child to the gods on occasion, together with the first-fruits of the harvest. In the economic field they continued to use barter long after the introduction of coinage by the Lydians and Greeks.

From Spain and North Africa they received silver, tin and other precious metals. In exchange they normally offered perishable goods, cloth, including cloth dyed with the famous Tyrian purple, and foodstuffs of various kinds.

The Greeks arrive

The Greeks arrived at much the same time as the Phoenicians. They probably made their first trading contacts with South Italy. Indeed, their name for the land, *Italia*, was derived from a tribe that lived in the 'toe' of Italy.

When, however, they established colonies, they began much further south along the coast

---

[1]It was from the Phoenician alphabet that the Greek alphabet was derived.

than had the Phoenicians, nearer to their prospective customers. The first such town was Cumae, founded according to the Greeks' own tradition in 750 B.C. Archaeological investigation has suggested that this date is approximately correct.

Ionian Euboea supplied most of the settlers for Cumae, and the Euboeans founded a number of other colonies. These included Naxos and Zancle in Sicily, and Rhegium, which was situated on the tip of Italy just across the strait from Sicily.

Dorian foundations were also important, especially Syracuse, Tarentum, Sybaris and Croton. Actually, the southern bay of Italy came to be studded with Dorian colonies, many of which came from land-starved Achaea.

The Greeks were no more noted for their interest in political power than the Phoenicians, and no unified Greek state emerged in Italy. Only in Sicily did the threat of the nearby Carthaginians eventually produce some cohesion. As a rule the Greek colonies were separate entities, each pursuing its own interests.

Yet there was a difference between the two peoples. The Phoenicians were almost wholly concerned with trade and with the sea. Their colonies were little more than the points at which their ships touched land. The Greeks, especially the Achaeans, had also an interest in owning land for its own sake, in order to till the soil and harvest the produce. As a result, the Greek settlements gradually spread into the adjoining territory, whereas the Carthaginians kept their settlements concentrated at the port.

When the Greeks first arrived in the West, trade was dominated by the Greek city Corinth. Colonies, including Ionian Cumae, were agents, selling to the people of the area Corinthian products, which were transported from Greece in Corinthian ships.

About 600 B.C. the Corinthian monopoly of trading products began to wane. At first Ionia took Corinth's place. Then from 560 B.C. Athenian pottery became important and rapidly drove all competitors from the field. Dunbabin suggests that the Corinthians allowed this intrusion because for approximately a century (until 480 B.C) Corinthian merchant vessels conveyed the Ionian, then the Athenian pottery to the western ports.

The Etruscans appear, but from where?

The third people of importance at this time are the Etruscans and they pose a special problem. They appear in Latin literature and histories, and to a lesser extent in Greek writings. To the Romans they were early enemies and at one time conquerors of Rome, to the Greeks they were pirates who were a constant threat to their shipping. In modern times archaeologists first found their remains in the eighteenth century, and our knowledge of them has continued to increase ever since.

The central problem is the origin of the Etruscans. Herodotus claimed that they came from Lydia in Asia Minor, and he said that this was the view of the Etruscans themselves. Dionysius of Halicarnassus, writing in Roman times, asserted that they were native to Italy itself.

Modern scholarship has been deeply divided. British writers have tended to favour the view of Herodotus. They argue that Etruscan civilisation did appear suddenly in Italy in the eighth century and that inscriptions in a language similar to Etruscan have been found on the Island of Lemnos, off the coast of Asia Minor. They also observe that the earliest Etruscan settlements lie near the coast, which is what we should expect with an invading people, coming from the sea.

Italian scholars have in general suggested that the Etruscans were indigenous to Italy. The most recent exposition of the Italian view appears in the Pelican book, *The Etruscans*, by Pallottino (see 'Further reading'). Pallottino suggests that the old opposition between the view favouring an Eastern origin and that favouring a native Italian origin is simple minded, and that the truth lies in between. He points out that Herodotus in fact places the Etruscan invasion just after the fall of Troy, long before the eighth century, where scholars of the British school set the event. Indeed even the advocates of an

2.1 *A hut-urn from Vetulonia.*

in Southern Etruria the Villanovans in an earlier period had buried their dead.

Were the Etruscans Villanovans?

What then is Pallottino's view? He suggests that the Etruscans were actually the same people as the Villanovans, and that the Villanovans simply represented an earlier stratum of inhabitants of Italy. He suggests that there was a shift of population from Asia Minor to the west via Lemnos, but that this probably took place in the Bronze Age or even earlier. This view, if accepted, is consistent with Herodotus' statement about the Eastern origin of the Etruscans, but whereas the British school puts the migration later than Herodotus did, Pallottino sets it earlier. Later migrations over the Adriatic and the Alps of people speaking languages of the Indo-European family drove the Villanovans to the western side of the peninsula of Italy, just as the Anglo-Saxon invaders drove the Celts in Britain to the West, to Cornwall, Ireland, Scotland and Wales.

How then do we account for the sudden emergence of an advanced civilisation in the eighth and seventh century BC.? Pallottino suggests that it was not as sudden as all that. It was in fact the flowering of the Villanovan civilisation. The Villanovans began at this time to work their abundant supplies of bronze and iron, found especially at Populonia and the island of Elba, which lay just off the coast. No doubt migrants from Greece and Asia Minor lent them their skills to exploit their mineral wealth, but that does not presume an invasion. These same migrants, to be precise the inhabitants of the Greek settlement of Cumae, gave the Etruscans their alphabet, so that their inscriptions all begin at this time. Moreover, the inscriptions themselves are consistent with either theory. They could equally well be the work of new arrivals or the work of a native people that had just learnt the art of writing. The proponents of an Eastern origin hold that the Villanovans spoke an Indo-European language, but there is no proof of this.

All in all, Pallottino is very persuasive, but those who are interested in this question would

Eastern origin are struck by the fact that the Etruscan cities rose on sites previously occupied by the Villanovans. (Although this, they say, suggests a small-scale invasion, in which the invaders imposed themselves on the native inhabitants and took their cities.)

In favour of an Eastern origin, it is pointed out that the civilisation of the Etruscans had a very Eastern character. Against this Pallottino says that the whole of Italy was then strongly under the influence of the East as the result of trade, helped by the fact that the Greek colonists who arrived in the seventh century to settle in Italy, were strongly influenced by their neighbours in Asia Minor.

Another argument put forward is that the form of burial changed from cremation to inhumation at the time the Etruscans are supposed to have arrived, about 750 B.C. Pallottino points out, however, that this change was by no means uniform throughout Etruria. Northern Etruria actually continued to practise cremation, while do well to read H.H. Scullard, *The Etruscan Cities and Rome* (see 'Further reading'), for an up-to-date exposition of the opposing view.

It is now time to examine the Etruscans themselves, a very interesting people whatever one's views. For this task we have some accounts of them in the writings of the Greeks and Romans, and we have the archaeological remains, which are most extensive and valuable, but with the inevitable limitation of archaeological evidence. Finally we have the evidence of Etruscan inscriptions and the manuscript found with the Zagreb mummy, and some few writers in Latin. Our story runs parallel to that of the Minoans and Mycenaeans (see M. Kelly, *View from Olympus*, second edition, Longman Cheshire, 1986, pp. 7–22).

With the Mycenaeans the script was the main obstacle to understanding the inscriptions. In the case of the Etruscans the script was no problem as it was basically the Greek script, but the language was unknown. As we shall see the language can now to a large extent be read, but as was the case with the Mycenaean inscriptions the Etruscan writings, although useful, do not tell us as much as we should like.

The Etruscan cities

The Etruscan cities that became powerful earliest, and in which archaeologists have found the richest remains are those of South Etruria. First there is Tarquinii (called by the Etruscans *Tarchuna*), which city must surely have some connection with the Tarquin family that conquered Rome. Its history goes back to Villanovan times, and it had a huge cemetery area, most famous for its wall paintings. We have now sixty of them, more than half of which have only recently been discovered. Etruscan inscriptions have also been found there, some of considerable length, and some Latin inscriptions commemorating Etruscan dignitaries. The port of Tarquinii, recently excavated, is Gravisca.

Not far from Tarquinii to the north-west was Vulci (known as *Velch* to the Etruscans). It is particularly famous for its bronze work and for its Greek pottery. Our main source for Greek vases is not Greece itself but the tombs of the Etruscans, and probably more Greek vases have been found at Vulci than anywhere else. Here too is the famous François tomb, named after its discoverer. In it were found wall paintings, dated to Hellenistic times, depicting a contest between the Vipsina brothers, Macstrna, (whom we know to have been the Roman king Servius Tullius), and Tarchunies Rumach, that is Tarquin of Rome! The heyday of Vulci was the sixth century B.C.

Rome (Rumach to the Etruscans) was for a period undoubtedly an Etruscan city, but because Rome has been constantly occupied ever since, not much archaeological material has survived. We do know that in Rome the Etruscan inhabitants lived mainly in the area known as the Velabrum, through which ran the *vicus Tuscus*, the Etruscan road, and some vases bearing Etruscan inscriptions have been found there.

Not far from Rome lay Veii, a famous Etruscan city, which also flowered in the sixth century B.C. Apart from its tombs a temple has recently been unearthed, which had facilities for its worshippers to bathe in healing springs. In that city too were found fine terracotta statues made life-size for the roof of a temple. The most famous of these is the statue of Apollo. Veii had close relations with Rome during the Etruscan period of Rome, and it had a noted sculptor, Vulca, who fashioned the statue of Jupiter for Rome's great temple of Jupiter Optimus Maximus and also a statue of Hercules. Veii had an excellent drainage system, of which traces still remain. This was an art for which the Etruscans were justly famous, and Rome's great drain, the *Cloaca Maxima*, was made originally by the Etruscans.

West of Veii was Caere (known to the Etruscans as Cisra or Chaire). It is now known to the Italians as Cerveteri or 'old Caere'. This city existed from Villanovan to Roman times, but it was at its height during the seventh and sixth centuries B.C., at which time it was probably the largest and wealthiest city of Etruria. A vast quantity of bronze artifacts have been found there and it developed an important local pottery school that manufactured pottery in a style

The northern Etruscan cities

We now come to the northern towns. Many of them developed later when the Etruscan influence had spread. Being some distance from Rome, a number of them continued to flourish in later Roman times and some do so even today, in the area we still know as Tuscany or Toscana.

Vetulonia (in Etruscan Vetluna or Vatluna) lay inland, in line with the island of Elba. It was founded in the eighth century B.C. and was most prosperous till the end of the sixth century, when it suddenly collapsed and after which it never recovered. Its vast cemeteries form the basis for the Etruscan collection in Florence. It also produced notable bronze work and statues of stone.

West of Vetulonia lay Populonia, called by the Etruscans Pupluna or later Fufluna, that is, the city of Fuflum, the Etruscan equivalent of Dionysus, the god of wine. It was the only coastal city of northern Etruria and it was most important. Near it were ore-bearing mountains, from which the Etruscans extracted and smelted copper. Later iron became more important, the bulk of it coming from the nearby island of Elba. Populonia was a typical mining town and it continued to work its ores throughout Etruscan history, with the Romans taking over and continuing the work in later years. Even in modern times, because the ancient method of extraction was inefficient, the slag has been melted down to produce more of the valuable metal. These huge piles of slag stretched over a large area, and in fact in recent times archaeologists have found that they covered an old cemetery of the Etruscans, including some beautiful vaulted tombs, often in the shape of houses. One of our more recent discoveries, Populonia is most significant in showing the source of Etruscan wealth and power.

Far inland, in the centre of Italy, lay the city of Chiusi (Clevsin or Camars to the Etruscans), which developed much later. It reached its peak

2.2 Terracotta statue of Apollo from Veii, c. 500 B.C.

derived from the Greek masters. Its cemeteries are impressive, and in one area, literally, a city of the dead may be seen, with rooms carved out of the tufa (porous volcanic rock).[2]

---

[2] The word for these cemeteries is *necropolis* which was a Greek word meaning 'a city of the dead'.

2.3 *Italy c. 750 B.C.*

in the fifth century B.C. and has been occupied continually ever since, right up to modern times. As we shall see, it was the city of Lars Porsenna, the king who appears in Roman history at the beginning of the Republic. Owing to continuous occupation no very large finds have been made in the area, but it is noted for its *Canopic* urns, which have a helmet or head surmounting them.

To the east of Chiusi lies Perugia, another city with a continuous history from Etruscan to modern times. Its Etruscan period extended from the fourth to the second century B.C. Perugia has been the main centre for Etruscan studies in modern times and important discoveries have been made there. They include some fine bronzes, a number of inscriptions, some in Etruscan, some in Latin, and a gravestone that bears the longest Etruscan inscription written on stone yet found.

So much for the north. Etruscan settlements south of Rome were more sporadic, and the settlers seem mainly to have come from the sea. We now know that Pompeii was once Etruscan, but the main centre for Etruscan influence in the south was Capua, where recently was found the Capuan tile, a roof tile that bears an inscription even longer than the one on the Perugian gravestone.

The life and society of the Etruscans

When considering the life and society of the Etruscans, we must keep in mind that evidence from Greek and Roman sources, although it is most important, is very prejudiced.

Etruscan cities were grouped in a federation of twelve, which must be related to, may even perhaps have been inspired by the Greek *amphictyonies*, which were of ancient origin and had a religious character. The first such federal grouping in Etruscan history centred on Voltumna, where there was a very important temple, which we know about from Roman writers but which archaeologists have not yet discovered. As with the amphictyonies, the Etruscan federations had as their most important function an annual festivity, religious in character, which took place at the temple of Voltumna. As Etruria expanded, a second federal group of cities arose in the north, then a third in the south, which centred on Capua.

Etruscan society was aristocratic, ruled originally by a monarch, known as a *lucumon* (*lauchume* or *luchume* in Etruscan), a term also

used to designate the aristocratic families generally. As in Rome, the monarchy fell in time and was replaced by a republican constitution. In the republic there seems to have been a chief magistrate, the *zilac* or *zilath*, equated to the Roman *praetor*, who was the chief magistrate in early Rome. There was another chief magistrate, the *maru*, who seems to have had a religious function. Like the Romans the Etruscans seem to have grouped their magistrates in colleges[3], and indeed it is clear that the Romans were heavily indebted to the Etruscans for their political framework. They owed to them all the ceremonial trappings of their consul, including the *fasces*, (axe and rods), that his *lictors* or officers carried to symbolise and, very practically, to carry out the floggings and executions he ordered, the curule chair on which he sat, his toga with its purple border, and the ceremony of the triumph celebrated by a victorious general.

Etruscan religion

In religion too the Romans owed an enormous amount to the Etruscans, and in this field, unlike many others, they willingly acknowledged their debt. The Etruscans had a somewhat primitive belief in predestination, and their powerful priesthood observed lightning and other heavenly phenomena, the flight of birds, and the entrails of animals to predict the future. We have found a terracotta model of a liver marked out with the names of Etruscan gods, showing their influence in each area. These practices have obvious parallels in the Middle East.

The main books of divination of the Romans were translated from Etruscan originals. We have some idea of their character from the linen book found wrapped round the Zagreb mummy (found in Alexandria in Egypt and preserved in the Zagreb Museum), and from the Capuan tile, both of which set out ritual procedures in calendar form. Some of the main gods of the

---

[3]Thus in Rome there were two consuls, elected at the same time, with equal power, and they constituted a college. They were, as we should say, colleagues.

Romans have obvious Etruscan counterparts: Juno and the Etruscan Uni, Minerva and Menrva, Mars and Maris, although Jupiter's counterpart had a distinct name 'Tins'. What we do not know is whether the Romans took the names of their gods from the Etruscans or they both drew on a common Italian inheritance.

As in so many matters, Etruscan mythology fell strongly under the influence of the Greeks, and a number of Greek deities were borrowed by both Etruscans and Romans. Examples of this were Hercle (Herakles in Greek, Hercules in Latin), Apulu (the Etruscan equivalent of Apollo), and Aritimi (Artemis in Greek). Other Etruscan deities had distinct names but owed much of their nature to the Greeks. Amongst them were Turan, who corresponded to Aphrodite or Venus, Turms to Hermes or Mercury, and Fuflum to Dionysus or Bacchus (see p. 11).

The Etruscans usually worshipped their gods in trinities, and their temples reflected this practice. The Romans while under Etruscan rule built their famous temple on the Capitoline Hill to Jupiter, Juno and Minerva, with a triple *cella*. The central one, dedicated to Jupiter, contained a terracotta statue of the god, make by the famous Veian artist Vulca.

Archaeologists were puzzled when they excavated an Etruscan temple and found only stone foundations and terracotta figures that were set along the roof-line of the temple like gargoyles. They came to the conclusion that the body of the temple was made of wood and so perished. Recent work has found another explanation. It now appears that the body of the temple was made of blocks of tufa, a volcanic stone that proved irresistible to Italian builders of later times. They used it for their own purposes, leaving only the foundations and the gargoyles!

The private lives of the Etruscans

In their domestic life the Etruscans did not differ remarkably from the Romans. The Roman house owed some features to the Etruscans, particularly the *atrium*, the central room with the insloping roof, in which the rain water came through the *impluvium* and fell into a pond in the centre of the room.

There was one important difference. In Etruscan wall paintings women were portrayed reclining beside their husbands, to the scandal of the Romans, who deduced that they were women of loose morals. They were always willing to think the worst of the Etruscans. An intimate impression of Etruscan home life may be gained from the Tomb of the Stuccoes at Cerveteri, which portrays in relief a host of everyday objects, from kitchen knives, spits and tongs to weapons of war.

The Cerveteri wall reliefs show another aspect of Etruscan life. The Romans claimed that they took over the idea of the gladiatorial games from the Etruscans and this is confirmed in the wall reliefs, which portray gladiators, wrestlers, audiences and even chariot races. Etruscan armour and arms are also shown, and they suggest what seems probable on other evidence, that in the military sphere too the Romans imitated their one time masters, even perhaps in the layout of the Roman camp.

Etruscan attire owed much to the Greeks. The men, who in the wall paintings are portrayed as red in skin (women being white, and the fiends of the underworld blue!), often appeared in earlier times as naked to the waist, later in a tunic. In both cases they usually had a cloak slung over their shoulders. One Etruscan specialty was footwear. The pointed Etruscan shoe was finely made, and Romans often referred to Etruscan footwear to denote high quality, in modern times a place generally held by the Italian shoe for women. An interesting thought!

In art the Etruscans were past masters in portraying the human face. It seems more than likely that the Roman custom of displaying the busts of one's well-born ancestors along the walls of the atrium came from the Etruscans. Whereas the Greek artists were primarily concerned with delineating the human form and until Hellenistic times paid less regard to the individual expression of their subject, the Etruscans conveyed human character in stone with great fidelity and the Roman skill in portraiture owed them a debt.

2.4 *The Necropolis in Cerveteri, Tumuli, each built by an aristocratic Tuscan family to shelter its members in death.*

What the Etruscans wrote

Recently we have managed to a large degree to read the writing of the Etruscans. Since they wrote using Greek characters there was not the original problem that the linear B[4] texts presented. They did use some characters of their own, but we are fairly sure of their meaning also. The bilingual texts, such as those found at Pyrgi, written in Etruscan and Phoenician, helped, as did some very long inscriptions that have recently come to light. In addition a new technique has been developed, which has proved invaluable. In many cases we know the subject matter of an Etruscan text, whether it is a funerary notice (very commonly), a religious rite and the like. It has been observed that the texts tend to follow a similar pattern to Roman inscriptions of a like nature, so by comparing the two it is often possible to work out the significance of the Etruscan inscription.

As was found in the linear B inscriptions, we are still not sure of the meaning or the precise meaning of a number of words, especially religious terms and those indicating such things as social rank. This is worse in Etruscan because, whereas linear B is Greek and from this fact we can make some guess at a number of words, Etruscan has no related languages, except for the few Lemnian inscriptions, so that when a word is not known we have very little chance of interpreting it.

Like the linear B inscriptions those of the Etruscans are useful but at the same time disappointing. They give us no literature, only mundane information, such as funeral details, family trees and religious rites. This is a pity, for we are tantalised, as with the Mycenaeans, by a vivid pictorial representation of a most interesting race. Still we do learn some things.

We find that the Etruscans used a personal name and a surname, a practice they passed on to the Romans who gave it to the Western world. Everywhere else at that time the practice was to

---

[4]This was the method of writing used by the Mycenaeans, described in *View from Olympus*, Chapter 2.

2.5 *Two of the three inscribed sheets of gold-leaf found at Pyrgi: that on the left is in Phoenician, that on the right in Etruscan, c. 500 B.C.*

use the personal name followed by that of the father. In general, as with us, the name had three components, the personal name followed by the clan name and one denoting a subdivision of the clan. It is also interesting to see a number of the actual names passed on to the Romans, as in the first names Marcus (Etruscan Marce), Aulus (Aule), and surname, Fabius (Fapi), Petronius (Petruni). Needless to say this was no coincidence. There was a significant Etruscan population in Rome and a number of famous Romans are said to have been of Etruscan descent, including Sulla and Maecenas. Actually Roman surnames ending in –a were thought to denote an Etruscan origin, as in the case of Sulla.

The Etruscans did not differentiate between *U* and *O*, hence *Rumach* for Rome and *Petruni* for Petronius. They wrote from right to left, or sometimes, in early years, from left and right alternately, like the early Greeks. This is as a man ploughs, hence the term for it, *boustrophedon*, which means precisely that.

The Capua tile, which was recently discovered, and the linen book found wrapped around the Zagreb mummy both dealt with religious ritual. It is now suspected that such linen books were not uncommon, and that they were often rolled up and put under the head of the dead, but naturally, except in the chance affair of the Zagreb mummy, they normally perished, going to dust with the body they accompanied.

We are not even sure if the Etruscans had a written literature. It could have been an oral tradition, like the epics of Homer. There is no suggestion that there was ever an Etruscan epic. However they were thought to have been interested in drama, and the Latin word for an actor, *persona*, came from the Etruscan word, *phersu*, denoting a masked figure. They also liked music and dance and the Romans claimed that the trumpet was an Etruscan invention, as was the double pipe.

The history of the Etruscans

Of the actual history ot the Etruscans we know pitifully little, and what we do know comes mostly from the Greeks and Romans. We know from the Hymns of Homer and from the Romans that the ships of the Etruscans were widely feared as pirates, but then most ships of that time were piratical when the opportunity offered. They flourished and had command of the sea in the eighth and seventh centuries. It is worth noting that the sea to the west of Italy is called after them the Tyrrhenian Sea, and that the Adriatic takes its name from the Etruscan city Adria.

When the Greeks arrived to colonise south Italy and Sicily they came into conflict with the Etruscans. At first the Etruscans managed to keep them from northern Italy and from the western Mediterranean.

The Etruscans seem to have had more amicable relations with the Phoenicians, indeed they combined with them to keep the Greeks at bay. This is strikingly confirmed by the discovery at Pyrgi of the bi-lingual temple dedication, in Etruscan and Phoenician. In these inscriptions Thefarie Velianas, whom the Phoenician inscription called the 'king of Cisra' (Caere or Cerveteri, as we know it) dedicated the temple to the goddess Uni (whom the Phoenician inscription identified with their goddess Aštarta). This inscription has been dated at the end of the fifth century B.C., and it is thought that the ruler in question was a puppet ruler set up by the Carthaginians to hold this Etruscan town. The whole century was marked by close cooperation between the Carthaginians and the Etruscans.

Polybius notes that there was a treaty made between Rome and Carthage at the end of the sixth century, when Rome was Etruscan, and Aristotle mentions treaties made between the Etruscans and the Carthaginians.

In 540 B.C. the two countries combined to attack the Greek colonists from Phocaea off Sardinia, a battle often wrongly called the battle of Alalia.[5] The Greeks were defeated and went to settle in south Italy, but after that date Etruscan sea power diminished.

There were a number of other engagements where Etruscan met Greek. A Latin inscription from the Imperial period mentions an attack made on Sicily by an Etruscan commander Spurinna of Tarquinii, in which he won a gold crown for his victory. The exact date of this event is unknown, but it probably does belong to the sixth century B.C.

In the fifth century all Italy suffered an economic downturn and Etruscan sea power and general influence declined. This was hastened by the rising power of Syracuse, whose forces beat the Etruscans at Cumae in 474 B.C. just after they defeated the Carthaginians at Himera.

Date table

B.C.

*c.*750   Phoenician settlement in the west: first Greek settlement at Cumae: Etruscans first heard of in northern Italy.

600   Corinthian monopoly yields to Ionians then to Athenians; Etruscans spread to Po Valley and Campania; Phocaeans found Massilia (now Marseille).

540   Etruscan and Carthaginian force defeat Greeks by sea off Sardinia.

474   Syracusans defeat Etruscans in Battle of Cumae.

Select quotations

1 Herodotus 1, 94:
In the rule of Atys, son of Manes, there was a great famine throughout the whole of Lydia . . . (this lasted eighteen years). When the trouble did not abate, but grew even more oppressive, their king divided the Lydians into two parts, drawing lots, one to remain, one to leave the country. He stayed with those who remained, while over those who left he put his son Tyrsenos. The latter passed through many peoples and reached the Ombrikoi (Umbrians) where they founded cities and still live. Instead of Lydians they gave themselves the name of Tyrsenoi after the king's son who brought them there.

2 Dionysius of Halicarnassus 1, 29 and 30:
To me all those people seem to be wrong who believe that the Tyrrhenian and Pelasgian races are one and the same. . . . Rome itself many historians took to be a Tyrrhenian city. . . . I believe the Tyrrhenians are different from the Pelasgians. Nor do I think the Tyrrhenians were Lydian colonists. They do not speak the same languages as they do, nor can one say that even if they do not use a language like their mother-country, they retain other souvenirs of their origin. They do not worship the same gods as the Lydians, nor do they observe similar laws or customs. . . . Those people are probably nearest to the truth who say that they did not arrive from anywhere else but were indigenous to the land, since they are found to be a very ancient race whose tongue and way of life resembles that of no one else.

---

[5]Alalia was a town on the east coast of Corsica, also inhabited by Phocaeans.

3 Scullard, *The Etruscan Cities and Rome:*
As praetor (Spurinna) led an army against
Caere. He took another to Sicily, as the first
Etruscan to lead an army across the sea, and
was decorated with an eagle and a gold crown
for his victory.

4 *Corpus Inscriptionum Italicarum II, Supplement*
III, 322:
Alethnas Arnth Larisal zilath Tarchnalthi amce.
(Which means: Arnth Alethna, son of Laris
was zilath in Tarquinia).

5 Zagreb Mummy, column 8, line 3 ff.
The month of September, the twenty-sixth day
(?) all the offerings to the god Neptune shall be
declared and should be made.

(Both these inscriptions are taken from Pallottino, *The Etruscans*, pp. 218, 224)

Further reading

M. Pallottino, *The Etruscans*, Pelican, 1978.
H.H. Scullard, *The Etruscan Cities and Rome*,
    Thames and Hudson, 1967.
D. Harden, *The Phoenicians*, London, Thames
    and Hudson, 1962.
B.H. Warmington, *Carthage*, Pelican.
J. Boardman, *The Greeks Overseas*, Pelican,
    1973.
A.G. Woodhead, *The Greeks in the West*,
    London, Thames and Hudson, 1962.

Chapter 3

The foundation of Rome and the Regal Period

GREAT CITIES often have humble beginnings. Like Attica in Greece, Latium in Italy was at first a backwater. None the less much was written by the Romans and the Greeks about the early years of Rome. This is not surprising. When cities and countries achieve greatness people become interested in their origins, often altering the facts in the process. The historians of Rome were no exception.

The historians of Rome

It was during the rule of the emperor Augustus (27 B.C. to A.D. 14), the Golden Age of Latin literature, that writers, encouraged by the emperor, wrote the history of Rome from its beginnings to their own time. The most famous is of course Livy, and his work will be vital for our study of the whole history of the Roman Republic. It should be kept in mind when using Livy that he held no public office and took no part in the politics of his time. He was wholly a writer and scholar. Although this removes him to some degree from the partisanship of the

political arena, it also means that he is not very familiar with the way Roman politics worked, and this, like the Greek historian Herodotus' ignorance of battle strategy, will need to be kept in mind.

A Greek writer, Dionysius of Halicarnassus, came to Rome in Livy's time. He wrote a history of early Rome, intended to serve as an introduction to the history of another Greek, Polybius, who wrote of Rome during the time of the Punic Wars. Dionysius is a somewhat pompous writer, far less attractive to read than Livy, but he was an enthusiastic scholar, and he can be useful, like Plutarch, where he preserves material that we do not otherwise possess (including, as we should expect, Greek writers), and that was not used by Livy.

Yet this was not the first age to be interested in Rome's past. During the Punic Wars, after the Romans' disastrous defeat in the battle of Cannae (216 B.C.), one of the city's rising young men, Fabius Pictor, was sent to Delphi to consult the god Apollo in Rome's hour of need. While in Greece Fabius found that Hannibal had encouraged Greek historians, particularly in Sicily, to write histories favourable to Carthage and hostile to Rome.

On his return to Rome Fabius Pictor set himself to redress the balance, and wrote in Greek a history of Rome from its origins to his time. His work has not survived except in fragments, but it was basic to the works of both Livy and Dionysius of Halicarnassus. Fabius performed an invaluable task, but at the same time created immense problems. His work was wholly patriotic, and he portrayed Rome as foreshadowing its future greatness from the very first. He accepted without question many heroic tales that had no foundation in fact, and on occasion made some up himself.

For these he drew in considerable part on the stories preserved by the aristocratic clans, of which the Fabian clan was a prominent member. His clan loyalty had one unfortunate effect. The Fabian clan had an age-old enmity towards the old aristocratic clan of the Claudians, and Fabius had no compunction about blackening the name of every Claudius who appears in his history. As a result of these factors there is an immense amount of the history of early Rome that must either be discarded, or examined without the bias of the original, if we are to arrive at the truth. This is not always an easy task.

From the period of the Punic wars comes also the *Origines* of Cato, unfortunately also only surviving in fragments. Cato, too, wrote of Rome from its beginning to his time, and as he was a leading public figure his views would have been very useful. From these fragments we do glean some information that has not otherwise been preserved.

A new light is thrown by archaeology

In recent years important work has been done on the early history of Rome, of which the most significant has been Gjerstad's archaeological research. A very full account of his work has been published, but a briefer exposition of his discoveries may be found in *Fondation Hardt*, vol. XIII, *Les origines de la République Romaine*, Vandoeuvres-Genève, 1966. This volume also includes very interesting articles by other leading historians concerned with the early history of Rome. The only problem is that although Gjerstad's article is written in English, many of the others are written in French, German and Italian. I will, however, be presenting a number of their theories in this chapter.

One of these writers suggests that as well as the new archaeological material, there is another source that we may consult with new eyes. Hannel[1] points out that modern historians used to accept Livy's statement[2] that the early records of Rome were completely destroyed when the Gauls sacked Rome in 387 B.C. and those that do appear are fabrications. It is now considered that the destruction of Rome was not as complete as used to be imagined and that these early records can be trusted. The most important of these were the *Fasti*. These were a list kept by the Roman priests of the sacred holidays of each year, the year being headed by the name of the consul who gave his name to the year, imitating the Greeks, who used the archon for this purpose. They included brief statements of important events that took place in the year in question.

Rome's early beginnings

The earliest signs of settlement at Rome go back to Chalcolithic times, when the Stone Age was giving way to the Bronze Age. The Iron Age began in the eighth century B.C. and at this time the population seems to have been at least in part Villanovan. Dwellings were of the wattle and daub variety, which we know from Villanovan hut-urns. A notable hut of this time, dated to about 750 BC., was found on the Palatine Hill. Naturally the hut itself had long since rotted away, but signs of the foundations were found, and they fitted exactly those that would be made in constructing a hut of the type shown in the hut urns.

The huts were built mostly on the hills of *Roma Septimontium* (Rome of the Seven Hills). These were not the seven hills of later Rome, but consisted of the Caelian, the Palatine's three peaks, and the three peaks of the Esquiline. The area where the Forum was later built was still swampy and used only as a burial ground. A very old religious ceremony called the *Septimontium* was performed at Rome in classical times and

3.1 *Reconstruction of a hut of the Villanovan period which is characteristic of the early Iron Age on Etruria, 800 B.C.*

[1]*Fondation Hardt*, pp. 177–96.
[2]Book VI 1.2.

3.2 *Overhead view of the Iron Age cemetery in the Roman Forum. It contains cremations (round) and graves (trenches).*

looked back to what must have been a loose federal link between the original villages. Even then Rome was, in a very small way, growing in importance.

The Romans themselves claim that they were of dual origin, Latin and Sabine, and archaeology gives some confirmation to this. In the Palatine area the dead were burnt and put in hut urns, the Villanovan practice, while on the Esquiline, the Quirinal and the Viminal they were buried, the practice followed by the tribes that lived to the south and east of Rome, where the Sabines lived in historical times.

Life continued in this fashion until *c.* 575 B.C., and from the whole of this period only twenty-eight imported vases have been found.

Despite this, even at this stage the position of Rome had some significance. The Tiber was not a big enough stream to encourage the development of a large-scale trade along its course, but

Rome was well sited on the routes for land traffic. The Tiber at this point was easily forded by those travelling north or south. In addition there was a pass not far away leading over the Apennines into eastern Italy.

Thus Rome, like many other famous cities, grew up on a junction. Its strategic position was to become more important later.

Romes becomes a city

The change that occurred about 575 B.C. must be linked with the expansion southwards of the Etruscans, for although Rome was not conquered by the Etruscans at this time it did undergo the influence of this essentially urban people.

Basically Rome now became a city, not a collection of villages. The Roman Forum was created, Rome's central market place, and in it two small terracotta temples were built. One was sacred to Vesta, the goddess of the hearth, the other was the Regia, which despite its name was not a palace. It was mainly devoted to the worship of Janus, the god of the city gate, represented by a god facing front and back. The door of this temple was open in times of war, closed in peace. It also contained a sanctuary to Mars, the god of war, the main god worshipped in early Rome.

The huts of wattle and daub were gradually replaced by mud-brick houses, with stone foundations and tiled roofs, similar to those the Etruscans built. Roads grew up, all leading to the Roman Forum. Another forum, the Forum Boarium or cattle market was built beside the Tiber, making use of Rome's position, and the two forums were a sign of the increasing trade of Rome.

This early period of Rome's history is linked with King Numa, who according to some accounts was the founder of Rome, and to his successors, Ancus and Tullus. Romulus and Titus Tatius come from a later tradition and are clear fabrications. It is interesting too that Numa was credited with being a Sabine, so the first king was of Sabine race, another motive for inventing a Roman Romulus to precede him. Numa is said to have built the Temple of Vesta

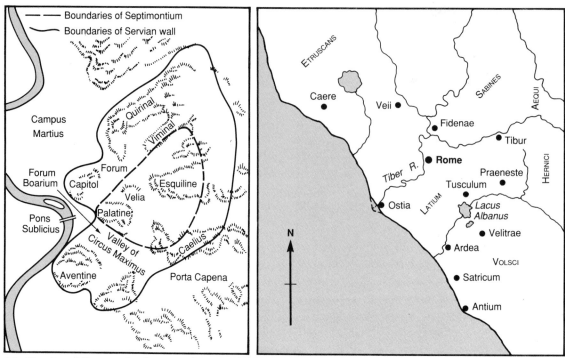

3.3 *The city of Rome and adjacent settlements, eighth to sixth centuries* B.C.

and the Regia in the Forum Romanum and later a temple was built to Jupiter Feretrius, possibly by Tullus, enlarged by Ancus. This temple had a triple *cella* in Etruscan fashion, sacred to Jupiter, Mars and Quirinus.

The Etruscans conquer Rome

About 530 B.C. a new phase began. Archaeologists note that from the period between 530 and 500 B.C., 203 imported vases have been found, a huge increase. It is to 530 B.C. not to the earlier traditional one of 616 B.C. that the conquest of the Romans by the Etruscans should be assigned and the beginning of the rule of Tarquinius Priscus.

The name Tarquinius (Tarchun in Etruscan), is associated with Tarquinii, an important early settlement of Etruria. There is also a link with Vulci, for in the cemetery of this town the François tomb was discovered. In this tomb, which was mentioned in the last chapter, there was a fresco, executed perhaps one hundred

years later than the events it portrayed. It showed an Etruscan, labelled as Tarchunies Rumach (Tarquin of Rome), being slain by a man described as Macstrna.

An important achievement of Tarquinius Priscus was the building of the temple to Capitoline Jove on the Capitol Hill, on which the Temple of Jupiter Feretrius had earlier been constructed. It had a triple cella, sacred to Jupiter, Juno and Minerva. Pliny quotes Varro as saying that Tarquin summoned the famous artist Vulca from Veii. He had him make a terracotta statue of Jupiter for the central cella and chariots of terracotta to set on the roof.

Tarquin also built the Circus Maximus, where the Romans held their chariot races throughout their history. He instituted the Great Games, the Ludi Magni, which were celebrated there, and the ritual of the triumph, held to celebrate victory in war. The triumph proceeded along the Sacred Way to the Temple of Jupiter on the Capitol. Tarquin is said to have carried out this building programme with the spoils he gained from the conquest of Apiolae.

When doctors disagree!

These facts are not without dispute. The dedication of the temple is set at 509 B.C. and the Romans believed that this was the year the Etruscans were expelled from Rome. According to their tradition the temple was begun by Tarquinius Priscus, whose rule they set back to 570 B.C., and finished by Tarquinius Superbus.

Two groups of magistrates with Etruscan names appear between 500 and 450 B.C. One group, between 500 and 490 B.C. included the names of L. Tarquinius Collatinus and Spurius Larcius. Then between 461 and 448 B.C. there was another such group including L. Tarquitius and in 448 B.C. Lars or Spurius Herminius. After this date no magistrates with Etruscan names appear.

The error may have arisen from a confusion of the two Tarquins and from the desire of the Romans to make the dedication of their most famous temple coincide with the beginning of the Republic.

Tarquinius Priscus, if we accept the revised dates, built a new Regia about 530 B.C., on the foundations of the old one. This reverence for the old temple, observed also when new temples of Vesta were built, is the main reason we have been able to discover and identify the old temples.

In 509 B.C. Rome made a treaty with Carthage, defining the respective spheres of influence of the two states. The treaty is similar in tone to the treaty made between the Phoenicians and the Etruscans in this period. Rome appears in this treaty as the head of a number of Latin towns. This is significant. Undoubtedly it was under the Etruscans that the Romans first achieved a position of some power in Latium, and after the Etruscans left it was a position they regained with difficulty.

Tradition would have it that Rome was attacked by Lars Porsenna the Etruscan king of Clusium. Although the main account claims that he was defeated, Tacitus preserves a tradition, which is probably the correct one, that he was victorious, although how long he stayed in Rome after his victory is not certain. The attack probably occurred at the end of Tarquinius Priscus' rule.

Servius Tullius, the reforming king

The next ruler of Rome was Servius Tullius. Tradition relates that he was not a Tarquin, and it seems most probable that he was a Roman king, ruling with Etruscan support. This would explain the fact that he is usually given as one of the Etruscan kings. At this point the fresco in the François tomb, which portrays Tarchunies Rumach being slain by Macstrna, is of interest.

The Emperor Claudius (the first century A.D.), whose first wife was Etruscan, was very interested in Etruria. He claimed that Mastarna (*sic*) was the Etruscan name for Servius Tullius; this could be important evidence. On the other hand, it is possible the Claudius' remark was simply an intelligent guess, based on the fact that he too had seen the François tomb. Present knowledge will not permit a solution of this problem.

Servius Tullius is said to have been responsible for reorganising the Roman army, and there is no good reason for rejecting this tradition. The Etruscans, like the Greeks and perhaps (as in so many things) imitating them, had developed the hoplite method of warfare, and this they brought to Rome.

In early times the Roman people met in the *Comitia Curiata* (Assembly by Curies[1]) to discuss and decide public affairs. Servius Tullius introduced a new assembly, the *Comitia Centuriata* (Assembly by Centuries). Unlike the earlier assembly it drew on the new population that had swelled Rome as a result of its recent growth. It met on the *Campus Martius* (Field of Mars) outside the city walls. This was appropriate, for the original function of the assembly was to assist in the levying of soldiers for Rome's wars, each century providing one hundred soldiers, but it came almost entirely to replace the Comitia Curiata as the regular assembly at which public matters were decided.

---

[1]We are not certain what the Curies were, but they probably were a small clan unit, consisting of a number of families.

Roman historians also attributed to Servius Tullius the later organisation of this assembly on the basis of wealth, into classes. This is an obvious anachronism as at this stage money was not invented and the assembly of this period would have been much simpler in its composition.

The same king is said to have divided the citizens on a regional basis into tribes, and in support of this tradition the Roman writer Varro claims that the names Ramnes, Tities and Luceres were the names of the original three tribes and all three names are Etruscan. In the ensuing period this division of the Roman people gave rise to yet another assembly, the Comitia Tributa (Assembly by Tribes).

The Etruscan rulers of Rome also had senior officials, whose central function was military, corresponding to the zilath of the Etruscan republic (see p. 13). They were called praetors, and as we shall see in the next chapter, they gave rise in the Republican period to the Roman consuls and praetors, who continued to be the senior officials of Rome.

Rome's position is threatened by its neighbours

The beginning of the fifth century had many problems. Etruscan power was waning and Rome, as one of the custodians of Etruscan power in Latium, felt the effect. In 497 B.C. the Latin states rebelled against Rome, led by the city of Tusculum. The Romans were led by Spurius Cassius. The details of this rebellion are somewhat fanciful, but it is clear that Rome at least survived the encounter, and in 493 B.C. Spurius Cassius for the Romans was able to make quite a favourable treaty with the Latin states. In terms of this treaty, they and Rome were to combine in a league to provide an army to protect their borders. The important feature was that Rome was to appoint the general.

Certain external factors helped to give Rome this diplomatic victory. It was not only the Latins who noted the collapse of the Etruscans. The hill tribes from the country adjacent to Latium hastened to take advantage of the new state of affairs. In particular, the Volsci, who occupied the land south of Latium, and the Aequi, whose territory lay further inland centring on Mt Algidus, made repeated forays. Both the Volsci and the Aequi had earlier been subject to the Etruscans, a control now lost. These foes helped to promote internal unity in Latium.

A new ally emerged at this time, which was to prove most useful. The tribe of the Hernici occupied an unenviable position between the Volsci and the Aequi. To protect themselves, they sought an alliance with the Latin League. This alliance was willingly accepted; for it had the result of driving a wedge between the Volsci and the Aequi, so that they could be dealt with separately. So Rome early in its history learnt the value of the principle that it applied so often later, 'divide and rule'.

Etruscan power declines

Meanwhile some events far away from Rome had their repercussions. In 480 B.C. the power of the Phoenicians was doubly crushed. The Carthaginians were defeated in Sicily in the battle of Himera by King Gelon of Syracuse. At the same time the battle of Salamis saw the defeat of the king of Persia's fleet by the Greeks. The Phoenicians contributed one-quarter of this fleet. As a result, the Carthaginians and the other western Phoenician towns were to a large extent cut off from the eastern Mediterranean and lost some power even in the west. Archaeological excavations in Carthage have revealed that in this period the importing of Oriental manufactures and Attic red-figure vases practically disappeared.

The Romans' own account of these years is falsified largely by magnification. They saw them as the period in which Rome took the first steps in the conquest of Italy. We know that in fact they were much less important and that Rome often found it hard to hold its own.

In 468–67 B.C., according to their own chronology, they took from the Volsci the coastal town of Antium, and established a colony there. They had from time to time also been harassed by the Sabines from the nearby hills, whom also they severely defeated, probably in 449 B.C. A large proportion of the Sabine people migrated to Rome.

Another hill tribe was also beginning to expand. Although more distant it was to be a more formidable foe to Rome than any of the nearer dangers. These were the Samnites, an Osco-Umbrian people, who had also some Illyrian blood. Their first move was southwards, where they defeated Tarentum in 473 B.C. Then in 445 they extended beyond their northern borders, took Capua, which up till then had been an Etruscan town, and swept over the whole of Campania.

Later, they turned their attention southwards once more, and occupied Lucania and Bruttium. The result was that they now populated most of the western portion of Italy south of Latium, in addition to Samnium itself in the central east. The Samnites were great mercenaries, and as such they were imported into Sicily both by Dionysius I and by the Carthaginians.

An interesting point to note is that even at this early period Rome had begun to establish colonies to hold down newly acquired territory. Antium was such a colony. These colonies were to be one of the secrets of Rome's successful expansion. They were definitely military in character, yet the colonists did not live in their new domain as an idle, armed garrison, for the Romans were farmers. They cultivated the land and developed as a community. At the same time they retained their links with Rome and their rights as citizens, and did not, like the normal Greek colony, break away from the place that founded them. They were more readily assimilated into their environment than the cleruchies of Athens, and did not rouse the fierce opposition that brought the Athenian venture to an end.

These external events the Roman historians attributed to the first years of the Republic. If we accept the new chronology they would belong instead to the last years of the Etruscan rulers. Yet, in fact, if we accept that these events did take place, it does not make an immense difference if they are regarded as taking place during the monarchy. Their relation to specific kings must, however, if we do make such a change, remain somewhat conjectural.

The end of the Etruscan kings

To return to Servius Tullius, we do have some record of his public works. He is said to have built the temples of Fortune and of Mater Matuta in the Forum Boarium, and in support of this their remains have been found in that area, dated to the early fifth century B.C. To him also should be credited the Temple of Saturn built in 496 B.C. and one dedicated to Ceres, Liber and Libera, again in the Etruscan triple tradition, built on the Aventine in 493 B.C. Two later temples were built, one to Mercury, one to the Dioscuri or the Heavenly Twins. He is also said to have built the grey tufa walls, which in Etruscan style once surrounded Rome, walls that were completed by Tarquinius Superbus. Archaeology again confirms this, as remains of such walls have been found belonging to two periods, consistent with this tradition.

The last Etruscan king of Rome was Tarquinius Superbus, Tarquin the Proud. The stories told about him make him a typical tyrant of the Greek type, and they are suspect. This does not mean, however, that there is no basis whatever for them. We really cannot be sure of the truth about the man. Some facts, however, are less contentious. He is credited with completing the walls of Rome, and there is support for this story. He also fought and conquered the people of Gabii and with the booty gained built a temple to Semo Sancus, dedicated in 466 B.C.

In any case, whatever the real truth about the man, Etruscan power in Italy was collapsing, and Tarquinius Superbus was driven out of Rome, and the Republic established.

Etruscan influence in Rome

Despite the comparatively brief duration of the Etruscans' domination of Rome, their influence was far-reaching. To the building activities already mentioned, such as the Cloaca Maxima and the temples, could be added the *Porta Capena*, which is said to have been of Etruscan origin, and the *Vicus Tuscus*. The name of this, one of the main business streets of Rome, suggests either that the Etruscans built it, or that they populated that area. Roman historians claimed that the *Circus Maximus* in its original form was likewise constructed by the Tarquins, even though it was rebuilt in republican times.

Apart from specific buildings, the Etruscans left their mark on the general character of Roman architecture. The Greeks did not make use of the arch; for them the column served to support the roof, as well as adding grace to the external appearance of a building. On the other hand, the arch, and the related phenomenon, the vault, were well known to the Etruscans. They used them in drains, in tombs, and in the triumphal arch. The temples the Etruscans built owed much to the Greeks, as did most of their art, but the raised base of the temple was distinctive and was maintained by the Romans.

One function fulfilled by the Etruscans was to pass on to the Romans at this early stage their love for Greek culture. This influence was reinforced subsequently by Rome's contact, first with the Greeks of South Italy, then with Greece itself. It is no wonder that Greek culture was so dominant in Roman thought.

The alphabet, which was once believed to have been adopted from the Greek, is now known to have come from Etruria, though that country in turn owed it to the Greeks of Cumae. This is shown both by the position of the letters in the alphabet, and by the redundant letters C, K, O, (C duplicating K and O duplicating U (V)).

The three names the Romans bore, as in Gaius Julius Caesar, corresponded to the Etruscan pattern, and differed sharply from the Greeks, whose general practice was to use two, the name of the person and that of his father. It is also suggested that Roman names ending in *a*, such as Sulla and Catilina, were Etruscan in origin, *a* being the normal noun termination in that language.

The *atrium*, the central room of the house, with its *impluvium*, was Etruscan, as was the habit of preserving on the walls the death masks of distinguished ancestors. Actually, Roman interest and skill in realistic portraiture owed much to this people. The Greeks were in general much more concerned with the grace of the human body.

Public life bore the same imprint. The senior Roman officials were called curule magistrates because they sat, like Etruscan princes, on the ivory curule chair. They also wore the purple-edged *toga*, once the costume of the kings' attendants, and they were escorted by the lictors with their fasces, whose Etruscan origin has already been discussed.

Some of the most characteristic features of Etruscan life were their relations with the gods. In victory the Romans celebrated a triumph in a manner derived directly from them. The triumphing general was attired like an Etruscan king in a purple robe, and wore a golden crown. He too rode in an ivory chariot, led by oxen with gold-tipped horns. The procession followed the ancient Sacred Way up to the original Etruscan temple of Jupiter, Juno and Minerva. After the ceremony, in some cases, the Etruscan custom of sacrificing the prisoners was observed.

The traditional amusement of the Roman populace, the gladiatorial games, derived from the funeral games of Etruscan princes, either directly or indirectly, by way of the Campanians.

It has already been noted that the hoplite form of fighting was an inheritance. Others in the realm of warfare were the Roman eagle and the trumpet. Indeed, the Roman camp, with its regularly marked streets set to the four corners of the compass, was based on the plan of an Etruscan town.

In the art of divination, the *haruspices*, who foretold the future by examining the sacrifice, remained with the Romans as a central part of their religion. They also continued to observe lightning and the flight of birds. Finally, the Sibylline books, which according to Roman legend came to Rome in the rule of Tarquin, contained many Etruscan elements, though they embodied as well much Greek and Latin religious lore. Throughout their history the Romans had a great respect for the art of Etruscan seers, which they called *disciplina etrusca*, and in times of crisis it was not unusual to send to Etruria for one of their priests.

It is apparent then that the influence of Etruria was widespread and significant. Their most important contribution was possibly the fact that they made Rome a city and gave its people a desire for leadership. The Romans were quick to learn and they did not suffer the handicap that crippled their masters. They were a practical race, and though they used the ceremony of religion, they did not allow it to dominate their lives and stultify their development.

Rome's beginnings: its own story

Among those who first wrote about the origin of Rome were its poets, especially Ennius in his *Annales*. Some portions of this survive and much of it was used later by Virgil when he wrote the *Aeneid*. The poets in their turn drew on legendary material. The Romans had few actual records from their early days.

Historians in the past were very scornful of this tradition, just as they gave little credence to any country's legends of its early days. They were said to have been simply the imaginative tales of Greek artists made up to please their Roman masters.

Events of this century have led historians to modify their views. The kingdoms of Minos, Troy and Mycenae were all shown by archaeologists to have really existed. Once men scoffed at that imaginary people the Hittites, who were mentioned in the Bible. The civilisation of the Hittites has also been unearthed. So now scholars are much more prepared to believe that legend may have a substratum of fact, however much it has been distorted in the telling.

It may then be of interest to present briefly the Roman legends of their foundation and early history, noting where recent investigation gives confirmation to the account.

Roman history, like that of Greece, was linked with Troy. When that city was sacked, one of the Trojan princes, Aeneas, was rescued by the goddess of love, Venus, and set off with a band of his followers to find a new home in the west. They had many adventures. At one point they came upon Dido, who was just founding the city of Carthage. Aeneas stayed with her and the queen was seized with a fatal love for him. When he left to continue his quest, Dido killed herself, and this incident provided an explanation for the later enmity between Rome and Carthage. Many

3.4 *Terracotta statuette of Aeneas carrying Anchises from Veii, fifth century B.C.*

of Aeneas' troubles were caused by the hatred of the goddess Juno, who was an avowed enemy of Troy and all the Trojans.

Finally Aeneas reached Latium, where he was welcomed by the old king Latinus. His chief opponent now was Turnus, king of the Rutuli. Ultimately Aeneas defeated and killed Turnus, and founded the city of Lavinium.

This story obviously contains many elements. Part of it derived from accounts of Greek migrations to the west, both in the Geometric Age and in the subsequent age of colonisation, but mainly from the former. The link between Aeneas and Latium used to be regarded as a conceit of Greek writers of historic times, intent on creating a venerable ancestry for Rome.

Recently, however, at Veii, near Rome, terracotta statuettes and other relics have been found, some dated to the sixth century B.C., which show Aeneas bearing his father on his shoulders as he fled from burning Troy. This shows that the connection between Aeneas and Latium-Etruria was very early indeed. It still does not reveal what historical facts lay behind the story. Two explanations seem possible. It could be Etruscan in origin as the Etruscans themselves said they came originally from Asia Minor. It could also, and this has been proposed as a solution, refer to a migration by the Phocaeans, an Ionian race, to the western Mediterranean, the venture that finally led some of them to found Massilia. Whatever the truth, at least the legend has a venerable history, and cannot be dismissed lightly.

Some generations later, so the story continued, the twins Romulus and Remus were born, in romantic circumstances, to Mars, the god of War, and Rhea Silvia, a descendant of Aeneas. They were suckled by a she-wolf and grew up to found Rome. Romulus slew Remus and became the first king of Rome. Of Rome's first four kings, some were Latin, some were Sabine in race. The fifth was an immigrant. His name was Lucumon (the title of an Etruscan prince, as was noted earlier), but when he ascended the throne he took the name of Tarquinius Priscus (Tarquin the Old). He was succeeded by Servius Tullius (the son not of Tarquin but of a slave woman), who instituted many reforms. Last

came Tarquin the Proud, an arrogant tyrant. His son's rape of a noble Roman matron, Lucretia, led to his final deposition. In his stead the Romans set up two consuls to rule the city, and with the help of brave Horatius they repelled the ensuing attack by Lars Porsenna.

This story then contains much that is at least partly authentic, and time may reveal more correspondences. The falsification, a natural one, is to picture Rome as more important than it really was in those days. Also the fact that they were actually conquered by the Etruscans was glossed over, though superficially only, in the official account.

A variant view

Controversy surrounds almost every aspect of this period of Rome's history, and it is worth examining yet another account of this age, which differs radically from Gjerstad's, but could for all that be correct. Alföldi, who was a contributor to the *Fondation Hardt* book, wrote a *History of Early Rome and the Latins*. He would propose a much less ordered history of this period.

He points out that Latium and Rome were important to the Etruscans not so much for themselves but because they guarded the way to the wealthy valleys of Campania, into which the Etruscans had expanded. This was especially necessary because the Greeks were a rival power in that area, where they had already founded Ischia and Cumae, and they would have seized any opportunity to block the Etruscans' access to Campania.

An inland route led from Etruria to Campania, via Gabii, Tibur and Praeneste, all of which show signs of Etruscan influence, especially Praeneste, which was a very wealthy Etruscan city. The coastal route to Campania was developed later, and it went through Lavinium and Rome. Thus Rome and these other cities were of value to the cities of southern Etruria, who were engaged in this trade: Caere, Vulci, Tarquinii and Veii.

Alföldi suggests that there was not a settled Etruscan dynasty in Rome, but that the city was seized and held by a number of these cities in

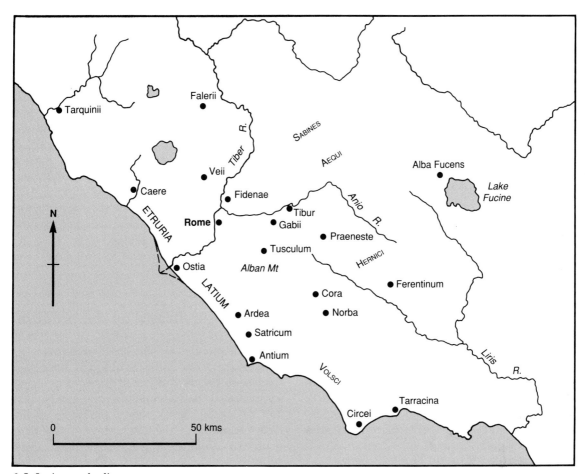

3.5 *Latium and adjacent areas.*

turn, a fact partly discernible even in the traditional account. The Tarquins probably came from Caere, where archaeologists have found a number of instances of the name, a town that was in early times the dominant city in south Etruria. The Etruscans then would have seized Rome and Tarquinius Priscus' rule begun at about 600 B.C.

The François Tomb suggests another incursion. It portrays Marce Camitlnas from Vulci slaying Gnaeus Tarquinius from Rome (Cneve Tarchunies Rumach). Aulus Vibenna (Aule Vipinas) from Vulci slays another man. Now independent evidence suggests that Aulus Vibenna was a king in Rome, and possibly also Mastarna, another of the François figures.

(Alföldi, however, will not accept the view that Mastarna was Servius Tullius.) Alföldi places the Vulci takeover at about 550 B.C.

After 600 B.C. Veii replaced Caere as the most powerful south Etruscan city. It managed a large salt works at the mouth of the Tiber and transported the salt up the river with Rome as one of the ports.

Alföldi notes that in 524 B.C. a large Etruscan army came south through Latium and made an unsuccessful attack on Cumae, which was defended by its tyrant Aristodemus. He suggests that it was probably this army that drove the Vulcan king from Rome and put Tarquinius Superbus on the throne. Our tradition notes that this king had close relations with Veii and used their sculptor when he built the Capitoline Temple. He finished the temple in 509 B.C. and was driven out by Porsenna in 505.

Alföldi argues that the Romans did not know what the first Tarquin did, and arbitrarily assigned to him some of the deeds of the famous Tarquin.

This brings us to Lars Porsenna himself, the man who according to one tradition was triumphantly repelled, while another acknowledges that he succeeded in becoming their ruler. Alföldi here makes use of an ancient Greek historian of Cumae, whose account is preserved in the writings of Dionysius Halicarnassus.

Lars Porsenna swept down on Rome in 505 B.C., driving out Tarquin, who fled to Cumae. In 504 Porsenna sent a force under his son Arruns to attack Cumae. However, Cumae's tyrant Aristodemus again repelled the Etruscans, killing Arruns. He then led an army, which contained forces from some Latin towns and the exiled Tarquin, to attack Rome. This attack was beaten off. Nevertheless Porsenna's power was weakened by his defeat. He had to make concessions to the Romans, and they, like many of the other Etruscan cities of the time, set up a Republican constitution headed by a zilath or praetor. This fits the tradition of the Roman Annals which include Etruscan names among the consuls (as the Romans came to call the senior praetors) of this period.

This is an interesting version. It still accepts that the Tarquins were the main rulers during the Etruscan overlordship, but holds that their rule was interrupted by rulers of different origins.

Alföldi also says that the traditional account distorts Rome's position in the Latin League, making Rome its leader. In fact this was not the case until 338 B.C. when Rome did impose its will on Latium. Before that the League members met at Alba Longa or Lavinium, and chose their leaders in succession from the thirty towns which made up the League. After Porsenna's defeat Aricia was made the centre of the League. The battles of this time were in reality battles between the various cities of the League, of which Rome was only a member, even though quite a vigorous one.

Alföldi makes one final point, which is also hotly disputed. He asserts that at this time the cavalry was the main part of the army, and was supplied by the aristocracy, and that the Senate and the officers of Rome came from the ranks of these aristocratic cavalrymen. Gjerstad and other historians oppose this, saying that the cavalry was never an important part of the Roman army, which relied basically on its infantry, tending to use foreign cavalry. Yet the primacy of the cavalry was a very general feature of those early societies, and we still have to explain why the top order in the *comitia centuriata* were the *equites* or horsemen, and that the middle class of Rome continued to be called the *equites* long after they ceased to be mounted. So this could be correct.

New light is thrown on the problem

In this chapter two accounts have been presented of the Regal period. Modern historians have been faced with the difficulty that the Romans themselves placed the beginning of their Republic at 509 B.C., while archaeology, and some of the facts preserved in the Romans' own tradition, point to a continuation of Etruscan rule to about 450 B.C.

Gjerstad's solution, which was the one first presented in this chapter, was to move the whole history on 50 years, so that Tarquin the Proud was expelled in 450 B.C.. Alföldi, on the other hand, follows the Romans' own account in putting the expulsion of Tarquin at 509 B.C., then suggests that during the next 50 years Rome was under the overlordship of Lars Porsenna, but that he, like a number of other Etruscan rulers of the time, granted the Romans a republican constitution. This theory has been lent important support by a recent archaeological discovery. Mr Treloar drew my attention to this discovery and provided the translation of the inscription which I use below.

Not far from Rome was the small town of Satricum, a Roman dependency, which according to Livy was destroyed by the Volsci shortly after the foundation of the Republic. In 1978 archaeologists working at the Satricum site found a stone which had been reused by being built into the wall of a later temple. Its reuse enabled the archaeologists to date the stone itself to about 500 B.C. and on it was the inscription in very old Latin 'the companions of Publius Valerius dedicated this (temple) to Mars'. According to Livy, when Tarquin was expelled from Rome one of the first pair of consuls was Publius Valerius!

The temple then was built shortly after Rome became a Republic, but destroyed by the Volsci. When the Volsci were driven back the temple was rebuilt, and because the stone, as a foundation stone, had religious significance it was built into the new walls. This is very useful confirmation of the Romans' own account, and consequently of Alföldi's version.

We still have to deal with the problem that Gjerstadt dates certain temples built by Tarquin to the period between 500 and 450. Either Gjerstadt's dates are wrong or the buildings were erected by Lars Porsenna. Nonetheless we can now feel considerable confidence in the view that Tarquin was expelled from Rome in 509 B.C., but that the Romans did not win complete independence till 50 years later.

The discovery was first announced in the archaeological supplement of the *Journal of Hellenic Studies* of 1978, then a full discussion was published in book form as follows:

C.N. Stibbe, G. Colonna, C.de Simone, H.S. Vernsnel, introduction by M. Pallottino, *Lapis Satricanus, Archaeological, Epigraphical, Linguistic and Historical Aspects of the New Inscription from Satricum*, Archaeologiche Studien van het Nederlands Institut te Rome, Scripta Minora 5, 1980. (In fact publication was delayed and it did not appear till 1987.)

Date table

B.C.
753	Traditional date for Rome's founding.
c.575	Etruscan influence on Rome begins. Its first kings.
c.530	Tarquinius Priscus becomes first Etruscan king of Rome.
509	Rome makes treaty with Carthage. Traditional date for expulsion of Tarquins from Rome.
497	Latin Revolt led by Tusculum.
474	Hiero beats Etruscans at Cumae.
c.450	End of Etruscan rule.

Select quotations

1 Polybius, III 22:
The first treaty between the Romans and the Carthaginians was made in the consulship of L. Junius Brutus and M. Horatius, who were the first to be made consuls after the expulsion of the Kings. . . . I have written down the text of this, translating it as accurately as I could; for there is such a difference between the old language and the new that the most skilled even among the Romans find some of it hard to unravel: . . . 'On these conditions there shall be friendship between the Romans and their allies and the Carthaginians and their allies: the Romans and their allies shall not sail beyond the Fair Promontory, unless driven by a storm or an enemy . . . . If any Roman comes to Sicily in the portion ruled by Carthage, he shall enjoy the normal rights. The Carthaginians shall not harm the people of Ardea, Antium, Laurentum, Circeii, Tarracina or any Latin town subject to Rome.'

2 Livy, VIII 40:
It is not easy to prefer one account or one source to another. I consider that the records have been falsified by funeral orations and false inscriptions attached to family portraits, as each family by lies tried to appropriate the ownership of great deeds and magistracies to its members. As a result the deeds of individual men and public records have been confused. Nor have we extant any writer of that period who is a reliable enough authority for us to depend to him.

3 Servius' Commentary on Virgil *Aeneid* I.373:
*Each year the chief pontiff had a whitened
board, headed by the names of the consuls and
of the other magistrates, on which he used to
note day by day memorable events at home and
at war, by land and sea.*

Further reading

Fondation Hardt, vol XIII: *Les origines de la
République Romaine*, Vandoeuvres-Genève,
1966.

A.Alföldi, *Early Rome and the Latins*, Ann
Arbor, University of Michigan Press,
1965.

H.H. Scullard, *The Etruscan Cities and Rome*,
Cornell University Press, N.Y. 1967.

Topics for essays or discussion

1 Examine the geography of Latium in general
and Rome in particular. What effect would
this have had on the original foundation of
the city and its later fortunes?
2 To what extent did Rome's legends give a
true account of its early history, and in what
way were they false? Base your examination
on the account as found in Livy I, or
Virgil's *Aeneid*.
3 What were the effects of the Etruscan
domination of Rome? Would you regard
them as superficial?
4 What influence did the Greeks have on
Rome in the regal period?
5 The Dorians took over the Messenian land of
Sparta, as the Etruscans took over Rome.
Why were the results so markedly different?

Chapter 4

The beginnings of the Roman Republic

Constitutional developments in early Rome

THE GOVERNMENT MACHINERY that the early Republic inherited from the Regal Period largely conformed to the type found in many primitive Indo-European countries, including Greece. It also had certain peculiarities, which played an important part in subsequent developments.

It must be noted that just as much disagreement exists in the constitutional field as in the other history of early Rome. Different theories have been advanced as to the exact nature of the assemblies and offices, their origin and the time at which they came into being.

There were, as in Greece, a privileged and an unprivileged class, and the aristocratic class consisted of the noble families or clans, called *gentes*. The ruling class had an assembly, corresponding to the *Areopagus* and the *Gerousia* in Greece. It is called the *Senate*, a word which has a similar origin to *Gerousia*, that is, 'a gathering of the old men'. The Senate had considerable power, especially in establishing and interpreting the laws. The laws themselves were at first

handed down orally and no written record of them existed.

The aristocrats were known as the *patricians* (those who had fathers, that is, fathers of note), the commoners as *plebeians*, or as the *plebs*, a collective term. The exact origin of this division has been a matter of dispute. Some think that it rose from a racial difference, that the patricians were the old Latin stock, the plebeians the foreign Sabines. There is no sound evidence for this view. Others think that the patricians were the Latins while the plebeians were the other settlers, of diverse origin, who according to the Romans were invited to help found Rome. This is probably nearer the truth, but not the complete picture.

It seems most likely that the division was similar to the one existing in other communities of the period. The patricians would then be the members of the leading clans, supported by their armed retainers. The latter were known as *clients*, while their aristocratic protectors were called their *patrons*.

The term 'plebeian' would be essentially negative in character. To this class would belong those people that came to the community from elsewhere and as a result were not allowed into the ruling body. To it would come clients who had lost a patron, the masterless men, as well as those who had simply fallen behind in the struggle for survival.

Some scholars have the theory that the division arose only after the Republic began, with the Struggle of the Orders see p. 35. This is unlikely. The division does seem to have begun earlier, although the struggle probably deepened the cleavage.

Again, some think the Senate was composed only of the heads of the clans, and it was they who sat in the *curia* or senate house. But this would then have been a very small body, and it is more likely that it consisted of all the male adult members of the noble clans.

The assemblies

The common people also had assemblies: the oldest of these was the Comitia Curiata, the 'assembly by curies' which was mentioned in the last chapter and is thought to have existed in Rome even before the arrival of the Etruscans. The exact significance of the curies is not known, but they were probably clan divisions of some kind. From the earliest days of the Republic the Comitia Curiata possessed no real power, its functions being ritualistic in character, the relics of some past greatness. When a senior magistrate was elected he then went to this body, which formally conferred on him his *imperium*. This implied the right to command, and especially to command an army.[1] It is in this connection that historians usually speak of the Comitia Curiata.

The Comitia Centuriata, which Servius Tullius founded, was a very important body. As was noted earlier, although its original function was to levy the army, it very soon became an assembly in which the people discussed and decided state affairs. It was probably from the start conservative, giving power to the middle class, which supplied the army, but by about 450 B.C. its structure became more elaborate, and it was then a timocratic body, in which those who had wealth had power. It is no coincidence that by this time Rome had adopted a rather primitive form of currency, based on the use of bronze, with the *as* as the basic unit. The following is the structure of the assembly as the Roman historians describe it.

At its upper end were the eighteen centuries, which supplied the cavalry. They included the wealthiest citizens. Next came the first division, or 'class' at it was called, which supplied eighty centuries of heavily armed infantry. The three following classes each provided twenty centuries of infantrymen, and then came one that furnished thirty centuries of lightly armed troops. At the bottom of the scale were the musicians and workmen (four centuries) and one century that was exempt from military service.

The lower the class, the more belonged to it. Each member was accordingly required to provide less for the army, but at the same time he had less voting power. The cavalry class and the first class were the least numerous divisions, but between them they possessed ninety-eight votes, in short a majority in the assembly. In addition, the vote was by custom first taken from the most senior class, and this vote had a religious binding force on the whole body. It can be seen then that although this assembly possessed some new features, and, being timocratic in basis, gave privileges to some otherwise denied them, it was by no means a popular assembly nor likely to support the giving of rights to the less privileged part of the community.

Comitia Centuriata	
Cavalry	18 Centuries
1st Class	80 Centuries
2nd Class	20 Centuries
3rd Class	20 Centuries
4th Class	20 Centuries
5th Class	30 Centuries
Unclassified	5 Centuries
Total	193 Centuries

It should be noted that voting in Roman assemblies differed in an important respect from the Greek practice, where the election was by counting individual members. With the Romans it was a block vote, by the curie in the Comitia Curiata, by the century in the Comitia Centuriata, by the tribe in the *Concilium Plebis* and the *Comitia Tributa*, which we will be discussing later. This form of voting seems to have arisen naturally from the nature of these assemblies, but it did in time make the manipulation of votes very easy.

The magistrates and the family

Next we must consider the executive officers, the magistrates. It is now generally agreed that the senior officers were originally called *praetors*. Their main function was to lead the army and they were chosen annually by the comitia centuriata. In time, certainly by the middle of the

---

[1]For this purpose the auspices were taken, that is a sacrifice was performed to ascertain if the gods accepted the candidate the people had chosen. If the auspices were favourable, the imperium was conferred.

century, the two senior magistrates came to be called *consuls*. They acted as colleagues, with equal power, and each had the power of *veto* (I forbid) to block the actions of the other. Clearly there would be problems if the consuls disagreed.

In times of crisis the two consuls were replaced by a single magistrate, the *dictator*, who himself chose a deputy, his master of horse. The dictatorship was a normal Latin magistracy, and has been found elsewhere in Latium as the title for the chief magistrate of a town.

This account would not be complete without considering the family, which formed the basis of the Roman state. By law the family was completely under the control of the father of the household (*paterfamilias*). He possessed the power of life and death over any member of it, his wife, his children, his household slaves. In theory, he retained this control while he lived, even over his grown-up sons. When he died each of them became a paterfamilias. With the daughters it was different. They remained under the control of their fathers until they married. Then they were under the control of their husbands.

Despite this autocratic framework, the wife held a much more respected position than her Greek counterpart. She did not live shut up in women's quarters. She appeared in public freely, and her opinion weighed with her husband to a degree inconceivable in Greece.

Religion also centred on the home, where the father performed the sacrifices to the household gods on behalf of the family. State religion was family religion magnified. Even the family hearth reappeared as the temple of Vesta. This building, round in shape like an antique house, centred on a fire, which the Vestal Virgins guarded and never allowed to go out.

Much of the Etruscan ritual was maintained, but it was subservient to the running of the state, instead of dominating it. Sacrifices were performed before most acts of importance, whether a harvest or a war, and the favour of the gods was requested. Yet this ritual was not accompanied by servile, superstitious fear. Instead, it came to be a useful tool in the hands of the ruling class. A rebellious official would find that the omens were against him, and

heaven would hamper his impious innovations. Yet good Roman commonsense did not allow such impediments to strangle the working of the state, or even to prevent a sensible compromise with the forces of change.

The Struggle of the Orders

The fifth century was marked by a fierce struggle for power between the classes, called by the Romans the Struggle of the Orders. In the traditional view this struggle began when the Republic was set up. If we accept the later dates for the kings (see p. 30) then the struggle must have begun during the Regal period, which is not impossible. It will be observed, however, that the contest became much more bitter in the second half of the fifth century after the expulsion of the kings. In short the Republic did not bring more favourable conditions to the common people but rather an aristocracy determined to preserve its privileged position.

Early in this period the plebeians won the right to have *plebeian tribunes*, officials to defend them. (The Romans called the leaders of the tribal divisions in battle *military tribunes*.) The tribunes were assisted by *plebeian aediles*, who were keepers of the Temple of Ceres, Liber and Libera, which was situated on the Aventine Hill. This hill, which was at first outside the city walls, was closely associated with the struggle. It had a strong population of traders and it was to this hill that the plebeians withdrew in protest in the so-called First Secession.

The tribunes of plebs

The tribunes had at first been appointed by the Comitia Curiata, but in 494 B.C. they withdrew to the Aventine Hill and threatened to found a city of their own. The patricians persuaded them to return and now a separate assembly was set up to elect the plebeian officials. It was the *Concilium Plebis*. It was constituted on a tribal basis, but with no patrician members.

Staveley, whose analysis of the institutions of the early Republic is referred to at the end of this chapter, has some comments to make on the tribunes. He suggests that their position and the basis of their authority began in a much less regular and legal fashion than Roman historians assert, and that the laws followed.

The main power of the tribune himself was that of the veto. When a noble seized a citizen, often for debt, and dragged him off to slavery, or to some other punishment, the tribunes could forbid this and give the arrested man their protection. So that they themselves would not be harmed while they did their duty, they were declared sacrosanct, that is, anyone who harmed them would be accursed. Both the effectiveness of the veto and the sacrosanctity of the tribune probably depended at first not on a law or an oath, but quite simply on the mob of angry citizens who accompanied him, ready to protect him if need be.

An early right possessed by Romans, which was recorded as the *lex Valeria* (Valerian Law), declared that if any man were arrested on a capital charge he could appeal to the whole citizen assembly (probably the Comitia Centuriata). Staveley suggests that here we have originally not so much a formal law as one of those compromises, at which the Romans were so adept. If a citizen were wrongfully arrested, a tribune could interpose his veto and rescue the man, but he would expect that when he restored him to his family the noble would return. A compromise could then be arranged, whereby the tribune would hand back the accused man to the noble, provided that his case were heard before the whole people.

The fifth century was a troubled one. Apart from the social unrest there were a series of plagues, affecting cattle as well as people, and a number of famines for which corn had to be imported. This must have exacerbated the social problems of Rome.

The Twelve Tables

The middle of the century was a time of crisis. If the revised dates are accepted it would have been the time of final transition from a regal state to a republic. There were also vigorous attacks

from the Volsci and the Aequi. The patricians desperately needed unity, and concessions had to be made to the plebs, who provided the rank and file of the army. As in early Athens, the people bitterly resented that there were no written laws, that they were tried and condemned on what the patrician magistrate said was the law of the land.

In 451 the patricians gave in on this issue, and the *decemvirs* (body of ten men) were appointed to commit the laws to writing, being given supreme power for this purpose. They drew up a list of ten tables of laws. The next year another committee was set up, which drafted two more, thus producing the *Twelve Tables*, which were regarded as the basis of future Roman law.

But the same thing happened as when Dracon drew up the laws of Athens. They only put in writing what were the current laws, and the laws themselves produced opposition. In 449 there was a secession of the plebs, caused, according to the Roman historians, by the tyrannical conduct of the second body of decemvirs, and in particular of Appius Claudius. This may be historical embroidery. In any case the secession won more formal recognition of the rights of plebeian tribunes.

In 445 there was another attack on privilege, led by a tribune, Canuleius. One of the Twelve Tables invalidated marriage between a patrician and a plebeian. The *Lex Canuleia* of 445 established that if a patrician married a plebeian woman, the children should be enrolled in the father's clan, that is, be patrician.

The plebeians also challenged the patricians' monopoly of public office. Here too, external wars helped them, as the continued wars made it necessary to have more generals and more officials to conduct the wars. The chief officer or consul had long possessed an assistant, the *quaestor* (investigator). The function of this official is not quite clear. The quaestor was in charge of finance, and that is the function of the quaestor in the later Republic. Yet there was also in these early days a quaestor who investigated cases of homicide on behalf of the consul. Perhaps there were two different officers who bore this name, or more likely the man had two tasks.

In 447, the appointment of the quaestor was made elective (there were by now two quaestors) and was entrusted to an assembly called the *Comitia Tributa* (assembly by tribes). This body was distinct from the *Concilium Plebis* but was organised in a similar way, and the two bodies were closely linked in their history. It is likely that the quaestors were given official status because the consul was so often away fighting for the city that some leader was needed to maintain order at home. The quaestor was not given imperium, (the power to lead an army). His *potestas* (authority) was civilian in character. He did not have the ivory chair, which marked out the curule magistrate, nor was he preceded by lictors bearing the rods with which to beat offenders, enclosing an axe with which to execute.

The plebeians win the right to public office

In 445 a further change was made. It was declared that the consulship could be suspended in any year, and instead a larger number of military tribunes with consular power be elected. This post was open to plebeians. Thus a concession was made to the plebs. Probably also, as Rome became involved in more extensive fighting, it was being found that sometimes two military leaders were not sufficient. After this the dispute arose annually: should there be consuls or consular tribunes? If consular tribunes were appointed, should any plebeian candidates be accepted? The conservative Comitia Centuriata, which elected these officers, was most reluctant to choose any but patricians.

In 443 another office was created, the *censorship*. The two *censors* were appointed by the Comitia Centuriata, and this body, not the Comitia Curiata, gave them their auspices. That was fitting; for the censors were primarily intended to fill a military need, the recruitment of Rome's growing army. They had a five year appointment, and drew up a list of citizens, who would then be eligible to fight in the army. They also drew up a list of senators. These were important powers and only very senior men were

given the task. In addition, it was soon decreed that they should hold the office only for eighteen months of the five years, for fear that, if they stayed in power the full five years, they might abuse their power.

Some historians have seen in the creation of these new posts a political move on the part of the patricians, creating more posts so that the consulship, when it finally became open to the plebeians, would not be all important. The other view is more likely, namely that Rome's increasing commitments, especially in war, made it vital to have more executive officers. Obviously, however, this increase would give added hope to the plebeians that they could win at last some entry into the official caste.

In 424 an important concession was won. The number of quaestors was increased from two to four, and it was declared that plebeians could compete for that office. This was a minor office but it was significant, especially as quaestors could be made members of the Senate.

So, very early, we see emerging some of the characteristic features of Roman government. Their habit of electing two consuls, two quaestors, two censors with equal power,[2] was a peculiar feature. This, together with the annual election, prevented any individual from gaining too much power. It made it especially hard for a consul to become a king. On the other hand, if the officers disagreed, a deadlock could result and sometimes did, and the system did mean a lack of continuity.

The powers of the Senate were not clearly defined, but it did possess continuity and it was consulted. This meant that, as time went on, it became a more dominant force in Roman politics.

It should be noted also that the plebs were not a united body. The unprivileged were in part those who had money but no political power, in part those who had neither wealth nor importance. The poor plebeian wanted to be free of debt and to possess land. He also wanted to be

---

[2] Such a group of two or more magistrates was called a 'college'.

protected from arbitrary arrest. The rich plebeian had less modest claims. He wished to enter the social caste of the patrician. It was important to him that he could hold public office, marry into patrician rank, and take part in the religious life of the state. It was obvious then that at some stage it would be possible for the patricians, if they were adroit, and made certain concessions, to win over part of the plebeians, namely the wealthy section, to their side and so weaken the plebeian party. This did happen.

Again, agreement is not general in this period. Some hold that the Comitia Centuriata was set up only in 445, the time when its machinery (in the account of this chapter) gained a more formal organisation. Others try to deny the truth of some of the secessions, saying that the early ones, especially the first, were fictitious. The reason for creating the consular tribune, as has been remarked, is in doubt.

None the less, whatever the truth on individual points, the pattern of Roman public life does begin to emerge, very different from the Greek, not fixed immutably by lawgiver or god, but flexible and capable of infinite adaptation to the needs of the moment. Yet this adaptability was itself protected from headlong change by a strong reverence for the *mos maiorum* (customs of the ancestors) which felt that the established practice should be respected if possible.

Having said this it is worth noting that the Romans always admired the Greek expertise in law and government and made constant use of it. Even at this early time the Roman historians have a story that an embassy was sent to Athens to seek advice when the Twelve Tables were drawn up. This may be a fabrication but it does seem true that the plebeian reformers looked to the Greeks, with whom they would be in contact in Italy and Sicily, for inspiration, and one of the Twelve Tables, attacking luxurious living, is very close in substance to Solon's law on the subject.

So too when they set up their own assembly they were not unaware that the Greeks used their popular assemblies to give power to the people. However, although the *Concilium Plebis* played an important part in their struggle, it never assumed the importance of the Greek bodies.

Date table

B.C.
494	First Secession of the plebs (?)
451–50	Decemvirs write out the Twelve Tables
445	*Lex Canuleia*
424	Censorship created
421	Quaestorship open to plebeians

Select quotations

Remains of Old Latin III, Loeb, 1935, p. 438 and 482.
(Portions of the XII Tables):

1 From Table 3:
Unless they came to an agreement debtors were kept in bonds for sixty days. During that interval they would be brought to court on three successive market days, and it would be announced what was the debt for which they were indicated. On the third market day they would be executed or be sold across the Tiber.

2 From Table 8:
Whoever burns down a building or a heap of corn near a house should be bound, lashed, and burnt to death, if he did the act wilfully. If it happened through chance or negligence, he should make good the damage, or if he is too poor, receive a lesser punishment.

Further reading

R.M. Ogilvie, *Early Rome and the Etruscans*, Fontana, 1976.
E.S. Staveley, *Journal of Roman Studies*, 1953 pp. 30–6, 'Significance of the Consular Tribunate'.
E.S. Staveley, *Historia*, V, 1956 pp. 74–122, 'The Constitution of the Roman Republic 1940–1954'.
E.S. Staveley, *Historia*, III, 1955 pp. 412–28, 'Provocatio during the Fifth and Fourth Centuries B.C.' (An important article, which discusses recent research on the most important constitutional problems of the early Roman Republic).

Topics for essays or discussion

1 Why did Etruscan power collapse in Rome? What were the consequences?

2 In what way did the threat from the Volsci and the Aequi benefit Rome?

3 Examine Rome's position in Latium after the expulsion of the Tarquins. To what extent have historians falsified the picture?

4 Did the collapse of Etruscan power in Italy have any feature in common with the collapse of the Mycenaean hegemony in Greece?

5 Analyse the constitution of early Rome and compare it with the institutions found in Greece before the rise of the tyrants.

6 'The Roman plebs early found that unity was the only way to combat privilege.' Discuss.

7 What was the importance of the Twelve Tables in the Struggle of the Orders? Why did it lead to further demands?

8 Examine the early magistrates of Rome. What was their function and what relation did they have to the functionaries of Regal Rome?

9 Examine the use of compromise as a weapon in the early stages of the Struggle of the Orders.

10 Rome like Sparta was faced by a national threat and a need for political reform. Yet their response to the crisis was very different. How do you explain the difference?

Chapter 5

The Struggle of the Orders and the Samnite Wars

IT IS PROBABLY no coincidence that after 450, the time when Rome achieved a measure of internal unity, it also enjoyed more success in the wars it was waging with its neighbours. The reorganisation of the Roman army would have helped in this success.

The stronghold of the Aequi had always been Mt Algidus, and in 430 they were dislodged from this area. By the end of the century the Volsci were driven from the coastal plain south of Rome.

Rome conquers Veii

Perhaps these victories gave the Romans courage to attack an enemy nearer home. In 405 Rome quarrelled with its powerful Etruscan neighbour Veii. The ground for the dispute was control of Fidenae, which was situated between the two cities on the banks of the Tiber. The details of this siege have been given a poetic flavour and are greatly exaggerated. None the less, it did represent an undertaking beyond any the Roman army had yet made.

Veii was a walled city, as was normal for the Etruscans, and the Romans had to conduct a lengthy siege. This meant that they could not follow their earlier practice of calling up their male citizens for a short summer campaign. The army now had to remain under arms all the year round, and as a result it was found necessary to pay them, to make some compensation for their absence from their farms. Even this concession was to prove inadequate.

Eventually the Roman general, Marcus Furius Camillus, was successful. He gained entry to the city, making use of the drainage tunnels Veii's own inhabitants had constructed, and took it. The traditional account makes the siege last ten years, like the siege of Troy. This is an obvious poetic fancy, and in fact it seems to have taken about six. However, in the absence of certain dates the traditional dates are preserved and the capture set at 396.

The city was destroyed and its territory divided among the citizens of Rome. This was a new practice and was doubtless an attempt to meet the problems caused by the lack of arable land for the sowing of corn. As we shall see, the demand for land was to be repeated throughout the Republican era.

The Celtic invasion

Meanwhile a new threat appeared north of Italy—the Celts, a nomadic Indo-European people, who at that time were seeking new land, either as a result of their own expansion or of pressure from tribes yet further north. This event is usually known as the Gallic invasion, as the Gauls were the Celtic people that occupied the area north of Italy, including the region that now constitutes France.

They reached Italy about 450 B.C., and their repeated if unsystematic onslaughts destroyed the northern possessions of the Etruscans, and even threatened the main cities of central Etruria. This would have made it hard for Veii to obtain help from the Etruscan League. Even when there was an opportunity, the cities of Etruria were remarkably indifferent to an attack on one of their number, a fact that contributed to their eventual conquest by Rome.

The Gauls, if we may so call them, were no more disciplined in battle than in daily life, but the wild charge of these tall, scantily clad figures (they wore no body armour) was unnerving to those unaccustomed to it. They also introduced the mass chariot attack for the first time. Finally, they had invented the nailed horse shoe, which gave their horses more endurance. It is interesting to note that many of the Latin words for horse-drawn vehicles, whether used in war or peace, were of Celtic origin.

In 391, the Senones, a tribe led by Brennus, made their leisurely way into Italy. When they attacked Clusium, which lay just north of Rome, the Romans tried to intervene. This only meant that their own city, which at the time did not possess very solid fortifications, was the next objective.

5.1 *The Forum Romanum was the centre of the ancient city. Its temples, halls, triumphal arches and oratorical tribunes marked Rome's rise to world power.*

A Roman army tried to head off the Senones at the River Allia, but were decisively defeated (387–86 B.C.). The city was taken, except for the walled Capitoline hill, and the invaders withdrew only when they had been paid a ransom of gold. Archaeologists have found evidence of this occupation in the area of Rome. In the place where the old senate house had stood in the Forum, charcoal and broken roof tiles have been found dated to the early fourth century.

The disaster was a salutary lesson. The Romans determined that they would be safe from future attacks, and they built a wall round the whole city, including this time the Aventine. They took as their model the solid fortifications of Veii, which were built of tufa stone. This wall was to be their salvation when Hannibal later appeared on the soil of Italy.

Revolts soon sprang up among the recently defeated Volsci and Aequi. Even the Hernici joined the rebels for a time. Camillus led the Roman army that defeated them. In 360 the Latin League staged a rebellion but it was also crushed. Finally the towns of south Etruria made a united attack, but they were defeated in 350.

In point of fact the danger from these rebellions was less than might appear. Although the victories of the Gauls weakened Rome, the Gallic threat, which had only temporarily ceased, tended to unite the people of Italy in case of further invasions. Therefore Rome, which gave most promise of successful resistance, finally achieved an even stronger position than before.

The Struggle of the Orders continues

The external threat to Rome imposed a further strain on its internal structure. The plebeians had not ceased to demand the right to hold magistracies, and an economic crisis made the struggle even more bitter. Rome's constant wars meant that its armies were seldom idle. But the soldiers were also farmers. Inevitably the farms were neglected and their owners fell into debt. The siege of Veii, the sack of Rome and finally the revolts of Rome's neighbours combined to bring this to a head.

In 367 at the plebeian assembly two tribunes passed the laws which bear their names, the Licinio-Sextian Rogations.[1] This bill had two aspects, one political, one economic. On the political side, the office of military tribune was abolished and the consulship reintroduced. One of the consuls, however, must be plebeian. On the economic side, the plebeians were allowed to deduct from their debts the interest they had paid and to repay the balance in three years. Finally, a limit was set on the amount of public land which could be held by one man (120 hectares, according to Roman historians). Rome's victories had greatly increased the quantity of this *ager publicus*, as it was called, which was confiscated from conquered territory. It was officially set aside as grazing land for general use, but it was soon occupied by the wealthy and powerful, and this was a grievance for the land-hungry poor.

Meanwhile the number of magistrates was increased. This was a necessary step, for the expanding power and territory of Rome meant more administration. An even more urgent problem was the continued absence of the consuls on military duties. Magistrates were needed to carry out their civil duties in Rome while they were away.

As a result two *curule aediles* were appointed, corresponding to the two plebeian *aediles*. They were responsible for the local administration of Rome itself, a type of function fulfilled in modern times by town councils. At the same time a *praetor* was appointed, a junior official who was attended by only six *lictors*. He too had *imperium*, and consequently the right to lead armies, but his main task was to cope with the legal business of Rome in place of the frequently absent consuls. The very next year it was conceded that the curule aediles should be plebeians in every alternate year.

In 366 Sextius, one of the proposers of the Rogations, became the first plebeian consul. The struggle was not, however, ended. Staveley has a theory to explain this.

---

[1] A rogation was a technical term, meaning strictly a proposal to pass a law.

Comitia Centuriata
(Assembly by centuries)

Elected the following curule magistrates, given in order of seniority:
— Two praetors who had imperium. After their year of office, they could be appointed as propraetors (having the rank of praetor) usually for one year.
— Two curule aediles, who were in charge of Rome's corn supply.
— Two consuls who had imperium. After their year of office, they could be appointed as proconsuls (having the rank of consul) normally for one year.
— A dictator in times of crisis to replace the two consuls. He had imperium and chose a deputy (magister equitum). He could not be vetoed.
— Two censors who drew up lists of citizens for the army. This was a five-year appointment but a censor would only serve the first eighteen months.

Concilium Plebis
(For plebeians only and membership was based on tribes)

Elected plebeian officials:

— Two (later five, then ten) tribunes of the plebeians who had the power of veto
— Two plebeian aediles, who assisted the tribunes and kept the records of the Concilium Plebis.

Comitia Tributa
(Assembly by tribes)

Elected two (later four) quaestors or junior officers who:
— Assisted the consul.
— Had civilian authority rather than imperium.
— Could become senators for life unless dismissed by the censors for misconduct.

Note: Imperium gave its holder the right to command an army.
Any magistrate could veto a magistrate of equal authority (a colleague) or a lesser magistrate.
No one could veto a dictator and a tribune could only be vetoed by another tribune or a dictator.

5.2 *Magistrates of early Rome.*

Some scholars hold that the consuls were originally called praetors or perhaps praetor consuls (Scullard's suggestion). Praetor means literally 'he who goes before', that is, 'leader'. The general's quarters in a Roman camp were called the *praetorium*. Then again, in verse the general of an army was often called not consul but praetor. If this were true, what was in effect created in 366 was a third praetor, junior in status to his colleagues. Staveley suggests that the patricians obeyed the letter of the law by electing a plebeian praetor, but made him the junior praetor.

The army mutiny of 342 showed that the people could be tried too far. A law was passed that decreed that two of these officials could be plebeian, and one senior praetor or consul must be plebeian. The patricians had also been appointing the same man year after year. It was enacted in the same legislation that no man could hold the same office again until ten years had elapsed. This provision was not to prove effective, although Sulla did incorporate it later in his laws.

If Staveley's theory is correct, and it has plausibility, the distinction between senior and junior official must have proved confusing, and they soon came to be known as consul and praetor respectively.

The opposition to the plebeians' holding the consulship now collapsed. The plebs continued to press their advantage. In 339 the *leges Publiliae* we're passed, whereby one censor had to be plebeian. Again, the Senate had been refusing to ratify laws which it disliked, after the Comitia Centuriata (see pp. 34, 36) passed them. One provision of these laws insisted that senatorial consent must be given to a bill before it went to the Comitia Centuriata. Finally, the *plebiscita*, the resolutions passed by the *Concilium Plebis*, were given the force of laws. This provision was for some time evaded, and only really enforced by the *lex Hortensia* of 287.

In 312 was the famous censorship of Appius Claudius. While holding this office he is said to have enrolled sons of freedmen in the Senate. He also redistributed the plebs among the tribes. There had been a tendency to enrol all new citizens, whether freedmen or allies, in the four urban tribes, where their vote counted for little. The rural tribes on the other hand were constantly increasing in number as the territory of the city expanded. The peasant votes were assured to their aristocratic landlords. This produced a most inequitable position in the Comitia Tributa, which was now replacing the more cumbersome Comitia Centuriata as a legislative assembly.

The reason why the distribution of citizens in the tribes was so important relates to the Roman block voting system, so different from the Greeks where individuals voted in the assemblies. Each tribe had one vote, no matter how small or large it was. So the overcrowded city tribes had one vote each, and so did the sparsely settled country tribes with their population of clients, loyal to the patrician overlord. In effect then the system is very similar to our electoral system, where we elect members to parliament from electorates, which can also differ enormously in the number of voters. Yet the elected member has one vote whatever the population of his or her electorate.

Appius Claudius' move was a democratic one, but it roused fierce opposition from the conservative factions. They had long been used to the Comitia Centuriata, where the wealthy were favoured, and they were anxious that the Comitia Tributa, as far as possible, should favour them in the same way. An interesting parallel to this problem can be seen in the Athenian Council, which Cleisthenes reformed in order to remove this very abuse.

The reform, however, was before its time. Ten years later, Fabius Maximus and Decius Mus, as censors, revised the lists once more, and restored the underprivileged group to the urban tribes. It took many years and a bitter struggle to remedy this injustice.

One important issue that remained to be decided in the Struggle of the Orders was the control and composition of Rome's priestly class. It is true that with the publication of the Twelve Tables a written law was secured. None the less the aristocracy still had a solid weapon to use against the plebeian litigant. Roman religious practice abounded in restrictions on the conducting of law-suits. One of the most important was that on any of the numerous holy days or *dies nefasti* no legal business could take place. The priests, who were patricians, kept the list of these days.

In 300 the patricians tried to win favour by passing the *lex Ogulnia*, using a tribune Ogulnius for this purpose. This law gave the plebeians the right to stand for the important priesthoods of *pontifex* and *augur*.

In the same year legal sanction was given to a right long exercised in fact. As was noted earlier, when the tribunes interceded, taking away a man whom the patricians wished to arrest, they could later reach a compromise, returning him to the patricians on condition that his case was heard before the Comitia Centuriata. It was now stated explicitly that a citizen had the right of appeal from a magistrate to the assembly in the case of a capital sentence.

The outcome of the Struggle

It is time to conclude the account of Rome's internal struggle. It was conducted in a very different way from the reforms that took place in Greece. There we repeatedly hear of a reformer such as Solon, who would draw a specific code of laws, or of a revolution, which at a single blow would radically alter the constitution of a state.

In Rome the process was rather a protracted struggle, punctuated by compromises. For this very reason it has not been possible to separate Rome's internal and external history into neat compartments.

Again and again the Roman populace used external pressures in order to secure internal change. Threats of wars would enable the plebeian leaders to demand concessions under pain of non-cooperation in the field of battle. A set-back in the war would produce economic distress, which in turn would create new demands.

Yet it must not be thought that the Struggle of the Orders eliminated privilege. At the beginning of the struggle the discontented comprised two elements. There were the politically underprivileged. They possessed wealth, usually through trade, but owing to their lack of land, or because they were not members of privileged families, or for both reasons, they were debarred from holding office. The second group were the poor. To them the ability to vote or hold office was only of importance in so far as it helped them win the most fundamental rights, to eat and live in comfort without fear of debt and unjust condemnation.

The struggle, as so often happens, was of most benefit to the first group, who were the more powerful. They were helped by the fact that the patricians did not spare themselves in warfare, so that their ranks were thinned progressively in Rome's battles. In the end new recruits to the privileged group were a necessity to the upper class itself.

It is significant that by the end of the Republic, when candidates were sought for the few offices still reserved to the patrician class, they had the utmost difficulty in filling them. Many noble families had died out, others were impoverished. The old had given place to the new.

Yet the new ruling class was to be no less arrogant. It consisted of the families whose ancestors had held consular office. A man not so honoured who tried to enter the charmed circle was a 'new man' (*novus homo*). For him the road to the consulship was at the best difficult, at the worst impossible.

Occasionally a novus homo of ability would be supported by one of the noble families, which was on the lookout for talent, and he would rise to the consulship. Nevertheless he would never be allowed to forget his upstart origin. Such men were among the foremost figures of Rome's history, including Marius, Cato and Cicero, to name three of the most famous. Yet one could set against this sprinkling the list of magistrates where the same family names recurred year after year with monotonous regularity.

The upper section of the plebs was helped to victory by the decline in the ranks of the patricians. It was further assisted by the need for more and more officials. It has been suggested by some historians that the patricians created new offices such as censor and praetor in order to evade the demands of the plebeians. This is only a part of the truth.

Rome's increasing power and expanding territory kept requiring more men to control them. The army was also increasing and needed officers. You will observe that the Romans, right to the last part of their history, did not separate the role of wartime officer and peacetime magistrate. A man had to be adept at both. The result was inevitably some unwarlike generals and some incompetent magistrates, but it was the tradition.

In any case more were needed. The demand was partly met by the creation of new offices, or by increasing the number of people who held them. It was met also by a new development, the prorogation of a magistracy. A Roman magistrate (apart from the censors who held office for eighteen months) was appointed for one year. After 327, it became the custom to extend an office for a further year or even years. These magistrates were called *proconsuls* or *propraetors*. The main crisis that demanded prorogation was war. A general's command might be extended because the war was continuing and it would be dangerous to change leaders in the middle of the campaign. Later on it became normal for a magistrate to hold office in Rome for one year, then to go as a promagistrate to other duties in the following year. But this was yet to come.

The First Samnite War

The 350s marked Rome's recovery from the Gallic invasion. Common fear of the Gauls induced a number of people at this time to ally themselves with it. Tibur, Praeneste and Caere did so in the latter half of the decade. The same motive led the Samnites of the hill-country above Latium to make an alliance.

This alliance was not to be long-lasting. Rome's desire to spread south into Campania is thought to have helped create the war with Veii. A similar motive brought Rome into conflict with the Samnites.

The Samnites were a mountain people, who practised a primitive form of agriculture, and were ruled by a body of their chieftains under the leadership of a meddix. Each year the Samnites sent out their excess youth to seek new pastures in foreign lands. This custom they called 'the Sacred Spring', and it meant that they continually expanded into neighbouring countries, such as Campania. They were hardy soldiers, greatly favoured as mercenaries. During this period the people of Tarentum, making a virtue of necessity, had built up an army of Samnites to help them hold their own.

The Samnites had in earlier years been kept in some sort of order by the Etruscans, but with the decline in Etruscan power the Samnites quickly spread over the whole of Campania, except for some Greek colonies like Cumae. Capua they did occupy, but in time they were won over by its pleasant way of life and did not welcome further waves of invasion from later and less civilised Samnites. In 343 B.C. they became involved in such a dispute with the invading Samnites and appealed to Rome for help, handing over their city as a whole to Rome. Rome, welcoming the opportunity of winning a foothold in Campania, agreed.

Alliance with Capua

In recent years some historians suggested that the First Samnite War never took place. They pointed out that this war was not mentioned by Diodorus Siculus and found unlikely some of the events in this war, such as the change of sides by the Samnites in 341. Their view has since been discounted. Actually Diodorus Siculus was very cursory in his treatment even of the Second Samnite War, and we now feel that our accounts of this war contain enough convincing detail to make it acceptable. Moreover our archaeological research has made us wary. So many places which we said were a figment of the imagination of the Ancients have now proved to exist. So if there is a tradition that a war took place like the Trojan War or the First Samnite War, it is usually the case that such an event did take place, even if the details of the event are not always accurate.

As a result of the earlier expansion of the Samnites, Campania was now largely occupied by people of this race, but the pleasant life of the traditional holiday area of Italy, combined with new trade interests, loosened the ties of kinship.

Capua had a disagreement with Samnium, and appealed for help to Rome. Rome, seeing a chance to win a foothold in Campania, agreed. Thus in 343 began the First Samnite war. It was the briefest of wars. In 342 the Roman troops mutinied in the field, leaving Rome in a very awkward position. Luckily, Samnium was also involved in a dispute with Tarentum, and this fact induced it to make peace with Rome in 341. The terms of the peace left intact the Roman alliance with Capua.

It is not hard to see a connection between the Roman mutiny of 342 and the law of 341, which corrected the anomaly in the application of the Licinio-Sextian Rogations. Once again, an external crisis enabled the plebeians to win a compromise in their internal conflict.

Other trouble was brewing. In 341 the Latin allies revolted with the help of the Volsci, who were not reconciled to their recent defeat. The Volsci were beaten at Antium. The Carthaginians, who had also made an alliance with Rome (*c.* 348 B.C.), assisted in the attack, for the inhab-

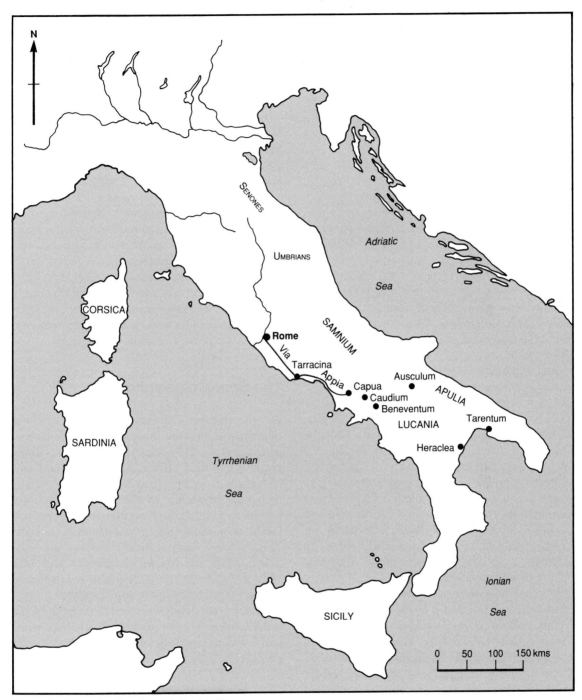

5.3 *Italy during the Samnite and Pyrrhic Wars.*

itants of Antium had been pirates, a notorious hazard for passing traders. When the fleet of Antium was routed, the beaks or *rostra* of their ships were set up as ornaments to the speaker's platform in the Roman forum, which in consequence itself came to be called the Rostra.

In 338, the Latins were crushed with the help of the Samnites, now Rome's allies. This gave the Romans the opportunity to reorganise the towns of Latium on a new basis. The old Latin League was dissolved. About six of the leading towns were incorporated in Rome. Their citizens were granted full civic rights, even to the holding of office. The remaining towns were granted a less privileged status.

Post-war reforms

This was the time that the *municipium* (hence our word 'municipality') was developed. When a town was recognised as a municipium, the type of franchise granted to it was based on that given to the town of Caere after the Gallic invasion. Its citizens were given private rights, that is the right of intermarriage, and trade with the Romans. They also retained full control of local government.

An important limitation was placed on the *municipia*. They had no rights of intermarriage or trade with one another, so that trade, for example, would have to pass from a municipium to Rome then to another municipium. Thus the towns were effectively isolated from one another by their very privileges.

Rome also made good use of the system of rewards. Men who held public office in these communities could be requited by the bestowal of full Roman citizenship, which included the public rights of voting and holding office. In addition, a member of a municipium who came to live in Rome was granted full Roman citizenship. This type of alliance was not new, but its systematic and successful application was.

Rome likewise developed another old Latin concept, that of the colony. From the beginning of their expansion the Romans had established Roman colonies, usually at strategic coastal points. The citizens of a Roman colony enjoyed full private rights, and, if they returned to Rome, could exercise the complete rights of a Roman citizen.

After the conquest of the Latins, Rome began the idea of the Latin colony, many more of which were founded than of Roman colonies.

They were usually established in inland areas and were much larger than the Roman colonies. Their constitution was similar to that of the municipia, and gave the same privileges. As the name suggests, these foundations were composed of Rome's Latin allies.

All the relationships so far described, between Rome and the colonies and between Rome and the municipia, imply communities that dwell in cities. When Rome conquered peoples who organised themselves on a tribal level only[2], a different procedure was needed. These states were called *civitates foederatae*, 'states bound by treaty', and their relation to Rome was governed by the particular treaty drawn up between their leaders and the Roman Senate.

So far we have been discussing the rights enjoyed by these communities. But rights imply obligations. What Rome required of its subjects, and required more and more as time went on, was the use of their citizens in its armies.

The Second Samnite War

By the timely concessions it made to the plebeians in 341, and by the conquest and reorganisation of the Latins that followed, Rome found itself in a strong position. It used this advantage in order to launch a new assault on the Samnites, regardless of the help the Samnites had given in crushing the Latin revolt. This was hardly admirable, but it was realistic, and the Romans were always realists.

In 334 Rome made an alliance with the Samnites' enemies, the Tarentines, and protected Capua by establishing a colony at Cales.

In 328, the Volsci were driven from the Liris Valley which lay between Latium and Campania, and a colony was placed at Fregellae to secure the area.

---

[2]We are now speaking of tribes in the sense with which we are familiar, as when we speak of a tribe of Red Indians. The tribes of Rome, who constituted the *comitia tributa*, did descend from a tribe in this sense in prehistoric Rome, that is a family or clan grouping, but by the historic period they were simply recognised divisions in an urban community.

The Samnites saw the developing threat. In 327 they made peace with Tarentum and declared war on Rome. Disaster followed quickly. The First Samnite war had not really involved a serious engagement between the opposing forces. Now the Romans found how ill equipped they were to deal with mountaineers in their own country.

In 321 a Roman force marched inland, heading for Apulia. They were trapped in a mountain pass, the Caudine Forks, and surrendered ignominiously.

Despite Livy's attempt to gloss over the results, it is apparent that the Romans were forced to make peace and no operations are recorded until 315. In this year the Romans once more tried to go through Apulia and take the Samnites in the rear. The Roman army, led by Rullianus, was again severely defeated at Lautulae.

Obviously Rome needed to consolidate its position. The task was undertaken by the famous censor, Appius Claudius. At this time we begin to see more clearly the outlines of those clan struggles that probably, as in the case of Athens, always played a part in Roman politics. Appius Claudius, himself an aristocrat, seems to have linked himself with the progressive party, while the opposing interests were led by Q. Fabius Maximus.

One feature of Appius Claudius' policy was to strengthen the ties with Capua. To this end in 312 he built the *Via Appia*, which linked that town with Rome. This was the first of the famous roads, which played such an important part in assuring Rome's control over its subject peoples. These roads, as the Romans' knowledge of engineering advanced, came to be built with such skill that they have survived even till modern times. They advanced undeviating over hill and plain, bearing Rome's armies in time of war, traders and travellers in time of peace. Persia had made use of roads in order to maintain its empire. Rome was to do the same.

Appius Claudius also built the first of the aqueducts that were to supply water for the ever-increasing population of Rome. The water was brought from the River Anio, not far from the city. The internal conflicts that occurred at this time, and the part played by Appius Claudius have been treated earlier in this chapter. Once again external reverses meant that Rome had come to terms with the discontented section of its own population.

After the defeat at Lautulae new troops were levied at once. No major operation was attempted, but the Romans began to retake some of the towns the Samnites had captured. The building of the Via Appia also made it easier for them to move their forces.

None the less the set-back served in the first instance to increase Rome's foes. The Marsi and Paeligni and even the Hernici rebelled and in 311 the Etruscans were brought into the alliance. The Romans concentrated their efforts on Etruria first, and brought it into subjection by 304. When they followed this by an attack on the Samnites, the latter asked for peace, which was granted.

The Third Samnite War

The pact served only to give the Samnites time to rally their strength. In an effort to increase their forces they appealed to Lucania for assistance. Despite their kinship the Lucanians refused, and when the Samnites threatened to win their adherence by force, they appealed to Rome for protection. This began the Third Samnite War (298).

Scipio, an ancestor of the famous generals of the Punic Wars, led an army to Lucania to protect it. His initial venture was successful, but stretched Rome's lines of communication to breaking point. Before this they had always been in the centre, and had the inner lines, but now the Samnites enjoyed that advantage.

Egnatius, the Samnite general, profited by this to make his way north past the Romans, winning over some northern peoples, especially the Umbrians and the Gallic tribe of the Senones. A few Etruscan cities also joined him. Scipio set out in pursuit, but was severely defeated at Camerinum (295).

Desperation spurred on the Romans, who levied yet another army. They even granted slaves their freedom, if they would enlist. The armies met at Sentinum in the same year. It was a bloody battle, and one of the consuls, Decius Mus, was killed. (Tradition claims that he actually sought death in an effort to win the favour of the gods.) Finally the Samnites were beaten.

The Umbrians and Senones capitulated, as did the rebellious Etruscan cities. Next the Romans turned on the Samnites. Their land was devastated savagely until in 290 they sued for peace. It was again accorded them, on no worse terms than in 304. However, Rome had set many colonies to hold down the troublesome area, and this, together with the new road, assured that at least for the time being the conflict was ended. None the less, as we shall see in the Social War, the Samnites never accepted final subservience.

These wars were most important. They secured for Rome the main portion of the Italian peninsula and consolidated its hold over such territory as Etruria, which had before been only partially subdued. In addition, the very arduousness of the conflict made the Romans modify their tactics and some of their equipment.

Finally, as we shall see in the next chapter, the conquests brought Rome to the door of the Greeks of South Italy, which led to new encounters and finally to Rome's bitterest and most difficult war.

Date table

B.C.
445   *lex Canuleia.*
443   Creation of censorships.
421   Quaestorship available to Plebeians.
406   War with Veii.
387–86 Battle of Allia.
367   Licinian Rogations.
343–41 First Samnite War.
327–4 Second Samnite War.
321   Roman defeat at Caudine Forks.
312   Censorship of Appius Claudius. Via Appia built.
298–90 Third Samnite War.
287   *lex Hortensia.*

Select quotations

1 Livy IX 5 ff.:
(The Roman army is sent under the 'yoke' after the defeat at the Caudine Forks.)
First, each with a single garment, they were ordered to come out beyond the rampart unarmed. Hostages were first handed over and taken into custody. Then the lictors were ordered to leave the consuls and their generals' cloaks were taken off. . . . First the consuls, practically half-naked, were sent under the yoke (two spears fixed upright in the ground with a cross piece tied above to join them). Then those below them in rank were humiliated in their turn. The legions followed them, one by one. The enemy stood round them, armed, abusing and mocking them; many even had the sword drawn against them, while some were wounded and killed if their expression showed too much indignation at their treatment, and offended the victor.

2 Livy VI, 35:
Gaius Licinius and Lucius Sextius were elected as tribunes and promulgated laws which were all against the power of the Patricians and to the advantage of the Plebs: One about debt, that the money which had been paid in usury should be subtracted and the rest paid off in three equal annual portions; the second limiting the size of landholding, that no one should possess more than five hundred iugera; the third that there should be no election of military tribunes, and that at least one of the consuls should be appointed from the Plebs.

Further reading

E.S. Staveley, *Historia* VIII (1959) pp. 410–433, 'The Political Aims of Appius Claudius Caecus'.
A.N. Sherwin-White, *The Roman Citizenship*, Oxford University Press, 2nd ed. 1973.
E.T. Salmon, *Samnium and the Samnites*, Cambridge University Press, 1967.

Refer again to H.H. Scullard, *History of the Roman World 753–146 B.C.*
M. Frederiksen, *Campania*, British School at Rome, 1984.

Topics for essays or discussion

1 Why did Rome succeed in dominating Latium? Contrast its position with its role in the Regal Period.

2 Who was the aggressor in the Samnite Wars? Could one side be named as an aggressor and what factors led to the conflict?

3 What effect did the Celtic Invasion have on the history of Italy in the fourth century? Compare this with the Celtic invasion of Greece and Asia Minor.

4 What factors led to the later extension of the Samnite Wars? What difficulties did the Romans encounter and how did they overcome them?

5 What was the importance of the Licinio-Sextian Rogations? What grievances did they seek to remedy and to what extent did they succeed?

6 Analyse the method of government and control of subject peoples evolved by the Romans during the Latin and Samnite wars. How effective was it?

7 Discuss the multiplication of magistracies during the Struggle of the Orders. How do you explain it?

8 What weapons did the plebeians have in their fight for extended privilege? How did they use them?

9 A Roman magistrate had to serve his state in military and civil capacities. Do you think that this fact was of any significance in the Struggle of the Orders?

10 In the fourth century Rome extended its power over most of Italy. A century earlier Athens failed to achieve the same result in Greece. Can you explain the difference in the fortunes of the two states?

Chapter 6

Rome moves beyond Italy: the Pyrrhic War and the First Punic War

THE SUCCESSFUL CONCLUSION of the Samnite Wars brought Rome for the first time into conflict with powers whose sphere of influence extended beyond Italy.

Sources

For this period we unfortunately do not have Livy, as it occurs in books 11 to 19, which are not extant. We therefore have only the summaries of these books. We do, however, have Polybius. His first two books serve as his introduction to the Hannibalic Wars. They mention but do not give an account of Pyrrhus, but they do treat the first Punic War and the period between the two wars.

Polybius was a Greek who was taken prisoner in the Macedonian wars and brought to Rome. There he was befriended by Scipio and Fabius and devoted himself to writing a history which began with the Punic Wars. We possess the first five books and fragments of the rest. He was a conscientious historian, although without any great depth of historical perception, and he was a very poor stylist. Livy made considerable use of him in his history of Rome. Polybius has this advantage that he actually took part in the Punic Wars and knew the places he wrote about. He was also careful to check the geographical details of any action he described.

For Pyrrhus we have to be content with Plutarch's life, which suffers from Plutarch's usual limitations, in particular that of being a biography not a history, and therefore not covering the period thoroughly.

Apart from these two writers we have only the fragments of some other historians, who treated the period in works that have not survived, and Frontinus, who in his *Stratagems* discusses battles which he found interesting.

The Pyrrhic War

From time to time, the Samnites had been diverted from their struggle with Rome by the need to hold their own against Tarentum, the most powerful Greek city state on the Italian mainland. Rome, by conquering Samnium, inherited its enemy.

The wealth of Tarentum depended on trade, and on the manufacture and dyeing of woollen cloth. Like the Hellenistic states generally, it relied for its protection on mercenary troops. The highlanders of Lucania served in this capacity whenever opportunity offered. Unfortunately, when it did not, they passed the time in banditry. They were therefore uncomfortable neighbours.

When Rome conquered Samnium, the Greek cities saw a possible new champion against the Lucanian raids, and availed themselves of the opportunity. Thurii requested and was granted assistance.

Rome declares war on Tarentum

In 282 B.C. while helping Thurii, a small Roman fleet of ten ships appeared before Tarentum. Without warning the Tarentines descended on them, sank some, and drove the rest off in confusion. The motives of the Greeks are not clear. There was an old treaty that forbade the Romans to sail in Tarentine waters, but it was half-forgotten by this time. Some historians on the other hand saw it as the result of the faction struggles in the town. There was, they argued, a pro-Roman party there, whose opponents, when they caught sight of the Roman fleet, suspected a plot, and with true Greek precipitation sprang to crush it. This raises the further question: was the Roman arrival an accident, or was the anti-Roman faction right in suspecting mischief? The whole truth is unlikely to be known.

The Romans were forced, much against their will, to declare war, especially as Tarentum followed this initial deed by marching on Thurii, and forcing the town to send away its Roman garrison. When this happened, Tarentum as usual looked for a general who should conduct the war in which they had embroiled themselves. They chose Pyrrhus, Alexander's successor in Epirus, who had a high military reputation.

During the early period of the Samnite Wars, the Tarentines had engaged Sparta to defend them. Later they turned to Alexander, King of Epirus. His rugged and inhospitable land had produced very little but valiant warriors and he was related to Alexander the Great. Unfortunately, his ambitions eventually made him dangerous to the Tarentines, who treacherously allowed him to be killed.

Pyrrhus answered Tarentum's summons, but when he arrived, he insisted that a garrison of his troops be admitted to the citadel of Tarentum. This would be some surety that the Tarentines would not treat him as they had treated Alexander.

The Battle of Heraclea

Pyrrhus then set off to give Rome its first taste of Hellenistic warfare. Besides the Greek phalanx and cavalry, he had an elephant division, by now a regular feature of Eastern armies. Thus equipped, he met the Romans at Heraclea in 280

6.1 *A bust of Pyrrhus, King of Epirus, who came to Italy and Sicily with his army and elephants to help the Greek cities, but was eventually defeated by the Romans.*

B.C. The Roman army was defeated; for it was no match for Pyrrhus. In particular, their cavalry would not face the elephants. None the less, the Romans had learnt to make their forces more flexible during their campaigns against the mountaineers of Samnium and they acquitted themselves honourably.

Pyrrhus followed up his victory by marching north upon Rome, as Hannibal was to do in later years. He could not hope to take the city itself. Since its capture by the Gauls, Rome had been protected by a solid wall. What he did hope for was a revolt among Rome's Campanian allies. There he was disappointed. The Campanian cities shut their gates. Rome, by a combination of fear and rewards, had built a solid system of dependencies in cental Italy.

Further south it was different. The Greeks of south Italy joined him, and so did the Lucanians and Samnites.

The Battle of Asculum

Pyrrhus' next move was attack on the west coast, in the hope of winning over Apulia. In 279 the Romans met him at Asculum. This time, as it was a wooded area, the elephants could not be used to full advantage, and although he won the victory, he lost so many troops that the value of his success was nullified. Hence the term, *a Pyrrhic victory*, which came to be a proverbial term for a victory in which the winner was in no better state than the loser.

Pyrrhus lacked one quality necessary in a general, and that was patience. He saw now that hopes of swift success were vanishing, and his interest in the Roman campaign diminished accordingly. At this moment the Syracusans sent him a call for help against the Carthaginians.

Pyrrhus turns his attention to Sicily

Pyrrhus succumbed and accepted the invitation. First, however, he sent an embassy to Rome to negotiate a pardon and immunity for Tarentum. The Carthaginians, who did not relish the prospect of his arrival in Sicily, sent their admiral Mago to urge Rome to refuse. Mago made a treaty with the Romans on behalf of Carthage, and urged them to refuse Pyrrhus' demands. This they finally did: they gave no guarantees to Pyrrhus, but he went all the same.

In Sicily the story of Pyrrhus' Italian campaigns was repeated. At first there were sweeping victories. The Carthaginians were driven out of the whole of Sicily except Lilybaeum. This stronghold could not be forced. It became evident that final success would be a protracted affair. Pyrrhus grew impatient, and his Greeks allies grew weary of the demands of warfare.

While Pyrrhus was away, the Romans brought back into subjection the Lucanians, the Samnites and the wild Bruttii, who lived in the 'toe' of Italy. This meant that Pyrrhus, if he returned, as he was soon to do, would have to begin all over again.

Pyrrhus' return, defeat at Beneventum and death

Pyrrhus did come back in answer to an appeal from Tarentum, but the Carthaginians attacked his fleet and destroyed half of it as he was crossing to Italy. As a result, he arrived with sadly depleted forces and dwindling hopes.

Again he moved northward, and in 275 at Beneventum tried to crush half of the Roman army before it could be joined by the remainder. M. Curius Dentatus, the consul who opposed him, held his ground until the other consul arrived, and the combined army was too much for the Greeks.

Pyrrhus withdrew, and soon after returned to Greece, where he was later killed during a struggle for the rule of Macedonia.

For the first time the East became aware of Rome as a power. Pyrrhus had enjoyed a high military reputation, and it was felt that any people that could defeat him must be worthy of respect.

Rome gains control of south Italy

In 272 Tarentum was finally taken. The Romans were lenient, as they were indeed to all the cities of Magna Graecia. Pyrrhus' garrison was driven out, but the town was not sacked. It did, however, have to admit a Roman garrison as a guarantee of loyalty, and so did all the main Greek cities of the south. They were then classified as naval allies and had to supply ships to Rome. Rome's navy had not previously enjoyed any importance and in fact, it later continued throughout the remainder of Rome's history to play a very subordinate role.

Colonies were established in Apulia to prevent future rebellions in that area.

Finally, in 268 Rome at last issued a silver coinage. Bronze coins had been struck since the Latin wars, but hitherto Rome had made use of Greek coins for any silver currency required. Its wider commitments and increased connection with the East now made it essential for Rome to have an established coinage of its own.

In a sense the Pyrrhic campaigns were little more than an interlude. The fighting was never arduous, nor was Rome at any time seriously threatened. Nevertheless, they did have important consequences. By gaining control of south Italy, Rome came into contact with both Carthage and the Hellenistic East. In short, the Punic Wars were brought a step closer. The campaigns were also a hopeful augury for Rome's success in a wider field. Rome's armies had met troops trained in the best tradition of the Hellenistic mercenaries and had held their own.

The First Punic War

Each time Rome solved a frontier problem a new one was created. The war with Pyrrhus proved no exception. As a result of this war Rome gained control of the rather unstable Greek communities of Magna Graecia. At the same time it was brought indirectly into the sphere of activity of the Greeks who lived in Sicily across the Straits of Messina. In consequence Rome was also very soon at enmity with Carthage.

The situation that arose had resemblances to the one that developed between Athens and Sparta before the Peloponnesian War. Here again were two nations, one almost exclusively a land power, the other devoted to trade and protecting itself with a powerful navy. Yet this divergence, which should have prevented conflict, failed to do so, because a sea power has to build its cities on land, while a land power has boundaries that impinge on those of the sea power.

Carthage's government and its empire

First, however, let us glance briefly at Carthage and its empire before the Punic Wars. Mention has been made earlier of the Phoenician activities in the western Mediterranean, and of those of Carthage in particular. Since the early days, the policy of Carthage had changed little. The city, like Tyre itself and many of the other Phoenician settlements, was built on a peninsula readily defended from mainland assault. Thus it had a much easier task than Athens to make itself impregnable against a continental foe.

Carthage was ruled by a group of powerful families. In that it was not very different from Rome. It too had a supreme council dominated by these families, and it possessed two main executives, the *suffetes*. Carthage, like Rome, forced the countries it ruled to supply troops, but in addition demanded a very heavy tribute. In fact Carthage was concerned far more to exact all it could from its possessions than to win their goodwill and cooperation. Although this harsh policy was advantageous economically (a primary consideration for the trade-minded Phoenicians), it produced unwilling subjects, and this fact contributed to the city's final defeat.

Carthage relied for its defence mainly on the navy. The disastrous series of defeats this navy suffered in the First Punic War at the hands of the inexperienced but determined Romans is interesting. Two factors could have contributed to this turn of events. Carthage may, as a result of years of power, have allowed the quality of its fleet to fall dangerously low. It also seems to have had no answer to the new battle tactics employed by the Romans.

For its armies Carthage, like the Hellenistic Greeks, recruited mercenaries. This procedure had many advantages. Such troops were efficient soldiers, and they only had to be called on—and paid—when war actually threatened.

Yet there were disadvantages. A mercenary soldier was primarily concerned with making a living. Desperate heroism in a lost cause had few attractions for him. He much preferred easy victory and booty.

Through Sicily Carthage impinges on the Romans

Carthage, even in the early days of Rome, had desired to gain control of the western Mediterranean. This goal the Carthaginians had achieved in combination with the Etruscans. Now, with the collapse of the Etruscans, they ruled those seas alone, with little opposition. Being situated in North Africa opposite Sicily, Carthage controlled access to the west by the straits that separated it from that island. The Carthaginians' possession of bases in Sardinia and Corsica gave them control of the upper basin in the west.

They also, as we have noted, had control of part of western Sicily and would have liked to conquer the rest of the island, an ambition frustrated by Syracuse. If they won Sicily they would also dominate the Straits of Messina between Sicily and Italy, the normal and safest routes by which ships passed between the eastern part of the Mediterranean and the west.

Rome could hardly view the presence of Carthaginians in Sicily with equanimity. It constituted a threat to the new Roman dependencies in Magna Graecia, and Pyrrhus' campaigns had underlined this danger. Moreover, the possibility that Carthage could hem Rome in by means of the three island masses was also a threat.

To what extent the Romans were aware of all the implications of Carthage's sea power is doubtful. Probably it was only to a limited extent. But at least they did know Carthage as a powerful force, which had successfully defied Pyrrhus, just as they had, and which was on their new frontier. The Romans were also now in control of the Greek states of the mainland, who would not be slow to confirm their distrust.

Messana leads to open conflict

The incident that led to open conflict concerned Messana. The Sicilian tyrants, like most Hellenistic tyrants, had made much use of mercenaries in their wars, and often recruited them from the Samnites. The Campanian Samnites were popular as mercenaries. Although they were originally infantry fighters, they had learnt the art of horsemanship from the Greeks and they provided the main cavalry contingents to the Greek cities of the south. Rome also made use of them and on this occasion sent a garrison of Campanian mercenaries to hold Rhegium. They, however, got out of hand and in 270 B.C. seized Rhegium for themselves. Rome promptly sent down an army, which crushed them and executed their ringleaders.

However, in 289 B.C. another band of Samnite mercenaries had seized Messana, on the opposite side of the straits to Rhegium. They had encouraged the rebels in Rhegium and took for themselves the name of *Mamertines*, 'the warlike ones'. They used their position to block the Straits of Sicily. The Syracusans could not allow that and appointed Hiero II to deal with the emergency. He led an army against them in 268 B.C. and defeated them.

The Mamertines felt that their plight was desperate and sent embassies to both the Carthaginians and the Romans, neither of whom had any cause to love them. However, politics are a practical matter. The Carthaginians decided that a Messana under their control would be useful and sent a garrison to occupy the city.

The Romans hesitated. They had their treaty with Carthage, according to which they should leave Sicily to the Carthaginians, and Carthage had helped them with money in their war with Pyrrhus. The Senate could not decide, so those who favoured intervention, including a number of Campanian senators, took the matter to an assembly, probably the Comitia Centuriata, which voted for action.

Rome expels the Carthaginian garrison from Messana

A force was sent under Appius Claudius. The faction in Messana that favoured Roman help made the Carthaginian garrison withdraw and admitted the Romans. A combined Carthaginian and Syracusan force attacked Messana, but Appius Claudius defeated them and set siege to Syracuse. Hiero held out for a while, but finally proposed terms for peace.

Hiero had no love for the Carthaginians, who occupied a large part of Sicily and were a constant threat, and an alliance with Rome gave him a chance to defeat them. He offered to hand over any prisoners he had taken and to pay one hundred talents of silver. His terms were accepted and from this time till his death Hiero remained a staunch friend of Rome.

It is interesting that Rome was so hesitant to intervene in Messana. This indecision suggests that again there was conflict between rival groups in the state. The older families saw that war and its necessities tended to break down the old aristocratic exclusiveness. Concessions had to be made to the soldiers who fought the wars, and new men came to power through their skill as generals.

On the other hand, the conquests were proving attractive to another section of the community, the middle class, known as the *equites*. This class took its name from a division in the Comitia Centuriata. In that assembly the equites were the richest citizens, who could afford to provide cavalry for Rome's armies. In time the term lost its exclusively military connotation. It was then used to refer to the social class that derived its wealth mainly from business and trade.

This class was already developing, gaining power and making demands. It is significant that after the Pyrrhic War Rome struck its own silver currency. The commercial interests and the leading families who supported them could see much to gain by extending Rome's influence over to Sicily itself.

It is interesting too that there were a number of Campanians in the Roman Senate. Their fellow-countrymen had for many years fought as mercenaries in Sicily, and they would be well aware of the advantages to be gained by controlling so rich an island.

Carthage was just as reluctant as Rome to involve itself in open war. When the Roman force arrived, the Punic garrison withdrew. Yet inevitably war did eventuate between Rome and Carthage.

War in Sicily. The siege of Agrigentum

In 262 B.C. the Romans attacked Agrigentum, the main Carthaginian city on the island of Sicily. They besieged it for five months, at which time, in response to appeals for help, the Carthaginians sent a force to the rescue under Hanno, which surrounded the Roman force in turn. The two sides held out grimly for two more months, but finally the Carthaginians in Agrigentum grew desperate and Hanno was forced to give battle. He was defeated.

6.2 *A Roman warship showing the inventions of grappling irons and gang-planks for boarding enemy ships. Warships like this were built by Rome to establish sea-power over Carthage.*

The Romans now determined to build a fleet, a necessary step, if they were to defeat the Carthaginians. It consisted of one hundred quinqueremes and twenty triremes. The quinqueremes were the mainstay of the fleets at that time, and Polybius said that the Romans used a captured Carthaginian quinquereme as a model, which may well have been the case.

The Romans also, with Syracusan assistance, added a device that was to be invaluable to their ships. It was a boarding plank, attached to the base of a mast at one end, and armed with an iron spike at the other. It was known as the 'raven', and when the enemy ship came close it was dropped onto its deck and held there by the spike while the Roman forces swarmed aboard. Thus a naval engagement was turned into a land battle, a field in which the Romans were supreme. In 260 B.C. this Roman fleet met the Carthaginians off Mylae and defeated them.

The Romans invade Africa and are defeated

In Sicily the situation degenerated into a dead-lock. Finally, in 256 the Romans decided that success could only be achieved by attacking Carthage itself. They beat the Carthaginian fleet off Ecnomus and landed safely.

The Romans ravaged the countryside, then as winter was approaching, returned home with a large part of the army, leaving Regulus in command of the remainder to hold out for the winter. Regulus defeated that Carthaginian force sent against him, and when peace terms were mooted proposed such harsh conditions that the negotiations collapsed. Regulus, with foolish optimism, determined to take Carthage before his fellow commander returned with the spring.

Unfortunately for him the Carthaginians had engaged a new mercenary commander, Xanthippus, a man of great military ability.

Xanthippus made use of the Carthaginian superiority in cavalry and of their elephants. He met Regulus in battle, drove the Roman centre back with the help of his elephants, then surrounded Regulus' army with his cavalry. The Romans were utterly defeated and most of the army was either destroyed or captured, Regulus being among the prisoners.

A stalemate ensues. Finally a peace of exhaustion

The Romans did manage to rescue some of the survivors of the army and they built a new fleet. Their misfortunes, however, continued. Their fleet was caught in the Syrtes quicksands off the coast of Africa and had to jettison most of its cargo. Then it was overtaken by a storm and half of the ships were lost.

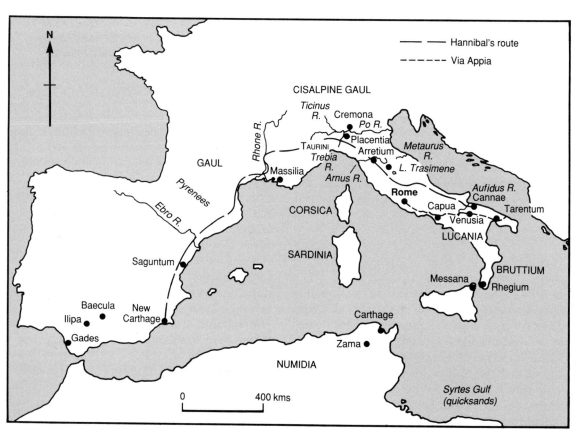

6.3 *The First and Second Punic Wars.*

6.4 *A coin from New Carthage, c. 220 B.C. The obverse side shows what is generally regarded to be Hamilcar Barca, the reverse shows an African elephant with a cloaked rider.*

Roman morale was at a low ebb. All that saved them was their own obstinacy, coupled with the desperate state of their enemy's resources. Despite the defeat and capture of their army and its general, Regulus, in Africa, and despite the disasters at sea, they refused to make peace.

The Carthaginians were in no fit state to take advantage of their enemy's weakness. They were content to hold Sicily by means of the towns of Lilybaeum, Drepana and Eryx. Hamilcar Barca, a member of the family made famous by the Second Punic War, continued resistance to the Romans by means of guerilla warfare.

On sea the Romans' disasters continued. They were defeated by the Carthaginians off Drepana, and a fleet sent from Rome as a reinforcement was wrecked by a storm. The treasury had no money with which to pay for more ships. In desperation, an appeal was made to private citizens. A fund was raised and a last fleet was built.

This fleet met the Carthaginians off the Aegatian Islands in 241. The Punic fleet was the product of an equally exhausted nation. It was poorly equipped and its crews ill trained. The Romans won the day and the war.

The Carthaginians, whose treasury was, like the Romans', utterly exhausted by twenty years of war, asked for peace. After some wrangling this was granted. An indemnity of three thousand two hundred talents was imposed, to be paid in ten years, and Carthage was forced to evacuate Sicily.

Thus the war ended. Rome's superior manpower was the decisive factor, but it had been hampered again and again by the annual change of generals. This problem was to be remedied during the Second Punic War.

Date table

B.C.

282	Attack on Roman ships by Tarentum.
280	Battle of Heraclea.
279	Battle of Asculum.
275	Battle of Beneventum.
272	Capture of Tarentum by Rome.

264	Capture of Messana begins First Punic War.
262	Capture of Agrigentum.
260	Roman sea victory off Mylae.
255	Regulus defeated in Africa.
242	Roman victory at the Aegatian Islands.
241	Peace with Carthage.

Select quotations

1 Plutarch, *Lives*, 'Pyrrhus' 21:
(The origin of the term a 'Pyrrhic Victory'.)
He met the Romans at Asculum, and being forced to encounter them near an area ill suited for cavalry, and a wooded an inaccessible one which made it impossible for the 'beasts' (i.e. the elephants) to gain a passage, he engaged with his phalanx. Many were wounded, many killed and night came without decision. Next day, the generals fixed the battle on level country, mixed the elephants with the hoplites and avoided difficult ground. In addition he distributed javelin throwers and archers among the beasts and created a closely knit strong force. After a long time the rout began when Pyrrhus pressed on against his adversaries, but the biggest part was played by the might of the elephants. And Pyrrhus is said to have declared to someone who congratulated him, 'If we win one more battle against the Romans we will be utterly destroyed'. For he had lost a large part of the force that he brought, and all his friends and generals with a few exceptions.

2 Polybius I, 22.
Since their ships were badly equipped and slow moving, someone suggested to them a contrivance to help them in battle, which subsequently got the name 'raven'. This is how it was made. A round pole was set up in the prow, twenty-four feet in length, nine inches in diameter. On the top it had a pulley, and attached to its base was a gangway thirty-six feet in length and four feet wide. At its end was set an iron spike and a ring. The whole thing looked like a baker's machine. A rope was attached to the ring, with which when the ships met they raised the 'raven' by means of the pulley, and dropped it down on the ship's deck. (The men then swarmed across and boarded the enemy's ship.)

Further reading

Plutarch, *Lives*, 'Pyrrhus'.
Cornelius Nepos, *Lives, Hamilcar*.
T. A. Dorey, and D. R. Dudley, *Rome Against Carthage*, Doubleday & Co. New York, 1972.

Topics for essays or discussion

1 'The Pyrrhic War was the inevitable outcome of Rome's victory of the Samnites.' Discuss.
2 The Pyrrhic War was the first clash between the Roman legion and the Hellenistic mercenary army. What did this encounter reveal?
3 'In the Pyrrhic War the Greek cities displayed their characteristic fickleness and disunity.' Discuss this statement with reference both to the Pyrrhic War and to earlier events in Magna Graecia.
4 What factors led to the outbreak of the First Punic War? Could either side be rightly considered the aggressor and if so, why?
5 Trace the history of Phoenician expansion in the western Mediterranean up to the First Punic War. What light does it cast on the events of this war?
6 What new problems, political and military, arose in the course of the First Punic War? How successful was Rome in solving them?
7 What were the results of the First Punic War for Rome and for Carthage?

Chapter 7

Between wars

THE COMING OF PEACE left Rome and Carthage with many problems to solve. The more immediate problems faced the Carthaginians. The terms of peace, and the huge sum of money which they had to pay as reparation, drained the treasury of Carthage and left them very little with which to pay the mercenaries who had fought for them. Unfortunately, the Carthaginians' solution was to try to cheat the mercenaries, and the result was a short but bitter struggle.

The mercenaries revolted, led by an Oscan called Spendius, and they were joined by the Libyans, who had long been oppressed by Carthage, and who had also supplied it with troops. The war was distinguished by great brutality on both sides. Prisoners were mutilated and massacred. On one occasion they were flung down to be trampled on by elephants.

At first the Carthaginian general was Hanno, a man of no great ability, who seems indeed to have been the one who provoked the war in the first place, by failing to pay the mercenaries. He had so little success that Hamilcar Barca was appointed with a second army. Hamilcar quar-

relled bitterly with Hanno and finally was given sole command, justifying the decision by defeating the mercenaries in 237 B.C.

Rome takes Sardinia

The Roman attitude to this war had been ambivalent, perhaps reflecting, as so often, conflict between the conservative party and those favouring expansion. At first the Romans kept the terms of their peace with Carthage. They refused to help the rebels, and when the Sardinians took the opportunity to revolt and kill their Carthaginian garrison, they also refused aid to them.

However, in 237 B.C. when the Carthaginians crushed the rebels and sent a force to Sardinia to recover the island Roman opinion changed. They seized Sardinia and Corsica and declared that Carthaginian opposition was an unfriendly act, demanding that they give up all claims on the islands, and pay a further 1200 talents. There can be no excuse for such standover tactics, for that was what they were, except the immoral one that they succeeded. Carthage was in such a desperate situation that it had no choice but to accept Rome's terms.

Although the Sardinians had wished to be rid of their Carthaginian masters, they liked the Romans no better. Many long campaigns had to be fought before they were crushed, and as a result Sardinian slaves became so numerous as to give rise to a proverb *Sardi venales*, 'as easy to buy as Sardinians'.

Conflict with the Gauls

Rome now began to have its share of the problems resulting from the war. Many of the mercenaries whom Carthage had hired were Gauls. They now returned home, their occupation gone, and began to stir up trouble. This resulted in the last big conflict between Gauls and Romans on Italian soil.

The Romans precipitated the conflict when Flaminius, a prominent member of the 'popular' (the People's) party, planted colonies in the territory of the Senones, a Gallic tribe. The malcontents could thus point to an actual breach of the peace by the Romans and they used their opportunity to the full.

The response was not immediate, but in 225 the tribes of the Gauls moved south and once more invaded Italy. The Romans were horrified. They had never forgotten that this people once captured Rome. In their desperation they even reverted to human sacrifice.

The Gauls managed to come within three days' journey of Rome itself, but then they were met and defeated in the Battle of Telamon. As a result they retreated towards their own territory.

The Romans now determined to take the offensive. They marched into the territory north of the River Po and crushed the Gauls. One of the consuls, Marcellus by name, met the opposing Gallic chief in single combat and slew him. The reward for this feat was the *spolia opima*. Roman legend claimed that this distinction had been achieved before but this is the most clearly authenticated occasion of its being granted.[1]

They then consolidated their victories in their usual fashion, establishing colonies at Placentia and Cremona to hold down the area, and building a road to it from Rome, the *via Flaminia*, along which its armies, its administrators and its merchants could travel.

The Illyrian pirates

Meanwhile trouble was brewing in the east. Across the Adriatic lay the coast of Illyricum, deeply indented, studded with islands, long the home of pirates. They had enjoyed unusual freedom in their forays while Carthage was engaged in its life and death struggle with Rome. Even the nearby Greek cities were weakened, as they were called on to supply ships for Rome's needs.

Now that the war was over they could no longer be ignored. Rome sent an army to attack them, not on their natural element, the sea, but by crushing the country which maintained them. The Illyrians were not a formidable power and Rome did subdue them after a number of small campaigns. What was significant was that Rome had now become committed in yet another area beyond Italy.

Rome adapts to governing an empire

These developments had their effect on the structure of Rome's government. As long as its expansion was confined to Italy, Rome had a formula for dealing with its conquests that proved successful. The citizen body, or its ruling class, were given a share in the rights of Roman citizens, they were left to manage their internal affairs, and were called on to supply soldiers to Rome's armies.

A revision was now needed. Even with the Pyrrhic War conditions had begun to change. Rome could see little use for Greek soldiers in its armies and certainly the Greeks would not have welcomed the idea. Rome compromised by using them to supply its naval needs.

With Sicily, Sardinia and Corsica it was different again. These lands lay at a greater distance and were separated from Italy by sea. Moreover they already had in existence a government which exacted a tax in the form of one tenth of the harvest.

This was just what Rome required. Its economy had been drained by the need to build fleet after fleet. Rome had to repay the private citizens who had lent the money which built the last fleet of all, and so brought victory. The war indemnities imposed on Carthage helped to repay these debts. The tax, which they continued to exact, helped further to restore Rome's prosperity.

The new areas were no recruiting grounds for Roman armies. Rather they needed an army of occupation themselves. A Roman magistrate was given as his field of responsibility or *provincia*, the administration of these territories. In conse-

---

[1] In 27 B.C. M. Licinius Crassus, the grandson of the triumvir, claimed this distinction for killing Deldo, King of the Bastarnians, but Octavian, who was never willing to grant military distinction to another, refused it, saying that Crassus was under his (Octavian's) auspices—a very niggardly excuse!

quence, the countries came to be called provinces. One province was Sicily, another Sardinia-Corsica. At first a quaestor was given the task, but he had no military authority. Then the number of praetors was raised from two to four, and the two additional magistrates were assigned the new provinces, which they governed for one year.

It soon became obvious that these governors, who belonged to the senatorial class, were in a position to reap immense profit for themselves, with no one to hinder them. In an attempt to prevent such abuses, the *lex Claudia* was passed in 219, which prohibited senators and sons of senators from taking part in trade. On the face of it this was a sensible step, but in fact it simply helped the development of two independent and often conflicting groups: the senatorial class, which enjoyed political and military power, but did not necessarily possess great wealth, and the equestrian class, the *equites* as its members were called, which had enormous wealth, but was without political power or responsibility.

The equites had increased rapidly in numbers and importance during the First Punic War. The need to build fleets and supply armies far from home called for the services of a business class. They had met that need magnificently and after the war they were rewarded. The newly acquired riches created an appetite for more. The provinces gave them their opportunity. True, the taxes were collected by local agents in Sicily, but even so there were many fields for self-enrichment, and they exploited these to the full.

Carthage recoups its losses

Meanwhile, the Carthaginians were trying to retrieve their shattered fortunes. They had lost Sicily and Sardinia in swift succession, and had been saddled with huge war indemnities. The latter were not the worst of their problems. The Carthaginians were experts at making money. On the other hand, if their trade was to prosper, they had to compensate in some way for the territory which they had lost in the First Punic War. They had to win new markets. Moreover, one condition of the peace was that Carthage

should no longer recruit mercenaries in Italy; so they could no longer look to the Samnites and Lucanians in the south, or to the Gauls in north Italy.

The answer was Spain. The Carthaginians had already set up some trading posts on Spanish shores, but their control of the country had suffered during the war. Hamilcar Barca and his son-in-law Hasdrubal set out to consolidate and expand Carthage's position there; with them went Hamilcar's son, Hannibal, who was still only a child. Roman historians give the impression that Spain was a Barcid venture (Barca was the name of Hamilcar's family) and did not have the full support of Carthage. Warmington doubts this view, which he claims to have been part of their attempt to make Hannibal and his family responsible for the outbreak of the Second Punic War.

True, differences of opinion had arisen in Carthage during the war against the mercenaries; true also, there had been a party in the city that favoured expansion into Libya. Yet the Spanish venture, which offered as its prize the Spanish silver mines and the hardy Spanish mercenaries, was too attractive not to have general support. Hamilcar gradually conquered an extensive area in the south and west of Spain. He consolidated his conquests by taking hostages and he imposed tribute on the conquered.

When Hamilcar died his son-in-law Hasdrubal continued his work. He had married a Spanish wife and was personally popular in the country. His diplomacy achieved results that had formerly required military operations. He extended the territory under Carthaginian control, although it still centred on the coast and the river valleys, and did not encroach on the mountainous terrain that lay further inland. He built as his capital New Carthage (Cartagena) in a strategic position on the east coast.

The Romans did not hinder them. After all, Spanish silver was helping pay Carthage's war debts. At the request, however, of the Greek town Massilia Rome made Carthage agree not to extend its territory further north than the River Ebro.

In 221 Hasdrubal was assassinated, and this left Hannibal. He was only twenty-five, but after all Philip and Alexander had been young when they began their careers. Moreover, he had already shown signs of the military prowess that in later ages was to be compared with that of Alexander himself.

Events now moved rapidly. Rome had earlier made an alliance with the town of Saguntum, which lay south of the Ebro, and therefore in Carthaginian territory. Rome, using a technique perfected in earlier wars, began to harass the Carthaginians. First they assisted a Saguntine anti-Carthaginian faction to power, then when the people of Saguntum attacked a neighbouring town, they sent ambassadors to Hannibal, intimating that Saguntum was under their protection and ordering him not to interfere. They found, however, a man who was not susceptible to such tactics. He refused to give any assurances, and when Saguntum continued to be troublesome, he besieged and captured it.

This occurred in 219. The following year, after some hesitation, the Senate protested to Carthage and requested that Hannibal be handed over to them, since he had violated their territory. Naturally Carthage refused, pointing out that Saguntum lay south of the Ebro and was consequently out of Roman jurisdiction. Both sides were left with no way of saving face, and war was declared.

The seeds of the Second Punic War

This raises the important question: what were the causes of the Second Punic War? The Romans' excuses were paltry to the extreme, and their attempts to make them sound more plausible only render this fact more apparent. On the other hand, their hesitation to use the chance when it was offered suggests that they were not consciously provoking open conflict. The Carthaginians themselves took no aggressive step, unless the capture of the troublesome Saguntum could be so called, and it would be unfair to charge them with deliberately provoking the struggle that followed.

It is perhaps nearer the truth to say that the second war resulted from the first and from the situation it created. That war left Rome in

possession of Sicily. Later events added Sardinia and Corsica. Yet the seizing of those two islands was itself significant. The ruthlessness of the first war, and the huge effort it demanded, had affected Roman attitudes.

Rome's eventual victory, after its conquest of most of Italy, convinced it that its armies and its methods of diplomacy were together invincible. The Samnites were ferocious and their mountain fastnesses hard to take. Yet the Samnites were beaten. Pyrrhus' well-trained Hellenistic army with its weird band of elephants on its flanks was a frightening sight. Yet it too had given way. In the First Punic War the Romans had ventured on a new element, the sea, and had beaten its traditional masters, the Phoenicians.

On the other hand, the latest war had frightened Rome badly. Regulus' defeat in Africa, the loss of one fleet after another, the stupendous effort needed to bring final victory, made them determined to avoid another such challenge. What was needed was to crush any possible foe before it became too powerful.

Yet Carthage could hardly abandon its role as mistress of the western Mediterranean. There was a party in Carthage that favoured developing the hinterland of Libya, but that could only be a part solution. Carthage depended on trade for its existence and this trade lay with the west.

The loss of the three islands to the north meant that Carthage had to expand elsewhere, and Spain, where it already had a foothold, was the logical choice.

There was a further issue at stake. Carthage had never been a big town. It lay on a peninsula, which made it easy to defend. It also meant that it could not expand. This did not worry the Carthaginians but it made their policy of using mercenaries in their armies not a preference but a necessity. In the past recruits from the mainland of Italy had supplied their needs. Now this source was explicitly forbidden. Spain could supply the deficiency. Between their own Libyan dependencies and the Spanish tribesmen they could fill their military needs.

It can be seen then that Carthage had to expand in compensation or perish. It is equally apparent that Rome, with vivid memories of the recent war, would regard Carthage's new venture as a threat. In short, there was no longer room in the Mediterranean for two powers of such magnitude. Ultimate conflict was only a question of time.

It might be added that the view put forward by Roman historians that the Second Punic War was instigated as a war of revenge by the Barcid family, with a reluctant Carthage in the background, is not a fair picture. It is true that this family played a central role in the war which followed, but events suggest that they had the backing of their government. When in the campaigns Hannibal seemed to be fighting a lone battle, that was not so much due to a lack of cooperation from Carthage, as to practical difficulties. Now that Carthage had lost command of the sea, it was no easy matter to send reinforcements from Spain to Italy. Indeed the whole theory was intended to excuse Rome of provoking the war by its actions. If it could be suggested that the Barcidae had been planning it all along, then surely Rome merely afforded them the opportunity they were awaiting.

Flaminius instigates reforms which are cut short by war

To turn from military affairs, it is worth observing that this period was also one of social and political reform, a movement cut short by the Second Punic War. The outstanding figure here is Flaminius, the man who fell at Trasimene. He is thought to have inspired the *lex Claudia*, which was one attack on senatorial privilege. The settlements he established in the newly conquered Gallic territory were for the benefit of the small settler, and like the Gracchan proposals later, roused the fury of the upper class.

Finally, in 220 (although there is some doubt about the date) he reorganised the Comitia Centuriata in such a way as to bring it in line with the Comitia Tributa. The Centuriate assembly had long been weighted in favour of the propertied classes. This maldistribution he modified. The details of his reforms are much argued, but it seems likely that he took the five classes

below the cavalry class and gave them equal voting power, seventy votes each class. Previously the voting power had been on a sliding scale, depending on the possession of property. Thus the assembly, which had once been the bulwark of privilege, lost the power to block the popular will.

As we shall see in the next chapter, Hannibal put an end to the aspirations of the reformers, and the move was not resumed until the time of the Gracchi.

Date table

B.C.
240 Rebellion of Carthaginian mercenaries.
238 Rome takes over Sardinia.
237 Hamilcar begins operations in Spain.
230 War against Illyrian pirates.
227 Four praetors established, two to be governors of provinces.
225 Battle of Telamon.
221 Hannibal succeeds Hasdrubal.
219 lex Claudia passed.
218 Outbreak of Second Punic War.

Select quotations

1 Polybius, *Histories* I 80:
(An incident from the Mercenary War.)
After this Autaritus the Gaul spoke saying that the one chance of safety in the affair was to reject any hope offered them by the Carthaginians. . . .saying this he advised them to mutilate and kill Gesco and those captured with him, and as well any of the Carthaginians who were subsequently captured. He was most effective in the councils because most understood him. For through his long service he knew how to speak Phoenician. Most understood this dialect owing to the length of their own employment by them. Many came forward from every race and tried to beg them at least not to mutilate him, owing to Gesco's past kindnesses to them. . . . When it was found that they were

dissuading them from revenge, and when one of the by-standers yelled out 'throw', they stoned all those who had come forward. And their relatives carried them out, looking as if trampled on by elephants. Spendius and his men led Gesco and his fellow-prisoners out of the fortifications. Taking them a little way from the camp, they first cut off their hands, beginning from Gesco. . . . Then they lopped off the wretches' extremities, broke their legs and threw them still living into a trench.

2 Livy XXI. 4:
(A description of Hannibal.)
He showed the utmost daring in taking risks, the utmost judgement in the midst of peril. No hardship could wear out his body or tame his spirit. He was equally enduring of heat and cold. His desire for food and drink was limited by his natural needs not by self-indulgence. In waking and sleeping he took no heed of day or night. What time remained from business he gave to rest. Nor was sleep wooed by soft couch or silence. Many often saw him covered by a military cloak lying among the sentries and guards. His clothing was no different from that of his companions. His arms and horses distinguished him. He was by far the first of cavalry and infantry: the first to engage in battle, the last to leave it. These great virtues were compensated by mighty vices. Inhuman cruelty, treachery unusual even for a Carthaginian, nothing true or sacred, no fear of gods, no respect for an oath, no sense of obligation.
(The last statements, coming from a Roman, must be treated with some caution.)

Further reading

Refer again to Dorey and Dudley, *Rome Against Carthage.*
Flaubert, *Salammbo* (An historical novel, to be read for interest rather than historical accuracy.)

Topics for essays or discussion

1 What were the main results of the First Punic War for Rome? What new policies were evolved as a result of its involvement overseas?
2 How was Carthage's position in the Mediterranean affected by the First Punic War?
3 What were the causes of the Second Punic War? Was it the inevitable result of the earlier conflict, or did other factors come into play?
4 Compare the conflict of interests between Rome and Carthage with those existing between Greece and Sparta before the Peloponnesian War, where also a sea and a land power were at enmity.

Chapter 8

The Second Punic War

AFTER he took Saguntum Hannibal at once began his invasion of Italy. He did not go by sea, as the Carthaginian navy was now smaller than the Roman one and dispirited by its recent defeats. Instead he chose to cross the Alps, a difficult route but one that gave him in compensation the element of surprise (see Fig. 6.3 p. 58). In addition, the Celts, after their recent wars with Rome, generally welcomed him and gave him assistance.

The Romans, as so often, were preparing for a war like the last one. One consul, Sempronius, was sent to Sicily, ready to cross to Africa; the other, P. Scipio, was sent to Spain. Scipio was very surprised when he landed at the mouth of the Rhone on the way to Spain to learn from his scouts that Hannibal's army was up the river. He set off after him but found that Hannibal had crossed the Rhone and was well away. Scipio then sent his brother Gnaeus on with the main army to Spain while he returned with a small force to Italy to be ready to meet Hannibal on his arrival. This was to prove to be a very wise decision. It meant that the Romans were able to stop reinforcements from Spain coming to Hannibal, reinforcements that he was to need desperately for final victory.

Hannibal crosses the Alps

Hannibal now prepared to cross the Alps. Some of the Celtic tribes tried to oppose him but they stood in some awe of his elephants, of which he had thirty-seven. However, when he reached the top of the mountains it was the snow that was to be his main obstacle. At one point he even had to make a road for his forces, especially the elephants. By the time he reached Italy his forces were sorely depleted. Through loss in action and through desertion he had lost almost half of the force that had originally left Spain, and he had now only 20 000 infantry and 6000 cavalry.

Hannibal had to sack the main town of one Gallic tribe, the Taurini, who were prepared to be hostile, but in general the Gauls welcomed him and willingly joined his army, thus helping make up for the losses he had suffered on his journey. This was to be a mixed blessing for Hannibal. His Gallic troops were not always reliable, and also they were heartily disliked by the peoples of Italy. This made it harder for Hannibal to appear as a liberator from the bondage of Rome, as was his plan.

8.1 *The reverse of a coin from New Carthage c. 200 B.C. showing what is generally regarded to be a portrait of Hannibal.*

The Battles of Ticinus and Trebia

Scipio on his return to Italy took command of the army on the Po, which he marched to Placentia. (Placentia and Cremona had been recently established as colonies to secure north Italy against the Gauls.) Scipio marched along the Po, meeting Hannibal at the junction of the Ticinus River. There a Roman force met a detachment of Numidian cavalry and a skirmish took place. The Roman force was beaten but managed to make its way back to the main body. Scipio, however, was wounded in the engagement, being rescued according to one story by his son, who as Scipio Africanus was to play such a decisive part in this war.

Scipio was now deserted by some of his Gallic troops and withdrew along the Po to its junction with the Trebia. There he was joined by Sempronius and his army, newly arrived back from Sicily, to meet the crisis. Scipio was incapacitated by his wound but Sempronius was eager for action and Hannibal was ready to give it. Hannibal drew his forces up in a flat area and in a watercourse concealed his brother Mago with an ambushing force of infantry and cavalry.

Sempronius led his men across the swollen Trebia and drew them up in the usual three lines with the cavalry on the flanks. Hannibal placed his Gallic troops in the centre and had his cavalry on the wings with the elephants before them. When the armies engaged the elephants threw the Roman cavalry into confusion. The Carthaginian cavalry then drove the Romans back and attacked them on the flanks. Finally Mago led his force from their ambush and took the Romans in the rear. The Romans fled, except for a force in the centre, which led by Sempronius fought its way through the opposing Gauls and made its way to Placentia. Here it was joined by Scipio, who had been left in the camp during the battle. Hannibal's losses were mainly from his Gallic troops, but in the snow that followed he lost most of his elephants. By the end of that winter only one survived.

Roman accounts of the battle put the blame heavily on Sempronius, and in the two defeats that followed they also had a scapegoat. Yet Sempronius' army was larger than Hannibal's and the real truth was that it took some time for the Romans to realise just how formidable an opponent Hannibal was.

The Battle of Trasimene

The next spring saw the two new consuls, Servilius and Flaminius, preparing to meet Hannibal. This time Flaminius was to be blamed for the defeat that followed, and he was portrayed as one of the popular party, and headstrong. Yet he had beaten the Gallic tribe of the Insubres in 223 B.C. and had the *via Flaminia* built north from Rome to the troubled area of the Gauls. He was no novice. Servilius with his army guarded the coastal route, while Flaminius at Arretium (Arrezzo) was ready in case Hannibal went through Etruria. This was what Hannibal did, hoping for support from the Etruscans, with some justification. However, he took a short route along the Arno, aiming to surprise them. Unfortunately the Arno was in flood and most of the pack animals perished as they struggled through the marshes. Hannibal himself caught ophthalmia and lost the sight of one eye.

Undeterred Hannibal made his way to Arretium and tried to lure Flaminius into battle. Flaminius took up the challenge and set off in pursuit of Hannibal. Since Servilius was coming to meet him, he hoped that Hannibal would be caught between the two armies. By Lake Trasimene Hannibal posted his men in ambush in the hills that lay along the lake and waited. The Romans arrived in early morning when everything was covered by mist and walked right into the trap. The army was surrounded on all sides and did not even have time to change into battle formation. It was a massacre. Flaminius fell early and apart from those who were killed on the spot, some tried to wade out into the lake, where they either drowned or were easily killed. After the battle Hannibal set free all the allied men he had taken, keeping only the Romans. Servilius' cavalry did arrive just at the end of the battle, but it was easily beaten.

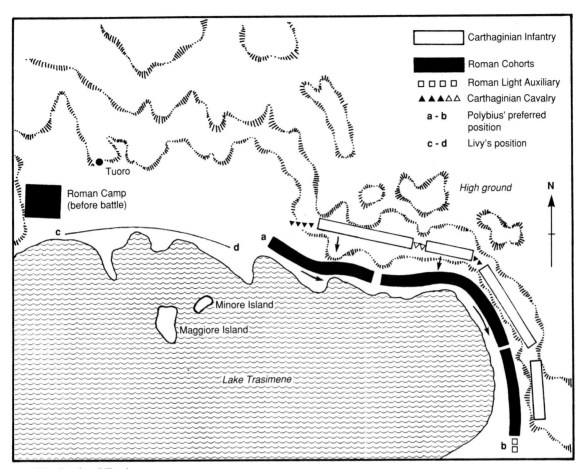

Carthaginian Infantry

Roman Cohorts

□ □ □ □ **Roman Light Auxiliary**

▲ ▲ ▲ ▲ △ **Carthaginian Cavalry**

a - b Polybius' preferred position

c - d Livy's position

High ground

N

Tuoro

Roman Camp (before battle)

Minore Island

Maggiore Island

Lake Trasimene

8.2 *The Battle of Trasimene.*

New tactics with Fabius the delayer

The Romans were appalled by the news and appointed a dictator, an office which had long fallen into disuse. Q. Fabius Maximus was appointed, an aristocrat of the ancient Fabian clan. He led his army down to south Italy where Hannibal tried as usual to provoke a battle. This Fabius refused. He marched his army along the higher ground beside Hannibal, harassing any detachments that left the main force. These were the famous tactics that gained him the name of *Cunctator*, the Delayer.

Finally Hannibal led his army into fertile Campania and began to ravage it. Fabius was now under enormous pressure, but still he resisted. He simply posted his men to block the pass Hannibal would have to go through when he returned south. Hannibal was equal to the occasion. He drove a herd of cattle with lighted torches tied to their heads up the foothills by night, and when the Roman guards came down, thinking it was the enemy, he slipped through the pass.

Fabius' policy now fell into disfavour and the next year he was not elected consul. Paullus and Varro were chosen, and again Varro was to be blamed for the coming defeat. He was a *novus homo* and probably supported by the Scipionic clan. Hannibal was in south Italy, but in June he came north in search of corn supplies and headed for Cannae, where the Romans had a corn depot. There the Roman army met him.

The Battle of Cannae

About the manoeuvring leading up to the Battle of Cannae the Roman historians made much of the different attitudes of Varro and Paullus, but their account is of doubtful worth. What is certain is that the Roman practice of the two consuls commanding on alternate days when they were both with an army was a fatal one, as was the practice of changing generals each year with the consular elections. Only bitter experience taught the Romans what was needed in order to face a professional general, let alone one who was a military genius.

The River Aufidus flows by Cannae, and the two armies encamped by it and several days were spent skirmishing. It was Varro's day of command when the two armies were finally drawn up for battle. The Roman army faced south, with its right wing near the Aufidus. Paullus commanded this wing and he had the Roman cavalry drawn up between his force and the river. The centre was immensely strong, perhaps as many as fifty men deep. In the centre

were the veteran troops. Varro commanded on the left and he had the allied cavalry drawn up by him.

Hannibal drew his men up following a special plan. He no longer had elephants to help him, but he still hoped to take the enemy from the flanks. His centre, drawn up more thinly, as his infantry were less numerous, consisted of Gauls and Spaniards. On each side of them he drew up his veteran African soldiers, a formidable force. Hasdrubal on the left wing led the Gallic and Spanish cavalry, while Hanno on the right commanded the Numidian cavalry.

Hannibal commanded the centre, and as they prepared to engage, instead of holding back the centre actually drew it up with a bulge in the middle, like a crescent, towards the Romans. Battle was joined. The Roman cavalry by the river were cramped and were soon routed by their opponents. The main army of the Romans advanced steadily, though the Gauls and Spaniards fought bravely and did not break. However, as the Romans continued to advance, the African detachments abruptly turned left and

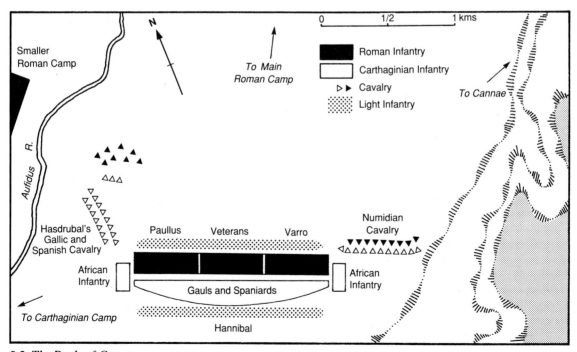

8.3 *The Battle of Cannae.*

right and attacked the Romans on their flanks. Hasdrubal too, after disposing of his opponents, led his Numidian cavalry round and took the Roman army from the rear. As at Trasimene, it was a massacre.

The Roman losses were immense. Livy gives it as 47 500 infantry, and 2700 cavalry. About 19 300 were taken prisoner and 14 550 escaped. With the officers it was as devastating. Paullus was killed and more than half the military tribunes. In all, eighty men were killed who were either senators or due to be senators. Some of the infantry escaped with the young Scipio. Varro escaped with some cavalry then gathered together all the survivors and took them back to Rome. Although Roman historians have been unkind to Varro, this was not the feeling of the Senate at the time. They thanked him for not despairing of the Republic and were to give him a number of commands in the years that followed.

Hannibal's losses were not heavy, and as in his earlier battles the Gauls suffered worst. In all he lost about 4000. Livy tells a story that Hannibal was urged to march on Rome after this victory but this was not really an option. Rome was too far away and still had ample troops to defend it.

After Cannae. Capua defects

After the Battle of Cannae, which ends Polybius' third book, we only have this author in fragments. This is a pity, but Livy did have Polybius and made constant use of him. The years that succeed are themselves less interesting. Hannibal's days of great victories were over, and he was to be subjected to a war of attrition, which in the long run spelled the end of his hopes.

Still, for the moment his prospects had never seemed brighter. Hannibal as usual released all the prisoners who were not Roman and defections came thick and fast. Most of Samnium joined him and, down south, Lucania and the Bruttii. Best of all, after some negotiation Capua came over to his side. Hannibal promised that when he conquered Rome, Capua would be his capital in Italy and he assured them that they

would not be called on to do military service. Philip of Macedon also entered into negotiations with him, but although this horrified the Romans when they heard it, in fact they managed to stir up enough trouble in Greece to keep Philip quiet, and he never took part in the war.

In Rome itself, although they did not abandon all hope, the mood was one of desperation. In the Forum Boarium they buried alive a male and female Gaul and a male and female Greek to propitiate the gods.

Otherwise it was business as usual. Fabius regained power as did his policies. Financially Rome was desperate, with an empty treasury. Luckily Hiero sent corn and enough money to pay Roman troops in Sicily for six months. It was a real loss when he died in 215 B.C.

Meanwhile Hannibal was concerned to win a sea port to give him easy access to Carthage. He did not try to take one by siege. Lack of siege equipment has been given as a reason for Hannibal's reluctance, but it is not true. He could easily have built it. The fact is that he wanted willing allies, and did not have enough troops to garrison towns taken against their will. The first Roman general to confront him was Marcellus, then a praetor. He was a tough soldier, who as we noted in chapter 7 in the Gallic war had killed the opposing commander in hand-to-hand combat, gaining for this the *spolia opima*.

Marcellus commanded the soldiers who survived Cannae, but no decisive battle took place. In the ensuing period both sides employed scorched-earth policies, with such thoroughness that agriculture especially in south Italy never recovered. As well, both sides built permanent camps to serve as bases for their campaigns, Hannibal on Mount Tifata north-east of Capua, the Romans a little south, a camp called *castra Claudiana* after Claudius Marcellus who built it.

Sicily. The siege of Syracuse

Fabius Maximus and Marcellus were elected consuls for 214 B.C. A total of twenty legions were put in the field, and the property qualification for military service was lowered. In Italy the Romans were holding their own, but in Sicily Hiero's grandson who succeeded him went over to the Carthaginians. Marcellus was sent over to hold the island. It was no easy task. The Carthaginians were desperate to win, as it would give them a stepping stone for sending reinforcements to Hannibal, and they sent an army and a fleet to help the rebels.

Marcellus tried to storm Syracuse, but the Syracusans, helped by the great mathematician Archimedes, who invented ingenious devices for them, foiled his endeavours. Finally he settled down to a regular siege. It was to take two years.

In 212 B.C. the Romans came to an agreement with the Aetolian League, which kept Philip busy in Greece so he could not help Hannibal. However, Hannibal had an important success when Tarentum joined him, giving the long desired sea port. The Roman garrison, however, held out in the citadel. The Romans were besieging Hannibal's other new ally, Capua, and he tried to divert them by marching on Rome, but Rome held out and the investing army stayed round Capua.

By the end of 212 B.C. Marcellus finally took Syracuse. He was helped by a plague that practically wiped out the Carthaginian force, and after he gained entry to the city the pro-Roman faction handed it over. The city was sacked, but the slaughter was moderated by the desire to spare the Roman sympathisers. Archimedes himself was killed although Marcellus had given orders for him to be spared. Capua too finally surrendered. Its senators were executed and the city was made a property of Rome, henceforth to have no political life.

Death of Marcellus

Marcellus was elected consul for 210 B.C., although his enemies saw that he was not given a triumph and that the other consul Laevinus was sent to complete the subjugation of Sicily. This he did successfully, taking steps also to restore its agriculture so it could supply Rome's armies with corn.

The year 208 B.C. saw the conquest of Tarentum by Fabius Maximus, but the same year saw a terrible disaster. The two consuls, Crispinus and Marcellus were reconnoitring a hill-top near Venusia in south Italy when they were surprised by a cavalry detachment of Numidians. Marcellus was killed and Crispinus was severely wounded, dying later that year. Hannibal, who was a great admirer of Marcellus, gave his body a funeral with full military honours.

The Spanish War. Death of the two Scipios

It is now time to see how the Romans fared in Spain. When Gnaeus Scipio was sent there at the beginning of the war, he was not recalled as the Romans did not want reinforcements to get through to Italy. Indeed they later sent Gnaeus' brother Publius to join him. The Romans won back the land north of the Ebro, capturing Hannibal's baggage train, which he had left behind, and in 213 B.C. they took Saguntum and won over the Celtiberians, Spanish mercenaries who had fought for the Carthaginians. It looked as if their fortunes were in the ascendant.

Unluckily, the Carthaginians saw the urgency of the situation and sent reinforcements. There were now three Carthaginian armies in Spain, led by Hannibal's two brothers, Mago and Hasdrubal, and by Hasdrubal Gisgo. The Romans did not realise that their opponents has been increased and came south to fight them. They split their army into two, Publius to lead the larger force against Mago and Hasdrubal Gisgo, while Gnaeus with the rest of the army and the Celtiberian mercenaries was to engage the other Hasdrubal.

Publius first met the Carthaginians, and was defeated, being himself killed. Gnaeus then found himself opposed by the whole Carthaginian army. His Celtiberians deserted him and he and his army suffered the same fate as the rest of the Roman force. It was a terrible disaster, and all that saved the Romans from utter catastrophe was that the three Carthaginian generals bickered with each other, and as a result they did not immediately invade Italy.

The young Scipio in Spain. New Carthage is taken

Rome sent Claudius Nero to Spain to keep the Carthaginians in check, then in 210 B.C. they put young Publius Scipio, later to be called Scipio Africanus, in command. This was a break in tradition, for Scipio was not yet even a praetor, but Rome had learnt that it had to be prepared to bend the rules. Scipio had proved himself in war, through his father he had Spanish connections, and he belonged to a powerful clan. It was to be a very wise choice.

Scipio brought reinforcements for Claudius Nero and spent the winter training his troops in new manoeuvres, which, as we shall see from the coming battles, involved more independent movement of the army during a battle, something that Hannibal was an expert in, while the old Roman army tended to keep to its rigid battle line. Some say that he introduced the use of the Spanish sword, but that we think was first adopted in the First Punic War.

With the spring Scipio prepared a surprise attack on New Carthage. This was the main base of the Carthaginians, but had only a small garrison. The three Carthaginian armies were scattered in various parts of Spain trying to hold down the native population, which was very restless. Scipio sent his friend Laelius with the fleet while he set off with the army, determined to take the town before any of the three Punic generals could come to its rescue.

The night before the battle he told his army that Poseidon, the god of the sea, would help him and that is what seemed to happen. It was no accident, however, as Scipio had learnt that at low tide New Carthage's walls could be approached through the lagoon. The attack went on all day by army and fleet, then late in the afternoon the scaling party set off with its ladders through the lagoon. A strong wind blew back the water and made the approach even easier. The walls were scaled and the city taken. It was a

great prize. It not only contained the main arsenal of the Carthaginians and 600 talents of silver, but the Spanish hostages were there whom the Carthaginians held to ensure their people's loyalty. They were all released by Scipio, and many of the tribes began to come over to him.

The Battle of Baecula

Scipio continued to prepare his troops and consolidate his position, untroubled by the Carthaginians. Then in 208 B.C. he marched south. Hannibal's brother Hasdrubal came to meet him and encamped in a strong position, near Baecula (Bailen). Scipio sent his cavalry to provoke battle, then when Hasdrubal's army emerged from the camp, he used a novel strategy. Instead of the usual three lines, Scipio divided his infantry in two, with himself on the right, Laelius on the left, and took the enemy on the flanks. Hasdrubal was defeated and he extricated what troops he could and hastened north to try to join Hannibal in Italy.

Some Roman writers blamed Scipio for letting him go, but there were still two Carthaginian armies in Spain, and in fact Scipio's victory meant that it was a sadly depleted army that did finally enter Italy. Scipio as usual released his prisoners, including the son of the Numidian prince Massinissa, a gesture that was to bring its reward.

The Battle of Ilipa

The next two years saw no major action, but in 206 B.C. Hasdrubal, Gisgo and Mago led their armies north to force an issue. They met the Romans at Ilipa. This was to be the site of Scipio's next big battle. Scipio led his forces out to meet Hasdrubal, who led the Carthaginians, and drew them up in conventional style. This he did for some days. Then he had his men breakfast early and come out before the Carthaginians were prepared. Hasdrubal hastened out, his troops unfed.

This time Scipio put his Spaniards in the centre, with his Roman infantry on the wings, and the cavalry beyond them again. He held his attack till midday, when his foe was hungry and hot, then attacked. The Carthaginian elephants took fright and hindered their own cavalry, while Scipio led his two infantry forces past the enemy on the left and right, then swung them round to attack the African troops on the flank. It was a strategy very similar to Hannibal's at Cannae. It would have been an utter massacre if a storm had not separated the combatants.

Scipio was one of the new breed of general, which was in due course to produce the emperors of Rome. He forged a very strong bond with his army, helped by his long command. He had also, as many writers note, an immense personal charm. It is interesting that when Spanish chiefs came to join him after the Battle of Baecula some hailed him as king. Scipio knew how hated that name was to the Romans, and told them not to use it but rather *imperator*, victorious general. This title was to be used regularly by the great generals that came later and was the title adopted by the Roman rulers in the imperial period, giving rise to our own word, *emperor*.

Hasdrubal enters Italy. The Battle of Metaurus

After the battle of Baecula in 208 B.C. Hasdrubal made his way over the Alps, hoping to join his brother. Unluckily, the letter he sent to Hannibal was intercepted by Claudius Nero, who was down south keeping watch on the Carthaginians. Claudius then left a masking force to conceal his absence and hastened north to join the other consul, Livius Salinator, who was facing Hasdrubal on the banks of the Metaurus. Hasdrubal fought bravely but he was outnumbered. His army was defeated and he was killed. Claudius then hurried back to Hannibal and Hasdrubal's head was flung into Hannibal's camp.

The Battle of Zama ends the war

Scipio returned to a jubilant Italy in 205 B.C. He was easily elected consul, but was denied a

triumph. He was given Sicily as his command, *provincia* as it was called, an ideal jumping-off place for the attack on Africa. Scipio enrolled his army, including many veterans of Cannae, and landed in Africa, where he attacked a number of towns. Carthage sent for Hannibal, but was so discouraged that it asked for peace. Scipio accepted their proposals subject to the confirmation of the Senate. This was not forthcoming. It would not grant peace while Hannibal was still in Italy. In 203 B.C. Hannibal did sail from Italy and 202 was to see the final battle.

Hannibal was at Zama, not far from Carthage. His cavalry was weak, but he had eighty elephants. Hannibal drew his forces up in the usual three lines with the Numidian cavalry on the left wing, the Carthaginian cavalry on the right, and the elephants in front of his whole army. Scipio drew his force up with his Numidians (whom Massinissa had brought when he joined his force) on the right, facing Hannibal's Numidians, and on the left his Italian cavalry, led by Laelius. He drew up his infantry, leaving corridors for the passage of the elephants.

The elephants did begin the battle, and some did charge through the gaps, but most of them swung round and attacked Hannibal's own cavalry, which combined with the attack of Massinissa and Laelius led to their speedy rout. The infantry were then locked in grim combat, pausing in the middle of the fight to regroup. Then the cavalry returned from pursuit of the enemy and took the Carthaginians in the rear. Most of the foe were killed in action, but Hannibal fled with a small force.

Once again Carthage sued for peace, urged on by Hannibal, who knew how hopeless their plight was. Scipio was again ready to comply, especially as even now the capture of Carthage itself was no easy task. The Senate made the original terms still harsher, but they too were willing to make peace.

The Carthaginians had to surrender their prisoners, almost all their fleet, all their elephants, and pay an indemnity of ten thousand talents over fifty years. The final clause was the one that was to be fatal to them. Massinissa, by joining Rome and bringing with him his Numidian cavalry, played an important part in Rome's

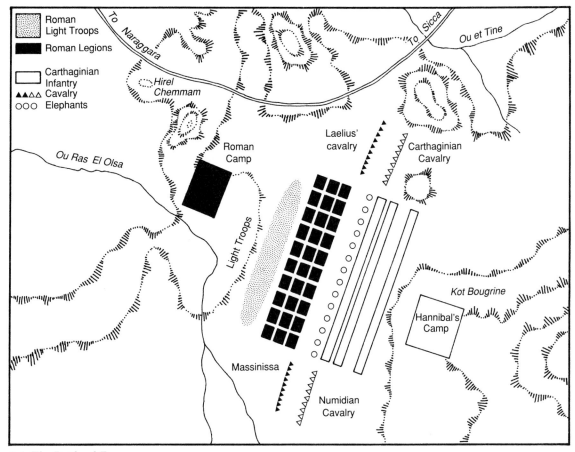

8.4 *The Battle of Zama.*

victory. All his land was to be restored to him by Carthage, and the city was forbidden to wage any war without permission from Rome. We shall see what use Massinissa was to make of this condition. Scipio went to Carthage and accepted the peace terms. He then returned to Rome and was finally given the triumph he so richly deserved.

Date table

B.C.
218	Hannibal invades Italy, Battle of Trebia.
217	Battle of Trasimene.
216	Battle of Cannae.
215	Beginning of First Macedonian War.
212	Syracuse captured.
208	Battle of Baecula
207	Battle of Metaurus.
202	Battle of Zama.

Select quotations

1 B.W. Tuchman: *The Guns of August* (Macmillan, 1962), p. 20
(The German plan of campaign for World War I.)
To achieve decisive victory, Schlieffen fixed upon a strategy derived from Hannibal and the Battle of Cannae. The dead general who mesmerised Schlieffen had been dead a very long time. Two thousand years had passed since

Hannibal's classic double envelopment of the Romans at Cannae. 'Field gun and machine gun had replaced bow and slingshot', Schlieffen wrote, 'but the principles of strategy remain unchanged. The enemy's front is not the objective. The essential thing is to crush the enemy's flanks .... and complete the extermination by attack upon his rear.'
(This passage was first brought to my attention by Professor L.C.F. Turner of the Royal Military College, Duntroon. Less well known is the fact which I learnt from Mr A. Treloar that an Australian general also made use of Hannibal's strategy. Brigadier-General Elliot was a classical scholar, and his attack with the 15th Brigade of the A.I.F. at Villers-Bretonneux in 1918 was modelled on Hannibal's attack at Cannae. Like Hannibal he was successful.)

2 Livy XXII, 38:
Before they set out from the city, the consul Varro delivered many fiery harangues, in which he claimed that the war had been brought to Italy by the nobles and would continue to devour the entrails of the republic if they had more generals like Fabius, while he would finish it the day he saw the enemy. His colleague, Paullus, made one speech the day before he left the city, more notable for its veracity than for its popularity. In it he made no harsh pronouncement against Varro, except just this, that he was surprised, not unnaturally, at a leader who before he came to know his or the enemy's army or the nature of the terrain, while still wearing his toga in the city was sure what

he would do when under arms, and could even predict the day on which he would join battle with the foe.

Further reading

Livy, _The War with Hannibal_, Penguin Classic.
Polybius, _The Rise of the Roman Empire_, Penguin Classic.
H.H Scullard, _Scipio Africanus, Soldier and Politician_, Thames and Hudson, 1970.
T.A. Dorey and D.R. Dudley, _Rome Against Carthage_, Doubleday and Co., New York, 1972.
J.F. Lazenby, _Hannibal's War_, Aris & Philips, Warminster, England, 1978.

Topics for essays or discussion

1 Was there any basis in the Roman claim that the Second Punic War was a Barcid affair? Why did they make this claim?
2 Why did Rome suffer such disastrous defeats in the first part of the war? How did they call a halt to this process?
3 Analyse the part played by the Senate in the Second Punic War.
4 Compare the Second Punic War with the Samnite wars. Had Rome learnt any lessons from the earlier struggle, which it could now apply?
5 What long range effects did the Second Punic War have on Rome's control over its armies? What caused these problems to rise?

Chapter 9

The Macedonian Wars and Spain

ROME was now to come in contact with the Greek homeland and the Middle East, homes of highly civilised peoples. As was explained in *View From Olympus* Greece of the Hellenistic age was very different from Greece of the Classical period. Athens was a university town, Sparta a backwater, while Greece was dominated by the Achaean League in the south, and the Aetolian League in the north. North of Greece was Macedonia, much weaker than in Alexander's day, while Asia Minor was shared between Syria and the vigorous state of Pergamum. Rhodes controlled the sea trade in the eastern Mediterranean.

We owe much to Polybius for the events we are to consider, as he and his father played an active role in them as leading citizens of the Achaean League. We have to be careful, however, as there is naturally a bias in favour of the Achaean League.

In fact Rome's involvement in this area began after the First Punic War, when some Italian traders complained of piracy by Illyria. Illyria in north-west Greece and Epirus in the south were much given to piracy, as was incidentally the

Aetolian League. Rome took action to curb the Illyrians and gave support to Demetrius of Pharos, who had helped them against the Illyrians.

Rome left the people of Greece free, but the Greeks and Demetrius were in a relation of clientship to the Romans. The relationship sprang from that existing between the patrician noble and his clients. He gave them protection and they owed him loyalty, having the same friends and enemies as he. Rome had used this client relationship within Italy with some success, but the eastern peoples could not conceive of such a vague bond, needing to have terms spelled out more exactly. So many misunderstandings were to arise.

The First Macedonian War

Demetrius was the first to learn a lesson. He tried to expand southward and, early in the Second Punic War, Rome expelled him from Illyria. He fled to Philip V, who had recently become King of Macedonia. Demetrius persuaded Philip to attack Illyria, which brought him into conflict with the Aetolian League. When Rome sent a fleet under Laevinus, to control him Philip, as we noted earlier, made an alliance with Hannibal. Luckily Laevinus managed to get the Aetolian League to keep Philip busy in Greece, and Philip was never a threat to Rome.

The Second Macedonian War

It was not till after the Battle of Zama that Rome again tackled its eastern problem. It sent Laevinus to investigate and found that Philip was not only attacking Illyria but also Rome's friends, Pergamum and Rhodes. Laevinus took Philip to task, and when Philip refused to keep the peace Rome formally declared war.

At least that was the Senate's intention. When, however, the matter was put to the Comitia Centuriata for ratification approval was refused. The citizens of Rome were weary of war and did not want another.

The approval was not given till the Senate agreed that none of the troops that had fought Hannibal would be required to serve, but a new army enlisted. This in effect meant a heavy reliance on allied forces, a practice that Rome was to pursue after that, causing strong dissatisfaction and then revolt by the allies. It was a motley army that eventually set out under inferior commanders. Needless to say they had little luck.

In 199 B.C. Flamininus was sent out to take command. He was a protégé of the Scipios, an experienced commander, and a lover of Greek culture, as were the Scipios. He set to work to restore discipline to his army, then went round the Greek cities, proclaiming his policy of winning them freedom. He won much support, from the Achaean League among others. Philip began to be anxious and offered peace, but the terms were too much for him. They involved among other things leaving Greece free, and giving up the key garrison towns whereby he had maintained control, 'the Fetters of Greece' as he called them, namely Chalcis, Demetrias and Acrocorinth (the citadel of Corinth). War then was resumed.

The Battle of Cynoscephalae. Greece is declared free

In 197 B.C. the opposing forces met at Cynoscephalae in Thessaly and Philip's army was annihilated. Flamininus then carried out his promise. He attended the next Isthmian Festival and amid enthusiastic applause declared Greece indeed free.

However, the satisfaction was not general. Although Philip had been humbled he was not crushed completely, in line with Rome's general policy of keeping a balance of power. In addition, he was a useful bulwark between Greece and the barbaric tribes to its north. The Aetolian League was not happy, as it had not been given a licence to plunder, as it would have liked, and it felt that the Achaean League should have been granted much less than it was, the Achaean League being only a recent ally of Rome.

Rome also had its worries, which delayed the promised departure from Greece. Antiochus III of Syria had become a threat in Asia Minor, and Rome sent a message to him declaring that the Greeks in Asia Minor should also be free. This, however, was only a bargaining counter, as they were far more worried by his moves against Thrace and Thessaly in north-east Greece. In addition in 195 B.C. when Hannibal was driven out of Carthage he took refuge with Antiochus. None the less, Rome did not want to be permanently in Greece and finally they did evacuate it and return home.

This did not mean that Antiochus was forgotten. Protracted negotiations followed, and Antiochus tried to win support in Greece. He found a ready listener in the Aetolian League, which felt it had not been well treated by Rome. At the same time Eumenes of Pergamum was urging Rome to take action as he was afraid that Syria had designs on him.

War with Syria. The Battle of Thermopylae

It was the Aetolian League that precipitated action. They took Syria's 'feelers' as meaning more than they probably did and fell on the 'Fetters of Greece'. They succeeded in taking Demetrias, and a somewhat reluctant Antiochus came to Greece to support his ally. He too proclaimed that he had come to liberate Greece, but he was only believed when the presence of his army made disbelief dangerous. The Romans sent an army against him led by Glabrio. It met Antiochus' forces at Thermopylae in 191 B.C. and defeated them. Antiochus now withdrew to Asia Minor.

Glabrio's lieutenant in the battle of Thermopylae had been Cato, the ex-consul. Indeed it had been he who had taken his men, like the Persians, over a mountain pass and attacked the Syrians in the rear, thus putting them to flight. Glabrio and Cato were a different breed from generals like Flamininus and the Scipios. They were ardently nationalistic, suspicious of the Greeks and hostile to the Romans who embraced Greek culture.

Glabrio showed this attitude. He was so savage in his reception of the Aetolians when they came to ask for peace that they continued fighting and Glabrio could not pursue Antiochus into Asia. Rome then sent over Flamininus, who was more diplomatic towards the Aetolians, and then Laelius and Lucius Scipio were sent over to conduct the war, with Scipio Africanus to advise Lucius. They made a truce with the Aetolian League and went over to Asia Minor, defeating Antiochus' navy in the process.

The Battle of Magnesia. Antiochus is defeated. Galatia crushed

Antiochus tried to come to terms with the Romans but they refused. They met him at Magnesia in 190 B.C. and defeated him. Scipio Africanus was sick and took no part in the battle.

Antiochus was ordered to pay an indemnity of 15 000 talents, and to surrender his fleet and elephants.

Rome's allies received their due reward. Rhodes was granted some territory on the coast of Asia Minor, the land assigned to them coming from the possessions of the Seleucids. But Pergamum was given even more, indeed it was given control over most of the rest of the coast.

In Asia Minor Rome discovered its traditional Gallic foes, in the shape of the trouble-making state of Galatia. It was decided that Galatia must be crushed immediately, and they did not even wait for legal justification. This was bad, but even worse were the demoralising effects of the huge plunder obtained from this last conquest.

The booty, combined with the indemnity paid by Antiochus, convinced Rome that war could be profitable, and that the East in particular was a vast source of wealth for enterprising generals and administrators. The lesson was learnt only too well. Asia Minor was to be bled white in the years which followed, and was to see no final respite until the advent of Augustus.

None the less the Scipios were as determined as Flamininus that Greece should be left free. The aim of their peace settlement was simply to redistribute areas in Greece rather than take them over. Yet this ideal of non-interference was doomed to failure. The Greeks themselves, by their constant bickering and by their ceaseless stream of complaining envoys, finally exhausted Rome's patience.

Cato fosters anti-Greek sentiment

At the same time a reaction was setting in at Rome against the pro-Greek sentiments of men such as the Scipios and Flamininus. The spokesman for this group was Cato, Glabrio's lieutenant and a 'new man', whom the family of the Valerii had supported.

Cato won respect for his honesty and determination. He was a capable man, but of incredibly narrow vision. In the early stage of his career he had won esteem by his exploits in Spain, and by the time of Antiochus' defeat he was ready to challenge the supremacy of the Scipios.

In 187, at Cato's suggestion, Lucius Scipio was asked to give an account of five hundred talents which Antiochus had handed over to him towards the pay of his troops. Scipio Africanus intervened and refused the demand. This haughty rebuff, though successful, was not forgotten. From this time the popularity of the Scipios declined rapidly.

Cato's group next attacked at a different point. Greek influx into central Italy, as a result of the Punic and Macedonian wars, brought as well the practice of their religions. In particular, the worship of Bacchus was now conducted in the licentious Eastern fashion to the scandal of the more conservative Romans. As a result the Bacchanalians were accused of conspiring against the state and between 185 and 181 their worshippers underwent a thorough purge. Then only was the religion permitted once more, provided that excesses were avoided.

There is one account which says that Scipio Africanus was subsequently prosecuted too. This may be a fabrication. It is, however, certain that he recognised his clan's loss of favour and, being himself in failing health, retired from Rome. He died in 185.

Scipio's ancient enemy Hannibal did not long survive him. At this period he took refuge with the king of Bithynia. When the Senate began to pay unwelcome attentions to his host, Hannibal saw there was only one course left open to him, and took poison.

In 184 Cato enjoyed his hour of triumph, which was employed in a fashion typical of the man. In that year he was made censor. He revised the Senate rolls and passed rigorous laws which limited luxury especially among women. He also bore down with a heavy hand on the letting of state contracts. There had been much corruption in this field, but his action roused vigorous protest from the equites.

The Third Macedonian War

Meanwhile all was not well in the East. Philip had helped Rome fight Antiochus, but his services had been ill-rewarded. He may himself have been planning renewed warfare, but when he died in 179, this task was undertaken by his elder son Perseus. It was of course a vain hope, and Perseus was not the man to achieve success. His nature was more suited to intrigue than action, and when war broke out in 171 he was only saved from immediate disaster by the incompetence of the commanders sent against him.

As usual, Rome ended by taking the step that should have been taken in the first place, namely sending a capable commander, in the person of Aemilius Paullus. He met Perseus at Pydna and defeated him. Perseus fled, but was captured not long after, and died in captivity in 164.

The final settlement of the East

The Romans now perceived that in the East their earlier policy of leaving the states their independence was impractical. Moreover the anti-Greek reaction was still strong. This time they tried the plan that had served them well in earlier wars, especially in Italy, namely, divide and isolate. Macedonia was split into four districts. These states were forbidden marriage and trade with each other on the pattern of Rome's Italian possessions. An annual tribute was also imposed

on them. At Rome itself direct taxation was abolished at this time. It was no longer needed.

Pergamum and Rhodes, despite the help they had given Rome, were seen as potential threats. To their great indignation, they had taken from them many of the possessions they had been given earlier. The island of Delos was also developed as a port in rivalry with Rhodes, ruining Rhodes' commerce.

The pro-Roman elements were encouraged to send the names of any disloyal citizens to Rome, and they responded with enthusiasm. There was a wholesale purge of Greece, and huge camps of exiled Greeks were set up at Rome. Among those so exiled was Polybius.

Paullus plundered any state that he interpreted as opposing Rome's will, and he set off homewards laden with plunder. He celebrated a magnificent triumph, leading Perseus and his family in chains.

Rome's policy of division could succeed in Italy, because Rome provided a centre of strength. In time Italy had become unified in dependence on Rome. In the East it was different. By splitting up the powerful states Rome simply exaggerated the tendency to disunion that had for so long plagued this area. It also made the states less able to defend themselves from attack by their barbarian neighbours. In short Rome was still shirking its responsibility. If these people could not rule themselves, Rome had to supply the government.

This soon became apparent. In 150 a pretender rose in Macedonia and was welcomed by the inhabitants. Rome was forced to intervene, and when it finally put down the revolt, recognised the inevitable and made Macedonia a Roman province.

'Carthage must be destroyed.' The Third Punic War

The forces of reaction in Rome, once again led by Cato, resolved that Carthage must finally be eliminated as a source of danger. This attitude was strengthened by the sight of Carthage's amazing recovery from its military disasters. Carthage's trade revival roused the enmity of the

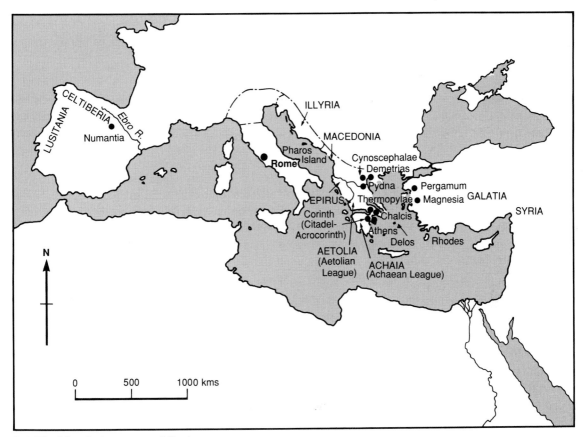

9.1 *The Macedonian wars and Spain.*

business class of Rome and they in their turn played on the fear of the senators.

Rome had an excuse ready to hand for intervention in Africa when it wished. After the Second Punic War Carthage had been forbidden to take part in any future wars, and Massinissa of Numidia had been rewarded for his services by the purposely vague permission to regain his ancestral domains.

This permision he interpreted liberally, and made it an excuse for constant encroachment on Carthaginian territory. In vain Carthage appealed to Rome. The spectacle of its humiliation was only too welcome to its former foe. Indeed when Cato was sent in 157 to act as mediator in one of these disputes he took alarm at the signs of Carthage's new prosperity and began to din into Roman ears 'Carthage must be destroyed'.

By 150 he prevailed on the Senate to take direct action. This took the form of protests to Carthage at their resistance to Massinissa. At first Carthage tried to comply with Rome's demands, but, as was to be expected, the demands never ended. In desperation they turned to active resistance. The resultant campaign is known as the Third Punic War, although such a title rather over-estimates its importance.

As usual, the Carthaginians, now that they were in a desperate situation, fought with fanaticism, and the siege dragged on for three years. Ultimately the Senate had recourse to Publius Cornelius Scipio Aemilianus. He was the son of the Paullus who had defeated Perseus, and was Scipio Africanus' son's adopted son. He was very young, below the age at which he could legally hold such a command, but the Punic wars had gone far to break down tradition in such matters.

He made a determined onslaught on the city and finally took it in 146. Carthage was utterly destroyed and its walls levelled to the ground. Now Numidia found that it was not to be the beneficiary. Instead Rome continued its new policy, and made the territory round Carthage into a new province, which was called Africa.

Savage destruction was repeated in the same year in Greece. Achaea had for some time been ripe for revolt as the result of the wholesale deportation of their leading citizens as hostages. In 146 they did declare war on Rome. The result was their swift defeat and the dissolution of the Achaean League, which was broken up into the states that originally formed it. Corinth, which had been one centre of this revolt, was like Carthage razed to the ground, and its inhabitants sold as slaves.

The Spanish Question

One troublesome heritage the Punic Wars left to Rome was Spain. In 197 the section of this warlike country that the Carthaginians had ruled was divided into two provinces called Hither and Further Spain. The number of praetors was increased from four to six in order to provide a governor for each of these new domains.

When the Spaniards proved ungrateful to their new rulers, and an uprising occurred in Hither Spain, Cato, who had already won some reputation, was sent as governor to settle the problem. It was a situation that brought out the best in the man.

He was firm with the trouble-makers and forced the revolting towns to pull down their city walls. Then, once order was achieved, he tried to find some way of preventing the abuses that had caused the disturbance. He drew up peace terms that dealt fairly with their problems, then proceeded to put the silver mines in working order once again, thereby helping to restore prosperity in the country.

The Romans had no illusions that mere justice would ensure lasting peace in Spain, and they established there the first standing army to be stationed outside Rome itself. As the Roman soldiers proved reluctant to enlist for an area that offered more danger than the East, and none of its glamour and prospects of rich plunder, allied forces were used. When they too were unwilling, they were conscripted forcibly to serve for a period of sixteen years.

This was an unwise move, for it helped to foster the disgruntlement that came to a head finally in the Social War. It was unfortunate that the same period saw the introduction of a new regulation whereby allied soldiers were allotted only half the booty granted to Roman troops. This added another solid grievance for the men who were increasingly being called on to fight Rome's battles.

Tiberius Gracchus gives good government

The Spaniards were fortunate to secure as governor in 179 Tiberius Sempronius Gracchus, a man of real enlightenment. He put an end to the riots which were again raging and then examined their complaints. It is interesting that he, the father of the two famous Gracchi, brought peace by settling the inequitable land distribution in the province. It is hard to avoid the conclusion that these events led his sons to think of similar land reforms in Italy. Gracchus was a lover of Greek culture, and his wife, who was a very well-educated and cultured woman, was a daughter of Scipio Africanus. Gracchus won such devotion from the Spaniards that his name was one to conjure with in the land for years afterwards.

Bad government, peace without honour

It was Spain's misfortunate that, although it was given a Cato and a Gracchus it was also allotted some governors whose stupidity was only equalled by their brutality and lack of any moral scruples. Gracchus' successors fell into this category and by 155 war flared up again.

Galba, the Roman governor, offered peace to the Lusitanians, then took advantage of their surrender to conduct a wholesale massacre. Cato was furious at this act of black treachery and had Galba put on trial. The Romans, however, were not concerned with principles and granted an acquittal.

A Spanish chief called Viriathus, who had escaped from the Lusitanian massacre, raised a new revolt. The Romans then bribed some Spaniards to assassinate him.

The murder of Viriathus brought peace to part of Spain, but the Celtiberians continued to fight, angry that the Romans would not give recognition to Gracchus' land reforms. Their main stronghold was the town of Numantia.

Although the Romans continued to use every means, fair or foul, they were unable to crush this last centre of rebellion. Finally, in 134 they called on Scipio Aemilianus to help them again.

He raised a volunteer army, making use of his own prestige to secure enlistments. (Marius, incidentally, served under him in this expedition, as did his future enemy, Jugurtha.) He invested Numantia, and finally did take it. The town was sacked and burnt to the ground, following the custom that was becoming popular with Roman generals since the sack of Corinth and Carthage. Thus Spain was at last brought peace, but not with honour.

In Scipio Aemilianus we have another commander of the style of Africanus, who owed his position to his own personal qualities of leadership. Thus a pattern was being set for men such as Marius, Sulla, Pompey and Caesar to follow.

Date table

B.C.
200	Outbreak of Second Macedonian War.
196	Peace signed with Philip.
190	Battle of Magnesia.
186	Bacchanalian Conspiracy.
185	(? 184) Death of Scipio Africanus.
184	Death of Hannibal.
171	War with Perseus of Macedon.
168	Battle of Pydna.
146	Destruction of Carthage and Corinth.
133	Capture of Numantia.

Select quotations

1 Polybius XXXI, 23:
Since my narrative and the course of events have led me to consider this claim, I wish to carry out for my reader a promise made in a previous book. For I promised to explain the reason and manner of the unprecedented rise to eminence of the house of the Scipios in Rome, and at the same time the reason why their friendships with Polybius grew to such a point that not only report of them spread through Italy and Greece, but their choice of a friend became even more widely known. This intimacy began, as I have explained, from the lending of a book, and the resultant conversation. But when the friendship grew, and the hostages began to be sent out to various towns, Fabius and Scipio, the sons of Lucius Aemilius, begged the praetor to allow Polybius to stay in Rome.

2 Plutarch, *Lives*, 'Titus Flamininus', 10:
The Isthmian Games were being celebrated, and a great crowd was seated in the stadium viewing the contest, now that Greece at long last was done with war and had hopes of freedom, so that it could hold holiday in safety. Then the herald, after a trumpet had called for a general silence, came into the centre and proclaimed that the Roman senate and Titus Quinctius, general and proconsul, having conquered King Philip and the Macedonians, were setting free, without garrison or tribute, to use their own national laws, the Corinthians, the Locrians, the Phocians, the Euboeans, the Achaeans of Phthiotis, the Magnetians, the Thessalians and the Perrhaebians. (The announcement was not heard at first and was repeated.) Then a shout incredibly loud rang out, which could be heard right to the sea, and the assembly rose, and gave no more thought to the contest, but all vied with one another in leaping up, clasping his hand and calling him the saviour and champion of Greece.

Further reading

R.M. Errington, *The Dawn of Empire*, Cornell
    University Press, N.Y., 1972.
Plutarch, *Lives*, 'Flamininus', 'Cato the Elder',
    'Aemilianus Paullus'.
Polybius, *The Rise of the Roman Empire*,
    Penguin Classics.

Topics for essays or discussion

1 Why did Rome make war on Philip in 200,
  and why was it reluctant to do this?
2 What effect did the Macedonian Wars have
  on the Roman army?
3 What was the balance of power in the East
  in 200? How was it affected by Rome's
  conquest of Macedonia and Syria?
4 Divide and rule! Why did that policy fail in
  the East?
5 Explain the anti-Greek reaction in Rome,
  which Cato led. How did it affect Rome's
  foreign policy?
6 What problems did Rome face in Spain?
  How successful was it in solving them?
7 Compare the Macedonian and Syrian wars
  with the wars of succession that followed
  Alexander's death. Why was the result
  different?

Chapter 10

The development of Rome in the second century B.C.

THE SECOND CENTURY saw a rapid development of Rome in the social, political and cultural fields. The city was now virtually ruler of all the lands around the Mediterranean, and was forced to adapt itself to meet this new position. For the first half of the century the change was comparatively slow, but after 150 a tremendous acceleration took place, which finally became uncontrolled.

Administration grew ever more complex as the territory to be administered increased. At the same time the division between the senators who governed, and the equites who controlled the financial side of the new empire, came to be more sharply marked. A similar division became evident between the Roman citizens and the allies.

The Senate and the *cursus honorum*

One reason why Rome was able to win the Punic Wars was that the Senate took control of the state and created a well-organised administration.

As a result, in the second century the Senate enjoyed a position of greatly increased power and prestige.

At the same time, in order to bring victory the Senate had given unprecedented powers to individual generals, such as Scipio Africanus. The senatorial class rightly saw that these powers endangered their own position. After the war they brought in a number of reforms, which they hoped would remove this danger.

It was determined that ten years' military service should precede a public career. Then the magistracies had to be taken in the normal order (known as the *cursus honorum*). They began from the quaestorship, then proceeded to the offices of praetor and consul. The minimum age for a consul was set at forty-two. The number of quaestors appointed annually at this time is not known, but was almost certainly more than eight. There were four praetors, and, as ever during the republican period, two consuls.

The office of curule aedile fell between that of quaestor and praetor but it was not a necessary step. That was as well; for there were only two curule aediles, and to make that office a compulsory step would have created an impossible bottle-neck in the ladder of promotion. Censors were also a special case. They were usually appointed from the most senior members of the Senate who had already served as consuls.

A further measure was added, stipulating that no one could hold a second consulship until ten years had elapsed since his first tenure of office.[1] Thus the too swift rise to supreme power by an able young general was in theory precluded. Unfortunately, however, whenever a war reached a critical phase, the Senate was forced to break its own rules and appoint the best general available, whatever his age or station.

Roman magistrates rule the provinces

Rome's magistrates had always fulfilled a double role, administering the city in peace and leading

---

[1] This was a re-enactment of the 341 law.

its armies in time of war. Civilian and military careers had never been separate and they continued to be linked throughout Rome's history.

So it was that when peace came its generals were to rule any new conquests. The area of command of a general was called his *provincia* and in peace this was used for the area he administered, the province as we call it.

It has been seen in the case of Athens that empire brings wealth, and that the imperialists do not wish to share this wealth among too many. That happened also in Rome.

During the wars Rome's conquests brought it wealth in the form of booty and war indemnities. In the time of peace that followed the administration of the new provinces brought wealth through taxes.

Now in 197, when the two Spains were made provinces, two additional praetors were appointed to administer them, raising their number to six. In 146 Macedonia and Africa became provinces. The obvious move would have been to increase once more the number of praetors, but this the Senate was reluctant to do, just as they never consented to alter the number of consuls. Such a step would dilute their ranks at a time when they were becoming increasingly exclusive. In addition, the provinces would be a source of profit to their administrators.

Accordingly, the principle of prorogation (invented during the Samnite wars to meet military emergencies) was adapted to serve a civil purpose. A praetor after his year of office could be appointed as a propraetor, to serve a further term, and a consul as proconsul. Thus the number of privileged was not increased, but their power and opportunities were.

Finally, the quaestor, who had gone to war to pay the general's troops now went to the provinces to handle the general's finances, in cooperation naturally with the equites. Thus the Senate grew in importance and exclusiveness, until, towards the end of the century, the consuls were drawn from about twenty-five families, and the holding of this office by a newcomer or novus homo (whose family before him had not enjoyed this rank) became increasingly rare. Beyond the inner circle of the consular group were the prae-

torian families who likewise had held that office for generations, and resisted any intrusion into their field.

The Senate controlled all foreign affairs, and met all foreign embassies that came to Rome. When the prorogation of magistrates became normal the Senate organised this procedure too, and at the end of each year allotted to the outgoing magistrates their respective provinces or tasks.

As the result of a law passed by Scipio Africanus at the beginning of the century the senators were allotted the front seats at the games or other public spectacles, which were becoming ever more popular as the century proceeded.

The Senate was the one body that sat continually, like our parliament, and it effectually controlled Rome. It had also increased its powers enormously during the Punic Wars. Unlike our parliament its members were not elected but taken from the magistrates when they became quaestors, but their entry had to be approved by the censors. Unlike our parliaments the Senate had no parties, but the families, especially the more important families, made a formidable voting block, and also there was a tendency for certain families to combine, so the end result did have a certain resemblance to the working of a modern parliament. The Fabii and the Cornelii (the Scipios) were two important families who had produced great generals, also the Claudii, who were not great generals but good administrators.

The role of the equites in the provinces

The equites, or equestrian class of Rome, who constituted its business people, were likewise becoming more powerful with the development of the city. The Punic wars had placed an enormous strain on the Roman economy and had forced them to raise capital in a way undreamt of earlier. The business men responded to this emergency, and in due course had their reward.

They supplied the money that built the fleet that defeated Carthage in the First Punic war. After peace was signed they were repaid from the war indemnities imposed on Carthage. In the Second Punic war they were given contracts to deliver supplies to the army. After the war they continued to serve the army's needs, and they also helped to collect the taxes from the provinces. As their tasks grew in complexity, they became too much for the individual, and the equites began to group themselves in companies or societates for business purposes.

The lex Claudia, as we have noted earlier, by making it illegal for senators or senators' sons to trade by sea, prevented one dangerous combination. If a section of the ruling body combined the privileges of both upper classes it would have wielded absolute power. Thus the senatorial class was to some extent preserved from corruption. The measure did, however, have some unfortunate consequences. For one thing, the senators, now being debarred from investing in trade, bought up huge tracts of land instead. By so doing they aggravated the growth of huge estates, which was to be one problem of the age.

At the same time the removal of senatorial competition meant that the equites enjoyed a very useful monopoly, which they exercised to the full, as the increasing number of provinces brought ever more business opportunities.

In the case of Sicily, Sardinia and Corsica the custom, which the Romans did not alter, was to allow the local commercial class to act as tax gatherers. In this area, although the Roman equites doubtless played their part, they did not as yet have supreme control.

In poverty-stricken Spain there was no rich harvest to be gathered, and in some cases the Spaniards were asked to supply troops, rather than taxes which they could not furnish. Yet in 187 the equites of Rome were given the management of the Spanish silver mines, which were perhaps the country's most profitable enterprise.

More important for them was the inclusion of Africa and the East among the provinces. Here was a real source of profit, and in these countries the *publicani* or tax gatherers of Rome, and of Italy generally, were given control from the start.

This increase in business activity was reflected in the development of Roman currency. Once the only Roman coins minted were bronze (the

as being the basic coin). In 269 B.C. the first silver coins were produced. In 217 the silver denarius was minted, which for the first time bore its value stamped on the coin itself. By 170 the denarius had replaced copper as the basis of Roman currency. Better known was the 'quarter' of the denarius, the *sestertius*. As Roman influence extended in the East its coinage also gained prestige, so that in time the Attic drachma was put on parity with the denarius, and coinage of other Eastern countries followed suit.

The unenviable plight of the provinces

The position of the provinces themselves was not enviable. Roman administration brought one great blessing, namely the cessation of those constant wars which had for so long racked the area. On the other hand, Rome's ignorance and neglect of naval affairs meant an increase in piracy to offset the decrease of devastation on land.

But Roman administration took the heaviest toll. Roman magistrates received no pay, and were called on to give increasingly lavish displays in order to secure election. This outlay could only be recouped when the magistrate went out to administer his province.

Some attempt was made to check the rapacity and dishonesty of governors, and in 149 the *lex Calpurnia* was passed which set up a permanent court or *quaestio* to which provincials could bring their complaints. As they had no legal standing, they would make use of their patron, a Roman aristocrat who had an association with their country and who would represent their interests in Rome. They would be expected to reward generously his services on their behalf. Badian gives information on the patron-client relationship between Romans and foreign states (see 'Further reading').

Yet this law was not very effective. It meant as a rule that the governor simply needed more money, so that he could by bribery avoid being convicted by the quaestio. So the saying arose that a governor needed to make three fortunes in his province, one to pay his election expenses, one to bribe the jury on his return, the third to keep.

So there began the process of constant depletion which the provinces were to suffer, from governors and tax-gatherers, until the end of the Republic brought them some relief.

At the lower end of the social scale, the ordinary Roman citizen came to occupy a different position in the course of the century. In particular, his status contrasted more sharply with that of members of the Italian allied communities.

The allies: all work and no pay

The Punic wars had made enormous demands on manpower both from Rome and from the rest of Italy. In the ensuing period the Roman citizens, unlike the allies, were able to resist further such demands. As a result, troops for the Macedonian wars, for Spain and for other campaigns or garrison forces, were drawn more and more from the allies.

Yet the allies were at this time suffering a great loss of manpower and wealth. Many of the towns, especially those of Latin status or the municipia, had long enjoyed the right of entry to Rome as Roman citizens. During the Punic wars Italy was ravaged by the armies which for so long tramped over it, and it was slow to recover. Rome on the other hand was flooded with new wealth. No wonder the Italian youth flocked to the city, leaving their small and unattractive holdings. It was an instance of that drift from the country to the city, which is a problem to so many lands when they reach a certain state of development.

This move was not welcomed by Romans or allies. The heads of the Italian cities saw their youth departing, while they were still expected to supply the same number of soldiers to the Roman armies, and of course to work their farms.

It was actually the Italians who made the first protest, although it undoubtedly fell on receptive ears.

As a result it was decreed that no citizen of these towns could migrate to Rome unless he left a son behind to take his place. Yet though the allies began the move, it was continued and Rome pursued a policy of limited immigration, so as to have fewer to feed and entertain.

Moreover, the same period that saw the allies supplying an ever-increasing proportion of Rome's soldiers also witnessed the introduction of an invidious distinction. Roman soldiers were now to have allotted to them twice as much booty after a campaign as was granted to an allied soldier.

Finally, the attack Rome made in 186 and the years following on the worshippers of Bacchus had an unfortunate effect on its allies. When Rome had dealt with the Bacchanalians within its own borders it sent commissions to stamp out the practice in the rest of Italy. The cult of Bacchus had long been established in the south of Italy, with its large Greek population. As a result many innocent people fell victims to the uncomprehending magistrates from Rome.

The city mob

Meanwhile the city populace, swelled by the constant addition of freedmen, manumitted by their owners, was benefiting from its country's growing power. The distribution of cheap corn from Rome's new provinces (especially Sicily) was becoming more and more regular. This, incidentally, had a depressing effect on the farming districts of the Italian countryside and made it more difficult for them to win back their old prosperity.

It has been noted that the Comitia Centuriata was reformed by Flaminius and made more like the Comitia Tributa: Yet these bodies, although they were used to elect magistrates and to pass laws, did not develop into responsible organs of government. They met infrequently, they were overshadowed by the Senate with its greater prestige, and they were very vulnerable to bribery. So, although the comitia could be used as a means of protest against injustice, and at times were so employed, only too often they simply furnished another opportunity to corrupt the populace.

Games, especially gladiatorial displays, were also becoming more frequent, and were used to win popularity. Thus the formula of 'bread and circuses' to appease the people of Rome was already being evolved.

Cultural development in Rome: the Scipionic circle

A more pleasant result of Rome's eastern expansion was the growth in this century of a Latin literature. Its more enthusiastic patrons were the family of the Scipios. The beginnings were humble enough: a translation into crude Latin verse of Homer's *Odyssey*, written by a Greek schoolmaster, Livius Andronicus. He also translated some Greek plays.

The Latin people did not for long have to rely on the Greeks to create their literature, but at this stage the actual city of Rome did not make any contribution. A playwright of note emerged, Plautus of Umbria (254–184), a man of humble origins. He had a copious output and enjoyed considerable popularity with his audiences. He made use of Greek plays, but adapted them boldly to suit local taste, with more action, with mime and with music. These plays were called *fabulae palliatae* because the actors wore the *pallium* or Greek cloak. They used a Greek setting. *Fabulae togatae*, which were set in Italy, were later written but we have no surviving examples of them.

Ennius (*c.*239–169) came from Calabria in Greek south Italy. Ironically, it was that opponent of Greek culture, Cato, who discovered him, but he was later taken up by Scipio Africanus. He is known for his *Annales*, an epic telling of the rise of Rome up to his own times. In it he adapted to the Latin language the Greek hexameter, a great advance on the clumsy local Saturnian metre. Ennius was long admired, and helped to inspire Virgil's *Aeneid*.

The next generation of writers gathered around Scipio Aemilianus. He was actually the son of the general Paullus who won the battle of Pydna, but he was adopted by the son of Scipio Africanus. He was the patron of the Campanian Lucilius (180–102), who wrote satires, and of the second notable play-wright, Terence, a Carthaginian. Terence was a dramatist for the intellectual, and was not a great stage success. Yet we owe some excellent plays to him and he had an enormous influence on the growth of modern European drama.

Also a friend of Scipio Aemilianus was the historian Polybius. Polybius was a Greek, brought to Rome as one of the hostages of the Achaean League. He soon came under the protection of the powerful Scipionic clan and conceived a great admiration for the Romans. He wrote a voluminous history—in Greek—which is an important source of information on the Punic wars. Even though much of it has been lost, we still have an indirect debt, as Livy made generous use of it in composing his history of Rome.

The same circle also became interested in Greek philosophy, especially in Stoicism. The Stoic teachings were brought to Rome by Panaetius, a very shy but sincere philosopher who roused the utmost enthusiasm in his new converts. Stoicism, with its emphasis on duty, appealed to the Romans. Perhaps, too, its theory of a world state and of the brotherhood of man appealed to Rome's vision of itself as founding such a state. One of its more notorious beliefs was that suicide was justified if existence had become profitless, through disease, dishonour or some other catastrophe.

Some opposed the Greek influence

But Greece was not to take over Roman culture without a struggle. The opposition gathered strength, led, as in the political field, by Cato. Twice (in 173 and 161) Greek philosophers were banished from Rome. Attacks were made on the performing of plays, attacks from which Roman drama was never to recover completely. As part of the same reaction, astrologers were banished from the city.

The reaction was not wholly negative. Cato

himself wrote, and helped found a Latin prose literature. His most famous work is his book on agriculture, a work somewhat severe, even savage in its advice at times, but presented with clarity and vigour.

To conclude, Rome had still a long way to travel before it achieved an independent culture of its own, but this century saw a promising start made, which laid the foundation for future more ambitious works. Even at this stage the note of pride in Rome's national achievement was evident, the conviction of the city's great destiny which was to dominate Roman literature and life.

Date table

B.C.
c. 220   Reform of Comitia Centuriata.
218   lex Claudia.
194   Senators given separate seats at games.
186   Bacchanalian Conspiracy.
167   Polybius brought to Rome.
149   lex Calpurnia.

Select quotations

1 Plautus, *Menaechmi* 1–20:
Now first of all, spectators, I bring best wishes—to me and you. I bring you Plautus on my tongue not in my hand, and beg you give a kindly hearing. Now hear the plot and pay attention. I'll give it to you as briefly as I can. Poets have this habit in comedies of saying that everything happened at Athens, so it may seem more like Greek to you. I will say nothing but as it occurred. Accordingly, although this plot has a Greek flavour, it is not Attic, but Sicilian rather. . . . There was an old merchant at Syracuse who had twin sons so similar that their foster mother could not tell to which one she was giving suck, nor even the mother who bore them.
(Shakespeare's *Comedy of Errors* owes much to this play.)

2 Cato, *de Agricultura* 2:
(Instructions to a man who has just bought a farm.)
Bring the overseer back to an account of the tasks and of his workmen. When it was rainy, tell him what tasks could have been done when it rained, washing vats and caulking them, cleaning out the villa, moving the corn, sweeping out the manure and making a pit for it, cleaning the seed, making and mending harness. . . . When the slaves were sick, they could have been given smaller rations. . . . Obtain whatever is needed for the year, and sell anything of which there is an excess. . . . Look over the stock and hold an auction. Sell the oil if it will fetch a good price, and also the wine and any corn that is left over. Sell old oxen, blemished cattle or sheep, wool, hides, an old cart, old tools, an old slave or a sick slave, and anything else that is superfluous. A householder should be a seller not a buyer.

Further reading

M. Grant, *Roman Literature*, Cambridge University Press, 1954. Consult also the Loeb editions of Plautus and Terence, and in the same series, *Remains of Old Latin*.
H.H. Scullard, *A History of the Roman World, 753 B.C. to 146 B.C.*, London, Methuen, 1961.
E. Badian, *Foreign Clientelae*, Oxford University Press, 1958.
F.R. Cowell, *Cicero and the Roman Republic*, Penguin, 3rd ed., 1964, pp. 94–104 for a discussion of Roman coinage.

Topics for essays or discussion

1 Explain the rise in power of the Senate in the second century B.C. Why did it become such an exclusive body?
2 Examine the development of the equestrian class during and after the Punic Wars. What was its importance and from what limitations did it suffer?

3 'The Second Century B.C. saw the growth of a pampered proletariat in Rome and a dissatisfied allied community.' Discuss.

4 Compare and contrast the political and social position in Rome of the second century B.C. with that which prevailed in the early republic.

5 Read a play of Plautus. Although it is set in Greece, does it throw any light on Romans, their life and attitudes?

6 Which was the more typical Roman, Cato the Elder or Scipio Aemilianus?

7 What part did nationalism play in the rise of a Roman literature after the Punic wars?

Chapter 11

The Gracchi

THE STAGE was now set for the entrance of two men whose zealous pursuit of reform revealed the weakness of the Senate and began some of the conflicts that were to put an end to the Republic.

For some time economic, social and political inequalities had been accumulating in Rome and Italy, and, as was noted in the last chapter, the allies who were supplying an ever-increasing proportion of Rome's armies were finding that they enjoyed every year a lower social status compared with the Roman citizen.

Furthermore, the uneven distribution of land was affecting the position of the individual citizen (and also army recruitment because only land-owners could serve in the army). In earlier years Rome had satisfied its people's need for land by sending out colonies, and by confiscating a portion of any conquered territory.

In the second century they ceased to send out colonies. Moreover the confiscated land, *ager publicus* as it was called, was denied the small landholder. In theory it should have been for general use, but in fact it was thrown open for squatting, normally to the benefit of the large landholder, who paid little or nothing for the privilege.

At the same time the rich were buying up huge tracts of land (or, in the case of ager publicus, simply squatting on it) and developing farms of a new type. These were called *latifundia* and were given over to the cultivation of vines or olive trees and to the rearing of sheep and cattle, none of which required intensive labour. Such labour as was required was supplied by slaves, of which Rome had such an abundance. Most of these rich land-owners, whether senators or knights, were absentee landlords and left the running of the estate to a bailiff. Slaves usually worked under harsh, even sub-human conditions.

The senators made money in the Eastern wars. Yet they were forbidden to invest this money in trade. The obvious alternative, as was noted in the previous chapter, was land, and the ravages of the Punic wars meant that large areas had been laid waste, and were available cheaply to a cash buyer. The equites too, although they could and did invest their money in commerce, were interested in acquiring property because of the prestige land-ownership gave them.

This was not all. The continued wars brought a flood of slaves on the Roman market. Sardinia was a notorious source of this commodity. The example of the United States in modern history has shown what a depressing effect the existence of a slave class has on the small free farmer.

Finally, a number of Rome's provinces, and in particular Sicily and Sardinia, supplied corn as their tribute. Whereas, while the war lasted, this corn went to feed the armies, and fulfilled an important need, now it went directly to Rome and also helped in the small settler's ruin.

The more long-sighted Romans had already realised some of the dangers that threatened the state. We have seen that Flaminius created an uproar in 232 when he suggested that the newly acquired territory in Cisalpine Gaul be distributed in individual lots.

Throughout the second century there were repeated efforts to reform the method of alloting ager publicus. According to ancient authorities the first attempt to ensure fair distribution was made in 367 B.C., forming part of the Licinian

Rogations. At that time it was declared that no citizen should be allotted more than 500 *iugera* (about 120 hectares).

A number of scholars doubt the accuracy of this tradition, and some think that the limitations an ager publicus were not proposed until the second century, not long before the Gracchi. At least we are certain that a law existed in 167 BC, for in that year Cato made a reference to such an enactment.

Sources for the Gracchi

This brings us to the time of the Gracchi. Here our sources are meagre and very unsatisfactory and this is regrettable, for it is a most important period, both in itself and for the effect it had on the later history of Rome.

Of Livy we have only the brief and unsatisfactory summary, and we have mainly to rely on Plutarch and on Appian's *Civil Wars*. Plutarch as always gives us excellent material mixed with anecdotes of doubtful authenticity. However, he was writing a biography not a history, so he was not concerned with giving events in correct historic sequence nor in giving a full and accurate account.

Our sources are also much subject to prejudice both in ancient and modern times. The orators, notably Cicero, refer to the Gracchi, but Cicero was most opposed to the Gracchi because they attacked the *boni*, the worthy members of society. With modern historians we have the danger that some of them portray the Gracchi as revolutionaries in a modern sense, taking them out of the context of their age.

The origins of the Gracchi

In fact the Gracchi were very typical of the upper class of their day. They were plebeian in origin, which is interesting, but their family had been highly successful. Their great-grandfather had taken Sardinia from the Carthaginians after the First Punic War. Their father had an even more notable career. As tribune he protected Lucius Africanus Asiaticus from the attacks of Cato, and on the death of Scipio Africanus he married Scipio's daughter Cornelia, a very intelligent and well-educated woman.

Gracchus was then, as praetor, governor of Hither Spain and won much commendation from the Spaniards for his fairness. As we noted in the last chapter Roman nobles achieved a patron-client relationship from the provinces where they governed and undoubtedly Gracchus had particularly grateful clients. After his consulship he governed Sardinia and helped pacify it. Gaius Claudius Pulcher served with him as consul and later as censor. It is interesting to see this association with the powerful family of the Claudii, and we find that Tiberius Gracchus married Appius Claudius' daughter and his brother Gaius married a daughter of another member of the family.

Their early years

In their early years the Gracchi brothers seem to have been quite close also to their mother's family, the Scipios. Sempronia, the sister of Tiberius and Gaius, married Scipio Aemilianus. Moreover, their mother (their father died when they were quite young) had them educated in the best traditions of the Greeks, and they were doubtless familiar with the Scipionic Circle, with its great love of Greek culture. The two brothers were taught Greek oratory and were most eloquent speakers. At the end of the Third Punic War Tiberius Gracchus served under Scipio Aemilianus, and was said to have shared his tent.

The break with the Scipios came later. When Tiberius was elected quaestor he was sent with the consul Mancinus, who had to quell a revolt in Spain centring on Numantia. Mancinus was incompetent and his army was of poor quality. He was utterly defeated and at the mercy of the leader of the Spaniards, Viriathus. Tiberius with his Spanish connection rescued them. The Spaniards trusted him and he was able to negotiate a treaty that gave the Romans their freedom. To Tiberius' horror when they returned to Rome the treaty was repudiated and Mancinus disgraced. Tiberius' own career was badly affected. It seems likely that the Scipios had a hand in this repudiation, and indeed Scipio Aemilianus was sent forthwith to Spain to deal with the rebellion.

The 130s were a troubled period for Rome. In the previous decade the Macedonian Wars had brought immense wealth to Rome and, with it, inflation. The wars in Spain brought no profit and a slave rebellion in Sicily was disastrous in itself and also crippled Rome's corn supply. There was no major building project in Rome in this period till 125 B.C. The Sicilian revolt was not ended until 132 B.C. Archaeology has provided interesting confirmation of Rome's economic plight. H.C. Boren[1] analysed the coins which have been found in Rome in the 140s and the 130s. He found in the 140s a huge increase in the number of *denarii* in circulation. The 130s saw an equally dramatic drop, suggesting an economic recession.

Tiberius is elected as tribune on a reform platform

There was urgent need for reform and with Scipio, one of the leaders of the conservatives, away in Spain the time was opportune. Tiberius rose to the occasion, being elected as tribune for 133 B.C. He was a man of great eloquence and he spoke movingly of the plight of Rome's poor. It was not so much the urban poor that moved him, but the soldiers, such as those who served under him in Spain. In theory only men with land could serve in the army, but the level of wealth at which they were called up was making a mockery of this. It seems likely that by the time of the Gracchi the soldiers also included tenant farmers and even itinerant workers, which makes sense of Tiberius' statement that Rome's soldiers had no home to live in when they defended it.

While they served away from Rome in the Spanish Wars, which brought little booty, their wives and children were left to struggle on alone. At the same time the rich, as we noted, were buying up huge tracts of land, which they worked with slave labour.

Tiberius saw a way to solve at the same time Rome's economic and military problems. The excess land should be taken away from the rich and distributed among the less well-to-do. Actually, this was not a new idea.

In 140 B.C. Laelius, a friend of Scipio Aemilianus, had tried to reform the method of land distribution, but the Senate had opposed him so bitterly that he had abandoned the idea, leaving the task to a younger and more determined man.

Although Tiberius was young, he had older men of experience to advise and help him. His father-in-law, Appius Claudius, belonged to a family that had a long tradition of progressive reform. Two of the leading jurisconsults of the day, Scaevola and Crassus, drew up his bills.

The time for action was well chosen. The Scipios, who had once had radical moments, were now thoroughly conservative. When Scipio Aemilianus went to Spain in 134, he left the field clear for the *populares*.

Tiberius' revolutionary character lay not so much in the scheme he proposed as in the means he used in achieving his goal. Normally such a proposal would have gone to the Senate for approval, but although Tiberius, as we have seen, had powerful friends in that body he did not trust it. He had been disillusioned by the part it played in the Numantine affair, and he knew well its power to cripple legislation by using stalling tactics.

Tiberius by-passes the Senate and goes to the people

He therefore took a step that was legal, but rarely used in practice: of presenting the bill to the *concilium plebis*, the plebeian assembly. Here too the aristocrats had their traditional methods of opposing change, the veto of another tribune. In this case they used Octavius, persuading him, even though he was originally a friend of Tiberius, that the law was dangerous.

---

[1]'Numismatic light on the Gracchan crisis', *American Journal of Philology*, 79, 1958, pp. 140–55.

Octavius imposed his veto and this led Tiberius to take another step which was against tradition. Having first taken the bill to the Senate, where it was predictably defeated, he returned to the assembly and proposed that since Octavius had opposed the will of the people he should no longer hold office. The assembly concurred, Octavius was deposed and the bill passed.

The law was in fact in many ways a re-enactment of the Licinian Rogations mentioned above, limiting the public land any one citizen could own to 500 iugera and also limiting the number of cattle that could be pastured on it. In the original draft there were some ameliorating modifications, notably that 250 iugera should be added for each child of the owner to a limit of 500 iugera. These modifications were dropped when the bitterness of the opposition made him feel that it was impossible to win their acceptance. The land in Campania was excluded from this law. The land taken from those who exceeded the limit was to be distributed among the landless in small lots, perhaps to a limit of 30 iugera. The land was to be inalienable so the rich could not immediately either buy it back or take it back by force.

Tiberius uses the treasury of Pergamum to finance his scheme

Three commissioners were to supervise the work, Tiberius and his brother Gaius and Appius Claudius. However they soon had problems. The Senate had lost the first round but it now tried to nullify the reform by voting a miserly grant to the commissioners, who in fact would need a lot of money in order to equip the new settlers with what they needed to work their farms.

At this moment a messenger came to Rome bearing the news that Attalus of Pergamum had died and left his kingdom to Rome. Tiberius immediately announced that Attalus' wealth rightly belonged to the people and that his treasury should supply the needs of the commission. To make matters worse he declared that the assembly of the plebs not the Senate should control the affairs of the province which

would be created as a result of Attalus' gift. This was a blow to one of the most important powers of the Senate and made the breach irrevocable.

Tiberius stands for re-election and is killed

The only hope for the Senate was that the tribunate of Tiberius was nearing its end, and after that his work could be undone. Tiberius dashed these hopes when he announced that he was standing for re-election. Magistrates were not normally allowed to hold office in successive years, but the tribunate was not a normal office and in any case the rule had often been ignored in practice. The Senate naturally took the view that he should not stand.

The election was marked by violence from the start. Tiberius did not have his full number of supporters, as it was harvest time, but there was no doubt what the upshot of the election would be. Disruptors scuffled with supporters on every side. The Senate was in session on the nearby Capital Hill, but the consul presiding, Mucius Scaevola, refused to intervene. It was then that the high priest, Scipio Nasica, called on those who would help him and set out from the Senate to take direct action. They broke up benches to make weapons, forced their way into the assembly, beat Tiberius to death and flung his body in the Tiber. It was a black day for Rome.

At this point the Senate did intervene. A commission was set up which punished Tiberius' supporters, though no one of note seems to have been condemned. Scipio Nasica was tremendously unpopular, and had to be sent abroad on a mission to Pergamum to save him from the populace. He died the same year while abroad.

The years of stalemate. The land distribution has problems

The events of the years that followed are very poorly documented, but we can trace some developments. The commission was allowed to continue the land distribution. As we noted, other members of the Senate had been worried by the land problem, and also the Senate did not wish to rouse the people by too readily destroying Tiberius' work. When two of the commissioners died they were replaced, but the commission began to run into trouble.

Protests flooded into Rome from allies whose land been taken and in 129 B.C. Scipio Aemilianus called on the Senate to take from the commission the power of arbitration in disputed cases. This move roused the people's ire, but then Scipio suddenly died.

One of the commissioners Fulvius Flaccus stood for the consulship and tried to counter the allies' complaints by promising them citizenship or at least the right of appeal against unjust condemnation by a magistrate. This was too much for the Senate. When he was elected consul in 126 B.C. they promptly silenced him by sending him north to deal with a Gallic uprising. The disaffection of the allies then blew up in the revolt of Fregellae. It was ruthlessly crushed and the city obliterated by Lucius Opimius, who was later to head the opposition to Gaius Gracchus.

Gaius Gracchus reluctantly heeds the people's call

And what of Gaius Gracchus? Here again there has been mythology. In particular it has been suggested that he was eager to avenge his brother's death. The truth seems rather to have been that he dreaded the inevitable struggle, which was to lead also to his death. He himself said that he avoided public life after his brother's death, and this is borne out by the fact that he did not become quaestor till 127 B.C., two years later than the normal time.

On election he was sent to Sardinia, where his family had a patron-client relationship with the people. This was lucky, for the army was in desperate straits, lacking both food and clothing. Gaius used his influence in Sardinia to get them clothing, and got corn from Africa. This made him popular and the Senate suspicious. The Senate tried to keep him away from Rome by

extending his commander's term of office for three years. Gaius then broke tradition by coming back to Rome. He was attacked for that but defended himself and stood for the tribunate of 123 B.C.

Gaius tries to learn from his brother's mistakes

He had enormous popular support and was easily elected. He was a brilliant speaker, even better than his brother, and the people needed him— in Rome because the corn problems continued, and outside Rome because the allies felt that no one heeded their problems. For the events that follow we are still dogged by our poor evidence, especially by the difficulty in putting Gaius' measures in their correct time sequence. Yet it is vital to do this if we are to understand him, so we must do our best.

It does seem, however, that Gaius, far from rushing into conflict with the Senate, tried to head off the earlier confrontation. For one thing, as we shall see, he tried to find land for the people away from the areas that had aroused the anger of the allies. Our ancient sources suggest too that initially there was a period when the Senate cooperated with Gaius.

None the less he was determined to break the stranglehold the Senate had on the freedom of the people, and this was finally to lead him to the same end as his brother. The Senate had grown fond of setting up commissions, *quaestiones*, from whose decisions there was no appeal. One such commission had punished Tiberius' followers. Gaius legislated that no commission with the power of life and death should be appointed except by the people.

Next he moved to set a ceiling on the price of corn. This was timely, for although the revolt in Sicily was over there had been a locust plague in Africa, and the price of corn was skyrocketing. This did not please the Senate, as one of their means of winning popularity was supplying corn to their clients. Now Gaius was to get the credit.

His service in Sardinia had given him first

class insight into the plight of Rome's soldiers. He brought in a law that the state should provide a uniform for its soldiers and that no one should be recruited under the age of seventeen.

Gaius makes moves to stop corruption in the provinces

One of the Senate's important powers was the allotment of provinces to ex-magistrates. Gaius brought in a law that the consuls' provinces should be decided by the Senate before the election. In that way a favoured son could not be rewarded, nor could one who had proved difficult be given a less desirable post. Incidentally, the Senate had also used this power to spirit away from Rome a consul who wanted to move a law they did not approve, in the hope that while he was away the law would lapse. Gaius' law also made it harder for them to use this device.

When Gaius came back from Sardinia he had complained bitterly at the way Rome's officials lined their pockets. A *quaestio* had been set up in earlier years to deal with the extortion of magistrates in the provinces. Unfortunately the senatorial jury defended its own and the unfortunate provincials received little help at its hands.

Gaius determined to remedy this. Here our accounts are very confused and contradictory, but it does seem likely that Gaius regulated the membership of all the commissions or *quaestiones*, making the normal procedure an equal membership of senators and equites. However, in the case of the *quaestio de repetundis*, which dealt with provincial corruption, equal membership would not be enough. To ensure justice in this case the jury should consist of equites only.

The province of Asia was very important to him as its revenue was to finance his central reforms. Hitherto the revenue had been collected in the province then sent to Rome. This had left much room for corrupt practices, especially on the part of the governor. In future the contracts were to be let in Rome, where the Roman equites could bid for them.

Gaius' remarkable energy rouses admiration

Like all reformers Gaius needed a great deal of money, not only for his land settlement but to stabilise the price of corn. He therefore increased the harbour dues for incoming ships.

He now turned his attention to practicalities. To make his corn laws effective he saw to the building of underground silos in Rome, and as well he built new roads to convey the corn from the harbours to Rome, and while he did so brought the roads themselves to a degree of excellence never before achieved. Plutarch speaks in admiration of the immense energy and capability Gaius showed in these and in his other activities. He really seems to have been a most remarkable young man and it was tragic that he had so short a time to exercise his talents.

The power given to the equites has been criticised

One aspect of Gaius' legislation has attracted much criticism, and that is the power he gave the equites, both through the courts on which they sat and through their activities as publicani or tax gatherers. In the later republic the greed and corruption of the equites was one of Rome's besetting problems, and Gaius was blamed for this. That is not quite fair. The system Gaius replaced was itself both corrupt and inefficient. The senators were no angels nor were the provincial tax collectors, where they were used. There was no public service that he could turn to and until this did come into existence from the time of Augustus, there was no way of calling on a body of capable and disinterested men to handle Rome's affairs.

None the less, apart from the question of blame, undoubtedly Gaius did pave the way for a very dangerous dual power structure in the years to come, with the Senate having control over office, while the equites had complete power over money, but no real responsibility for the consequences of their actions.

Gaius' second tribunate

Gaius now stood for re-election as tribune in 122 B.C., having an ex-consul Fulvius Flaccus as one of his colleagues[2]. This event did not itself trigger the kind of violence that had led to his brother's death. The Senate had found the unleashing of mob violence on this occasion unnerving and had for the moment no wish to repeat the experience.

None the less his re-election marked the end of the period of truce between Gaius and the Senate. This was soon evident. Gaius and Flaccus introduced a bill to give Roman citizenship to those of Rome's allies who had Latin citizenship, and Latin citizenship to the rest. Immediately Livius Drusus, a fellow tribune and a member of the Scipionic circle, interposed his veto. Gaius made no move to expel Drusus from the tribunate and the bill lapsed.

He did manage to pass a bill to establish colonies. The plan to settle the poor in the public land of Italy had caused too many problems with the allies. The *lex Rubria* established a colony, Iunonia, on the site of Carthage and colonies were also to be set up at Tarentum and Capua. Archaeologists have used aerial photography to establish the details of the colony Iunonia. The allotments marked out were of considerable size, suitable for middle class settlers. This agrees with our other evidence. Flaccus went off immediately to oversee the first steps in founding Iunonia. When he returned Gaius went himself to see how the colony was faring. That was the signal for the opposition to make its move.

The Senate counters Gaius by outbidding him

The counter-attack was led by Livius Drusus, helped by the consul Fannius, also a Scipionian, whom Gaius had thought favourable to him. They roused mob hostility by telling the people that Gaius' plan to give citizenship to the allies would mean less for them. This was a bad move, however useful politically, as it made the fight with the allies more bitter and led on to the Social War.

Drusus now offered twelve colonies (they probably were never in fact founded), and promised that unlike Gaius' colonies no rent would be charged for them. Flaccus lacked Gaius' eloquence to counter these moves and when Gaius returned he found that public opinion had swung solidly against him. The opposition also used Rome's anti-Carthaginian feeling and played on popular superstition by saying that the site of Iunonia was cursed and there were frightful omens. This was readily believed.

Gaius fails to win a third tribunate

Gaius moved his house from the Palatine to a poor quarter and tried, again unsuccessfully, to introduce the bill to give the allies citizenship. He also made a frontal attack on the Senate by proposing that in the Comitia Centuriata the order of voting of the centuries should not begin with the rich first centuries but at random. As the first votes had a binding quality on the whole vote this was an important issue. The bill was not passed.

It was now time for the elections for 121 B.C. Gaius stood again. The election was a bitter one full of recrimination, with Gaius' opponents bringing out all the issues that had inflamed the mob. Gaius failed to be re-elected and in the consular elections, which took place at the same time, a bitter opponent of Gaius, Opimius, the destroyer of Fregellae, was made consul.

Gaius still had some months left of his tribunate, but he was not to enjoy them. The opposition moved immediately to annul the *lex Rubria*, which established the colony Iunonia. Feelings ran high and in the resulting disorder a herald of Opimius, Antillius, was killed. This was enough. Opimius demanded from the Senate the right to take action on its behalf, *senatus ultimum consultum* (literally, the final decree of

---

[2] As noted earlier in this chapter Fulvius Flaccus had been an agrarian commissioner and in 126 B.C. as consul tried to gain citizenship for the allies. He was a most useful ally for Gaius, and no doubt his main aim as before was to win justice for the allies. Incidentally, it was most unusual for an ex-consul to stand as tribune.

the Senate). This gave him unchecked power, and was the first instance of the decree that was to take the place of the dictatorship in the late Republic.

Opimius had forces ready at hand, including Cretan archers. Gaius and Flaccus took refuge in the Temple of Diana on the Aventine, but it was in vain. There was a wholesale slaughter and the heads of Gaius and Flaccus were cut off and presented to Opimius. About 3000 were killed in all.

Opimius then in supreme irony built a temple to concord. In an early use of *graffiti* someone scrawled on the temple by night that the Temple of Concord was founded by discord!

Attempts were made to put Opimius on trial for his actions, but they failed. It was not till 110 B.C. that he was condemned on a different issue, namely bribery in the Jugurthine Wars.

How do we evaluate the Gracchi?

The Senate then left the equites in control of the courts, but the people never received the promised colonies, and a law was passed making the land grants alienable. The rich then speedily either bought or seized them back.

The Gracchi were defeated but they left behind them a legacy for good or ill that long survived them. The power given to the equites was to create a social division that haunted the rest of the Republican period. The frustration of the allies was to lead implacably to the bitter Social War. Likewise the desire to win a better deal for the ordinary citizen was to continue as a division between the *optimates*, the conservatives, and the *populares*, the reformers, also to the end of the Republic.

The Gracchi tried unsuccessfully to create a new ruling body in Rome, the Popular Assembly chaired by the tribunes, inspired, as was natural for admirers of the Greeks, by the Athenian Assembly led by the archons and later by the generals. This did not work. The Roman Assembly had none of the continuity of the Athenian Assembly, let alone of its rival, the Roman Senate. But they did create a new role for the tribune, who was to appear repeatedly

after this as heading a body of reformers, or less creditably as a kind of Mafia boss.

Finally it must be kept firmly in mind that it was not just the reforms of the Gracchi that created all the problems. The problems—of the allies and the widening gap between rich and poor—existed and were getting worse. By their vigorous attempts to reform, the Gracchi brought these problems clearly before people and polarised society, a polarisation that continued until the imperial period created new forms of society, which alleviated some of these problems, although they did create their own.

Date table

B.C.
134   Scipio's siege of Numantia.
133   Tribunate of Tiberius Gracchus.
129   Death of Scipio Aemilianus.
123–22 Tribunates of Gaius Gracchus.
121   Massacre of Gaius Gracchus and his followers.

Select quotations

1 Plutarch, *Lives*, 'Tiberius Gracchus' 2, 2:
First of all, in appearance and behaviour Tiberius was mild and deliberate, while Gaius was high-strung and passionate, so that, when addressing the people, the former stood quietly in the one spot while the other was the first of the Romans to stride up and down on the platform and pull the toga from his shoulders as he spoke. . . . Gaius' way of speaking was violent and emotional to the point of exaggeration, while that of Tiberius was more pleasant and appealed to compassion.

2 Plutarch, *Lives* 'Tiberius Gracchus' 9, 4:
(Speech of Tiberius)
The wild beasts that inhabit Italy each have a cave or a lair to call their own, while the men who fight and give up their lives for Italy have air and light but nothing else, and without

house or home they wander about with their *wives and children. Their commanders lie when in battle they exhort the soldiers to drive back the foe from their tombs and temples. For they have no ancestral altar, nor have any of all these men a family tomb, but they fight and die for other men's luxury and wealth, and though they are called the rulers of the world, they have not one sod of earth for their private possession.*

Further reading

Plutarch, *Lives*, 'Tiberius Gracchus', 'Gaius Gracchus'.

Appian, *Civil War I*.

H.C. Boren, *The Gracchi*, Twayne, New York, 1968.

D. Stockton, *The Gracchi*, Clarendon, Oxford, 1979.

Topics for essays or discussion

1 Analyse the reforms proposed by Tiberius Gracchus. Were they necessary, and were they practical?

2 Compare the Gracchan proposals with those of Solon. Why were the Athenian's land reforms fruitful, whereas the Romans' failed?

3 How did Gaius try to avoid Tiberius' fate? Why did he fail to do so?

4 Discuss the effect of the Gracchan proposals upon (1) The Senate, (2) the equites. Do you think that the changes would have happened even without the Gracchi?

5 Some have seen in the Gracchan measures an attempt to introduce Athenian political concepts into Rome. Do you agree with this? Would there have been merit in such an ambition?

Chapter 12

The campaigns of Marius and the Social Wars

Sources

For this period our sources are extremely unreliable. We only possess the unsatisfactory summary of Livy. Moreover it was the age of the literate general. No less than three wrote at the time: Rutilius Rufus, who took part in the Numidian War, Catulus, who was less than brilliant in the war against the Cimbri and Teutones, and Sulla himself, who wrote his autobiography. All three were concerned to extol their own virtues, and each time at the expense of Marius. Their writings do not survive, but our later accounts draw on this highly prejudiced material.

Plutarch's *Life of Marius* is of very poor quality, mainly because he made extensive use of Sulla's autobiography. Sallust, who lived a generation later than these events, should be of more value than he is. He is very readable but, having had an unsuccessful political career himself, he was concerned to show recent times as degenerate. He was on the side of the populares, but he painted a gloomy picture of all his cast, including Marius. He wrote a *Jugurtha* and a *Catilinarian Conspiracy*.

Marius had one defender: Cicero. Cicero, like Marius, was a novus homo and came like him from Arpinum in Volscian territory. He also saw, not always accurately, some parallels between Marius' career and his own. Although he mentions Marius only in passing, he can on occasion serve as a useful counterbalance.

The lull before the storm

It is now time to return to our story. As was noted earlier, the Gracchi did not so much create entirely new political situations as bring to a head tendencies that had been in evidence for some time. One case in point was the division between the optimates and the populares. The optimates were the conservative faction, the bulwark of the Senate, who supported the selection of consuls from the few privileged families. The populares included a proportion of the senatorial class. They opposed the narrow restrictions of the optimates, and tried on a number of occasions to broaden the ranks both of senators and citizens. Inspired by the example of the Gracchi, they repeatedly used the office of tribune to further their reforms.

Another result of the Gracchan episode, which will be seen in this and later chapters, was the increasing use of mob violence in political disputes, ending sometimes in assassination. This was a practice markedly absent from the earlier Struggle of the Orders.

The Senate must have thought at first that it had successfully dealt with the threat to its privileges and position. No external danger was immediately apparent, and the death of Gaius Gracchus and his followers cleared the local scene of dangerous elements.

Rome had been asked for help by Massilia, which was troubled by incursions from its Gallic neighbours. In 121 the Romans subdued the area and created a new province, Gallia Narbonensis. This was later to be the most Romanised area of all Gaul, and is now the French district Provence.

Scaurus, a senator of some shrewdness and sense of the value of compromise, held power in Rome for the ensuing ten years.

What then happened to the colonies planned by Gaius Gracchus? A colony was established at Narbo, which helped to consolidate the new Gallic province. But the overseas colonies were abandoned, although the settlers who had gone to Iunonia were allowed to remain, and Neptunia, the colony near Tarentum, was established. That was all.

The Senate itself had learnt little from recent events. It did continue the corn dole. This helped to keep the peace within the city. Moreover it was in line with their own long established system of patronage. They also allowed the equites to keep their dominance over the law courts and the taxation system. One reason for this was that the Senate was not strong enough to dislodge them. In addition the senators in general entered into an unholy alliance with the equites. When the latter abused their taxation position, fleecing the provincials unmercifully, the senatorial governor did likewise and the loot was shared. The problem of the allies was also shelved. Those who had gained citizenship were enrolled in the four urban tribes, so that they had no political influence, and no further concessions were made. The Senate was soon to pay a heavy price for this neglect.

One attack was made on the optimates at this time. Opimius was prosecuted because of his summary execution of Gaius' followers. He was, however, acquitted, on the grounds that the Senate had given him supreme power under its emergency decree.

Meanwhile the Land Commission was coming to an end. This was not simply the result of senatorial opposition. Most of the new settlers, recruited from the streets of Rome, were not ideally suited to their new life. It was largely their complaints that inspired a law, passed in 120 B.C., which permitted them to sell their holdings. By 118 the Land Commission was dissolved.

Trouble brews in the East and in Numidia

Although superficially Rome and its dependencies were peaceful, in fact serious trouble was brewing in two places. In the eastern Mediterranean Rome had conquered the nations which once were powerful in the area, but, being a land power, took no steps to police the seas in their stead. The result was that piracy, which had always existed, grew constantly more serious.

It was then that a vigorous new ruler arose in the Kingdom of Pontus, Mithridates. He became king of Pontus in 120 B.C. and not long after was also given the lands of Crimea. Its inhabitants surrendered their freedom, hoping in return to be given protection. The rise of Mithridates offered some hope that order would through him return to this troubled area, but it also constituted a threat to the dominance of Rome.

The position in Africa was a more urgent problem. Rome had beaten Carthage with the help of Massinissa of Numidia. She rewarded him by the gift of large portions of Carthaginian territory. This enlarged realm he handed on to his heir Micipsa.

Unfortunately Micipsa had an excess of heirs. He possessed two sons, and an illegitimate adopted son, Jugurtha. Many chieftains in such a case made their choice, eliminating if necessary any possible rivals. Micipsa instead directed that when he died his kingdom should be divided between the three.

In 118 he died. Jugurtha, who was the most capable of the heirs, and certainly not the most scrupulous, immediately had one of his brothers, Hiempsal, assassinated. Adherbal, the other brother, fled the country and went to Rome to complain.

A Roman embassy was sent to Numidia. It was not unfavourable to Jugurtha, who had served under Scipio at Numantia, and it recognised his *fait accompli*, dividing the kingdom between him and Adherbal. Adherbal was, however, given the richer eastern portion, including the capital, Cirta. (This area falls within the modern country of Algeria.) Truth to tell, Rome was in no position to take a firm line just then, even if it had wished to do so; for shortly afterwards two Germanic tribes, the Cimbri and Teutones, threatened Italy from the north.

Jugurtha was encouraged by Rome's lack of determination and went on to conquer Adherbal's share of Numidia. The Italian merchants of

Cirta, who had given support to Adherbal, were massacred, and the prince was killed.

War with Jugurtha. A luckless beginning

Jugurtha was unwise to include the Italian merchants in his vengeance. This roused the Roman equites, who in turn put pressure on the government. As a result, Rome, despite all its other commitments, was forced to take action.

Unfortunately, as was proved in all theatres of war at this time, morale in the Roman armies was at a low ebb. There could have been many reasons for this. The Gracchan reforms showed that there was an ever-decreasing number of Roman citizens who could be enlisted in the forces. The Italians, who formed such a large part of Rome's armies, were becoming more and more discontented.

The Numidian wars posed one special problem for Rome: the excellence of the Numidian cavalry enabled them to harass the Roman armies from all sides and the Roman cavalry was no match for them. The cavalry had never been a strong point in the Republican army, and it had degenerated greatly since the end of the Punic wars.

The ensuing campaigns were to make only too clear this and other weaknesses of the Roman forces. In addition, it was claimed by Jugurtha himself, and by critics of the senatorial party, that Numidian gold in the form of bribes stopped many a Roman commander in his tracks, even when the military might of the enemy would have failed to do so.

The first general sent to deal with Jugurtha was signally unsuccessful, and finally returned to Rome after making an armistice. A tribune, Memmius, declared that the campaign had been a scandal. He demanded an inquiry, and arranged for Jugurtha to come to the capital in order to give evidence.

Jugurtha came, but another tribune interposed his veto to prevent him from giving evidence. Still the trip was not wasted. Jugurtha took the opportunity to arrange for the assassination of a cousin of his, who had taken refuge in Rome.

A consul was the next to be sent to Africa. He too had little success, but his brother, whom he left there with a holding force when he returned, was even less fortunate. During a winter campaign his army was defeated and made to go under the yoke, a humiliating reminder of the Caudine Forks.

Yet another tribune rose to denounce this incompetence, and a number of those responsible for the defeats were sent into exile. Finally, as so often in the past, the Senate was roused to send a man of ability. Metellus, a member of the family that dominated Roman politics in this period, was sent in 109 B.C. to crush Jugurtha.

Unfortunately the Senate had delayed too long, and public confidence was very low. Moreover, Jugurtha had not succeeded merely because his opponents were men of straw. Even though Metellus imposed much-needed discipline on his army, and captured Cirta, he was not able swiftly to bring the war to a successful conclusion, and that was what was demanded.

Marius enters the scene

When Metellus went to Africa he had on his staff Marius, a man of equestrian origins, born in Arpinum, a city in the Volscian district. A *novus homo*, Marius was helped in his career by the Metelli. He served with distinction under Scipio Aemilianus in the siege of Numantia. In 120 B.C., with the help of the Metelli, he gained the quaestorship, followed by a tribunate, then not without difficulty, a praetorship.

In his propraetorship Marius was given the province of Further Spain, where he did good service by putting down brigandage. That country also brought him financial advancement. He acquired a considerable interest in the mines of the country, where his descendants continued to be powerful in the later history of Rome. The mountain range, *Mons Marianus* (called in modern days Sierra Morena) bears witness to this fact.[1]

---

[1] T. Carney, *A Biography of C. Marius*, p. 23.

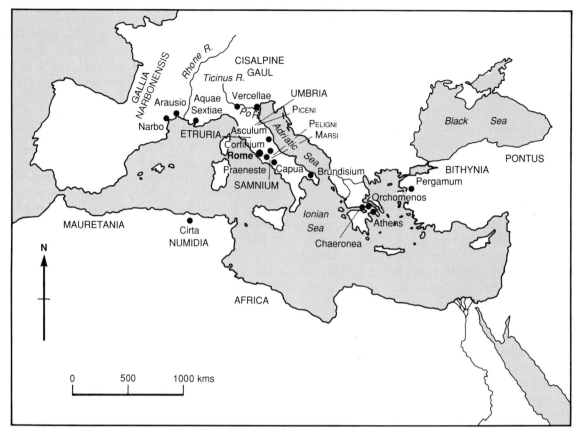

12.1 *The campaigns of Marius and Sulla.*

On his return to Rome he married a member of the Julii, a clan soon to be famous but then of little note. Still he now had social entry to the senatorial class, to which he belonged by virtue of his magistracies. This brings us to his service in Africa under Metellus. Our sources, notably Plutarch, suggest that Marius and Metellus quarrelled at this point, but this is a good instance of the fabrications of our sources.

In 108 B.C. Marius went to Rome—according to Plutarch, against Metellus' wishes, but probably just on a normal mission. On his arrival in Rome, however, just at the time the consuls were to be elected for the following year, Marius found a feeling of intense dissatisfaction at the long-drawn-out war, and saw his opportunity. He stood for the consulship, criticising Metellus and promising to bring the war to a successful

conclusion. The Senate was not happy, but it was powerless to intervene. Marius was elected.

The populares welcomed this new champion of their policies, and the Tribal Assembly gave Marius the command in the war against Jugurtha. This was an innovation, for since the Punic Wars it had been the Senate that decided what the spheres of duty of the consuls should be, especially in time of war.

Marius takes charge and Sulla comes on the scene

Marius then enrolled his army, but did so completely disregarding property qualifications. This was really the end of a long process. We saw in the last chapter that the property quali-

12.2 *Gaius Marius (c. 155–86 B.C.)*

fications had now been so eroded as to mean very little. None the less Marius took an important step, which was to have important consequences—of which, incidentally, he was himself not aware. He was simply a practical soldier enlisting the army that would serve him best. The result was that these landless soldiers felt more loyalty to their commander than to the state, and that they looked to him to provide for them at the end of their service.

Marius then set out for Africa with his new army. There he did not find Metellus, as he had retired in disgust and left his lieutenant to hand over the command. Back in Italy a young quaestor Sulla had the task of recruiting a cavalry force to take over to Marius.

Sulla was descended from the Cornelii, a once famous clan that had fallen on evil days. He had spent his youth in abject poverty, keeping company with the acting fraternity, for whom he even wrote some plays. It is significant of the man that in his days of fame he was never to forget the boon companions of his youth. A fortunate marriage and a wealthy mistress raised Sulla's fortunes and enabled him to gain the quaestorship. This mighty future champion of the Senate was a very dubious member of the class, but his misfortunes had filled him with a burning ambition, and sheer ability coupled with great personal charm helped him achieve his goals.

The war is won with the help of a little treachery

Marius spent the rest of 107 welding his army into an efficient fighting force, conducting only minor skirmishes and letting his men plunder on occasion to sample the rewards of war.

In 106 B.C. Marius took the offensive. He marched west and attacked a stronghold at Muluccha, which was perched on top of an almost inaccessible rock. He took it and with it Jugurtha's treasure, which was stored there.

Marius was now joined by Sulla, bringing the newly recruited cavalry, and he marched east again. Outside Cirta, which had at some time fallen again into Jugurtha's hands, he met the combined armies of Jugurtha and Bocchus of Mauretania. Marius won a decisive victory and Cirta opened its gates.

Jugurtha had won the alliance of Bocchus by promising him the half of his kingdom, but Bocchus wanted the best bargain he could get and also to be on the winning side. He entered into negotiations with the Romans, no easy task as Jugurtha watched him like a hawk. Sulla headed the negotiating team, and seems to have exerted his personal charm with some success. In the end Bocchus secretly accepted Rome's alliance, tricked Jugurtha into coming to his camp by the suggestion that they might negotiate a truce in the war, treacherously seized him, and handed him over to the Romans.

Bocchus' reward was generous, for Rome gave him large portions of Jugurtha's territory, and made no territorial claims for itself.

Jugurtha was taken back to Rome, together with many prisoners and considerable booty. He appeared in Marius' triumph and later died in prison. Thus Marius had achieved his first success.

A new threat. The Cimbri and Teutones invade Italy

It is not surprising that Rome took no further interest in Africa. There were problems closer at hand, and Marius was the only man who could solve them. Two north German tribes, the Cimbri and Teutones, came down to the north of Italy in 107. There they met the consul Longinus, whom they defeated and humiliated by making his troops pass under the yoke. The Roman forces were in a state of utter indiscipline and demoralisation. In 105, under the leadership of Caepio, they were defeated at Arausio and the resulting slaughter was second only to that of Cannae.

Marius, however, was now back again. The Comitia Centuriata appointed him to five successive consulships (104–100), and entrusted him with the campaign against the Cimbri and Teutones. The incompetent generals were attacked by a tribune, Saturninus, who had Caepio sent into exile. The Senate could do nothing to protect him.

Meanwhile the northern invaders had left Italy for the time being. The Cimbri ventured into Spain, where they were severely defeated by its tribesmen. The Teutones were unsuccessful in Gaul. What a commentary on the military ability of Rome!

Still this change of purpose gave Marius time to prepare. He took the army, consisting of his own forces and those of the defeated senators to a camp he set up on the Rhone and hammered them into shape with his usual efficiency. He also made the Roman legion more efficient. Previously it had been drawn up in three lines, each with different equipment, which the soldiers supplied themselves. This was obviously a cumbersome arrangement. Now that the soldiers were no longer men of property, the state supplied their equipment and Marius took the opportunity of making it uniform. He also made the tactical unit within the legion the cohort, instead of the smaller maniple. The cohort under him, and later under Caesar, was trained to manoeuvre more flexibly, even during the course of battle. In arms drill he borrowed the techniques developed in the gladiatorial schools.

To this revitalised legion he gave as its standard, the eagle, which it was to bear into battle throughout the rest of its history. It was during this time that he probably had the canal built, bearing his name, which takes the water of the Rhone through its muddy delta region[2].

In the meantime, Marius did not forget the veterans of his African campaigns. In 103 B.C. the tribune Saturninus passed a bill settling many of them in Tunisia.

Marius defeats the Gallic forces

By the time Italy was invaded again in 102 B.C. Marius was ready. The barbarians split their forces, with the Teutones marching down the west coast, while the Cimbri took the route east of the Apennines. Marius crossed the Alps and met the Teutones at Aquae Sextiae (near Orange), defeating them soundly.

Meanwhile the Cimbri had encountered Catulus, Marius' senatorial colleague, who hastily fled. Marius took his time, but in 101 he met them at Vercellae near the mouth of the Po not far from Rovigo. Plutarch's account of this battle derives from Catulus and Sulla, who naturally took all the credit for themselves, but luckily Zennari[3], using other sources, corrects the tale. He came upon the Cimbri early in the morning, with his advance obscured by mist, so the enemy were taken by surprise and could not draw up in full formation. Their plight was made worse by the dust and by the fact that they had the sun in their eyes. The troops of Catulus and Sulla were in the centre, and they pinned down the enemy, while Marius had the cavalry on the wings, and with his left wing he drove back the enemy cavalry and took the army at the rear, routing them utterly.

---

[2]L.A. Constans notes (*Esquisse d'une histoire de la Basse Provence dans l'Antiquité*, p. 44) that Marius' long stay in Provence did a great deal to Romanise it, and even now the popular folklore preserves his memory.
[3]See Ooteghem in Appendix, pp. 218–31.

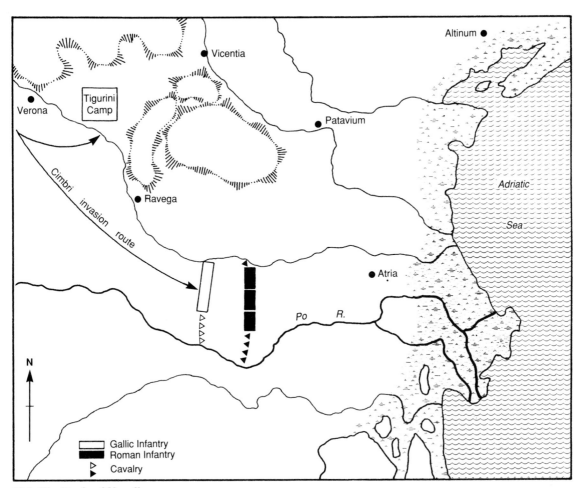

12.3 *The Battle of Vercellae.*

Marius' victory turns sour

Marius' return to Rome was followed by great rejoicing and by a triumph, which Marius shared with Catulus, less from any admiration of the man than to conciliate the aristocratic party.

At this point Marius had no further ambitions. It was not till later that generals conspired to take supreme control of the state. He did, however, have one pressing need, to provide land for his veterans. His opponents in the Senate saw to it that Metellus, now his implacable foe, was elected consul, and he solidly refused Marius' plans for his veterans.

Marius now turned to his old allies, the popular party and the tribunes. For the following

events our sources are solidly against Marius. In particular they paint a very black picture of his allies, Saturninus and Glaucia. The true situation was probably far more complex, but we have no way of arriving at it. In any case Marius helped Saturninus to a second tribunate, and his other ally Glaucia to a praetorship. He himself was elected consul for 100. These events were not without incident, for Saturninus had one opponent for the tribunate assassinated, an ill omen for the future.

Glaucia and Saturninus had a bill passed, assigning land to Marius' veterans in Sicily, Achaea, Macedonia, Corsica, Africa and Cisalpine Gaul. There was much dissension and in the end Metellus went into exile. Clearly Rome was now in a state of turmoil, such as led to the death of the Gracchi, and realising that they would not be safe as private citizens, Glaucia stood for a consulship, Saturninus for another tribunate. The elections were marked by violence and Glaucia had one of his rivals assassinated.

The Senate met and passed the *senatus ultimum consultum*, giving emergency powers to the consuls, Marius and Valerius. Marius heeded the call. He was no revolutionary. Glaucia and Saturninus fled with their followers to the Capitol, where they finally surrendered. They were shut up pending a trial, but senatorial extremists broke in and massacred them. It was a sorry story, recalling the worst excesses of the Gracchan period.

The Senate's troubles were by no means over. The equites, having been given control by the Gracchi of the courts that prosecuted corrupt practices in the provinces, made corrupt use of their power. This came to a head when they prosecuted and condemned Rutilius for misgovernment in Asia, when his only crime had been to protect Asia from the exactions of the equestrian tax collector. The indignant people of the province of Asia flocked to his support, and the case was an open scandal.

At the same time the allies were becoming weary. One after another, reformers who offered them some hope were defeated or met a violent death. Dissatisfaction was growing daily.

In 91 a champion rose who suggested a solution for these problems, M. Livius Drusus. His father had put forward the counter-proposals which helped to bring about the end of Gaius Gracchus. Similarly his son seems to have wished to win favour for the optimates by getting them to support a scheme of reform.

As tribune he revived the proposal to found colonies, and he also sought favour by arranging for a distribution of corn. Next he put forward a compromise solution of the problem of the courts. In future the jurymen who sat on them should be drawn half from the Senate, half from the equites. In compensation, the equites were to gain entrance to the Senate, which was to be increased from 300 to 600 members. Finally he brought forward a bill to give citizenship to the allies.

Neither the Senate nor the equites approved of his judicial reforms, and the city mob was alienated by his bill extending the franchise. When the Italians began to rise in support of Drusus, this was excuse enough. A mob gathered in the streets of Rome and lynched the reformer.

The Social (or Marsic) War

Both the names given to this are misleading. The word 'social' is not used in its modern sense, but because the Latin word for an ally was *socius*, and the war was an uprising of Rome's allies. Again the Marsi were prominent among the rebels, but the Samnites were equally important. Yet, although the war received scant mention in ancient histories, appearing as an interlude between Marius and Sulla, it was quite important, and was a real threat to Roman supremacy.

The allies were weary of fighting Rome's wars, then being constantly snubbed and ignored when the fruits of victory were distributed. Moreover, the Samnites had never grown reconciled to being Roman subjects. The weakness of the rebels was that they were in two senses divided: in their aims, for the Samnites wanted complete independence, whereas the Marsi and Paeligni only wished to be granted citizenship; geographically, for Latium and Etruria remained loyal to Rome, which drove a wedge between the Samnites and their allies in the south, and the Marsi and Paeligni in the north.

The rebels chose as their capital Corfinium, which lay in the territory of the Paeligni. They hopefully renamed the town Italia, and they issued coins which were equally symbolic of their ambitions.

This time the Tribal Assembly of Rome did not take charge of military operations. Their champion, Marius, had lost influence, and they had no substitute. This left the task to the Senate, a task made no easier by the fact that the rebels were the very people who normally made up their armies. In desperation, they even enlisted freedmen and slaves in the armed forces.

Nevertheless, although the enemy was formidable, not all Italy had risen. Not only Latium

12.4 *Coin struck by rebels, showing Italians taking an oath against Rome.*

and Etruria, but also the Greek cities in the south took no part in the proceedings. As was normal, the two consuls were given command. In the north was Lupus, who had Marius on his staff, in the south Lucius Caesar, who similarly had the assistance of Sulla.

In the first year the Roman forces just held their own. Capua was saved from the Samnites, but the rest of Campania was over-run. In the north Pompeius Strabo, Pompey's father, assumed command, bringing with him his retainers from his own estates. However, the decisive defeat in this area was that which Marius inflicted on the Marsi.

Rome makes concessions to the allies and ends the war

Even so, mere victories were not enough. Rome could not do without its allies, any more than in the early Republic the patricians could do without the plebeians. In 90, the first year of the war, the *lex Julia* was passed by L. Caesar,

offering citizenship to the states which had not revolted. Citizenship may also have been granted to any that surrendered, for the actual details of this and the ensuing laws are not known. Umbria and Etruria were the two states which gained most from that law.

Next year Sulla was in command in the south, and the consuls combined in an onslaught on the enemies to the north. Marius was not given an official post in these operations. His loyalty was not beyond suspicion, for as general he had endeavoured to win just rewards for his troops, and in recent years he had shown sympathy for their grievances. Pompeius Strabo was rewarded for his patriotism by a consulship. He conducted a vigorous campaign, capturing the enemy capital, and inflicting a decisive defeat on the northern army at Asculum.

In the same year further concessions were made by the *lex Plautia-Papiria*, passed by two tribunes. Amongst other measures, they offered citizenship to all the Cisalpine Gauls north of the Po.

Meanwhile, during the course of 89 and 88 Sulla dealt ruthlessly with the Samnites. He defeated them and devastated their territory.

The war was now over. Rome had won the battles, but the Italians had won the concessions for the sake of which they had made the war. From this time on Italy was a unit in terms of citizenship. Even the states that were most recalcitrant, and so were excluded, were admitted not long afterwards.

It should be kept in mind that the significance of this citizenship was not primarily political. It is true that many Italians came to Rome, where they were at first confined to the few urban tribes. (This final grievance they soon rectified.) But even for them, and all the more for the many Italians who never came to Rome, citizenship was first and foremost a matter of status. It meant that they were in the highest category when they enlisted in the Roman army, and that they had their full share of whatever prizes their commander had to distribute. In law and trade also they were entitled to all the privileges enjoyed by the people of Rome themselves.

By 88 the war was virtually ended, but Italy was a shambles.

Marius and Sulla clash over command against Mithridates

The new citizens of Rome were disgruntled when they found that they were enrolled only in the urban tribes rather than being distributed among all thirty-five tribes. In the urban tribes, their voting power, and in consequence their influence, was very small, compared with their numbers.

A friend of Drusus, P. Sulpicius Rufus, though himself an aristocrat, saw that the frustrations of the allies would have to be resolved. He therefore proposed that the allies be distributed among all thirty-five tribes. At the same time he tried to win Marius' support by promising him command of the war against Mithridates.

Sulla was not pleased. He had been made a consul in 88, and had opposed the redistribution of the new citizens. The war against Mithridates had been allotted to him. In consequences he set a new precedent by marching at the head of his legions against Rome itself.

Marius had no army with which to oppose him. Therefore he left in haste and crossed over into Africa, where many of his veterans had been settled. Sulla then reorganized the government, in a manner that foreshadowed his later reforms. When he had cancelled Sulpicius' measures, he gave the Senate final authority on whether laws should be passed. After that he set off to make war on Mithridates.

Laws that are backed neither by force nor by popular consent have little enduring power. One of the consuls of 87, Cinna, was a supporter of the populares. As soon as Sulla was gone, he reintroduced Sulpicius' law.

Rioting resulted, and Cinna was driven out of Rome. He called Marius to his aid, and Marius made haste to answer, gathering an army as he come. He promised freedom to any slaves who enlisted in his forces.

Cinna and Marius besieged Rome, which was struck by a plague and soon surrendered.[4] A second time Rome was captured by its own citizens. The victorious army was given licence to loot and murder, but when the moderates cut

down Marius' own bodyguard because of its excesses, a halt was called.

Historians exaggerated the massacre that occurred on this occasion in order to make some excuse for the Sullan massacres that followed.

In 86, Marius was elected to his seventh consulship. This was said to have been what was promised to him by the sooth-sayers, but it was an empty honour, for he died soon after.

Cinna continued in power for three years. He carried out his promise and redistributed the new citizens among all the tribes. This was a necessary remedy to a long-standing grievance and no attempt was made, even by Sulla, to undo it. Cinna, however, lived continually in the shadow of the absent Sulla whose ultimate return and vengeance was only a matter of time.

Marius: an evaluation

With Marius, Rome had taken a step further on the road to military despotic rule. The process had begun during the Punic wars, when the Scipios were given consulships out of turn, and on occasion enlisted an army of their own supporters. The Scipios, however, were true members of the senatorial class. Marius had no such loyalty. By removing the property qualification for army service he created the new soldier, who was henceforth to be characteristic of the Romans. He had few if any home ties, enlisted voluntarily for long periods, saw in his general the man to whom he owed his entire devotion, and looked to him for a gratuity and a land allotment to provide for his old age. With this new army the Senate lost control over the forces that held the empire it had won.

Marius himself is worth careful consideration. A number of modern writers have been persuaded by our ancient sources, and see him as uncouth, ignorant and politically incapable. Carney and Ooteghem (see 'Further reading')

[4]Pompeius Strabo had been called in by the Senate to defend Rome against Marius and Cinna, but he died of the plague.

oppose these views, and attribute to him considerable shrewdness, and some education.

Actually, he more than any other single Roman created the new Roman army, which was to control Rome's dominions for many centuries[5]. Again, despite his alliances Marius was no mob agitator. His sympathies were fundamentally with the equestrian middle class, to which he belonged. His other loyalty was to his soldiers, and that was one factor which made him such a half-hearted supporter in the Social War, in which he saw ranged against him his own former soldiers.

After his death his name was in disgrace, owing to Sulla. One man did defy it. When the young Julius Caesar, Marius' nephew, buried Julia, Marius' widow, he had borne in the procession the ancestral effigies of Marius, amid popular acclamation!

Date table

Select quotations

1 Plutarch, *Lives*, 'Marius', 22:
After the battle (with the Teutones) Marius chose from the arms and spoils of the barbarians whatever was undamaged and spectacular and likely to add distinction to his triumph. The bulk of the rest he heaped up on a large pyre and offered it up as a magnificent sacrifice. The army stood around him, armed and wearing wreaths, while he, clad in purple, as the custom is, seized a burning torch, and raising it in both hands to heaven, was about to kindle the pyre. Then some friends of his came into sight, riding towards him at full speed, so that all were filled with silent expectation. When they were close, they leapt off and saluted Marius, announcing that he had been chosen consul for the fifth time, and they handed him written confirmation of the fact. This gave added joy to the festivity, and while the army in delight clashed their arms and cheered and the leaders put the laurel wreath on Marius once more, he lit the pyre and completed the sacrifice.

2 Plutarch, *Lives*, 'Marius', 39:
(Marius, in flight from Sulla, hides in a cottage at Minturnae in Italy.)
The magistrates and council of Minturnae decided to despatch the man without delay. None of the citizens could undertake the task but a cavalryman of Gallic or Cimbrian race (both versions exist) took a sword and went in. The part of the cottage in which he lay was not well lit, and Marius' eyes are said to have seemed to flash at the soldier, and a loud voice came from the gloom, 'Do you dare, fellow, to slay Gaius Marius?' At once the barbarian took to his heels and, throwing away his sword, rushed out of doors shouting only 'I cannot kill Gaius Marius'.

Further reading

Plutarch, *Makers of Rome* and *Fall of the Roman Republic*, Penguin Classics.
Sallust, *The Jugurthine War and the Catilinarian Conspiracy*, Penguin Classics.

---

[5]Marius also modified the javelin, the hurling weapon of the Roman soldier. He substituted a wooden pin for one of the rivets in the shaft. The javelin then snapped off short on impact and could not be reused by the enemy.

T. Carney, *A Biography of C. Marius,*
Proceedings of the African Classical Ass.
Suppl. No. 1, 1961.

J. van Ooteghem, *Caius Marius*, Royal
Academy of Belgium, Brussels, 1963.

Topics for essays or discussion

1 Did the career of Marius represent a victory
over the senatorial clique? If so why did he
succeed?

2 Contrast the part played by the Senate in the
time of Marius with its role in the Punic
wars. How do you account for the
difference?

3 What is the importance of Marius in the
development of the military machine in
Rome?

4 What was the relation of Marius to the
populares? Who was the dominant partner of
the two?

5 What caused the Social War? Could it have
been avoided?

6 Contrast the Social War with Rome's earlier
struggles with the Latin League, noting any
significant resemblances and differences.

Chapter 13

Sulla

Sources

FOR SULLA we have to rely on Plutarch's *Life of Sulla* and on Appian's *Civil War*. Both Plutarch and Appian based their work on Sulla's highly suspect autobiography, and unfortunately we do not have any independent contemporary source to set against them.

In this connection Badian[1] is interesting. He notes, as a number of historians have done before him, that it was a little surprising that Marius should leave a young and untried Sulla to recruit a cavalry force for him to use in the Numidian War. Badian suggests that Sulla concealed the fact that Marius had some time back taken Sulla under his wing. Reversing the usual procedure, Marius, a *novus homo*, saw the advantage of making use of an able young man of aristocratic lineage, who had come on evil days.

It is noteworthy that although our sources suggest a coolness between Marius and Sulla after the Numidian War, there is no really firm evidence for a break between them until the time of Sulla's consulship after the Social Wars. In short Sulla wished to present himself as a self-made man, and deny the debt he owed the older man.

Sulla sets off to fight Mithridates

By 89 B.C. Mithridates had conquered most of Asia Minor and he ordered a massacre of the Italians in the province. The Italian *publicani* or tax gatherers were highly unpopular, so Mithridates was obeyed with enthusiasm and over 80 000 Italians were killed. Mithridates then besieged Rhodes and sent his general, Archelaus to conquer Greece. The Greeks, not least Athens, welcomed the invaders, and by the time Sulla arrived, Greece and Asia Minor were in the hands of the enemy.

Sulla had no easy task. He had an army of five legions, but his home base Rome was hostile to him, so that he could hope for no supplies and no reinforcements. He had, however, the ruthlessness which was needed to cope with this situation. The lack of supplies he countered by living off the land, thus imposing a heavy burden on Greece, the scene of his operations. He also seized the treasuries of the main shrines of Greece, promising to pay them back later.

He took Athens and with more difficulty its port, the Piraeus, and there was a terrible slaughter of those who had resisted. Archelaus set off from the Piraeus with his fleet to join Mithridates and his army. There he urged a war of attrition, but he was overruled. Sulla had gone from Athens to Boeotia, which offered more supplies for his troops, and Archelaus met him at Chaeronea, Sulla was victorious, but Archelaus withdrew to Chalcis, where Sulla, without a fleet, could not pursue him. There was a second engagement at Orchomenos, where the Romans were also successful.

[1]E. Badian, *Lucius Sulla, the Deadly Reformer*, Seventh Todd Memorial Lecture, Sydney University Press, 1969.

Mithridates has had enough. Peace is negotiated

All was not well with Mithridates. He had decided that the ruling classes of Asia Minor were against him, so he declared himself a champion of the poor, and cancelled all debts. There was wholesale slaughter of the well-to-do, and as a result dissatisfaction was widespread. In addition another force, sent by the Cinnan faction in Rome, had arrived. It was led by Fimbria, who had killed the original commander and it devastated the province of Pergamum. Mithridates felt he had had enough and opened negotiations through Archelaus.

The two negotiators were well aware of each other's need for peace. Mithridates to recover his losses, Sulla to go back to Rome; so after some parley a deal was struck.

Mithridates was to withdraw from Greece and his other conquests, giving back Bithynia and Cappadocia, and in addition he was to give Sulla 2000 talents as indemnity for the war, and seventy warships. Mithridates in return was to be accepted as an ally of Rome.

13.1 *Sulla (138–78 B.C.)*

Sulla then attacked the dissident Fimbria. Fimbria's troop deserted him and he himself committed suicide. This was the end of Sulla's military operations. His final task was to punish those who had opposed him and to gain urgently needed funds. The two tasks went well together, Sulla imposed a heavy war indemnity on all the cities that had opposed him. He had no publicani to collect his dues, so the army undertook the task. Asia and Greece were beggared, but by the end of winter Sulla's funds were replenished.

Sulla prepares to march on Rome

Sulla prepared to return to Rome. He left much undone, not only Mithridates but the pirates who now ruled the seas were unchecked, but he could do little till he settled his own position.

Sulla sent a message to Rome that he was returning to report on his proconsulship. Cinna gathered an army to meet him, but Rome and indeed Italy was not united.

The Senate led by Flaccus of the moderate faction, was eager to mediate and the Italian allies were willing to reach an agreement, particularly when Sulla sent a message that he would accept the redistribution of the tribes. Some of Cinna's own army deserted to Sulla and when he tried to stop them, they stoned him to death. However, Carbo remained to lead the Cinnan faction and he resisted all efforts to reach a settlement.

Sulla was in no haste. He spent some time in Athens, putting its affairs in order and even taking part in the Eleusinian Mysteries. Then only did he set out, accompanied by many senators who had fled to him from Cinna. In 83 B.C. his fleet set sail for Brundisium, which opened its gates to him. Sulla marched north, careful to avoid any pillaging as he went. That was an easy self-denial, as they were laden with the spoils of the East. Metellus and Crassus came from Africa to join him, and as Metellus was a leading senator of the highest nobility, this was important. Young Pompey, Pompeius Strabo's son, also declared his allegiance, and a number of senators, led by the moderate Flaccus, came to his camp. Crassus and Pompey were to dominate the political scene in the period immediately after Sulla.

The opponents met in Campania. Sulla first encountered Norbanus, whom he defeated, then he found himself opposed by the consul Scipio. Scipio tried to negotiate a peace, an idea welcomed by Sulla. But when Scipio sent his lieutenant Sertorius to consult Norbanus, Sertorius broke the truce. It was too late. Scipio's army had been fraternising with Sulla's men, and they deserted in a body. Scipio was given a courteous safe-conduct back to Rome.

Pompey raised two legions in his home country of Picenum and joined Sulla, and in 82 B.C. Sulla marched north. He met and defeated Marius' son of the same name who retired to Praeneste, which was a rallying point for Sulla's opponents, especially the Lucanians and Samnites. Next Sulla met Carbo, who was deserted by many of his Celtiberian cavalry and defeated. Norbanus too was beaten and fled to Greece.

The Battle of the Colline Gates

Finally the Cinnan forces led by Carbo and by young Marius decided to march on Rome and force a confrontation with Sulla there, the core of this army being the Samnites led by Telesinus. Sulla came hot on their heels and found them drawn up before the Colline Gate. It was late in the afternoon, but Sulla would heed no advice of caution, flinging his army into battle at once, though weary from the march. Crassus on the right wing of Sulla's army was victorious, but on the left a rout began. Sulla tried to stop it, almost being killed in the process. The fleeing men hammered on the gates of Rome, but they were shut to avoid a slaughter in the streets. Sulla's men now literally had their backs to the wall, and desperation gave them strength. The battle went on till late, but finally the enemy were driven back, Telesinus killed and Sulla had won.

The Proscriptions

Up to now Sulla had been in general conciliatory to his opponents, but this was at an end. His victory was followed by an unbridled massacre, in which the slaughter of three to four thousand Samnite prisoners was conspicuous. Sulla seems to have nourished a great hostility to this people, perhaps as a result of their determined stand in the Social War.

When he entered Rome, bloodshed continued in the city itself. Simultaneously his men devastated Etruria and Samnium in return for their earlier opposition. From a cynical viewpoint Sulla gained doubly here, as the land thus cleared of its occupants provided farms for his veterans, a need that by now no commander could afford to neglect.

At first there were no restrictions on the massacre in Rome, but when even his own associates became worried at the excesses, he drew up a list of those who were for their actions outlawed, and so could be killed with impunity. At least forty senators fell and fourteen hundred equestrians.[2] Some put the figure much higher. Their property was confiscated and their slaves were freed, a bounty being paid to the killers from the proceeds. The slaves were made Sulla's own freedmen, called as was the custom, Cornelii after him. They numbered about 10 000, a figure that confirms the magnitude of the proscriptions. The families of the proscribed were forbidden to hold office. Julius Caesar was put on the list, but powerful friends had his name removed.

These events had a further indirect result. When Marius pensioned off his veterans, he sent them, as was the custom, to distant places. Even so they were valuable supporters, linked by the bond of clientship to him, as patron, and they proved their usefulness when he went into exile. Sulla was able to settle his veterans in the neighbourhood of Rome. Thus, not only did he have a powerful body of clients, but they were placed strategically to give him their support immediately, any time the need arose, and to crush opposition.

---

[2]The common people of Rome were not his target. It was only in the allied communities such as Etruria and Samnium that the whole people was put to the sword.

Sulla reforms the Constitution

So far Sulla's labours had been destructive in character. He next turned with equal efficiency to restore and remodel the state which he, among others, had so cruelly mauled. In order to do this he assumed the title of dictator. That was an office long fallen into disuse, but he revived it in an altered form. The dictator had originally been appointed to fulfil a religious function, or to meet a military emergency. He made himself dictator for the purpose of revising the constitution, a role reminiscent of Greek law-givers such as Solon. Also, whereas the dictator had formerly been appointed for a set period, not exceeding six months, no such limit was imposed on Sulla.

He had seen the state threatened twice before he himself took it by force, once by the Gracchi, once by Marius. His ideal was the Roman state of old, in which aristocratic rule prevailed, centred on the Senate, in short, one where the optimates were all-powerful.[3]

One threat to the supremacy of the optimates had been the tribunes, who since the time of the Gracchi had been leaders in popular agitation. Sulla crippled their power in two ways. He took away from them the right of proposing laws to the people. He also made it illegal for them to hold a curule magistracy after their term of office was over. This meant that any man of ambition would think twice before taking on a post that ended his hope of future advancement.

The other threat to the state had been from victorious generals backed by an army full of loyalty and of hope for the rewards of victory. Such a general could be a praetor, a consul, a propraetor or a proconsul. Sulla simplified this situation. He decreed that only a pro-magistrate could hold office outside Italy, whether as general or governor. He had to stay within the bounds of the province allotted him, and the moment he set foot in Italy, he had to disband his army.

He also set obstacles in the way of the rapidly rising young general, such as Scipio had been. To do this he gave final form to a procedure that had been developing through custom. This was known as the *cursus honorum*. (The 'order of

The cursus honorum

Quaestors	— Thirty years of age minimum.
	— Twenty positions elected annually.
	— Automatically became senators.
	— Would be sent to assist a governor in a province after their year of office.
Curule Aediles	— Not necessary to hold this position for election to the praetorship.
	— Two positions elected annually.
Praetors	— Thirty-nine years of age minimum.
	— Eight positions elected annually.
	— Given a propraetorship to govern a province after their year of office.
Consuls	— Forty-two years of age minimum.
	— Two positions elected annually.
	— Given a proconsulship to govern a province after their year of office.
	— Plebeian tribunes could hold no higher office after their year of office.

(*Note:* for propraetors and proconsuls see Fig. 5.1)

13.2 *The Cursus Honorum of Roman magistrates as organised by Sulla.*

offices' might render the idea.) Offices were to be held in strict sequence. The first of these, the quaestorship, should not be entered on before the age of thirty, the praetorship before thirty-nine, the consulship before forty-two. To stop one man gaining too much power by holding an office (notably the consulship) year after year, as

---

[3]Like many conservative Roman reformers, Sulla abolished the corn dole.

Marius had done, it was reaffirmed that ten years must elapse before an office could be held for a second time. As applied to the tribunate, this law served to hamper yet further its use as a centre of popular agitation.

The curule aedileship, normally taken between the offices of quaestor and praetor, did not form a necessary part of the cursus honorum. As there were only two curule aediles, it was patent that the eight praetors could not be elected each year from retiring aediles. Nevertheless, the holding of that office could give an advantage later in the candidature for the praetorship. One important task of the aedile came to be the arranging of a gladiatorial show, and if he were wealthy, he could by his munificence gain valuable publicity.

If Sulla wished to restore power to the Senate, he had also to restore the Senate itself. Not only had many of its members fallen in the wars and in the proscriptions, but the families of those proscribed, as well of those who had fallen in battle while opposing him, were debarred from office. The body had in consequence fallen far below its statutory number of three hundred.

Nor did Sulla wish merely to restore the former numbers. While the size of the Senate had long been fixed, the citizen body had been increasing constantly, and with the admitting of the allies after the Social War had taken a mighty step upward. Likewise the other class of importance, the equites, had been growing ever larger. Therefore, in proportion, the Senate had been diminishing over the preceding period. This was most undesirable if the Senate was to govern effectively. It was also likely to be crippling, if the Senate was to be the source of the administrators of Rome.

Sulla took no half measures. He doubled the size of the body, raising it to six hundred. This measure also served the end of giving the equites some political role. In order to supply the additional senators, Sulla drew on the equites, not so much probably on the urban members of that class, who had been some of the main victims of his proscriptions, as on the small landed proprietors of the Italian communities. He had recourse also to the states which had been made part of the citizen body by the recent enfranchisement laws.

Having created a larger Senate, Sulla had to maintain it at that size. In former days the censors had drawn up the senatorial list. Such a task became increasingly difficult to fulfil as Rome grew, and their position was always open to abuse if it fell into unscrupulous hands. Moreover, the censors' other task, that of drawing up the list of citizens in order to recruit the army, was now an anachronism with the development of a volunteer army recruited much at the whim of its commander.

Sulla decreed that the Senate should be composed of all curule magistrates. In effect, this meant that a man became a senator automatically on gaining the lowest office, that of quaestor. To ensure an adequate supply, the number of quaestors to be elected annually was increased to twenty. This step achieved a further purpose. There were by now ten Roman provinces, two each in Spain and Gaul,[4] to which were added Asia, Macedonia, Cilicia, Africa, Sicily, and the islands of Sardinia and Corsica, which were combined in a single province. Ten of the quaestors were set aside for administrative duties in the provinces.

The number of praetors also needed to be raised, in order not to give too much power to too few men. So the number of praetors was raised from six to eight. The consulship was left unaltered, as an increase in the number of consuls would have lessened the power of the office. Now there were eight propraetors and two proconsuls available each year for the ten provincial commands.

The praetors had another task. Rome's judicial system had long been antiquated. The right of *provocatio* of appeal in criminal cases meant that magistrates saved themselves useless labour by automatically referring all such cases to the full assembly. This was most cumbersome. The special court, set up in 149 to deal with corrupt provincial governors (*quaestio de rebus repetundis*) had shown a possible new procedure.

Sulla used this precedent to establish eight additional courts of the same sort, using one ex-

---

[4]The second Gallic province, Cisalpine Gaul, was his own creation.

aedile as well as the eight praetors to preside over them. They handled all major criminal cases. He altered the composition of the courts by taking them from the equites and restoring them to the senatorial class. Their decisions were not subject to the traditional appeal. These *quaestiones* or permanent courts turned out to be the most lasting of Sulla's reforms.

Sulla's retirement and death

Sulla felt it was time to celebrate his triumph over Mithridates. He did so in fine style and in the process so denuded Greece that their Olympic Games that year were ruined.

Meanwhile the young Pompey had been covering himself with glory. After crushing opposition to Sulla in Sicily he was sent to Africa where he was equally successful. He was then ordered to disband his army, but the army refused to be disbanded. The same thing had happened to Pompeius Strabo, and one suspects that Pompey did not try very hard to let them go. Anyway Pompey came back to Rome with his army, a foretaste of things to come. Sulla was placatory, granting Pompey a triumph, and Pompey then divorced his wife and married Sulla's stepdaughter, Aemilia.

Two more triumphs were granted, to Flaccus, who had helped achieve a settlement in Gaul, and a most undeserved one to Murena, who had tried to create an unprovoked war with Mithridates. Mithridates protested and Sulla stopped Murena's war-mongering but when he came back to Rome he gave him also a triumph. Spain was still not settled. Sertorius had gone there as governor and was gathering opposition to Sulla. This problem was to be settled later.

Sulla's celebrations on top of the civil war left the treasury empty, so he replenished it with the money he brought back from the war with Mithridates and the money from the proscriptions. He also imposed new taxes on the provinces, making their desperate loss still worse.

Sulla now felt that his task was over. He stood for the consulship with Metellus as colleague and relinquished his dictatorship. He also divorced his dying wife and married the attractive niece of the famous orator Hortensius, Cicero's main rival in the law courts.

At this time Cicero defended Roscius against the wrong-doing of one of Sulla's men, and Sulla allowed the trial to proceed and Roscius to be acquitted of his charge.

After his consulship Sulla retired to his country villa and wrote his memoirs in twenty-two volumes, the last of which had to be completed after his death. The work was a political pamphlet, if a large one, and aimed to show Sulla as a favourite of the gods.

The question now was would Sulla's laws, imposed by violence, survive? For the moment it appeared that they would. A violent attack on Sulla in his retirement was unlikely to succeed, for Rome was encircled by his veterans, who would flock to his defence. He also had a solid core of support in those in the Senate who benefited from the privileges he had won for that body.

Yet there were ominous signs. In 79 B.C. Lepidus stood for the consulship, vowing to repeal Sulla's measures. Despite Sulla's opposition he won the post, then when he failed in his attempt to change the laws, he withdrew from Rome, preparing for more violent measures.

Then in 78 B.C. Sulla collapsed with a massive haemorrhage, caused by liver failure. He had been a strong man physically, but in the end his excesses caught up with him. He had a fine funeral, and Hortensius gave the funeral oration.

What sort of man was Sulla and what did he achieve?

Sulla is an interesting man. He is presented as a monster of cruelty, and he was both cruel and vengeful. Yet he had great personal charm, which he used successfully on women and on his troops, with whom he was on as easy terms as with the acting fraternity of his youth. His proscriptions were frightful, but up to the battle of the Colline Gate he was conciliatory to his opponents. After that implacable. He was not a great military innovator like Marius, though like Marius he was convinced of divine protection. Marius thought Hercules was his protector, while with Sulla it was Apollo and Venus. Great generals of all ages tend to such superstitions.

It remains to sum up his achievement. As you will see in the next chapter, nearly all his reforms barely outlived him. They were established by a law, and the law was repealed.

The trouble was that the Senate simply was not capable of governing in this new era. The radical changes which Sulla had made in its composition and the death of many of its traditional members would of course have weakened it. It needed to re-educate itself, and events were moving too fast for such apprenticeship.

More than that, Sulla had not found the real answer to controlling the army. He had tried to insist that provincial commands be limited strictly to one year. Yet, whenever there was a real crisis, this rule was inevitably broken, and inevitably gave a strong general his opportunity. Its only effect was that the provinces were plundered more than ever. The briefer a governor's stay, the greater had to be the speed of his looting operations. This, combined with the heavy reparations that Sulla imposed on Asia after the First Mithridatic War, created in the provinces of the late Republic a state of chronic bankruptcy and despair.

Nor did the tribunes long stay repressed. They and the disreputable gangsterism with which they had become associated, were a real power in Rome, and they could be very useful to an ambitious politician. It was obvious that their disqualification would have no more permanency than Sulla's other constitutional laws.

Sulla also failed to remove the cleavage that existed between the governing classes of Rome, a cleavage that was fatal to harmony. There still remained the Senate, which had political power, the equites, which had financial power but no political power or responsibility, and finally the military junta, which was subject in no real sense to any one but itself.

The legacy of Sulla was somewhat different from what he had planned. He left the reformed law-courts. That was his most valuable positive contribution. With it he did leave a more realistic civil service, owing to the increase in the numbers of magistrates, and the more sensible fashion of recruiting the Senate. He did away with the antiquated office of censor, and despite later revivals of the office it never came back as a normal part of the state.

He left a provincial system badly administered and bound to get worse. The limits he imposed on the movements and length of tenure of magistrates reduced efficiency and increased abuses. The balance of ten pro-magistrates and ten provinces would only last until another province was created, and Rome was still expanding.

His laws forbidding unconstitutional power were less effective than his own example, which encouraged it. The countryside of Italy he left devastated, so that southern Italy never fully recovered. Indeed, it has continued to be the depressed part of Italy up to modern times. Sulla was not to blame for this. Other factors contributed to make the decline permanent, but he did initiate the process.

Sulla brought to its logical conclusion the mass slaughter of political opponents. This practice had been in evidence in the time of the Gracchi, but had gathered momentum in the Social War. This war was essentially a civil war, and any such fighting is always particularly savage. Sulla carried on the tradition, but his very excesses also gave the Romans pause. As a result, even when the Civil Wars rent the country not long after, the Romans, with the one ghastly exception of the proscriptions of Antony and Octavian, tended to avoid more such bloodbaths.

Date table

B.C.
86	Battles of Chaeronea and Orchomenos.
85	Sulla signs terms of peace with Mithridates.
84	Cinna murdered by his troops.
83	Sulla lands in Italy.
82	Battle of the Colline Gate.
81	Sulla becomes dictator.
79	Sulla resigns.
78	Death of Sulla.

Select quotations

Plutarch, *Lives*, 'Sulla' 30:
When Sulla learnt . . . that most of his enemies
had perished, he went at dawn to Antemna and
when three thousand of them sent men to parley,
he promised to spare them if they turned on the
others, who were hostile, before coming to him.
They gave him credence and attacked the rest and
many were slain, on both sides. Nonetheless he
penned them up, with the rest of the survivors,
about six thousand in all, in the Circus, then
summoned the Senate to meet in the temple of
Bellona. Just as he was beginning to speak, those
he had assigned to the task began slaughtering the
six thousand. The cries made could be heard from
afar, which is not surprising, when so many were
being killed in so small a space. But when the
Senate was terrified by this, he continued to speak,
with no change of expression, and told them to
pay attention to what he said, and not to bother
with what was happening outside. Some trouble-
makers were by his orders being punished.

Further reading

A. Keaveney, *Sulla, the Last Republican*,
   Croom Helm, London, 1982.
J. Leach, *Pompey the Great*, Croom Helm,
   London, 1978.
Plutarch, *Lives*, 'Sulla'.
Cicero, *Pro Roscio Amerino*, Loeb.

Topics for essays or discussion

1 Why could the Senate not wield the power given them by Sulla?
2 'Sulla's reforms were made necessary because the Gracchi destroyed the harmony of the state.' Do you agree?
3 Analyse Sulla's reforms of the magistracies and the law courts. Why were they necessary and what advantages did they offer?
4 'Sulla's example was more effective than his precepts.' Discuss.
5 Compare and contrast Sulla with the Athenian law-giver Solon.

Chapter 14

Pompey and the breakdown of the Republic

THIS PERIOD, which leads on to the collapse of the Roman Republic, is of prime importance for the history of Rome. It is also one of the best documented.

Sources

We still have Appian's *Civil War* and Plutarch's *Lives*. In addition there are Cicero's speeches and, equally important, his abundant and revealing letters, of which the most important are those written to his friend Atticus. Caesar himself makes some reference to this period in his *Civil War* and Suetonius' *Lives of the Caesars* begins with the life of Julius Caesar. We also have Sallust's *Catilinarian Conspiracy*.

Although there is so much material it is a controversial age, and this is reflected in our sources. Suetonius was a public servant living in the time of the emperor Trajan. He was eager to disparage earlier emperors, so that Trajan would show the better, and he was willing to accept the most outrageous gossip. He also was

no historian. We have already noted Sallust's weaknesses as an historian. Cicero is particularly dangerous. As a lawyer he had a case to plead, and truth was of secondary consideration. The fact that he is such a brilliant writer and such a good lawyer makes his distortion all the harder to detect, and he has succeeded in prejudicing some of our modern historians. We are helped a little by the fact that his letters were private, and often reveal the truth that his public pronouncements concealed. Nevertheless we can be grateful to Cicero in that it is mainly through him that we know these times almost as vividly as a modern period.

Caesar was also an excellent writer, and this makes it necessary to treat him too with caution. His *Gallic War* and *Civil War* are political pamphlets, designed to put Caesar's point of view, but they are written with such clarity and apparent objectivity that their bias is easy to miss. The eighth book of the Gallic War, written after Caesar's death by his lieutenant Hirtius, shows some of the aspects of Caesar's generalship that he passed over.

Another source should be mentioned here. Dio Cassius lived in the late Roman Empire (A.D. c. 150–235) having the emperor Alexander Severus as his patron. He wrote a complete history of Rome up to his time. The portion surviving covers the latter period of the Republic from 68 B.C. till the death of Claudius in A.D. 54.

He was a most conscientious writer and we owe him much detail that has not survived elsewhere, but he is not noted for his integrity. He was eager to keep the favour of his patron and so had little good to say of the defenders of the Republic, such as Cicero and Brutus.

We do not have Livy except for the summary, and that is a pity, for we are told that Augustus chided Livy as being more an advocate for Pompey than for Julius Caesar. This brings us to the final cause of distortion. Augustus was a great patron of the arts, and he had a clear idea of what he expected in return. Any writing from the time of Augustus, whether extant or found in later writers who used this material, is heavily biased in Augustus' favour, and naturally too in favour of his ancestor Julius Caesar.

Sulla leaves a very dissatisfied Rome

When Sulla died, he left a legacy of great dissatisfaction. The populace was indignant at Sulla's cancellation of their corn dole, the equestrian class at the loss of their law courts, the populares at the curtailing of the powers of the tribunes. Even Sulla's veterans were finding agriculture uncongenial after a life of soldiering, and were eager for a war to rescue them from rural boredom and debt. Finally, there were the many who had lost their land and were debarred from public life because their fathers had opposed Sulla. On the other hand Sulla's laws had greatly benefited the Senate, which was eager to maintain the privileges Sulla had granted it. Unfortunately Sulla's proscriptions had eliminated many of its most gifted and energetic members. He had swelled its numbers by bringing into it many from the equestrian class. These new men would be most eager to enjoy the privileges of the Senate, but they lacked experience.

As a result the Senate showed little vision in this period. It made up for this by a great obstinacy, following blindly old and recalcitrant leaders like Catulus, and Cato the Younger, who was imbued with the prejudices of the old. In addition it was an age when corruption flourished, not least in the elections, details of which we learn from Cicero. Possibly the Senate could never have held out against the power of the new generals and the new armies they led, but its loss of effective leadership certainly made the end inevitable.

The uprising of Lepidus

The first man to take advantage of the situation was the aristocrat Lepidus. He had been convicted of malpractices while governing Sicily, and was anxious to stir up trouble so that he might earn his reinstatement. He was elected consul for 78 B.C. and brought forward laws that would remedy a number of the current grievances. The distribution of corn was to be recommenced, exiled citizens recalled, and confiscated land returned to its original owners.

Finally, the tribunes were to be freed of the restrictions imposed on them. The Senate was not altogether unfavourable and passed a number of his measures. It would not, however, tamper with land ownership or the position of the tribunes. When the exiles were allowed back, Julius Caesar, who, although not officially exiled, had fled from Rome during Sulla's dictatorship, took advantage of the amnesty to return to Rome.

Meanwhile armed revolts began. This was an evil omen for the Senate. Armies would be needed to crush the rebels, and the Senate soon found that it was an incapable as ever of handling ambitious generals backed by their troops.

The trouble began in Etruria, which was full of men who had lost their land through Sulla. Sulla's own veterans, who had farms in the area, were only too eager to join the insurgents. The Senate, following long-established tactics, sent Lepidus to quell the revolt. They hoped thereby both to deal with the uprising, and to send away from Rome a too-vocal citizen. They reckoned without the added lawlessness that the preceding period had inculcated. Instead of defeating the rebels, Lepidus joined them.

The Senate now needed another army to meet the new threat. It levied one and put it under Pompey and Catulus. Pompey's obvious military ability led to the choice, although he was too young to hold a magisterial position in the normal state of affairs. The *cursus honorum* was crumbling in the first emergency that arose to test it. Pompey and Catulus were successful, and Lepidus was crushed at Cosa in 78 B.C.

Pompey's next task: Sertorius and Spain

The Social War had produced one able general on the side of the populares, Sertorius by name. As often happens, his merits roused the jealousy of his associates. He was despatched to Spain in 83 to deal with rebellions in that country and not then recalled to help oppose Sulla. In Spain he was most successful and won victories not only by military skill but through diplomacy, following a policy of friendliness towards the Spaniards.

He was a remarkable man, who himself learnt from the Spaniards the art of guerrilla warfare, which made them such formidable opponents in ancient times and, indeed, in modern times as well. The ranks of Sertorius' followers had been swelled by many who fled from Rome during the proscriptions of Sulla. After the death of Sulla, Sertorius had tried to make peace with Rome, but his approaches had been rebuffed.

When Pompey returned to Rome after defeating Lepidus, he showed how little laws could prevail against unpalatable reality. Though he was too young to hold normal command, he arrived at the gates of Rome without disbanding his forces (in flagrant defiance of the Sullan laws) and demanded permission to march against the rebellious Sertorius. There was some ground for taking action in Spain; for Perperna, Lepidus' lieutenant, had fled there after the defeat of his commander, and also Sertorius had signed a pact of mutual aid with Mithridates. The Senate had no option but to give Pompey the command he asked.

Pompey had an army of 30 000 infantry and 1000 cavalry. He made his way to Spain and spent the winter preparing for his campaign. He was, however, not alone. In the south was Metellus, an experienced and distinguished senator, who was governor of Further Spain. The country between was held by Sertorius.

In the spring of 76 Pompey moved down the coast to join forces with Metellus, getting as far

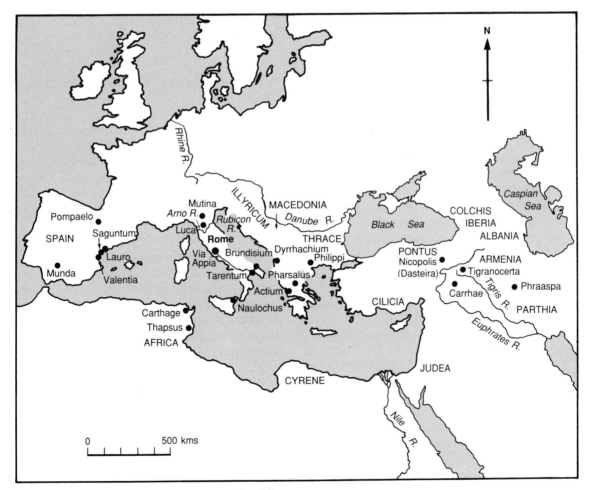

14.1 *The Mediterranean countries in the late Republic.*

as Valentia. Sertorius was waiting. He met him at Lauro, and Pompey was no match for his local experience and skill. Pompey was badly defeated, losing 10 000 men, and had to go back north to recover. Metellus was more successful, defeating a force sent against him, and then coming north to join Pompey.

The next year Metellus went back to his province and Pompey again went south to Valentia, this time defeating an army under Perpenna and Herennius and sacking Valentia. Perpenna withdrew to join Sertorius who was not far away and when Pompey met the combined forces at Sucro he was defeated, and himself wounded. At this point Metellus joined him and together they fought against the Sertorians, but without a decisive result.

The war swings in Rome's favour

So far it would seem that Rome had had little success, but Pompey sent an urgent message to Rome for reinforcements, and two legions and supplies soon arrived. Sertorius had lost two of his best generals in these engagements, and continued warfare was having an effect on the morale of his troops. At this point Metellus offered a large reward for the assassination of Sertorius, who had changed his Spanish bodyguard for a Roman one in the hope of escaping this danger. In the ultimate his hopes were vain, for it was Perpenna who had him assassinated, not for the reward, but in order to take over the leadership.

Metellus now retired to his province and Pompey continued his campaign against Perpenna, finally meeting and defeating him in 71 B.C.

Pompey's military achievements in this war were not spectacular, but in the settlement of Spain he came into his own. When Perpenna was captured he offered to hand over correspondence he had, which implicated many Romans who were sympathetic to Sertorius and could have led to a new proscription to rival Sulla's. Pompey burnt the papers and executed Perpenna.

Pompey was of the new breed of enlightened Romans, like Scipio, like the Gracchi. He had had a Greek tutor, the philosopher Posidonius, and was a great admirer of Greek ideas and in particular of Alexander, whom he aimed to emulate. The learned encyclopedist Varro was a close friend and came with him to Spain. He settled the affairs of Spain in a most statesmanly way, indulging in no retributions and settling many of Sertorius' veterans in two colonies, one in northern Spain, one named after him Pompaelo, in Gaul, just north of the Pyrenees. He gave Roman citizenship to a number of Spaniards who had helped him.

Spain suffered terribly at the hands of many of its Roman rulers but Pompey treated them well, gaining, as was customary, their loyal clientship. Caesar himself noted that the Spaniards showed great loyalty to Pompey in the Civil War that came later. Incidentally in 70 B.C. a law was passed granting an amnesty to Sertorius' followers, and many of them returned to Rome and even resumed public life.

Affairs in Rome. The Spartacus uprising

While Pompey was in Spain there was some political conflict in Rome. Julius Caesar, now back in Rome, had made some attacks on supporters of Sulla, helped by a young tribune, T. Labienus, who was later to be his ablest commander in Gaul. Caesar himself had no great power at this time, but had allied himself to the followers of Pompey.

Then in 75, the consul C. Aurelius Cotta passed a law permitting tribunes to go on to higher offices. This aroused no furore, for tribunes were not just the tools of revolution. The tribunate could serve as a handy office for a young politician, and a compliant tribune with his power of veto, could be a handy friend to a politician, even a consul.

Meanwhile fresh trouble had arisen in Italy itself. For some time now discord on Italian soil had had a tendency to spark off a slave revolt. Such a one occurred in 73 among the Capuan gladiators. Led by a Thracian slave, Spartacus, they fortified the crater of Vesuvius, then quiescent, and defeated no fewer than four generals sent to deal with them.

Pompey was still in Spain, but the Romans still had one man to fall back on (although they did not have full confidence in him), the banker Crassus. He had grown rich through buying up the land of the proscribed under Sulla, and was full of political ambition. He had not, however, proved himself in the field. Crassus was not a match for Spartacus, who broke through the cordon he tried to throw across his path. The rebel leader was joined by slaves from the latifundia and planned to fight his way north to his home country of Thrace. However, what the Romans failed to do, internal dissension did for them. Part of Spartacus' forces went off independently, met the Romans and were defeated. Later Spartacus with the forces that stayed by him met a similar fate.

Meanwhile, the Senate, which had not been very hopeful of Crassus, sent for Pompey. He arrived too late for the battle, but in time to join in the slaughter that followed. On his way he lined the via Appia with the crucified bodies of five thousand of the slaves.

Pompey and Crassus gain the consulship. Cicero prosecutes Verres

Our accounts suggest that Pompey and Crassus had little love for each other. Cicero in particular advanced this view, and although he had his own reasons for doing so, he was accurate in his observation. Their only resemblance was that neither belonged to established senatorial families and both were anxious to win favour with the inner clique of the Senate. In short they were rivals.

Pompey was not a novus homo but his father Pompeius Strabo was the first of his family to hold the consulship. Pompey aimed to achieve influence through his military successes, and up to now he had not sat in the Senate and taken part in its deliberations.

Crassus could not have been more different. His only military success, and that achieved with some difficulty, was against a band of slaves, hardly a recommendation in Pompey's eyes. His expertise was in the Senate, where he was a deft and if need be unprincipled schemer. He won

favour and gained clients, probably from among the new recruits to the Senate, by lending them money without interest and speaking on their behalf in the law courts. He did not have Cicero's eloquence but he was hard working.

Still at that time Crassus and Pompey had a common interest. They both returned to Rome with their armies and demanded the consulship for 70 B.C., even though Pompey was not the requisite age and had not held the normal lower offices.

In due course Pompey celebrated with Metellus a triumph for the victory in Spain and Crassus had a lesser celebration, an ovation, since his was only a war against slaves, and both of them were elected consuls. Pompey had never sat in the Senate before and he had his learned friend Varro write him a book on senatorial procedure, for he as consul would have to preside with Crassus in that assembly, and he did not want to disgrace himself.

Meanwhile the people of Sicily sent to Rome to launch a prosecution against Verres, who had oppressed their province as governor for the previous three years. Cicero was now making a name for himself as a lawyer and he had won favour when he was in Sicily earlier as quaestor. The Sicilians engaged his services, while Verres called on Hortensius, then the leading barrister of Rome and currently standing for the consulship for the following year. Cicero had no easy task, and if his opponents could drag the case out till Hortensius was consul, an impossible one. Cicero prepared his case with incredible speed and launched a brilliant prosecution which caused Verres to go into exile before the case was finished.

It was an opportune victory, for immediately after it L. Aurelius Cotta, a praetor and the brother of the consul who had passed the law allowing tribunes (see p. 124), to proceed to higher office to put forward a law to change the composition of the law courts. They were no longer to be in the hands of senators alone but consist in equal parts of senators, equites and *tribuni aerarii*. Who this last body was is uncertain, but it seems most likely that they were a lower grade of equites. How important Cicero's victory was for Cotta is hard to say. In fact there does not seem to have been much opposition, and it could well be that the senators had found jury service, especially with the new courts Sulla had introduced, rather burdensome, and were not sorry to share the task.

In the same year censors were appointed. They registered the many Italians who had gained citizenship as a result of recent events and expelled a number of senators, some probably on political grounds, many, however, quite justifiably for corrupt behaviour.

Lucullus and the war with Mithridates

We must now go back in time and look at events in the East. We noted in the Spanish war that Sertorius had entered into an alliance with Mithridates, and the latter was not resigned to subservience to the Romans. Nicomedes, the king of Bithynia, left his kingdom to Rome in his will. Mithridates was determined not to allow encroachment on territory to which he himself had laid claim. In 74 he invaded and took Bithynia, thus reopening hostilities with Rome.

He did not have to fight alone, for he had the assistance of his son-in-law Tigranes, of Armenia, and he had Sertorius' officers to train his troops. The Romans countered by making an alliance with the state of Parthia, which had arisen to the east of Alexander's former empire. They were a Scythian race, who had conquered a number of the countries Persia once ruled, including Persia itself.

The Senate chose a general of proven loyalty and ability to meet this crisis. Lucullus, who had just finished his consulship, was a proud aristocrat of ancient lineage. He was not only a good general but a stern disciplinarian.[1] He defeated Mithridates in his first engagement, and destroyed his fleet. In 72 Mithridates was beaten a second time, and fled to join his son-in-law in Armenia.

This left Lucullus to deal with an Asia that was reduced to a pitiable state. The country had been ruined by Sulla's exactions, and had made bad worse by having recourse to equestrian

money-lenders. Lucullus promptly cancelled two-thirds of the debt, and fixed a reasonable rate of interest, 12 per cent per annum, for the remainder. This step rightly won him the gratitude of the local population, but the eternal enmity of the equites.

At the same time he was incurring the displeasure of his troops by his strict discipline and by forbidding them to plunder at will. Lucullus invaded Armenia. When Tigranes refused to hand over Mithridates, Lucullus defeated him and took his capital Tigranocerta. When, however, Lucullus tried to press on further, the weary and disgruntled troops mutinied.

The next spring Mithridates and Tigranes took the field once more, but Lucullus' army would not oppose them. He demanded fresh troops from Rome, but this was the chance for which his enemies, the equites, had been waiting. They urged the Senate to send, not fresh troops, but a new general, Pompey.

It was at this time that the revolt of Spartacus broke out, finding the Roman Senate ill-prepared. It was finally crushed and both Pompey and Crassus returned to civilian life. But it was not to last. Affairs in the East demanded attention.

Lex Gabinia. Pompey crushes the pirates

Mithridates and Lucullus were in a state of stalemate, and Mithridates' allies, the pirates, were thoroughly out of hand. Indeed, they even intercepted a corn fleet bound for Rome and caused a food shortage, an action that helped to consolidate opinion against them.

So in 67 a tribune Gabinius, using his newly restored power to propose laws,[2] brought forward the *lex Gabinia*, as a result of which

---

[1]In private life, an interesting contrast, he had a reputation for enjoying the good things of life.
[2]Once again the tribunes were an invaluable ally in breaking the opposition of the Senate. Pompey, and after him Caesar, made full use of the tribunes as Marius had done before them.

Pompey was authorised to wipe out the pirates. Antonius, who had been sent earlier for this purpose, but failed, had been given an extraordinary command over the sea coast of all the provinces. This command inevitably contravened Sulla's legislation, which insisted that no governor be allowed beyond the borders of his one province. Pompey was to be granted a *maius imperium*, similar to that held by Antonius, an office which was to serve as a useful precedent when Augustus sought to legalise his imperial rule.

Although the tribunes put his law to the *concilium plebis*, it was also debated in the Senate, where there was ferocious opposition, led by the consul Piso. When the people heard of this they almost lynched the consul, who was rescued by Gabinius himself. Finally the law was passed.

Pompey's campaign was masterly. He divided the sea coast into thirteen sections, putting a legate in charge of each, with a fleet, infantry and cavalry, with which to sweep them from the area, attacking them if they landed. Meanwhile Pompey himself, with his own fleet, began sweeping the pirates eastward. He first cleared Sicily and North Africa so the corn fleets could bring relief to Rome, and soon had all the pirates bottled up in Cilicia, their home base.

Many of the pirates surrendered during the operation and were treated with Pompey's usual humanity, and when the final battle took place off Cilicia there too the pirates were half-hearted and soon surrendered.

As in Spain Pompey took no revenge on his enemy but saw to their rehabilitation, settling them as farmers well back from the sea coast with its temptations. Many were established in Cilicia itself, some in the deserted town of Soli, which he renamed Pompeiopolis, many in other parts of Asia Minor, others in Achaea and Calabria.

Lex Manilia. Pompey is given the command in the East

As we saw earlier Lucullus was in a desperate position in Asia Minor and in 66 B.C. Manilius,

another tribune, proposed a bill to give Pompey the command in the East. Like Pompey's command against the pirates this was to go beyond a specific province, and some historians, who thought that the lex Gabinia did not give Pompey overriding power, see this as the first instance of *maius imperium*. Hortensius and Catulus spoke against the law, but many supported it, including Cicero with his famous speech, *pro lege Manilia*. Cicero's friends, the equites, were very eager to see Pompey succeed, restoring peace to the area and with it their profits. The law was passed.

News of his command was brought to Pompey who had not yet returned to Rome, and he immediately sent a message to Phraates III of Parthia, asking him for support, and in the first instance to make an attack on Armenia. Then Pompey met Lucullus, a very unpleasant event naturally, and took over his command and his army. Counting his own and Lucullus' forces Pompey had 50 000 infantry to Mithridates' 30 000. The core of Mithridates' army consisted of Roman deserters.

Pompey sets out in pursuit of Mithridates

As Leach[3] notes, Pompey's campaign in the East bears a striking resemblance to Alexander's. To some extent this is because Pompey had the same objectives as Alexander, but it went beyond that and it was no accident. As we said earlier, Pompey had always admired Alexander and saw himself as a new Alexander. Like his hero he named towns after himself, and like him he took scholars with him, in his case including his learned friend Varro and a Greek historian Theophanes.

First Mithridates made an offer of surrender, which Pompey refused unless the king would hand himself and his Roman deserters over, conditions obviously impossible for Mithridates to accept. The king set off northward and made

---

[3]See end of chapter, Leach, p. 78.

his first stand at Dasteira, which Pompey besieged. Pompey took the city but Mithridates escaped and fled on. Next Pompey caught up with him at a place now known as Belgazi. There was a fierce battle, in which Mithridates lost over a third of his army, but once again he escaped. This time he sent to Tigranes of Armenia, requesting asylum. Tigranes' answer was to kill the messenger and set a price on Mithridates' head. Mithridates now fled north to Colchis on the Pontus.

Pompey deals with Armenia and Parthia

Pompey meanwhile settled his problems with Armenia. When he arrived Tigranes surrendered and was ordered to pay an indemnity of 6000 talents and to surrender all the lands he had conquered. Pompey's general Afranius was left to supervise Tigranes while Pompey went on.

He met with fierce fighting in Iberia and Albania, but conquered both peoples. He then went on to Colchis only to find that Mithridates had fled on to Panticapaeum in the Crimea, where Pompey did not try to follow him.

Phraates of Parthia was not pleased at the mild treatment of Tigranes and sent a message demanding that Pompey renew his treaty with him, but Pompey gave his messengers a cool reception. On the Roman principle of divide and rule he felt it would be wise to support the weaker Armenia against Parthia. Pompey marched onwards, while his scientists made discoveries, which are recorded by Pliny the Elder and Strabo. When a message came to him from Tigranes requesting help against Parthia he refused but sent envoys who worked out a settlement of their differences.

Pompey's last operation was in Judea, where he found two brothers Aristobulus and Hyrcanus fighting. He supported Hyrcanus and finally Aristobulus gave in, but his followers shut themselves in Jerusalem, leading to a three months' siege, which is very fully recorded by the Jewish historian Josephus. Finally Jerusalem was taken and sacked, but the temple was spared. Josephus speaks with admiration of Pompey's final settlement, which displayed his usual moderation and far-sightedness.

During the siege Pompey learnt of the death of Mithridates. The king had been trying to raise one last army, but there was an uprising and he took his own life. The body was brought to Pompey who gave it honourable burial.

Pompey settles the East

With Mithridates dead, Pompey set to work to organise the Middle East, taking 63 B.C. and the following year for the purpose. He kept the original provinces of Asia, Bithynia and Cilicia, but extended the last two considerably. He gave most of the cities independence, giving them a code of government to follow. Syria he also made a province. He also founded many new cities, including in Bithynia another Pompeiopolis, and Nicopolis (city of victory) near Dasteira where he first fought Mithridates.

The interior of Asia Minor he left as client kingdoms. He satisfied both the equites back home and the unfortunate Asians by adjusting the tax burden. He cut back the intolerable burden borne by the agricultural communities but abolished the tax exemptions which many of the cities enjoyed.

It was a great achievement, and Augustus was to use his settlement as the basis for his own organisation of the eastern provinces, making few changes. What Pompey failed to settle, and no Roman after him was to succeed, was the problem of Parthia and Armenia.

Pompey had now finished his mission. He paid off his troops, 16 000 talents in all, which still left him the richest man in Rome, indeed we suspect of the known world. On his way back he stopped at Lesbos, the birthplace of his friend Theophanes. He gave Theophanes Roman citizenship and freedom to Mytilene, the capital of Lesbos. At Rhodes he saw and talked with his old teacher Posidonius, and finally at Athens he made a presentation of fifty talents to rebuild their city, which had been sacked by Sulla. In December he reached Brundisium.

Affairs in Rome. Cicero gains consulate

While Pompey was in the East all was not well in Italy. Debt was oppressive, both in Rome and throughout Italy. Sulla's proscriptions had left the sons of those proscribed barred from public office, and finally there were many men who had lost their land, some having been expelled to make way for the veterans. The veterans themselves were also a problem, for many had not succeeded as farmers. The year before Cicero stood for the consulship the two consuls elected were convicted of bribery and two new consuls appointed.

Cicero had been praetor when he spoke on behalf of the lex Manilia, and when he stood for the consulship of 65, he could count on the support of Pompey's followers. The same year the ten tribunes, with an unanimity rare for that office, had prepared a proposal, the Rullian bill, after the name of their spokesman, which was to appoint a commission of ten (*decemvirs*) to divide land among the landless. There was a strong suspicion that Crassus and Caesar were behind this proposal, especially as it was also rumoured that they would take over Egypt in the process, a land which many had been eyeing hungrily for some time.

The equites and the conservative forces in the Senate were united against the proposal, and Cicero gladly championed them, even though it meant a divided loyalty, as it was thought that Pompey also was in favour of the bill. Cicero summoned his friend Atticus to Rome. He had strong connections in conservative ranks, and Cicero as a novus homo would need all the help he could get.

Two of the rival candidates for the consulship, Antonius and Catiline, were prepared to back the Rullian proposal, and they were thought to have financial backing from Crassus for their candidature. Cicero had chosen his cause wisely. He was elected, and although Antonius was his colleague, Catiline failed. Cicero then carried out his promise. He spoke vigorously against the proposal, and managed to get one of the tribunes to veto it. It was dropped.

The conspiracy of Catiline

Later that year Catiline stood for the consulship for the following year, but was again defeated. Catiline was painted in the worst possible colours by Cicero, but in fact his great crime was that he did not succeed. He seems to have had a great deal of personal charm and he was really attempting to do what a number of people were doing at the time, namely to use force to achieve a political object. He had before him the examples of Lepidus, who failed, and of Pompey and Crassus, who succeeded.

Catiline had now been defeated twice, which would have put him heavily in debt. Also Crassus would certainly not be throwing good money after bad. He therefore chose direct action and looked around him for allies. He found them, but unfortunately not of high quality. A forlorn cause does not attract successful men. His next move was to send envoys out to trouble spots in Italy, such as Lucania and Etruria, asking them to join him.

Cicero learnt what was happening from the mistress of one of the conspirators, but at first found it difficult to convince the Senate. Catiline himself had not yet made a move and attended the Senate, and he was an aristocrat, while Cicero, even though a consul, was still a novus homo. The Senate did acknowledge the disaffection outside Rome, and sent forces to deal with it, but that was all.

Then Cicero had a stroke of luck. The Allobroges from Gaul had sent an embassy to complain of their burden of debt. They were returning unsatisfied and the conspirators saw them as allies and approached them. Fortunately the Allobroges were cautious and told their patron who told Cicero. They were then told to pretend to agree and thus the conspirators were caught leaving Rome with them. Catiline himself had at last left, but before them so he was not caught.

The conspiracy is crushed

The Senate had earlier given Cicero the *senatus consultum ultimum* but (if we except Sulla's proscriptions) it had become very rare to execute a Roman citizen and Cicero wanted his authorisation spelled out. He summoned the Senate. In the debate Caesar urged that the conspirators only be imprisoned, but Cato the Younger spoke after him and urged the death penalty. The conspirators were executed immediately.

Meanwhile Catiline had raised two legions in Etruria, though very poorly equipped. They met an army led by Murena. The battle was fierce, for Catiline was no coward and they were desperate, but they had no final chance. They were beaten and many, including Catiline were killed.

Undoubtedly Cicero dealt with the conspiracy most efficiently, but he got no thanks for it. The Senate itself had been bitterly divided, and Pompey was not pleased. There is some suggestion that he originally was not out of sympathy with Catiline's proposed reforms. He would not have condoned his direct action, but it would have afforded him a chance of once more saving the state, and he would not have thanked Cicero for robbing him of the chance. Cicero could never understand this and in later years tried repeatedly and unavailingly to make Pompey grateful! But as we shall see he was soon to face a more urgent problem.

Date table

B.C.

76	Pompey sent to Spain.
73–71	Revolt of Spartacus.
70	Consulship of Pompey and Crassus, trial of Verres.
67	*Lex Gabinia*, conquest of pirates.
66	*Lex Manilia*.
63	Crushing of Catilinarian conspiracy.

Select quotations

1 Plutarch, *Lives*, 'Crassus' 2:
When Sulla took the city and began to sell the property of those he had put to death . . . Crassus was insatiable in taking and buying it. In addition, seeing how common, and indeed endemic in Rome, was the collapse of houses and their burning, because they were so heavy and crowded together, he bought slaves skilled as architects and builders. Then when he had more than 500 of them, he began buying up houses when they were on fire, or houses in the immediate neighbourhood of a fire, which their owners would let go for a song because of their fear and uncertainty. Thus he came to own most of Rome.

2 Cicero, *pro lege Manilia* 13:
Which do you think have suffered more in recent years, the enemy's cities through the arms of your soldiers, or the states of your allies through their winter quarters? . . . Are we surprised that Pompey so excelled all others in this respect that when his legions arrived in Asia not only did so great an army do no harm to those who surrendered, but they did not even leave a trace of their passage? Every day the reports of men and their letters tell us how the soldiers are behaving in winter quarters: not only is no one compelled to be out of pocket to supply the soldiers, but they are not permitted to do so if they wish. For our ancestors felt that the houses of their allies and friends should be a shelter against winter, not an excuse for avarice.

3 Cicero, *Pro Plancio*, 64–65:
I would say indeed that I thought then no one at Rome was speaking of anything but my quaestorship. During a real shortage I sent home a vast quantity of corn. I was courteous to the businessmen, just with the merchants, generous to the citizens, in no way grasping where the allies were concerned. I showed myself all round most diligent in all my offices and the Sicilians granted me unheard of honours. I came back thinking that the Roman people would show great appreciation. But when on my way back from the province I happened to drop in on Puteoli, because there are some of the nicest people there, I almost fell over backwards, gentlemen, when someone asked me on what day

I left Rome, and if there was any news. I replied that I was on my way back from the province. Goodness me, yes, he said, Africa, I believe!

Further reading

Those who wish to undertake further reading have a much bigger task than for earlier periods. There is much more ancient material and as it is such as important time, modern writers have written a great deal on it also. As there is so much classical material, I have recommended Lacey's book, which gives some well chosen extracts from Cicero, fitting them into the events of the time. I then suggest Gruen to give a general view. Finally, much recent writing has concentrated on the generals of the age who struggled for power, and many excellent recent biographies have been written. I especially recommend Leach on Pompey.

E.S. Gruen, *The Last Generation of the Roman Republic*, University of California Press, 1974.

W.K. Lacey & B.W.J.G. Wilson, *Res Publica*, Oxford University Press, 1970.

Plutarch, *Fall of the Roman Republic*, Penguin Classic.

Sallust, *Jugurthine War & Conspiracy of Catiline*, Penguin Classic.

J. Leach, *Pompey the Great*, Croom Helm, London, 1978.

D. Stockton, *Cicero, a Political Biography*, Oxford University Press, 1971.

B. Marshall, *Crassus, a Political Biography*, Hakkert, Amsterdam, 1976.

Topics for essays or discussion

1 'The rise of Pompey proved once more that the Republic could not control a successful general.' Discuss.
2 'Pompey's real genius lay less in the military sphere than in administration.' Do you agree?
3 Compare and contrast the careers of Pompey and Marius.
4 What problems had arisen with Rome's annexation of the East? To what extent did Pompey's settlement prove satisfactory?
5 'Sulla had tried to divide the provinces into compartments, but Pompey's history proved that they could only be dealt with effectively as a unit.' Discuss.

Chapter 15

Life and letters at the end of the Republic

WHEN WE LAST examined the literature of Rome it was gaining in confidence under the patronage of the Scipionic circle. Even so, the actual writers tended to be freedmen or foreigners rather than accepted members of the Roman community. In addition, there was still a fierce struggle between those who accepted and those who rejected the heritage of Greece.

Literature in the late Republic

By the first century B.C. the picture had changed. Roman literature had come of age. Its art was still modelled on that of Greece, but translation and adaptation now played a minor part. An independent literature was arising, even though still deeply indebted to the Greeks.

The authors of the new age were Roman citizens and proud of the fact. A national awareness is implicit in their work, although not given the open expression which was to characterise the Augustan age.

The poets Lucretius and Catullus

Two poets of importance emerged, Lucretius and Catullus. Of Lucretius, apart from his work, we know little. He lived from 95 to 52 B.C., and we think that he was a Roman aristocrat. He wrote a didactic poem in six books, *de Rerum Natura* ('Concerning the Nature of Things'). Lucretius was an Epicurean and in this poem he expounded that philosphy, which held an atomic theory of the universe, denied the possibility of life after death, and regarded the gods as being indifferent to the fortunes of mankind. It also held that the aim of man was pleasure, not bodily pleasure, but the intellectual satisfaction of the soul. Nothing would be further from the austere soul of Lucretius than the teachings of those who perverted and vulgarised Epicurus' ideas, saying that man favoured sensuality.

A science text-book in verse is a formidable thought, and one cannot deny that there are arid tracts in Lucretius' work, especially when he explains Epicurus' atomic theory. The marvel is that there is so much poetry in it. Lucretius did have a vivid poetic insight. Such phrases as *flammantia moenia mundi*, 'the flaming walls of the universe', come to mind. In addition, the missionary fervour with which he attacked the superstitious fears of death enhanced the quality of his writing. He used the hexameter and affected an archaic style, which owed much to Ennius. Virgil was in turn to be his debtor.

The short-lived Catullus (87 or 84 to 54 B.C.) was a very different person. He came from Verona in Transpadane Gaul, which was a late entrant to Roman citizenship, but he himself lived for most of his life in Rome. He was a lyric poet and in spirit an Alexandrian. This debt to the Hellenistic Age gave a certain artificiality to his longer poems, but his short pieces, on which his fame mainly rests, were no pedant's adaptations. They were vigorous and pithy expressions of his loves, his hates and his youthful adventures.

In his poems he called his love Lesbia, but she was in reality Clodia, a woman of no good repute, but apparently of considerable fascination. It was to her that he wrote his famous two-line epigram, 'I hate and I love; I know not why, but I feel it and it tortures me', lines very characteristic of the man.

Catullus was the leader of a poetic circle, but the work of the other members of his group has been lost.

Prose writers: Sallust, Caesar and Cornelius Nepos

So much for the poets of the period. In the field of prose the age was of considerable importance. Two Romans engaged in historical writing at this time. C. Sallustius Crispus (86–35 B.C.) was a man of Sabine extraction and plebeian family. Sallust took an active part in politics, supporting the populares and receiving the patronage of Caesar. At one time he acted as governor of Numidia. This experience was to be useful to him, when in the years of his retirement he wrote a history, *The Jugurthine War*. He also wrote *The Catilinarian Conspiracy*. Both these works have survived, but we have only fragments of his third work, *The Histories*.

Sallust's work is useful, for it covers events (especially in the case of the Jugurthine War) in need of documentation, but although his general account is clearly presented, his details are vague and often inaccurate. He was an admirer of the Greek historian, Thucydides, and in an endeavour to emulate him he introduced long commentaries of a moral nature in his work. Unluckily, he did not have Thucydides' acuteness of perception and his general observations are in consequence boring, having as their main theme the degenerate state to which Rome had sunk since its early days.

Yet elsewhere in his work Sallust possesses a certain epigramatic terseness, which makes him agreeable reading. His writings have a bias in favour of the populares, and of Caesar in particular. Cicero suffers in this process.

Caesar was also an historian, contributing his *Commentaries on the Gallic War* and his *Civil War*, which between them covered most of his military exploits. His work is important in its own right, for it gives a clear, accurate and comprehensive picture of the events it covers. It gains also by the eminence of the author, who played such an important part in the history of his age.

It would not be fair to describe his writings as propaganda. They were historical works of real scholarship. Yet equally it could not be claimed that they were quite free of bias. This is shown not so much in the distortion of events described as in the omission of incidents which would not reflect favourably on the author. The *Civil War* inevitably suffers more in this respect than the earlier work. It does tend to slant the truth in order to put the responsibility for starting the war completely on the shoulders of Caesar's opponents.

His style is lucid and deceptively simple, qualities which helped to increase the impression of truthfulness in his narrative. Yet we can see from the efforts of those who tried to complete his work that this simplicity was itself a work of art of no mean order.

Of less importance than Sallust or Caesar was Cornelius Nepos, who wrote the lives of some famous Greeks and Romans. They are childish efforts in comparison with Plutarch, and suffer from the fact that their author tried to write only the best about people. Their only use is in filling gaps where more reputable historians are not available.

Cicero, orator and man of letters

The most important of all the writers of this age was the orator, Cicero. We have noted that the youthful equestrian tried out his talents under Sulla in his speech *pro Roscio*. After this, ill-health, combined perhaps with prudence, sent him east, where he studied rhetoric at Athens and Rhodes, the classical equivalent of a University course.

By the time he returned, his style was at its peak. His only peer among orators of the Classical world was the Greek Demosthenes, whom Cicero greatly admired.

Cicero's opportunity came, as we have noted, in 70 B.C., when the Sicilians called on him to help them prosecute the infamous Verres for his three years' misgovernment of the province. The Verrine orations which resulted are considered by some his finest work. They are important not only because they helped produce a reform in the law courts but because of the admirable picture which they give of the administration of the provinces in the late Republic.

The years which followed saw Cicero's triumph and his disaster. When the triumvirate exiled Cicero they broke his spirit. On his return he played a much less prominent role and sought comfort in the writing of books on oratory and philosophy. His last great effort was the *Philippics*, in which he returned to all his early vigour in an attack on Antony, thereby procuring for himself a hero's death.

In addition to his more public work, Cicero engaged in a copious correspondence, which has been preserved for us. These letters, and in particular those written to his publisher and friend, Atticus, afford an intimate picture of the Rome of his time. In fact, between his speeches, which describe the public activities of Rome, and the letters, which, like Pepys' diary, introduce us to all the gossip, quarrels and trivialities of daily life, we are indebted to Cicero for a picture of this period fuller than any of an earlier age.

Life in the late Republic

The influence of the Greeks

It remains to consider what kind of city was the Rome in which Cicero lived. It had imbibed much of Greek culture, both at the upper and lower levels. At the lower end of the social scale, Rome abounded in Greek freedmen. They were to be found everywhere as traders, business-men and clerks, and their vocabulary had come to permeate the language of the ordinary people of the time. In higher circles Greek culture was very important. As we have seen, the Greeks supplied the Romans with universities and with many of the teachers who supervised their earlier studies.

Roman religion had become increasingly a

15.1 *Cicero (106–43 B.C.). His letters are an important source for his own life and character, and for contemporary events.*

formality, denoting family and national solidarity, but imbued with little religious fervour. In its place came the religions of Greece and the East. The Greek mysteries with their promise of salvation gave comfort to many, especially to the humble citizens. Even more popular at this time were the religions of Egypt and Asia Minor. They too preached salvation and happiness in the after-life but were more colourful in their ritual. Some of the cults of Asia Minor, particularly that of Cybele, were frowned on in Rome, but this did not prevent their spread in the city.

For those who despised these spectacular rites there was Greek philosophy, especially that of the Stoics, which with its emphasis on duty had a strong appeal to the Roman mind. Epicureanism had its followers, but was never a general favourite.

Senators and equites: a money-centred society

The Rome of Cicero's time laid great emphasis on position and wealth. The richest men were probably the equites, who had to have property valued at more than 400 000 sesterces. Yet there were among the senatorial class a number who were as wealthy, since they too could take part in business operations indirectly, even though this was strictly forbidden by law, and could also enrich themselves while governing the provinces. Two of the wealthiest men in Rome at the end of the republic were Pompey and Crassus. Crassus, as we have seen, though a member of the senatorial class, engaged in business activities with great profit, while Pompey was a landholder on a vast scale in Picenum, north-east of Rome. His wealth reached its peak, however, as we noted, with his conquest of the East.

The senators were in great need of money; for they required it in order to win the favour of their electors, either by putting on a gladiatorial show or by direct bribery. Then it was only too likely that they would need it to bribe their jury, if the province which they fleeced tried to bring them to justice.

In addition, the nobleman's prestige was measured in terms of the numbers of clients to whom he acted as patron. They would come to see him in the morning to pay their respects, receiving in return a gift of food, or later of money. They then would act as escort to their patron, vote for him, even applaud his halting verse. It was also the patron's task to speak for his clients if they were put on trial.

Cicero is a good example of a well-to-do Roman. As a lawyer he was not supposed to be paid, but he could accept gifts, and it was also a normal practice for a grateful client (in the ancient or modern sense of the word) to mention him in his will. In this way Cicero amassed a fortune, for which the most accepted use, then as in earlier days, was the acquisition of landed property. Like many of his wealthy contemporaries, Cicero had a number of country houses or *villae*. The *villa*, unlike the farm from which it developed, was devoted to pleasure rather than profit (except in the case of some old-fashioned Romans), and the shores of Campania were a favourite resort.

Rome's trade, like that of Britain, grew as a result of its empire

Northern Italy, from Campania upwards, was prospering at the expense of the southern part of the peninsula, which had not recovered from the Social War and Sulla. The roads, which the Romans were building with a view to military strategy, were also helping to expand commerce. Italy was producing fine wines and oil as well as that very popular pottery, the red-glazed Arretine ware. Campania also manufactured a fine black-glazed ware.

Trade with the East went through Brundisium, which was linked with Rome by the Appian Way, but most important of all was the city of Rome itself with its port Ostia. Rome was not a great exporter, but it was a vast importing centre. To it came the shipments of corn and other tax revenue, not to mention the goods sent to individuals in the city. They sent out in return armies and administrators.

Women, freedmen, slaves and the less privileged gain more freedom

It is now time to examine the social divisions of this period. Women had always held an honoured position in Roman society, much higher than did their Athenian counterparts, and Roman expansion was bringing them more freedom. In former days they had as children been subject to the legal authority of their father, which they left only to be ruled by their husband. Now legal subterfuges had been found which could save those who so desired from the second subservience. Divorce, which had never been difficult in Rome, used to operate in favour of the male. Now it came to the rescue of the enlightened female, and in particular of the wealthy heiress, of whom there were increasing numbers.

The business world, at its lower end, was largely the province of the ever-growing class of freedmen. The wealthier section consisted of the equites, but they themselves were to some extent recruited from the freedman class. Wealthy Romans would let their slaves buy their freedom, or would free them in their will, and this practice continued to swell the ranks of a hard-working, sometimes very well-educated class. As traders and scribes they were invaluable to the community, but they were inevitably also resented by the Roman citizen of impeccable ancestry but less industry.

Slaves too were important. Those who worked on the huge estates or in the mines had a wretched lot; gladiators led a brutalised existence though with a chance of huge profits; the household slave, on the other hand, could lead a pleasant existence with a chance of freedom in his later years. Cicero's letters to his secretary, Tiro, show how deep his affection was for that faithful if ailing servant.

Rome's buildings try to keep pace with its growth

The public buildings of Rome had not yet benefited from the wholesale reconstruction programme of Augustus. They counted among them a number of fine edifices raised in the time of Rome's expansion, alongside many older ones fallen into a decayed state. The arch had been adopted very early by the Romans, and from the second century it appeared in the triumphal arches, elaborately carved, which commemorated Rome's victories. The Romans had also adopted, and practically made their own, the Corinthian column, more slender and more ornate than the Doric or even the Ionic form. The arch and the column appeared in the construction of the basilicas and colonnades which sheltered their shops and their law courts, and of course in their temples. A number of aqueducts were built, which brought in water for Rome's increasing population. While the wealthy built fine town houses and elaborate villas, industrious businessmen constructed huge blocks of flats, *insulae* as they were called, where, at inflated rentals, the poorer citizens were housed.

As we shall see in the next chapter, Pompey made his contribution to Rome's beautification when he returned from the East. The most important was the Theatre of Pompey, but there were also his gardens and his own villa, built outside Rome.

Rome's laws develop under Greek influence

Meanwhile law had become more sophisticated. Civil law had developed very rapidly. Like

British law it grew on the basis of precedents. Jurisconsults, old and revered aristocrats, who without fee gave legal advice to the oncoming generation, kept stored in their memories a long list of such precedents. Each praetor, on beginning his term of office, would post his edict, which stated what legal principles he would follow. Naturally praetor imitated praetor, making such modifications as he thought fit, and in this way a legal basis was built up.

As more non-Romans flocked to the capital, a *praetor peregrinus* was appointed to deal with cases between Roman and non-Roman, corresponding to the *praetor urbanus*, who dealt with Roman citizens only. This praetor also published an edict. As, however, he was concerned with the customs and procedures of foreign lands, his edict was enriched with principles taken from the laws of other peoples, especially the Greeks. From his edicts there grew up the *ius gentium*, the code of international law. This code in turn began to have an effect on that of the *praetor urbanus*, and so too did a closer acquaintance with the writings of the Greek philosophers. Thus Greek legal thought enriched Roman law, but without taking from it the greater elasticity, which made it superior to that of the system-ridden Greeks.

The provinces

Finally, let us examine the government of the provinces in the late Republic. The system had many defects. The magistrates, sent annually, were not paid, either as governors or in the preceeding magistracy. They therefore had to cover their very considerable expenses and make a profit, at the cost of those they governed. This obviously left the door open to many abuses. Moreover, the governor in his province had no one to check his power or prevent misgovernment. The *publicani* likewise, when they collected the taxes, had every opportunity to make a profit, and very little to stop them from being exorbitant. The governor and the *publicani*, who should have been a check on one another, tended in general to work in collusion for the profit of both. As a result, the provinces, especially in the East, were drained of their wealth at a frightening speed. Cicero's speeches on Verres give a detailed picture of the behaviour of a bad governor.

Pompey did bring more stability to the East by his settlement, and as in the case of Roman law, he drew inspiration from the Greeks, in particular from Alexander. It is interesting to reflect that Alexander himself made great use of the institutions of the Persians, those great early imperialists, whose work was not always appreciated, because Greek writers were so keen to vilify them as the great menace to the freedom of Greece.

The military side of the provinces also left much to be desired. There was not as a rule a set garrison appointed to a province. The protection of the frontiers was left to the client kingdoms which fringed Rome's possessions, and they were by no means dependable. If a crisis did arise, then the governor, or the consul at Rome, had to gather his army as the need became evident, with more speed than efficiency. Hence the early defeats which the Romans tended to suffer in their wars.

Since the time of Marius it became the practice to recruit soldiers for a set time, probably of twenty years, instead of the earlier annual levy. As was natural in such disturbed times, the soldiers had a great deal of power and there was a real danger of the country turning into a military dictatorship.

The naval position was considerably worse. Rome, being a land power, had a blind spot in matters naval, and even after Pompey crushed the pirates the situation was not ideal.

On the credit side the provincials did have some chance of redress through the courts at Rome (*quaestio de repetundis*). Admittedly the chances of securing a conviction were slight and the possibility of real compensation remote. Still it was some brake on misgovernment. Moreover, not all the governors were corrupt. Some, like Cicero, took their task seriously and helped their subjects. In addition, Rome did bring peace to some extent and built roads, both of which assisted the peaceful development of trade, a necessary condition for prosperity.

On the whole, however, the picture was not a very bright one. The government of the provinces had developed in too haphazard a fashion, and was left in the hands of amateurs. It remained for Augustus and his successors to put the government and protection of the provinces on a professional, business-like footing.

Date table

B.C.

87	Birth of Catullus and Sallust.
80	Cicero's oration *Pro Roscio Amerino.*
55	Death of Lucretius.
54	Death of Catullus
50	Caesar's *Gallic Wars* published.
44–43	Cicero's *Philippic Orations.*
34	Death of Sallust.

Select quotations

1 Catullus 31:
Sirmio, pearl of peninsulas, or islands if you will, such as either Neptune bears in limpid lakes or mighty sea, how glad at heart I visit you, barely believing that I have left Thynia and the Bithynian plains, and see you in safety. What is more blessed than to be free of care, when the mind lays down its burden, and, weary from foreign toil, we come home and rest upon the longed-for bed. This is the one reward for such great labours. Greeting, lovely Sirmio, and rejoice in your master, and hail to you also, waves of the Lydian lake, burst forth, all the merriment of my home.

2 Lucretius III, 1060:
Often he goes out of doors, leaving his huge house, bored with staying at home, and as suddenly returns, because he finds nothing better outside. He rushes to his country estate, driving

*his ponies madly, as if bringing immediate aid
to a burning house; as soon as he sets foot
within it, he begins yawning immediately, or
abandons himself to heavy sleep in quest of
oblivion, or even hies himself back in haste to
the city. In this way each man tries to escape
himself, but naturally cannot do so, and is
enmeshed against his will, and full of hatred
because, though sick, he does not know the
cause of his illness.*

Further reading

Lucretius, *On the Nature of the Universe*, Penguin.
Catullus, *Poems*, Penguin.
Edith Hamilton, *The Roman Way*, Mentor Book.
D.R. Dudley, *The Civilisation of Rome*, Mentor
  Book.
M. Grant, *Roman Literature*, Pelican.
A.H. Macdonald, *The Roman Republic*,
  Thames & Hudson, 1966.

Chapter 16

Julius Caesar

THERE ARE NO NEW SOURCES for this chapter. They are the same as for chapter 14, but the question of bias needs to be stressed once more, especially in relation to the three main characters: Caesar, Pompey and Mark Antony.

Sources

Caesar is a most controversial character and we have two very differing views of him. The official version, found in his own writings and in the writers under the patronage of Caesar's successor Augustus, present him as a great man with extraordinary gifts, who by his achievements brought on the rule of Augustus. Another view is presented by such writers as Suetonius, a scandal-monger by nature, who was eager to denigrate the Julio-Claudians so that his patrons, the succeeding emperors, should shine by comparison. He portrays a most unscrupulous man, utterly immoral and eager to succeed at any price. Our contemporary source Cicero was well aware of this dual personality. The historians of the nineteenth century had a deep respect for

empire and, correspondingly, admired Caesar. Our own age is less reverent, and it may be possible now to achieve some kind of balance.

Pompey is another interesting case. He and (even more) his father were newcomers, and Roman society did not admire the novus homo. Moreover Pompey broke all the rules of the establishment, and received political advancement at every stage, to which he was not legally entitled. The establishment was jealous of his success and was eager to belittle him, and Augustus himself, whose adoptive father Caesar had fought against Pompey, was happy to encourage this attitude. Indeed he took Livy to task for being a champion of Pompey in his writings. It is all the more unfortunate that we do not have Livy's version of these events. Cicero is interesting. He speaks in admiration of Pompey in his famous pro lege Manilia, but as a novus homo himself he had hoped to have the friendship of Pompey, and he was very hurt that Pompey tended to ignore him. So he too is not very favourable to Pompey.

This brings us to Mark Antony. He was a gifted soldier and capable of real insight on occasion as an administrator. But in private life he was a womaniser, a drinker, with no respect for the conventions of civil government and those who ran it. Cicero loathed him from the start and when Antony turned his troops against Octavian, Cicero launched out against him in his *Philippics*.

Needless to say these speeches are hardly remarkable for their impartiality. For Octavian, Antony was the opponent he defeated to win the emperorship. He launched a vigorous propaganda campaign against Antony at the time, and later took every step he could to wipe out his achievements. In consequence some of the things Antony did can only be recovered from inscriptions.

Pompey returns

All was now prepared for the final struggle that was to end the Republic. When Pompey landed at Brundisium there was much trepidation at Rome. So often Pompey had come with his army to enforce his demands. This time it was to be different. Pompey had settled the affairs of the East, sending home huge sums of money to the coffers at Rome, and he saw no reason why he should not simply return and be received by a grateful people. He was to be sorely disillusioned.

He delivered his final speech to his troops and dismissed them, then made his way to Rome, accompanied by cheering throngs. But the Senate was in no welcoming frame of mind. The optimates, headed by Cato, had long resented Pompey's flouting of constitutional procedure. Lucullus had his own grievances at the young upstart who had replaced him and taken credit that should have gone to him. Finally Metellus, the most powerful man in the Senate, was indignant because Pompey had recently divorced his wife Mucia, a member of the Metellan clan, on the grounds of an affair with Caesar.

Pompey himself was singularly ill-equipped to deal with political manoeuvring. His life had been spent in the army where his word was law, and he had had little experience of the Senate. He was soon to see the senatorial intrigues in action.

16.1 *Pompey (106–48 B.C.). He formed the First Triumvirate with Crassus and Caesar but broke with Caesar and was defeated at Pharsalus.*

The Bona Dea Scandal

In 63 B.C. Caesar had been made *pontifex maximus*, a priestly office of considerable political importance. It usually went to a senior member of the Senate, and it was no small achievement that Caesar won the post when only a quaestor. In fact it required immense bribes, financed by Crassus, who as so often was eager to give financial support to young talent.

Because Caesar held this office in 61 the celebrations of *Bona Dea* were held at his house. This ceremony was open only to women, but Clodius dressed as a woman attended, as gossip held, in order to further an affair he was having with Caesar's wife, Pompeia, whom Caesar promptly divorced.

All of this happened just before Pompey's return and when Pompey arrived Clodius was being put on trial. Pompey was asked his opinion of the affair. He was anxious not to offend the optimates, who had yet to ratify his Eastern settlement and provide land for his troops. He

therefore refused to commit himself, saying that it was a matter for the wisdom of the Senate to determine. In this way he won the enmity of Clodius.

At the trial Cicero broke Clodius' alibi. At a time Clodius claimed to have been away from Rome Cicero said he had spoken to him. He too was not forgiven by Clodius. Crassus bribed the jury and Clodius was acquitted.

The frustration of Pompey

At first Pompey was not aware of the gathering opposition. He settled down to enjoy his new leisure, preparing for his coming triumph and planning the construction of two magnificent buildings. One of these was the Theatre of Pompey, Rome's first permanent theatre, which Pompey built on the Campus Martius and further adorned by the Pompeian Gardens, also very beautiful, which he built by them. Outside Rome near the Alban Mountain he built himself a villa, obviously inspired by his eastern experiences, for it was more like a palace than the home of a private citizen.

When Pompey did try to have his Eastern settlement ratified Cato thwarted him by prolonging the debate till it was too late for a decision in 61. Lucullus helped by insisting that the Eastern settlement should be considered point by point and compared with the settlement that Lucullus had earlier drawn up. Pompey had no hope.

Pompey was no more successful in gaining land for his veterans. He had hoped to push this measure through with the help of favourable consuls, and accordingly, with the lavish bribery which was a regular but regrettable feature of the elections of the time, he succeeded in having his general Afranius elected as one of the consuls of 60. Pompey had also made an outlay to have one of the tribunes, Flavius, elected, and Flavius brought forward a bill to provide the land required. The other consul, however, was Celer, one of the Metelli and his bitter enemy. The Senate led by Celer opposed the bill so violently that Afranius, who had no political skills, was powerless to stop them, and the bill was finally withdrawn.

Cato attacks the equites

It looked as if the Senate had succeeded in reasserting its authority, and Cato took advantage of this to make an attack on the equites, and on their supporter Crassus. The equites were trying to renegotiate a contract they had entered into for the taxes of Asia, where they had, they felt, made too high a bid. Cato managed to have the Senate refuse their request, and demanded an inquiry into the bribery of juries. Cicero was most unhappy. He had no illusions that Cato was right in his criticisms, but he felt that the Senate could not afford to fall out with the equites, breaking the *concordia ordinum* (harmony of the classes) which he felt was so important. His misgivings were justified. The Senate had made too many enemies and its triumph was to be short-lived.

Caesar's fortunes in Spain

It was Caesar who brought matters to a head. He had gained the praetorship in 62, but he was deeply in debt through the bribery needed to win that post and the office of pontifex maximus. In 61 he was awarded Further Spain for his propraetorship, but his creditors tried to keep him in Rome till his debts were paid. Again Crassus came to his rescue by standing surety for his debts. In Spain Caesar repaired his fortunes somewhat by conquering some parts of the province that had revolted, and he did bring some help to the unfortunate provincials by reducing by two-thirds the amount they had to pay in taxes.

Now in 61 Caesar was back. He desired a triumph to celebrate his Spanish victories, but he also wanted to stand for a consulship. To do this he was required to enter Rome and hand over his command, thus forfeiting his triumph. Cato led the opposition in the Senate, which would not let him stand for the consulship outside Rome. Caesar promptly laid down his command and forfeited his triumph.

Caesar won his consulship, but with a senatorial colleague, Bibulus. The Senate, as was the practice, settled the provinces that the consuls would have after their term of office, and instead of the normal province gave them the commission to oversee Rome's forests, an idle commission, which would bring Caesar no financial return.

Caesar realised that he faced ruin. Spain had helped his financial position but he needed much more, and he also wanted an opportunity to have his own army, so essential now as a power-base.

The Triumvirate is formed

There were now three dissatisfied and powerful men, Pompey, Caesar and Crassus. There was a problem. Crassus and Caesar had no love for one another, and indeed Crassus had taken part in the Senate's attacks on Pompey. However, Caesar was persuasive. He won the agreement of the other two, and the result was what we know as the First Triumvirate. Caesar as consul had the official power and he proposed a bill to award land to Pompey's veterans. Cato opposed it in the Senate, so Caesar took the bill to the assembly, with Pompey's veterans at hand to enforce his wishes. The opponents of the bill were removed forcibly and it was passed, although Caesar's colleague Bibulus declared that he would watch the skies for omens. This technically meant that no official business could be transacted, but the triumvirate was above technicalities.

Next Caesar had a tribune Vatinius propose a bill validating Pompey's Eastern settlement. This was passed, as was a further bill of Vatinius reducing by one third the taxes of Asia. Thus Caesar had met the needs of his two partners.

It was now his turn. Vatinius put through a measure giving Caesar a command of five years (far beyond the normal term) of Cisalpine Gaul and Illyricum. At this stage it was not clear whether more opportunities would arise for Caesar in the east or the west. Caesar then had a stroke of luck. Metellus was on his way to govern Transalpine Gaul when he dropped dead, and Transalpine Gaul was immediately added to Caesar's command.

Caesar has Cicero exiled and Cato sent to Cyprus

Caesar determined to eliminate any opposition in Rome before he set out for Gaul. He made overtures to Cicero, who refused them and he turned to Clodius. He put behind him the Bona Dea incident—after all his own reputation was not the best where women were concerned—and succeeded in having Clodius adopted into a plebeian clan, a necessary procedure if he was to stand for the tribunate. Clodius was now elected as tribune for 58.

Clodius' first move was to ensure his own popularity, and he passed a law providing for free corn to be distributed in Rome. Hitherto corn had only been sold cheaply to the people, and his move was naturally popular, but inevitably a heavy burden on the treasury.

Next he took steps to remove the enemies of the triumvirate. To Cato he offered the governor-

16.2 *Julius Caesar (102–44 B.C.)*

ship of Cyprus, and when Cato tried to refuse threatened to force him to accept it. Cato departed, and that left Cicero. Clodius had a private score to settle with him and he passed a law outlawing all those who executed Roman citizens without a trial. Cicero went into exile in Greece at once, and then Clodius passed a law specifically against Cicero, confiscating his house.

Caesar also cemented his bond with Pompey by giving him his daughter Julia in marriage. It was a political marriage, and Pompey had in the past a number of political marriages, but this turned out differently. Julia was about thirty years younger than Pompey, beautiful, charming and clever. Pompey fell head over heels in love with her.

Caesar begins his campaign in Gaul

Caesar now had affairs in Rome under control and he could take over his provinces. It was a Gallic people, the Helvetii, from the area of modern Switzerland, who gave him his opportunity. Pushed by German tribes behind them they wanted to come and settle in west Gaul, but Caesar refused them permission. They then changed their route to avoid Roman territory, but Caesar was still adamant.

It must be realised that at this stage Caesar would have had no firm plan to conquer the whole of Gaul, but that is precisely what the present situation was to lead to.

What Caesar certainly did want was a successful campaign; this would replenish his finances and at the same time enable him to build up an army loyal to him, which would be a counterpoise to Pompey's Eastern veterans. Various circumstances led him far beyond that.

In the first place, as he himself was to note, the Gauls were profoundly disunited, and they were under constant pressure from the German tribes to their north. At first Caesar seemed to them a real opportunity to gain assistance in their internal squabbles and help against the Germans. At that time the Aedui were the leading tribe, and their rivals, the Arverni and the Sequani were intriguing with Ariovistus, a German chief north of the Rhine, to help them against the Aedui.

Caesar's chief legate (or legionary commander) was his old political ally Labienus, who was to be his right-hand man in his campaigns. He now left Labienus on guard on the Rhine, and went back to collect three legions from their winter quarters and enrol two more. Here he set an important precedent. As we noted, the Transpadane Gauls had long agitated for full Roman citizenship, which would have made them eligible to serve in the Roman legions. Caesar enrolled his two new legions from them, in effect accepting them as Roman citizens, and from then on he drew the bulk of his army from there.

When he returned the Aedui called him to help them against the Helvetii, who were coming

their way. He met the Helvetii near where the town of Amercy now lies. It was a fierce battle that lasted all day but finally the Gauls were driven back from the wagons, which the Romans then took and removed. This meant that the Gauls were now without supplies. Some days later they surrendered and were sent back to their original home.

Caesar defeats Ariovistus

The Gauls were very impressed by Caesar's success and the chief of the Aedui, Diviciacus, asked for his help against Ariovistus. This had its problems, for the Romans, urged by Caesar, had recently called him a friend of the Roman people, but Caesar demanded that he not cross the Rhine, and when he refused went to stop him at Vesontio, the chief town of the Sequani. The Germans did not engage him for some days, but at last they drew up in line and engaged. Caesar led his right wing against their left, as it seemed unsteady, and after an initial fierce battle drove the Germans back on the Rhine, where many were killed and many drowned. Ariovistus himself escaped but his army was slaughtered.

The campaign of 57 against the Belgae

At the beginning of 57 Caesar learnt from Labienus that the Belgae of northern Gaul were plotting against him.[1] When Caesar came north some of the tribes surrendered but he learnt that the fiercest of them, the Nervii, were preparing to confront him, and they were closer than he realised. His advance legions were preparing their camp for the night on the river Sabis (Sambre) when the Gauls fell upon them unpre-

---

[1] If you are confused refer to the map of Gaul (p. 145). There you will see that the Belgae were one of the four main divisions of Gaul. Within them were the Nervii, the Atrebates and the Viromandui.

pared. Luckily the Romans' long training came to their aid. They drew up in line as they were and the Ninth and Tenth legions drove back the Atrebates who faced them. The Eleventh and Eighth legion also were successful against the opposing Viromandui, but the right wing faced the fiercest foe, the Nervii. Caesar rushed in to hearten them and at the same time the enemy were taken at the rear both by the Tenth legion, which had come from taking the camp of the Belgae, and by the Thirteenth and Fourteenth legions, which had been following in the rear of Caesar's army. The battle now became a massacre, and in the end, as Caesar wrote, only the old men and children remained of the Nervii. Caesar now, as was to be his annual custom, sent his troops into winter quarters and went to Italy to see that all was well at home.

Caesar as a soldier and tactician

An interesting evaluation of Caesar has been made by J.F.C. Fuller, himself a major-general, who wrote extensively on military matters (see 'Further reading' at the end of this chapter). He comments that Caesar was not, like his uncle Marius, a military innovator. He never really made effective use of the cavalry. He did have immense personal charm, which he had used before his soldiering days and with which he held his troops, and something soldiers also revered— he was utterly fearless, and relied for most of his success on the element of surprise, catching his foes unawares by an unexpected, often fool-hardy move, which threw them off their guard. At times this impetuosity left him without supplies or without sufficient troops, which then had to follow in haste, but till his last fatal encounter in the Senate House his reckless daring won out.

His charm had another side. Fuller spoke of him as a 'Jekyll and Hyde'. He could be most horribly cruel. At the end of his Gallic wars he had killed a million Gauls and enslaved a further million. He could be merciful, but there too in a calculating fashion. It is of interest that his oldest friend Labienus went over to the other side in the Civil War.

All is not well in Rome

With Caesar absent unrest began to develop in Rome. Clodius' gangs roamed the streets to the terror of all, and the optimates plotted. Pompey began to feel increasingly isolated although he did get an adventurer Milo to organise a rival gang which helped to check Clodius.

In August 57 BC. he received Caesar's permission to have Cicero recalled. The orator came back amid considerable rejoicing and looked to repay his debt. At Rome there was now a severe corn shortage, made worse by Clodius' free corn dole. The Senate, with Cicero's eloquent approval, gave Pompey a five year control of the corn supply. Unfortunately Cicero then went further. He felt that the triumvirate was breaking up and joined the intriguers.

Caesar and the Veneti

Meanwhile Caesar had further problems. The Veneti, who were a sea-faring tribe on the west coast of Gaul, heard rumours that Caesar was going to invade Britain (correctly) and plotted against him. Caesar then had a fleet built and sent it against the Veneti under Decimus Brutus (his future assassin). The Veneti had better boats but no archers and the Roman fleet was able to get alongside them and cut down their sails. Again Caesar was ruthless. He killed all the Venetian senators and sold the rest as slaves.

Conference at Luca

Again came winter and Caesar went to north Italy to find that affairs in Rome were critical. The optimates were planning to have a hostile consul elected, and to unseat the triumvirate. Caesar moved with his customary speed. He summoned Pompey and Crassus secretly to Luca in north Italy and a new agreement was drawn up. Pompey and Crassus were to be elected to the consulships of 55, and Caesar would send troops to Rome at election time to force through the election. In the following year they were to obtain as provinces Syria for Crassus and Spain

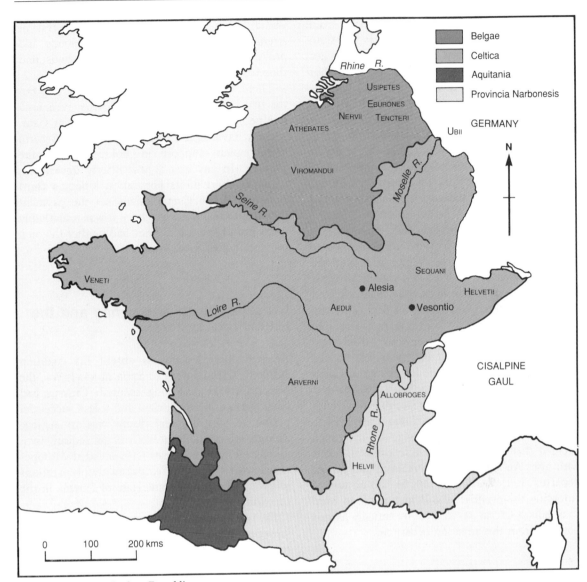

16.3 *Gaul during the late Republic.*

for Pompey. Caesar in turn was to have another five years in Gaul. Cicero's brother, who was serving under Caesar, was sent to warn him to toe the line in his speeches.

Caesar defeats the Germans and invades Britain

The year 55 B.C. was to be a year that brought little credit to Caesar. It began when he learnt that two German tribes, the Usipetes and the Tencteri were wanting to settle this side of the Rhine. He sent to protest and they asked him for land. He told them to settle in the land of the Ubii, then marched against them. A German cavalry detachment came upon a Gallic band of cavalry and routed it. The German leaders came to apologise to Caesar and he seized them and marched immediately against their leaderless followers, slaughtering the soldiers and driving the women and children into the Rhine, where they drowned. He then released the chiefs. Even the Senate was horrified and led by Cato protested, but there was nothing they could do.

The summer season was almost over but Caesar determined to make a sortie into Britain. He went with the Seventh and Tenth legions, and there was a fierce battle. The Britons negotiated for peace, but when Caesar was preparing to depart a storm overwhelmed his fleet, which was not properly beached, and finally Caesar returned to Gaul, with the ships remaining, achieved little, as the peace negotiations petered out.

In 54 B.C. Caesar made ready a second invasion of Britain and this time had a formidable fleet built for the purpose. When he landed the opposing force fled at once and Caesar with his army set out once more in pursuit, again without beaching his ships. Once more a storm came and destroyed many ships, damaging more, so that Caesar had to send for repair teams from Gaul to fix them. He then set out again against the British, who were under the leadership of Cassivelaunus. Using guerrilla tactics, Cassivelaunus had some success but Caesar decided that mildness would achieve more than force, and was so careful to restrain his troops that the tribesmen decided that it would be wise to come to terms with him. An agreement was reached and Caesar departed, but, needless to say, he had no way of enforcing the promises the British made to him; so although Caesar saved face, he actually gained nothing from this invasion of Britain.

The Gauls' final effort: the Battle of Alesia.

By 54 B.C. the Gauls were beginning to feel the weight of the Roman yoke and there was a widespread revolt, which was crushed with the utmost savagery. The defeat had a transient effect, but by 52 they were ready again, led by Vercingetorix of the Arverni. Even the Aedui joined the rebels, which was a blow as they had hitherto supplied Caesar's cavalry. Undaunted, Caesar called on German aid, and with German cavalry began his toughest campaign. Finally he besieged Vercingetorix in Alesia, where all the Gallic forces had gathered for a last test of strength. The battle of Alesia was bloody and prolonged, but finally Caesar was victorious, and thus won domination over Gaul.

There were some minor revolts after that but the real battle had been won. Caesar even used mildness, a weapon not used hitherto in Gaul, and by favouring the Aedui and the Arverni gained their support in holding down the country. In any case it was utterly devastated, with one-third of its population killed, a third enslaved. When Caesar finally set the payment they had to make as a province it was remarkably light, but of necessity. They had neither the men nor the money to pay more.

Crassus' death at Carrhae and the triumvirate suffers

Again, while Caesar was absent his coalition suffered. Crassus went to Syria in 54. It was the opportunity he had long awaited. Crassus had been a most able financier, and a less successful politician, but his real desire was to achieve military glory. This he set out to acquire with more eagerness than care. He invaded Mesopotamia with a large army, and made preparations to invade the troublesome state of Parthia in the following spring.

He was not only inexperienced in war, but a stranger to desert warfare. He took the direct route to Parthia, through waterless country, was lured by the Parthian horsemen into the intractable area of Carrhae, and there his exhausted and worn-out troops were wiped out by the Parthians with their horse archers. Crassus fell, and the standards of seven legions were lost, a terrible disaster, as the standards were held in religious reverence by the Romans, and their loss was a final disgrace.

Pompey did not go to Spain, but remained in Rome, ruling the province *in absentia* through his legates. In 54 Julia died, breaking an important link between the two triumvirs. At the same time the death of Crassus left the partnership one of two members only, which created dangerous possibilities of rivalry.

Caesar prepares to return to Rome

The year 52 was one of trial in Gaul and as well it was not peaceful in Rome. Milo and Clodius finally clashed and Clodius was killed. A state of emergency was called, but, instead of passing the usual decree, the Senate made Pompey sole consul, an interesting precedent. Pompey had Milo exiled, overawing Cicero's attempt to make a defence.

Meanwhile Caesar had been pouring money into Rome, much of it gained by plundering the Gallic shrines. He had a number of ambitious buildings undertaken, including the *Forum Julium*, which was to be the first of the imperial fora. His concern now was to gain further office without laying down his command, so he could not be prosecuted. He applied for another consulship in 51, accompanying his request with the publication of the first seven books of his *Gallic Wars*. This was a remarkable work, written with all Caesar's clarity and eloquence. It presented his campaigns with a great appearance of objectivity, but needless to say, utterly justified his actions.

Caesar's request was refused. The optimates hoped that at last they had a chance of separating Caesar from his army and his power, as when Pompey had laid down his Eastern command. But Caesar was not Pompey. He countered any attempt that might be made on the loyalty of his troops by issuing them with double pay on the spot and continued his manoeuvres. Meanwhile Pompey had gained a further proconsulship, as the Senate felt they needed him against Caesar. Cicero was at the time away from Rome, having been appointed as governor of Cilicia.

Caesar crosses the Rubicon and Pompey leaves for the East

Caesar saw that he needed to retrieve his position. He no longer had Clodius to guard his interests; so with lavish gifts he won the support of an impecunious and extravagant young aristocrat, Curio.

Curio in 50 called both Caesar and Pompey to relinquish their commands. Pompey refused.

Caesar sent asking permission to stand for another consulship without returning to Rome. Caesar did not dare to enter Rome, for to lay down his official command would put him at the mercy of his enemies. His request was refused, and Pompey, on the pretext that he was organising an expedition against Parthia, asked Caesar to send back one legion which Pompey had lent him and to contribute a second legion to the force. Caesar complied, thus relinquishing two legions.

The consul now called on Caesar to disband his army, and a battle of tactics began. The senatorial party seems to have thought that it could overawe him, but Caesar had taken warning from Pompey's earlier action. He refused to undertake a unilateral demobilisation, and finally marched on Italy, crossing the Rubicon (the river which bounded his province), thereby creating a proverbial phrase for taking an irrevocable step. Pompey did not have sufficient troops to meet Caesar on Italian soil (the two legions Caesar had sent him would be of doubtful loyalty), and in any case he had planned a strategy of withdrawal. He had control of the sea, and had all the East to draw on. Accordingly he withdrew, taking with him the bulk of the Senate and of the administrative class. He embarked his forces at Brundisium to land in Greece. He could now cut Rome off from its food supply and return like Sulla to retake Rome.

Caesar crushes resistance in Spain and follows Pompey to the East

Caesar's policy in the Civil War was far different from his savagery in the Gallic Wars. We know that it was a conscious policy for he explained it in a letter that still survives. He knew that if he was to win in a war of this kind he had to show himself merciful and have popular sentiment on his side, and this is precisely what he achieved.

In Spain Caesar was faced by Pompey's generals Afranius and Petreius and the learned Varro. They did have some initial successes but Caesar could have finally forced the issue.

16.4 *The Forum of Julius Caesar.*

Instead he kept close enough to them to allow the opposing troops to begin talking. Finally the Pompeian forces compelled their commanders to surrender.

Caesar had a different fate in Africa, where Curio, whom he had sent with unprepared troops, encountered the Numidian cavalry, which was too much for him and he and his force were massacred.

Caesar now made a lightning visit to Rome, where he settled the various magistracies and took the consulship, resigning the dictatorship which the Senate had granted him just before his return. He then hurried to Brundisium, for although it was now winter, Pompey had had nine months to prepare, and it was time to face him. We now see both the strength and weakness of Caesar's strategy. He did cross over to Greece, even though he did not have sea power and could only take a small force, but then he lost his surprise, because he had to wait for reinforcements from Antony.

When, however, Pompey managed to beat Caesar in taking the key port of Dyrrachium, the paucity of Caesar's troops became apparent. He invested them in a rather inadequate blockade, saddened still further by learning that his ships had been sunk on their way back. None the less, Antony did make his way over to join Caesar, but no supplies could be sent across, and when Pompey grew weary of the blockade, he had no trouble in forcing his way out. All these reverses on Caesar's part should be kept in mind by some historians who dwell on the theme of the invincible Caesar and the overrated Pompey.

The Battle of Pharsalus

Pompey's strategy would have been to fight a delaying war, and there he could have succeeded, but he could not handle the optimates, who were his senior staff. They became over confident and when Caesar retreated to Pharsalus in 48 they

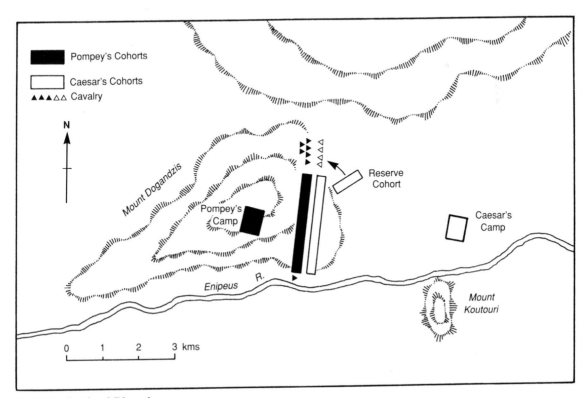

16.5 *The Battle of Pharsalus.*

insisted on giving battle. Even then he had an army twice the size of Caesar's. He drew up his forces with Labienus in charge of the cavalry on the left wing, instructed to defeat the opposing cavalry and take Caesar in the rear. Caesar, to counter this, had eight cohorts drawn up behind his right wing in support. Labienus failed in his task. His force advanced in massed formation, and when Caesar's eight reserve cohorts appeared they swerved aside and fled. The cohorts now fell on Pompey's left wing and attacked on the front and the flank; the Pompeians broke and fled. Pompey then fled to Egypt, where he was seized treacherously and beheaded by a man who had once served under him.

J. Leach (see 'Further reading' at end of chapter) suggests that Caesar's account of the battle of Pharsalus was superficial, attributing Caesar's victory entirely to strategy, and ignoring the very important question of morale, caused especially by the divided leadership. Some have criticised Pompey, who left the field at once when defeat loomed, but Leach suggests, agreeing with the poet Lucan, that Pompey felt that if he went the soldiers would not feel bound to fight to the death, but would surrender, and in fact this was what happened.

Caesar and Cleopatra

The next episode has again some of the unbelievable character that marked so many of this strange man's acts. Caesar went on to Egypt with a minute force of two legions. He found there a dynastic dispute between the 13-year-old Ptolemy and his sister Cleopatra. Caesar was convinced that he had defeated all his foes and that his will was law. He saw his next task as the settling of this dispute, aided by the fact that he fell headlong in love with the young queen, who was smuggled into Alexandria wrapped in a bundle of bedding in order to meet Caesar. He also demanded that the Egyptians supply the pay for his troops. The Egyptians were not as impressed as he expected and he was in fact forced to stand siege in Alexandria till Mithridates of Pergamum came to his rescue. Ptolemy and his forces were finally defeated and the

young king lost his life, whereupon Caesar took Cleopatra up the Nile for a two months' honeymoon! A son Caesarion was born of his union with Cleopatra.

The African campaign and the Battle of Thapsus

A rebellion in Syria roused Caesar. He crushed it in a whirlwind campaign which he himself described in his famous message to the Senate, *veni, vidi, vici*, I came, I saw, I conquered.

Caesar now returned to Italy and found great unrest. While he had been gallivanting in the East his troops had not received their promised pay, and they were not satisfied with his promise to pay them when he had finished his campaign in Africa. Even his Tenth Legion was in a state of mutiny at the prospect of further service. He quelled them by a single word. He rose to address them and used the term *Quirites*, best rendered in our language by 'civilians'. The Tenth Legion reacted like the troops of Alexander (with whom Caesar has been compared), and begged forgiveness. Caesar's next campaign was in Africa, where the Pompeians had gathered.

When he first arrived in Africa he was not in a good position. He had given his enemies a whole year to prepare, and when he did arrive it was with his usual impetuosity and too few troops. In his favour was the fact that the Pompeians had roused considerable discontent in the locals by their exactions and that the enemy leadership was not united. In particular Metellus Scipio, who was nominally in command, was not a decisive man. In his first operations Caesar was met by Labienus who had command of Numidian cavalry, and Caesar was quite unable to cope with their evasive tactics. On several occasions he came close to defeat, but finally he managed to obtain sufficient reinforcements and food supplies, which had also been short and seized the town of Thapsus where the enemy cavalry would not have scope. After some manoeuvring the enemy forces drew up opposing each other, with Scipio's army guarded on the wings by his elephants. In fact Caesar's army

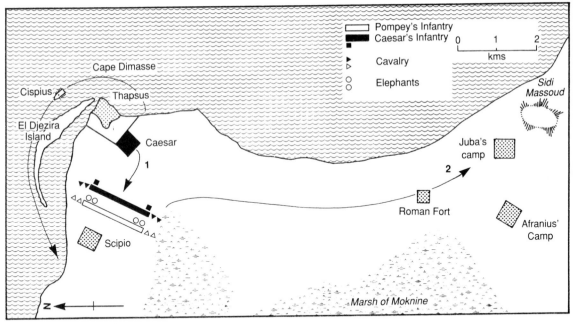

16.6 *The Battle of Thapsus.*

attacked even before it had its orders. Their archers and slingers frightened the enemy elephants, so often a dubious asset, which tram-

16.7 *The coin of Labienus.*

pled on their own forces. Scipio's army was routed and a massacre ensued, with 10 000 killed despite Caesar's efforts to stop it. Labienus escaped, but Cato the Younger committed suicide.

It was a triumph for Caesar and he celebrated it with the lavishness natural to him. He returned to Rome where he accepted a ten-year dictatorship. He celebrated four simultaneous triumphs, gave largess, and put on splendid gladiatorial shows.

The unfortunate Vercingetorix was at last killed and Caesar's troops received their promised prize money. All were not happy however. The bloodiness of Caesar's gladiatorial displays horrified many and eyebrows were raised when Cleopatra was installed in a house on the Janiculum with her infant son by Caesar, Caesarion.

The final campaign in Spain. The Battle of Munda

Meanwhile all was not well in Spain. Caesar had left a corrupt and greedy commander there,

Cassius. He was finally drowned at sea, on a ship he had laden with booty, but it was a final base of rebellion, with Labienus and Pompey's two sons, Gnaeus and Sextus, leading them. Caesar took eight legions to Spain, determined to end his opposition and finally forced the enemy to face him at the fortress of Munda. The details of this battle are obscure, for we rely on an anonymous historian of little merit, who wrote a book on the war in Spain. It would seem, however, to have been a bitter contest, the hardest fought of any in the Civil War, but it was decided by an attack on the rear of the Pompeian army by Moorish cavalry, led by King Mogud. About 30 000 were killed of the Republican army and Labienus was among the slain. Caesar then returned to Rome, bringing with him Octavius, the grandson of his sister Julia, whom he was to adopt as his heir, a decision of great importance for Rome.

Caesar's reforms in Rome. Did he wish to be king?

Reform of administration was now the need. To recruit an adequate civil service Caesar increased the Senate from the six hundred of Sulla to nine hundred, and to keep the proportion needed he raised the number of quaestors from twenty to forty—of praetors from eight to sixteen. In order to fill the senatorial ranks (which were further depleted by the civil wars) he appointed members from Italy and from the recently admitted Gallic citizens. As in the case of Sulla, the flooding of the Senate and the provenance of the new recruits met with bitter criticism.

Expansion was the keynote of Caesar's programme. He did reduce the corn dole, but he provided work for Rome's poor by ambitious public works. They included the *Basilica Julia* and the *Forum Julium*, which acted as law courts. These open spaces also made communication possible within what had been the most densely populated part of the great city. He hoped also to build a new Senate House to cope with the increased membership. Other public works contemplated were the new harbour for Ostia and the draining of the Pontine marshes, neither

of which he achieved. He added a gold coin, the *aureus*, to the currency, and made a definitive reform of the calendar, which was now practically the one we still use. The month of July at this time was named after him.

He was no less active abroad. He granted citizenship to all the towns of Sicily, to many Spanish towns, and to many other towns in the provinces. He also bestowed it on his troops from South Gaul. The principle that citizenship should be a reward for military service was not entirely new, having been used on a partial scale on a number of previous occasions, but it was to become a general principle of imperial administration. It had also long been and continued to be the theory of the ancients that city life was the means of civilisation and that the production of new Roman citizens should be their task.

Taxation in the East was reduced, and more than twenty colonies were planned. These included the important commercial colonies of Tarraco (in Spain), Carthage and Corinth.

The assassination of Caesar

The difficult question still was the position of Caesar himself. The senatorial body was not content to be pushed into the background, and he was not tactful enough to conceal the fact that for him the Senate was nothing but a recruiting ground of administrators. Caesar had too much flamboyance and possibly egotism for the difficult task of carrying out the transition from a republican to an autocratic state. He accepted the office of permanent dictator and also that of tribune. Although he refused the title of King (*Rex*) and the crown proffered to him, he wore regularly the scarlet robe of a triumphing general, which had been taken over from the Etruscan kings. He also allowed temples to be erected in his honour (a privilege usually reserved for the dead). In short, his desire for the reality, even the trappings of monarchy, was a little too apparent.

His end was hastened by a virtue of the man. One fear since Marius and Sulla had been a renewal of proscriptions. Caesar not only refrained from liquidating his opponents, but recalled exiles, and even reinstated his late opponents in positions of trust. He also disbanded his personal body-guard. He may well, like many great generals, have believed that a divine providence protected his personal safety.

If so he was over-confident. On the Ides of March 44 B.C. he was assassinated in the Senate House by a large number from that body, including his trusted Brutus.

Evaluation of Caesar's career

Caesar's career offers interesting parallels to that of Alexander. Like that youthful prince he had actually most distinguished himself in war. He undoubtedly also did have ambitious schemes for administrative reform, but like Alexander was cut off before he could do more than sketch out his programme. It remains to decide what would have happened had he been allowed to continue. Would the impetuosity and autocracy of a successful general have restrained itself to the patience needed in civil life? There is some room to doubt this. His schemes were grandiose, but would the empire's treasury have survived the strain he imposed on it? He did not succeed in conciliating the Senate. Could he in time have welded them and the equites into a working partnership?

It is hard to be sure if Caesar would even have waited for an answer to all these questions. Like Alexander he had up to the end further military goals in mind. For him it was vengeance on the Parthians, and the conquest of the Dacians. In any case it is interesting to see the lessons which Augustus drew from the career of Caesar, what he saw could be achieved, and what pitfalls he avoided.

Some Roman captives from Carrhae reach China

Mr Treloar, Honorary Fellow of the University of New England, drew my attention to an interesting series of events which followed the battle of Carrhae, a battle in which, as we know from Roman writers, including Horace, many Roman soldiers were captured (10 000 in all), and forced to serve their Parthian masters.

New evidence was found to continue the story. Pan-ku, a Chinese historian of the Han dynasty told how some of these captives were sent to guard the Eastern frontier of Parthia at Margiana[2].

About a hundred of these men, weary of their ignominious position, escaped from Margiana and approached Chih-Chih, prince of the neighbouring Hun kingdom, offering him their services as mercenaries. This offer he gladly accepted, as he was at war with the rulers of China.

The Chinese forces arrived to attack Chih-Chih's city, and the Roman soldiers played an important part in its defence. However Chih-Chih was finally defeated and he himself was killed. The Chinese commander, Chen-Tang, recognised the worth of the Romans as soldiers and took them back to China, settling them in a town which was given the name of Li-Chien, the Chinese approximation for Rome (actually for Alexandria, but the Chinese confused the two). There the descendants of these Roman exiles lived undisturbed for many hundred years!

Mr D. Harris of Adelaide University learnt of these events from Mr Treloar and went on an archaeological expedition to China, where with the assistance of the Chinese he is trying to unearth the ruins of Li-Chien.

Date table

B.C.

60	First Triumvirate.
58–57	Cicero's exile. 58 Caesar takes over his province.
56	Conference of Luca.
55–54	Caesar's expeditions to Britain.
53	Battle of Carrhae.

---

[2]The Chinese histories were translated and the story of the soldiers discovered by H. H. Dubs, Professor of Chinese of Oxford University, and independently by Professor J. J. L. Duyvendak of Leiden University.

49	Crossing of Rubicon.
48	Battle of Pharsalus.
46	Battle of Thapsus.
45	Battle of Munda.
44	Caesar assassinated.

Select quotations

1 Cicero, *Letters, ad Fam* vii, 5:
(To Caesar.)
*On this one man (Trebatius), my dear Caesar,
I should like you to bestow all that you could
be persuaded by me to give to my friends. I
guarantee that there is no better man, more
honest or more respectful. As well, he is the
head of his profession in civil law, he has a
remarkable memory and profound knowledge.*

2 *Ibid.* vii, 7:
(To Trebatius.)
*I am surprised that I do not receive letters as
often from you as from my brother Quintus. I
hear that there is no gold or silver in Britain. If
that is so, commandeer a chariot and hurry back
to me with all speed. But if, despite Britain,
you can obtain what we wish you to, try to be
one of Caesar's friends. My brother will be of
great assistance there, so will Balbus, but
believe me, your attitude and hard work most
of all.*

3 Suetonius, *Lives of the Caesars* I 37:
*When he had finished the wars he (Caesar)
celebrated five triumphs. . . . The first and most
outstanding was his Gallic triumph, then the
Alexandrian, the Pontic, the African and finally
the Spanish one, each showing different gear
and spoils. . . . He went up to the Capitol by
torchlight with forty elephants carrying lamps on*
*his right and left. In the Pontic triumph amidst
the display of the procession he set forth an
inscription of three words,* I came, I saw, I
conquered, *not to indicate what happened in
the war (as was usual) but the speed of its
execution.*

Further reading

J.F.C. Fuller, *Julius Caesar, Man, Soldier and Tyrant*, Eyre & Spottiswood, London, 1965.
M. Gelzer, *Caesar, Politician and Statesman*, Blackwood, Oxford, 1968.
Beryl Rawson, *The Politics of Friendship, Pompey and Caesar*, Sydney University Press, 1978.
D. Stockton, *Cicero, a Political Biography*, Oxford University Press, 1971.
Plutarch, *Fall of the Roman Republic*, Penguin Classic.
Suetonius, *The Twelve Caesars*, Penguin Classic.

Topics for essays or discussion

1 What caused the formation of the First Triumvirate? Could it have been avoided?
2 What was the nature of the First Triumvirate? Why did it prove an unstable combination?
3 What was the importance of the conquest of Gaul (a) for Caesar (b) for the provincial system?
4 Who, in your opinion, if any one, was responsible for the outbreak of the Civil War? What were the causes of this conflict?
5 Discuss (a) Caesar's organisation of the state (b) the role he assigned to himself. Give your reasons for his success.

Chapter 17

The end of the Republic

Sources

IN ALL THIS PERIOD, bias in our sources makes it extremely hard to achieve a wholly balanced account. As we shall see in the course of this chapter, Octavian or Augustus as he later became, made strenuous efforts to present himself in the most favourable light, and that did involve destroying accounts of these years that were critical of him, and even public inscriptions, especially in the East, recording work Antony had done there. We have to add to that Cicero's *Philippics*, which were in fact a political document, written in a highly volatile period, when passions were aroused, and when Cicero himself had little regard for the truth in his aim to vilify Mark Antony. Yet Cicero's excellence as a writer has meant that even these polemics have been treated with more reverence than would otherwise be the case and help to denigrate Antony's reputation. Writings from this age then follow a consistent line.

However, there were opposing feelings, and later writers, such as Suetonius, Plutarch and Appian, do make use of them on occasion, although naturally their main narrative comes from the highly biased writings of this period. Yet many modern writers of Ancient History follow what we might call the Augustan line.

I myself have been very indebted at this point to *Mark Antony* by Eleanor Goltz Huzar. Huzar, without denying the obvious flaws in Antony's character, takes pains to sift through the evidence and show where our traditional account is inaccurate.

Friends, Romans, Countrymen, Lend me your ears

Our own knowledge of these immediate events is inevitably coloured by Shakespeare's play, *Julius Caesar*, and it is interesting to see how accurate a picture the dramatist paints of these events.

The death of Caesar created a crisis for which the tyrannicides themselves were quite unprepared. They seem, somewhat naively, to have expected that with Caesar's death the Republic would revert to its normal functioning, but there were many reasons why this could not happen, among them the presence of Caesar's army in Italy, which had its own demands and would one way or another gain a new leader.

For the moment Caesar's man and his fellow consul Mark Antony took control. He obtained Caesar's will from his widow Fulvia and in the scene Shakespeare has made immortal whipped up the feelings of the mob at Caesar's funeral, with the result that they burnt down the Senate House and tried to find and lynch Caesar's killers. Brutus, Cassius and the other conspirators hurriedly left Rome.

Antony then took the money Caesar had ready for his Parthian campaign and began arranging land to settle Caesar's veterans.

Enter Caesar's heir

In his will Caesar had named as his heir his grand-nephew Octavius. Octavius was only 18 years-of-age, somewhat sickly and, as we shall see, a hopeless soldier. He had been waiting in

Greece to go with Caesar on his campaign. He could hardly have seemed much of a threat. Yet this youth changed his name to Octavian[1] as Caesar's heir and appeared in Rome to claim his inheritance!

When Antony refused to hand over Caesar's money, much of which he had spent, Octavian declared that he wanted it to pay Caesar's troops, sold some of Caesar's possessions and sent for money that had gone to Greece for the campaign. He also took steps to have the dead Caesar deified. He gained support from many in the Senate, who felt they would be able to manipulate him, among them Cicero, who began what was to be a series of speeches or pamphlets, attacking Antony, whom Cicero had always hated, as an enemy of Rome, and calling on the people to unite against him. They were the *Philippics*, which he modelled on Demosthenes' speeches, written when Philip threatened Athens.

Antony versus the Senate

Problems really began with the distribution of the provinces. The Senate had earlier distributed the provinces and the conspirators Brutus and Cassius had gone east to theirs, hoping to build up an army to support them. Antony now made a new distribution of provinces and gave himself Cisalpine Gaul, which was then held by Decimus Brutus (not the conspirator.) Antony took an army and set off to seize Cisalpine Gaul. In his absence, encouraged by Cicero, the Senate outlawed him and supported Decimus Brutus, sending also Octavian against him with his forces. Octavian was later joined by the consul Hirtius.

The opposing forces met at Mutina, and Antony was beaten. He then retreated to the West and finally won the support of a number of commanders there, including Lepidus, who was governing Nearer Spain. In the end he had twenty-three legions, a formidable force.

In the ensuing engagements both Hirtius and Decimus Brutus were killed, leaving Octavian. Cicero supported him and wanted the Senate to make him consul. But the Senate rashly felt that they could do without the young man and even

17.1 *The young Augustus (63 B.C.–A.D. 14). He became Rome's first emperor.*

began to support Cassius and Brutus in the East. It was a fatal move. The troops themselves took fright, as they feared they would be robbed of their promised donatives, and Octavian and Antony began to see the advantages of making common cause.

The Second Triumvirate. The Proscriptions

Octavian arranged to meet Antony at Bononia in North Italy and there in 43 B.C. the Second Triumvirate was formed, consisting of Octavian, Antony and Lepidus, for a five-year period. The

---

[1]To be exact, he took Caesar's name and added his own to it, becoming Gaius Julius Caesar Octavianus.

three were each to have consular power and had provinces allotted to them, and they were to make ready to face the conspirators led by Brutus and Cassius in the East. All the official positions were given to their followers.

First, however, money in abundance was needed to pay their huge army of sixty legions and provide for 80 000 veterans. The triumvirs entered Rome in triumph then organised a proscription, which rivalled Sulla's in ferocity and cold-bloodedness. Their enemies were to be liquidated and wealthy men were to be killed for profit. Cicero's fate was inevitable, and his head

and right hand were presented to Antony and Fulvia, whom he had pilloried. Cicero's friend Atticus had always been astute and he escaped. It was horrible, but it filled their coffers, and they were soon ready to lead forth their armies.

Conflict in the East. The Battle of Philippi

It still seemed incredible that the young Octavian, with no battle ability whatever could continue to survive in the deadly civil war. Yet

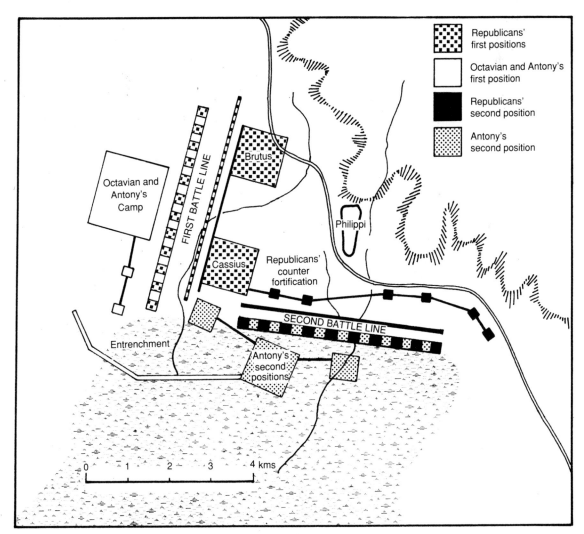

17.2 *The Battle of Philippi.*

he did. He had the prestige of Caesar's name, and that counted, especially with the troops, and they hoped that as Caesar's heir he would reward them, and he did. Unlike his opponents, he had an utterly ruthless will and a clear vision of his goal: that he would rule alone. The rest had no such determination. Then, although he lacked military skill, he constantly was able to call on the skill and the loyalty of those who did have this ability, among whom his friend Agrippa[2] was to be the most important.

For the moment, now that the armies' demands had been met, Antony and Octavian led out their army, leaving Lepidus, always the minor player in the triumvirate, to guard Italy. They met Brutus and Cassius in Greece at Philippi. For about a month the two armies stood face to face, each trying to out-manoeuvre the other. Octavian was ill most of the time and took little part in proceedings. In one of the attacks Cassius thought his men were defeated and fell on his sword, a grave loss for their side. In the end supplies ran short on Antony and Octavian's side and they forced a battle, in which still Octavian took no part through illness. The conspirators' army was easily put to flight, and about 50 000 were killed, Brutus also now committing suicide. The only opponent remaining was Pompey's son, Sextus Pompeius in Sicily and Sardinia.

Dividing up the tasks. Antony goes East

Antony and Octavian divided up their tasks, ignoring Lepidus. Antony was to settle the East, and carry out the invasion of Parthia planned by Caesar, while Octavian dealt with the West. Theoretically Italy was to be shared between them.

Octavian had a difficult task, for he had to settle the veterans on the land, and much ill-feeling was aroused. None the less his power steadily increased, while that of the absent Antony diminished. Antony's brother Lucius, helped by Antony's wife, Fulvia, observed this and led a revolt, for which they tried to gain Antony's support. He did not reply, and said

later that he did not hear of it. As we have observed Octavian was no soldier, but his friend Agrippa led an army against the rebels who were defeated.

Antony now did get news and came west. Sextus Pompeius wanted his support against Octavian, but Octavian outwitted them by a timely political marriage with Sextus' aunt Scribonia. Antony now landed at Brundisium, but although he was supposed to have open access to Italy the city refused him entrance, and Octavian brought his forces south.

Pact of Brundisium

It looked as if the civil war was about to break out again, but the soldiers themselves would not allow it. Officers and men alike from both sides fraternised and forced Octavian and Antony to come to terms. Octavian was not unwilling. Antony was a formidable fighter, and the outcome of a contest would be doubtful, while Antony was anxious to proceed with the invasion of Parthia. Negotiations were carried out through Octavian's other life-long friend and helper, Maecenas, and in 40 B.C. the Pact of Brundisium was signed. Again Antony got the East, Octavian the West, Lepidus Africa. Sextus Pompeius went back to Sicily. Antony was given in marriage Octavian's attractive sister, Octavia, who was to remain remarkably loyal to him in very trying circumstances.

Sextus Pompeius defeated at Naulochus and later killed

Although the triumvirate were supposed to have come to terms with Sextus Pompeius he still gave trouble and cut off Rome's corn supply. In anger Octavian divorced Scribonia and married Livia, who belonged to the ancient and powerful family of the Claudians, and was to be his wife and a centre of power for the rest of his life.

---

[2]Agrippa was with Octavian in Greece, waiting for Caesar and he was said to have been a school friend.

The triumvirate was an uneasy one but in 37 Octavia persuaded Antony and Octavian to meet at Tarentum to renew it. Antony agreed to supply Octavian with ships against Sextus Pompeius, while Octavian agreed to send Antony four legions for the war with Parthia. Antony sent the ships but Octavian never sent the promised legions.

Agrippa was a brilliant naval commander and he prepared Octavian's forces. Octavian went with him but in fact had few successes. In 36 B.C. the navies met at Naulochus and Sextus Pompeius was soundly defeated. He fled east but was killed some time after. At this point Lepidus unwisely tried to assert himself against Octavian who promptly sacked him from the triumvirate.

Antony's settlement of the East

Meanwhile Antony had to settle the affairs of the East, which had been hit hard by mismanagement and by the civil war, where successive generals had bled their treasuries to pay their armies. On the whole he was rather successful. He built on the work of his predecessors, especially Pompey. He founded a number of colonies, which helped the East and also his veterans who settled in them. He encouraged trade and lightened the taxes of the cities that were worst off. His good work was only marred by his personal extravagance and high living, which was a burden wherever he went. One problem requiring settlement was Egypt. Antony went to Egypt, met Cleopatra and like Caesar took her as his mistress.

Like Octavian, Antony organised Caesar-worship in the East. There king and god were regularly equated, and Antony enjoyed being worshipped himself as the god Dionysus. Antony also followed Pompey in controlling most of the East through client kings. One such king was Herod of Judaea, who made every effort to curry favour with Antony, sometimes supplying pay for his troops.

Antony marries Cleopatra. The first battle with Parthia

Meanwhile the Parthians were giving trouble and invading the client kingdoms. They invaded Judaea, where they helped Herod's opponents. Antony came to Herod's rescue and drove away the Parthians, much to Cleopatra's annoyance. She disliked Herod and wished to regain Egypt's old empire, including Herod's Judaea. Antony finally gave her coastal Judaea, but did not sacrifice Herod. In 36 Antony married Cleopatra.

The Parthians made a most determined attack on Antony's domain in 40 B.C. when he was confronting Octavian in south Italy. Luckily Antony had a very able lieutenant, Ventidius, who defeated the Parthians and killed their leaders. For the time being the Parthian threat was removed.

The invasion of Parthia

By 36 B.C. Antony was ready to invade Parthia. Octavian had not sent the promised legions and

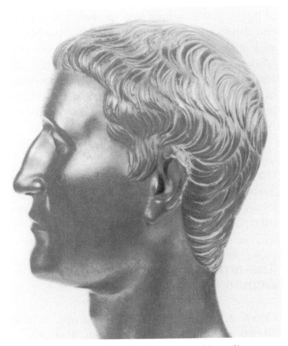

17.3 *Mark Antony (c. 82–30 B.C.). A bitter dispute arose between Antony and Octavian, Caesar's heir, for control of the empire. The defeated Antony killed himself.*

would not let Antony recruit soldiers in Italy, although that was a flagrant violation of their agreement. Antony, however, by recruiting locally, and including Asians in his draft achieved an army of 100 000 and 10 000 cavalry. Actually his marriage with Cleopatra had its commercial side, as he wanted Egyptian money to pay for his invasion.

Antony set out. He avoided the central plain that had been so disastrous to Crassus, going instead round by the north. Even so it was a slow and difficult march, especially for his baggage train. He besieged Phraaspa, the capital of the North, but had little success. The Armenians, who had supplied cavalry to his army, deserted and the Parthians attacked and destroyed his baggage train. Then the icy winter of the Parthian uplands came on and, just as Napoleon and Hitler found the northern winter of Russia their destroyer, so Antony had to retire. It took all Antony's superb generalship to save his army from the fate of Crassus and his forces, and even so when he got to safety he had lost one-third of his army. The Parthians gave him a farewell salute in recognition of his valiant fight.

Octavian's propaganda campaign using Cleopatra

Antony's defeat was a tremendous blow to his military prestige. Octavian's troops had been clamouring to be paid and Octavian had told them to wait until Antony was victorious in Parthia. Now he could tell them that the great general Antony had failed and put the blame on him. It was clear that he saw his way clear to winning supreme power.

He began a wholesale propaganda campaign against Antony. Antony's marriage to Cleopatra gave him an excellent weapon. He portrayed her as a monster and claimed that Antony and Cleopatra aimed to subordinate Rome to the East. Actually, Cleopatra was a very able woman. She was Greek by race, descended from Alexander's general Ptolemy, and she was the more successful in winning her people's loyalty in that she could speak the native language of her subjects, which no Ptolemy before had done. She

was very ambitious for Egypt and hoped to use Antony to gain back some of its past greatness.

Unfortunately, that made her try to keep Antony closely tied to her, which gave more credibility to Octavian's propaganda, and also alienated Antony's own Roman following. This was no small body, for there were many who did not love the Julian upstart, and the proscriptions had also driven many away.

Other actions of Antony played into Octavian's hands. He declared Caesarion and the children he himself had by Cleopatra his heirs, and he accepted deification for himself and Cleopatra as Osiris and Isis.

Octavian's affairs improve. He declares war

Octavian had been doing well in Italy. The defeat of Sextus Pompeius meant that there was no longer any problem with the corn supply. His private life with Livia was exemplary and could serve as a contrast to Antony's. Then helped by Maecenas and Agrippa he set in train a number of public works, which gave work to his veterans and enhanced his reputation. He filled the Senate with his supporters and spread abroad his own more modest form of deification. He did not aspire to be deified himself, but he declared himself the son of the divine Caesar. In addition he was under the divine protection of the god Apollo.

Even now there was quite a body in the Senate that preferred Antony to Octavian. So in 32 B.C. Octavian surrounded the Senate with an armed guard to quell dissent, denounced Antony and finally declared war, not on Antony but on Cleopatra; a clever move!

The armies gather and meet at Actium

Octavian now recruited a huge army, perhaps 80 000 men and set off, leaving Maecenas to guard Italy in his absence.

Despite her many trials Octavia had been loyal to Antony, but he now formally divorced her. He

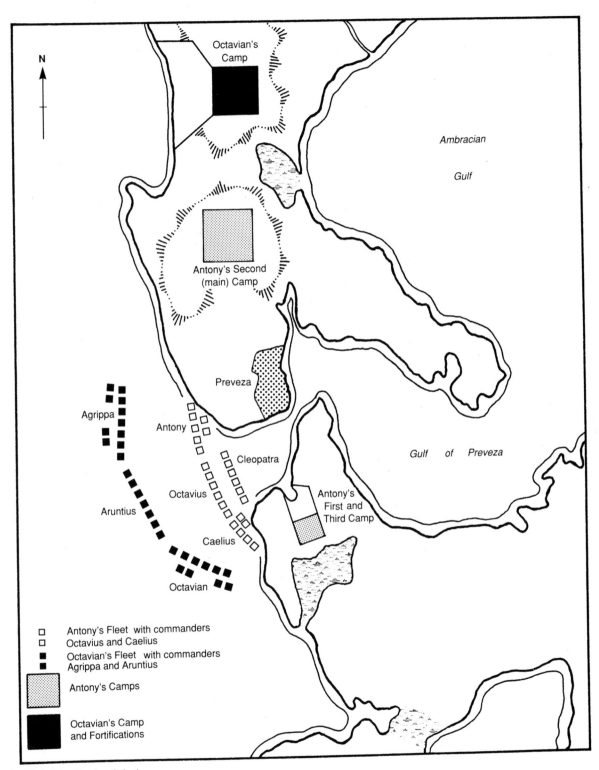

17.4 *The Battle of Actium.*

then recruited his army, Cleopatra supplying a quarter of the navy. He had to get the manpower for his army in the East, but it still had a core of Italian troops.

Antony then advanced to Athens. His camp was troubled by quarrels between those supporting and opposing Cleopatra. His Romans urged Antony to take the war to Italy, but Cleopatra argued with success that they meet the Roman army in Greece. Antony took his army to west Greece and camped at Actium, seizing all the main Greek ports from Corcyra to Methone to guard his supply line with Egypt.

In 31 the Roman army arrived. Octavian had more men and ships than Antony and in Agrippa an excellent naval commander. Agrippa encamped opposite Antony and his navy took all the ports Antony had fortified along the coast, cutting Antony off from Egypt. A stalemate situation then ensued for almost six months, with Antony's forces devastated by disease and hunger, as they were cut off from their food supplies, and also by desertion.

The Battle of Actium

Finally, in September 31 B.C. Antony decided to join battle with Octavian's navy. He had 230 ships to Octavian's 400, an unequal contest, and Antony had his ships equipped with sails, which made his men rightly suspicious. It was to be a battle not to win but to escape. Antony drew up his fleet, extended in the hope of outflanking his opponents, himself leading the right wing opposite Agrippa. His wings were strengthened, his centre weak, with Cleopatra and a force of sixty ships drawn up behind the centre. Octavian took no part in the battle.

Agrippa drove back Antony's forces then the rest engaged. Cleopatra with her sixty ships sailed through the weak centre and took flight for Egypt. When the battle was lost Antony followed her with forty ships. The rest surrendered and Octavian burnt their ships. In fact the battle was lost before it began, but Augustan propaganda tried to give the whole event a supernatural flavour, little connected with reality.

The land force saw that they had no hope and they surrendered to Octavian, who was very willing to be generous, taking them into his army with the same pay and privileges as his own men.

The end of Antony and Cleopatra

The client kings now went over to Octavian, including Herod. Octavian was hailed as *imperator*, and he had the gates of Janus closed to mark that there was peace throughout the empire. This had only happened twice before.

However, there was trouble in Italy. The troops were rebelling against Maecenas, wanting their donatives and their land. Agrippa was sent to help Maecenas, but it was clear that Octavian had to have the gold of Egypt to solve his financial problems.

So Octavian had every reason to set out for Egypt and finish his conflict with Antony. Cleopatra tried to organise resistance and also to bargain with Octavian, a vain endeavour, but for Antony it was all over. As Octavian advanced, ships and troops deserted to him. When he arrived Antony drew up his fleet against him but it, too, went over to Octavian on the battlefield.

Antony fell on his sword, but Cleopatra tried a little longer to bargain with Octavian. He, however, wanted her dead not alive and gave her the needed opportunity to end her life, whether with poison or poisonous snakes as the various versions tell.

Octavian now took control. He had all the records of Antony destroyed, saw that Caesarion and Antony's eldest son by Cleopatra were executed, sparing the younger ones as not being a threat, and seized the treasury of Egypt. At last he had the means of paying his troops, giving them the promised donatives and land, and could reduce his legions from seventy to twenty-six.

Octavian, master of Egypt, returns to Rome

Octavian was now master of Egypt and he kept tight control over it, as it provided him with the wealth he needed throughout his rule, and he was careful not to put it under the control of anyone who might rob him of this most valuable asset. In compensation he was a careful overseer. He kept in the main to the bureaucracy he found there, but he repaired the canals and roads which had been sorely neglected by the Ptolemies in recent times, and he also tightened up its administration.

In 29 B.C. Octavian returned to Rome and celebrated three successive triumphs.

An evaluation of Octavian and Antony

It is interesting to look over the career of the powerful men who lived in the last years of the Republic. The career of Antony bears some resemblance to that of Pompey, although he was a far rougher and less civilised man. Both these men aimed to become men of importance within the framework of the Republic. In contrast, both Caesar and Octavian after him were ruthlessly determined to win power for themselves alone. This singleness of purpose gave their opponents little chance.

Octavian set to work to destroy Antony's memory, which was already sullied by war propaganda and by Cicero's *Philippics*. Any account favourable to Antony was suppressed and he destroyed the monuments set up to commemorate Antony's work in the East. It was a consistent campaign and it was effective. It is now hard to find a really balanced account of Antony.

None the less some evidence has survived which enables us to set the record straight to a degree. In point of fact, although Octavian's propaganda was finally successful, his troops were not blind to his total lack of military skill, and the illnesses which, genuine or not, on so many occasions held him back from battle, did not win their hearts. They joined him because he paid them well, but there was a strong core of loyalty to Antony in the army, which took a long time to subside. Even in Rome, where Octavian was so successful, people looked on Antony, for all his faults, as being one of them, a traditional Roman, and there were

many among them who long favoured him against the upstart Octavian.

As a soldier Antony was outstanding, and in the East, although he spoilt some of his acts by his personal wastefulness and extravagance, he was not an unworthy successor of Pompey. It is significant that although Octavian ostentatiously obliterated Antony's memory, he actually kept on most of the arrangements Antony had negotiated. Octavian's settlement of the East he owed essentially to Pompey and Antony.

Date table

B.C.
44	Cicero delivers the first four of his *Philippics*.
43	Second Triumvirate. Cicero killed in proscriptions.
42	Battle of Philippi.
40	Pact of Brundisium. Antony marries Octavia.
37	Pact of Tarentum.
36	Antony invades Parthia, marries Cleopatra.
31	Battle of Actium.

Select quotations

1 Plutarch, *Life of Antony*, 1.3:
He was also of very noble appearance. He had a well-grown beard, a large forehead and an aquiline nose, giving him all round a bold, masculine look, that reminded people of the portraits of Hercules in paintings and sculptures . . . What might seem to some unendurable, his boasting, his jesting, his drinking in public; sitting down with the men as they were at meals, eating as he stood from the common soldiers' tables, made him the delight of the army. In love affairs also he was very amiable, and gained many friends by the help he gave them in theirs.

2 Virgil: *Aeneid* VIII, verses 675–88:
(Describes the illustrations made by Vulcan on the shield he fashioned for Aeneas.)
In the middle you could make out the fleets modelled in bronze, the battle of Actium; and you could see all Leucate foaming with the battle drawn up there. On this side Caesar Augustus leading the Italians into battle with the Senate and the people, the household gods and the mighty gods above, twin flames belching forth from his two temples, while his father's comet shone upon his brow. On that side Agrippa towered, favoured by wind and gods, leading on his fleet. His brows, a proud ensign of war, were set around with a naval crown. On that side Antony, with barbaric wealth and varied armament, came, victorious over the peoples of the East and the Red Sea, bringing Egypt with him and the strength of the East, and there follows, O sin indeed! his Egyptian bride.
(Octavian was present, but as an observer. He did *not* lead his forces!)

Further reading

Plutarch, *Lives of Antony*, 'Brutus'.
Eleanor Goltz Huzar, *Mark Antony*, Croom Helm, London, 1978.

Topics for essays or discussion

1 Compare and contrast the First and Second Triumvirates.
2 What factors enabled Octavian to defeat Antony despite his lack of military ability?
3 Compare and contrast Mark Antony and Pompey.

Chapter 18

Augustus

Sources

IT IS INTERESTING to analyse the sources for the age of Augustus. He made his own contribution. In the early years of his rule he began but never completed an autobiography, in which he defended himself against criticism, including his actions as triumvir and at the battle of Actium. This book is not extant but was used by other writers. Later he had a large inscription prepared. It was a political manifesto and listed all his achievements. It was displayed in Rome outside his family tomb, the Mausoleum, and in all the provinces. It is called the *Res Gestae* (things achieved) or the *Monumentum Ancyranum*. This name comes from the fact that the copy which has survived complete was the one set up in Ancyra. Like the tyrants of Greece, to whom he bore some resemblances, Augustus raised magnificent buildings to record his achievements. They will be discussed later.

The attitudes of the historians reflected their origins. The Latin writers, of whom the best known extant example is Tacitus, came mainly from the senatorial class. They looked back at the Republican era as the time of their greatness and resented the fact that Augustus ended the dominance of the Senate. This was Tacitus' view, although he did not include the reign of Augustus himself in his writings. Livy did not write about Rome in his own time, but told of Rome's rise to greatness, and he presented the Senate as the natural leader of the Roman people.

The Greek historians held a different view. Appian in his *Civil War* described the conflicts that tore Rome apart at the end of the Republic, and although the surviving part of his writing does not go beyond 34 B.C. he clearly regarded Augustus as bringing an end to a troubled era.

Even more important was Dio Cassius. Like Thucydides Dio conveyed his views in speeches. Thus in book 56 we have the important speech made by Tiberius at Augustus' funeral which tells of Augustus' achievements. Again in book 52 a speech of Maecenas analyses the institutions of Rome, showing Augustus' contribution, while the institutions themselves are described at more length in the following book.

Velleius Paterculus is an interesting case. He was of Italian origin and served under Tiberius during Augustus' rule. He wrote a long history of Rome up to his own time that is not extant, but a short account in two books survives. He was a man who owed his social position to the empire and like the Greek historians his sympathies were with his masters. He is especially interesting as giving the most favourable account of Tiberius. Suetonius lived much later under the emperor Trajan, whose secretary he was. In his *Lives of the Caesars* he presented the lives of Julius Caesar and of the emperors from Augustus to Domitian. His work is full of scandalous detail, which he obviously enjoyed, and he felt no restraint in the telling, as his stories served to contrast the evil deeds of the early emperors with the virtues of the emperors of his own time.

The year 27 B.C. The first division of powers

It is now time to return to our history. In 29 B.C. Octavian returned to Italy. He had the treasures

18.1 *The Mausoleum of Augustus.*

of Egypt to pay his debts, and he had all the prestige of the conqueror. On entering Rome he celebrated a triple triumph and solemnly closed the doors of the Temple of Janus, to indicate that peace reigned throughout the Roman empire.

The following year was spent in putting his establishment on a peace-time basis. He possessed seventy legions under arms, far too many for his needs. He retained twenty-eight and demobilised the rest. He was far from happy with the Senate. Despite its subservience, he remembered the fate of Caesar, and determined to end the task which his proscriptions had begun. For this purpose he removed from the Senate two hundred members of whose loyalty he was doubtful.

He was now in a position to consider his future. The warning of Caesar's end could not have been far from his thoughts, and his actions show that he was very anxious to avoid the errors made by his predecessor. Caesar had proved that magnanimity to his opponents was unwise.

Octavian followed the opposing course of extreme ruthlessness.

Caesar had made no attempt to disguise the autocratic nature of his position. He had held the office of dictator regularly and in no way conciliated the Senate. In this respect also Octavian was determined to follow a different principle. His aim, while ensuring that he never lost real control, was to disguise his absolute authority as far as he could, and to give the appearance of restoring Republican forms, by setting up a dual control—himself in partnership with the Senate.

In pursuance of this object he dramatically confronted the Senate (from which he had removed all fractious elements) in 27 B.C., and declared that he was prepared to lay down his power. The Senate did what was expected of it and refused to let him withdraw into private life. Instead it proceeded to draw up a scheme for control of the state by himself and the Senate in conjunction. He was to remain as consul, while the Senate in addition to its legislative function was to act as an appeal court in certain cases. To the Senate was returned the right to mint coins. The provinces were divided. The *princeps*,[1] as he was often called (a title of respect normally conferred on the man who directed and led discussion in the Senate), kept the new provinces, and those which required an armed garrison to protect them. The senatorial provinces were generally the older ones, and were rarely protected by arms. One judicial task assigned to the Senate was the trying of extortion cases in the senatorial provinces. Egypt was left to the emperor, and indeed was guarded by him so jealously that no one from the senatorial class was admitted within its borders.

The emperor instituted one necessary reform of the Senate, suggestive of the Athenian system. This body, even after his pruning of its ranks, comprised six hundred members, far too unwieldy a body for effective government. Accordingly he set up a committee of the Senate, which like the Athenian Prytany prepared business for the parent body. It consisted, besides himself, of the two consuls, of one from each of the other magistrates, and of fifteen senators. This committee of the Senate became a very important governing instrument. It was called the Imperial Council.

Administration under Augustus

The provinces were divided between the emperor and the Senate. The governors of the senatorial provinces held office as of old for one year, and had the rank of proconsul. The provinces assigned to the Senate were those where no legions were stationed, so they could not be used as a base from which to challenge the emperor's leadership. The governors of the emperor's provinces, the imperial provinces, were called *legati*, (the delegates of the emperor). They held office for five years with the rank of propraetor, being thus automatically subordinate to the emperor with his consular powers.

It is worth noting that although the Senate appointed the governors of the senatorial provinces the emperor sent out edicts to imperial and senatorial provinces alike, so that in practice his rule extended over all Rome's possessions. More and more inscriptions that were issued by Augustus have been found which show his concern for the administration of the provinces, going into the minutest detail.

One contribution made to administrative harmony was the creation of a *cursus honorum* for the equestrian class, which gave it a political role and responsibility in the state to match that of the senators. As you will remember, the lack of political responsibility on the part of this class helped considerably to bring about the downfall of the Republic.

The equites were at this moment a chastened body. Their numbers had been depleted to an appalling extent by the proscriptions, not least by those instituted in the Second Triumvirate. Moreover, they now no longer had a free hand in tax collecting and contracting. In many cases imperial officials took over their task, and where the tax companies were kept on, they were under strict control.

In compensation the equites were made much more important in the new administration. In the army the senators still filled the higher ranks in the legions, but the equites were used as military tribunes in the legions and as officers in the auxiliary forces.

The financial administration of the provinces was assigned to an equestrian procurator, and in his own sphere he could even call the governor to account. Some smaller provinces were governed by procurators (and this was one of the highest aims of the ambitious equestrian). The prefect of Egypt, most important of all provinces, came from this class. The equites also filled certain other important posts, such as the commander of the imperial bodyguard. The emperor was determined not to expose himself in as foolhardy a fashion as Caesar to assassination.

---

[1]From this title used by Augustus, the early empire came to be known as the Principate, in which, in theory at least, Augustus ruled as the leader of the Senate.

As will be apparent, a civil service was being built up, though not yet of a very complex structure, developed from the civil organisations which Pompey, Caesar and others created for their own purposes in the late Republic. In this civil service the equites played an important role, because they were not so elevated socially and so were less of a danger to the emperor. Similarly the freedmen class was found indispensable, being used extensively in the role of secretaries to the various departments. They often grew to be exceedingly powerful, but even more than the equites they were entirely dependent on the continued favour of their lord.

The equites were in fact a class to which Augustus paid a lot of attention. He was well aware that the senators would never give him more than a grudging support, but with the rising body of the equites, who were moreover grateful that thanks to him they could conduct their business affairs in peace, it was different. He expected and obtained much support from them.

He often referred to his equestrian origins, and he regularly supervised the annual parade of the equites, trying to restore their original link with the cavalry, and he drew on them to fill the gaps left in the Senate with men on whose loyalty he could rely.

The position of the emperor

The most important question of the new constitution was finally the role to be played by the emperor himself. He had to find a way of co-operating with the general administration, and he also had to achieve a special position for himself. The Senate took an important step at this stage (doubtless prompted). They bestowed on the emperor the appellation *Augustus*.[2] This he accepted and ceased to make use of Octavian, the only part of his name which linked him with his less distinguished past. This question of a name may seem unimportant but it was of real significance from the publicity viewpoint (on which he laid great stress). The name Octavian was associated with his equestrian origins, whereas he was anxious to link himself in the public imagination with the aristocratic Julian line. In addition it was connected with his highly unpopular activities as triumvir, including the proscriptions. On the positive side, the name Augustus held a vague religious connotation. It was linked with augury and even with Romulus the founder of Rome, who on that occasion took his famous *augurium* to decide the site of the future capital. These considerations, for a people who had as much regard for ancestral traditions as the Romans, weighed heavily.

Augustus, as he will hereafter be called, took other steps towards an identification of himself with religion. This tendency for rulers to be regarded as in some way divine was long established in the East. There the Greek conqueror Alexander had adopted the practice, but had found strong resistance among his fellow Macedonians. Augustus made use of a very delicate discrimination in the matter. In the East he allowed himself to be worshipped openly as a god, and temples were set up in his honour. In the West the practice of ancestor-worship was linked with emperor-worship. In Italy itself he was more cautious. Open emperor-worship was deprecated. On the other hand, shrines were set up to Augustus and Rome; by deifying Caesar, he was able to speak of himself as the son of the divine Julius, thus at least claiming divine ancestry; he also permitted the flattery of his poets to link him regularly with the gods in general and Apollo in particular. All of these procedures had the effect of removing him from being regarded as a mere common man, which is psychologically valuable for an absolute ruler.

Constitutionally Augustus still based his power on repeated consulships; he also held proconsular power in the provinces and had the personal immunity of a tribune. He had no desire to hold the actual office of a tribune, for a tribune had to belong to a plebeian family. Augustus was firmly determined to be associated with the senatorial aristocracy of Rome.

---

[2]At the same time they called the eighth month Augustus.

Troubles continue. A new power-sharing in 23 B.C.

Augustus, having as he hoped settled the constitutional position in 27 B.C., went abroad. One cannot help wondering if one reason was the desire to leave Rome to simmer down and accept the new arrangements without his distracting presence. His destination was Gaul and Spain. He found no difficulty in settling any administrative problems that required his attention in the Gallic provinces; for Caesar had done his work well. It was different in Spain. There he met stubborn resistance, and proved yet once more that he was not meant to cope with military problems. In the end Agrippa was sent for, who tamed Spain with a ruthless expenditure of blood. When Augustus went back to Italy, Agrippa remained, and set to work to provide Gaul with an excellent system of roads, which was to assist materially in the maintenance of order and prosperity in that area for future years.

Augustus' return to Italy in 24 B.C. was no happy event. His health was bad. It had never been good, and he had suffered from the rigors of campaign life in Spain. Indeed history relates that disease nearly ended his life that year. He was imperilled equally from another source. A conspiracy against his life was discovered which involved two senators, one being Maecenas' brother-in-law. This evidence of dissatisfaction, coupled doubtless with other evidence, made it clear to Augustus that the constitution of 27 B.C. needed revision. This in 23 he proceeded to do.

It was apparent to him that there was some discontent in senatorial ranks. One serious complaint was that Augustus regularly held the office of consul, which meant that each year only one man could attain to that highest of senatorial offices. Augustus therefore abandoned the office. It then became necessary to find some official position which would enable him to retain directive power in the state. This he did through the power of the tribunate. He already held tribunician immunity, but, as was explained, he had no wish actually to become a tribune. Accordingly he took for himself *tribunicia potestas*, the power of a tribune. This conferred on him, in addition to the immunity he already possessed, the all-important right to veto or forbid any law or act of which he disapproved. The same power enabled him to convene both the Senate and the tribal assembly and put measures before them. In his own provinces he still held proconsular authority which set him above his appointed propraetors; in the senatorial provinces his *maius imperium* (greater authority) put him above the proconsuls. This idea he took from Pompey.

Back to the provinces

Having arrived at a new formula of control, Augustus gave it in its turn a chance to prove itself in his absence. In 22 B.C. he set out to tour the Eastern provinces, and remained there until 19 B.C., examining the East and seeing that its organisation accorded with his plan for the empire. In general he kept very close to the settlement of Antony for these countries, namely central provinces with client kingdoms serving as buffer states. He had at this time one important diplomatic victory. He took advantage of dynastic trouble in Armenia in 20 B.C. to have a pro-Roman ruler put on the throne. At the same time he sent his stepson Tiberius, who forced Parthia, which was in a state of great internal turmoil, to acknowledge Roman hegemony and surrender the standards lost in the battle of Carrhae.

This was an important achievement. There had been a strong demand to avenge Carrhae, and now honour was satisfied without endangering a single Roman life. Augustus' coinage commemorates this event with the slogan, 'standards recovered'.

The Senate felt that it had won a victory, and when Augustus left Rome it at first tried to assert its authority. It soon found its limitations. On two occasions the consular elections were a disaster, the people openly demanding that Augustus be made consul. To add to the general gloom there was a corn shortage. When Augustus returned to Rome he found a very chastened Senate.

Agrippa returned with him. Agrippa had completed the conquest of Spain and was entitled to a triumph. This he sternly refused, and Augustus was to take this as a precedent for denying to his generals on future occasions the triumphs which in Republican times they would have celebrated.

Augustus took another important step in 19 B.C. Since the late Republic there had been a dangerous law, introduced by Saturninus and later used by Sulla. This was the *lex de maiestate*. Our nearest equivalent would be the law against high treason. By it anyone who by his actions diminished the majesty of the state was punished, sometimes by exile, in time of greater turmoil by death. Under an emperor the law obviously dealt with attacks on him.

Augustus took responsibility for the execution of this law from the courts and gave it to the Senate. This was in line with his general policy of making the Senate the high court of the land, but in the times of Tiberius and some later emperors it was to cause great problems, especially for the Senate itself.

Augustus tries to introduce moral reform

His next task was to be the least successful project of this generally most successful reign. Augustus decided that morals in Rome were in a low state and, as one result of this, that too few children were born in the governing classes. He himself had treated marriage vows very cavalierly when divorce suited his political advancement. This did not discourage him from the endeavour. In the *leges Juliae* which he promulgated in the years 18–17 B.C., he imposed penalties on bachelors and childless couples. He also gave rewards, including swift promotion, to couples who produced three children or more. These laws had little effect, beyond giving a profitable new field for the *delatores* or informers,[3] who extracted blackmail as a result. He also weakened the effect of his law by bestowing the privileges of those possessing three children on men who had merited well by him, but did not come in

that category. Even Virgil and Horace, who were bachelors, were given this honour. Still, for propaganda purposes he had to be successful, and in 17 B.C. he commemorated his success by celebrating Rome's centenary (a little early) with the Secular Games, as they were called. They were said to have been of Republican origin, but this is the first occasion we hear of them. They were to be performed after some calamity in hope of better times to come, and certainly Augustus and his people could feel the time very appropriate. For this Horace wrote his *Carmen Saeculare*, which was sung by the young men and women of equestrian rank before Augustus. Plays were also performed.

The succession problem

Another problem began to vex Augustus in 23, one which he found more difficult to solve than any other, that of a successor. The reason was that although he had a daughter Julia, he had no son, and he was most anxious to be succeeded by one of his own blood. He had two adopted sons, Tiberius and Drusus, Livia's sons by her previous marriage but he did not wish them to be his successors. At first he chose his young nephew Marcellus. He married him to Julia and raised him to a consulship well before his time, appointing Agrippa as his guardian. His own illness may have made him feel that a secure position had to be achieved at all costs. But in 23 B.C. Marcellus died suddenly. His sad end is alluded to in Virgil's *Aeneid*, and Augustus is said to have wept when that line was read to him and Livia. Augustus next tried to ensure a successor from his own blood by marrying Agrippa to Julia in 21 B.C. As we shall see, this solution was no more successful than his first attempt.

---

[3]Since there was no public prosecutor any citizen could charge another with some offence against the state. If the *delator*, as he was called, proved his case, he received a proportion of the malefactor's estate—such a system was unavoidable but was obviously open to serious abuse.

Rome's frontiers

Augustus now turned his mind to the question of Rome's frontiers. Rome's possessions had been generally organised, but some frontier areas of importance were not under Roman control, and it was time they were conquered. Augustus had the perennial problem that he was no military genius himself, and consequently needed someone, preferably related to him, who could fight his battles yet remain faithful. Agrippa had served in this role but he was growing old. Augustus now began to make extensive use of his stepsons Tiberius and Drusus.

One area which obviously needed to be conquered in order to maintain contact with Rome's provinces in the East and the West was the Alpine region (in which area Switzerland falls in modern times). The work of conquest had already begun in that region but in 16 B.C. Tiberius and Drusus were sent there, and by 14 B.C. they returned successful. Noricum and Rhaetia were established as imperial provinces.

Two further problems remained. The Danube formed an excellent natural boundary to the Roman possessions in the northeast. To Tiberius fell the task of conquering the tribes in the Danube area, and this he did successfully between 12 and 9 B.C. In the west the Rhine had been the boundary, and this river, like the Danube, was a good natural division. The disadvantage was that the Rhine-Danube frontier was very long and had a large elbow in it. A much shorter frontier could be achieved by extending the boundary beyond the Rhine to the Elbe River. Drusus undertook this task and, helped by the chronic disunity of the German tribes, succeeded in doing so in the same period (12–9 B.C.). Unhappily he fell from a horse at the conclusion of his campaign, and a broken leg with ensuing complications cost him his life. It was left to Tiberius in the years 8 to 7 B.C. to complete the conquest of this area.

More succession problems

It would appear on the surface as if all was well for Augustus, but this was far from being the case. The trouble lay in the other problem, that of succession. At first Augustus' plans seemed to be working out well; for Agrippa and Julia had two sons, Gaius and Lucius, whom Augustus duly adopted. It was a blow then when in 12 B.C. Agrippa died, while the two heirs were still children.

Augustus took no risks. Tiberius was husband to Agrippa's daughter Vipsania, whom he loved dearly. Augustus forced him to divorce her and marry the already much married Julia. Julia had, perhaps through natural wildness, perhaps in reaction to being a mere political pawn, begun already to gain a reputation. Tiberius was now merely a guardian to the two young heirs until they should reach maturity, a barren prospect. In 6 B.C. Augustus tried to conciliate him by giving him the all-important *tribunicia potestas*. This had already been bestowed on Agrippa, and was a means of establishing a successor in a position of authority. Tiberius was not propitiated. Weary of unrequited labour, and of intrusion even into his private life, he retired to the island of Rhodes, where for the next ten years he lived in seclusion and disgrace, as a private citizen.

Augustus' building activities

This would seem to be an appropriate moment to review some of Augustus' other activities. From Caesar he inherited a concern for the city of Rome, its streets and its buildings. Agrippa was first entrusted with this responsibility, and in 33 B.C., as aedile, undertook a programme of repair and reconstruction of Rome's public buildings. Augustus himself took over the water-supply, which he increased to meet Rome's rapidly growing population. As well he built the *Forum Augusti*, which assisted in the same functions as the *Forum Caesaris* of Caesar. Augustus' proud boast was that he found Rome built of brick and left it built in marble. This was not an idle claim. Temples especially benefited from his attentions, and assisted his effort to revive traditional Roman religion.

Augustus had another reason for his building activity. Like the Greek tyrants he found public

18.2 The theatre of Marcellus. This was built by Augustus in memory of his nephew Marcellus.

buildings an excellent means of advertising his achievements to the general populace, whom he would not have reached through the written word, and they were indeed an impressive sight.

In the middle of the Roman Forum Augustus built a temple to the deified Julius Caesar, decorating it in front with the *rostra* (beaks) taken from the enemy ships captured at the battle of Actium. Nearby stood the Arch of Augustus, which he dedicated in 19 B.C. Further on lay the *Forum Caesaris* beside which was the *curia* (Senate House), which he rebuilt after it was burnt at Caesar's funeral. Then we come to the *Forum Augusti* with its temple to *Mars Ultor* (Avenging Mars). This temple served an important purpose. As we noted earlier Augustus took from the senators the right to a triumph, which in Republican times had marked the pinnacle of a Roman aristocrat's success. To make up for this he set up in the Temple of *Mars Ultor* a row of statues, which went back to mythical times and the origins of his own family. Mars and Venus were there and the heroes of Rome's

history. Augustus gave those generals who would formerly have been awarded a triumph the right to add their statue, bearing an inscription giving their name and achievements. So a Roman senator could still celebrate his doings but strictly within the confines imposed by Augustus.

Beside the Tiber north of the city lay the massive but not very lovely building, the mausoleum of Augustus, his family tomb, first used for Marcellus. In the Campus Martius was the *Ara Pacis* (Altar of Peace), dedicated by the Senate in 9 B.C. Augustus always set great store by the fact that he brought peace to war-troubled Rome, and the altar records this fact. It depicts Augustus and his family advancing in procession, including the real warrior Agrippa, coming back from the wars in Gaul and Spain. Finally there was the Pantheon, built by Agrippa in 27 B.C. to the gods of the seven planets. It had huge statues of Augustus and Agrippa in front and contributed to Augustus' revival of traditional religion.

Finance and fire brigades

An important base for Augustus' power lay in his wealth, which owed much originally to Egypt. He had his own treasury, the *fiscus* while the Republican *aerarium* continued under the management of the Senate, although it very often had to be helped out of difficulties by the emperor. In 14 B.C. Augustus claimed the sole right to coin gold and silver in Rome, leaving copper coinage to the Senate.

The main revenue still came from the provinces, which paid both a poll tax on individuals and a land tax. One heavy burden on Augustus was providing for the pension payments to his army. The army in this period was changed in character from a mobile fighting force to a stationary army designed to hold the frontiers. Legionaries were Roman citizens, while the discharged auxiliary troops and their descendants gained the same privilege. That, incidentally, meant normally that the second generation of auxiliary troops filled the ranks of the legions. Augustus had experienced all the problems of settling retired veterans on the land, and he therefore took the wise step of substituting in 13 B.C. a pension in money for the earlier land grant. In A.D. 6 a fund was established for this purpose, into which went a tax on inheritance and on the freeing of slaves. Nonetheless the pensions of the troops were never easy to meet and throughout the empire we find emperors delaying their armies' retirement, and resultant uprisings.

Augustus used his coinage for another purpose. During most of the Republic no living Roman could appear on a coin. This rule broke down in the last years of the Republic. Julius Caesar issued coins in his name, and Augustus regularly issued coins with the portrait of himself and his family, a practice followed by all succeeding emperors, and adopted by coinage such as our own in modern times.

As well the coins served as a cheap and effective means of giving widespread publicity to the emperor's achievements. Augustus used them in this way and he was followed in this by his successors. We have noted that he announced the recovery of the standards from Parthia in this manner, and as early as 28 B.C. he issued coins with the inscription, 'champion of liberty'.

One of his senators, Egnatius Rufus, lent unexpected and unwelcome aid to Augustus. As aedile he founded a fire brigade to deal with the terribly prevalent incidence of fires in the city. Augustus treated this as a flagrant act of civil disobedience, and accused Rufus of trying to gather together his firemen with a view to securing a small private army in case of a chance of conspiracy. The fire-brigade accordingly collapsed, but the emperor himself founded one in A.D. 6.

Changes in the consulship and the role of the Senate

Although Augustus' reforms of 23 B.C. had brought general stability to his constitutional position, modifications were introduced later. He had abandoned the consulship as the basis to his power, but he claimed the right to take his seat officially between the two consuls. He also did take on the office of consul twice after this date for special purposes.[4] This had little significance. Of more importance was the change he introduced in 12 B.C. a practice used on occasion by Caesar before him whereby *consules suffecti* were created near the end of each year, replacing the ordinary consuls. Thus there were now four consuls in each year. This had a double effect. It meant that there were more men of consular rank to fill civil-service posts, and that was necessary; for there were new provinces to administer with the reorganisation of the empire, and there were other offices being created to fulfil special needs. At the same time it lessened the prestige of the consulship, thus making the office less of a threat to Augustus himself. Augustus did reserve to himself the right to recommend candidates for the consulship, but it was a power he rarely used.

---

[4]In fact, to introduce Gaius, and later Lucius, officially to public life.

At the same time he made some changes in the recruitment of the Senate. For many years senators' sons had become senators unofficially, but he made it official. The *comitia centuriata* and the *comitia tributa* thereby lost all importance. He also imposed a minimum financial requirement for senators of four hundred thousand sesterces, raised later to a million. The equites also had a minimum standard, probably of four hundred thousand, but naturally they normally far surpassed it. However, he gave financial assistance to worthy but indigent candidates so they could meet their requirements, a generosity which he claimed put him quite out of pocket at times!

The army

The army under Augustus eventually consisted of twenty-five legions and an equal number of auxiliary troops. There were eight legions on the Rhine, which was divided into the Upper and Lower Germany, there were five on the Danube, three each in Spain, Syria and Egypt, two in Dalmatia and one in North Africa.

The soldiers served normally for sixteen (later twenty years) while the auxiliary forces served for twenty-five. There were nine cohorts in Italy, the praetorian guard, who were Augustus' own bodyguard, and they were to become the only force recruited in Italy. They were commanded by two prefects.

Trouble abroad. Tiberius named as successor

So far, despite some set-backs, Augustus had carried most of his projects through successfully. This was not to last.

The departure of Tiberius to private life was followed by a series of events, many of them disastrous. In 2 B.C. Julia's misconduct could no longer be ignored. She was exiled to an island, and a number of her associates, including the poet Ovid, suffered a similar fate.

In A.D. 2 Tiberius came back to Rome, but in the same year Lucius died, while in A.D. 4 Gaius was wounded in action and likewise died. Augustus had now no choice, and reluctantly adopted Tiberius. This long delayed and unwilling acceptance of Tiberius as his heir, together with the break-up of Tiberius' family life should be kept in mind when one observes the latter's misanthropic tendencies in his principate.

Tiberius was granted the *tribunicia potestas* again and was sent out at once to resume his management of Augustus' military plans. He soon found that he was needed, not to make further conquests but to stave off imminent disaster. First, a huge revolt broke out in the Danubian area, which took three years to crush.

Meanwhile trouble was preparing elsewhere. The area of Germany between the Rhine and the Elbe had never been thoroughly subdued, and the densely wooded and often marshy country was ill-suited to Rome's usual policy of setting up a network of roads and cities. Then two circumstances combined to precipitate action. A nationalist leader arose, Arminius (compare the modern name Hermann, by which he is known in Germany itself), who managed to unite that notoriously disunited people. At the same time a governor Varus was appointed, who gave them their opportunity.

Varus has in some histories been accused of greed and injustice, but more recent research would suggest that his crime was rather over-trustfulness and lack of care. In any case, Varus, leading three legions, allowed himself to be ambushed in thick forest country. The area has been identified with the Teutoburg Forest, and a monument has been set up to commemorate it by the Germans, but, despite many searches, no certain identification of the battle area has been achieved. He was killed, the legions were almost annihilated, and disgrace was added to carnage when the standards were lost as well. As a result Augustus abandoned the Elbe frontier and set up his standing garrisons on the Rhine.

In the East Augustus consciously refrained from further conquests. The first prefect of Egypt, Gallus (29 B.C.), did, it is true, extend

Rome's territory to the First Cataract of the Nile, which was to be the limit of their possessions throughout the imperial period. He also embarked on further conquests, but his vainglorious attempt to claim the credit (he even set up statues of himself and recorded his victories on inscriptions in the province) brought upon him disgrace and not long after suicide.

The provinces

Elsewhere in the East Augustus kept to Antony's system of central provinces surrounded by buffer states under vassal princes. He did break up the province of Macedonia into smaller units, a practice he followed also in Spain and Gaul. Later, all the buffer states became provinces with their rulers' deaths. As a result of these two procedures as well as the conquests in the Danubian area, the number of provinces rose from eleven to twenty-eight.

The final result then was a larger number of smaller provinces, with a standing army guarding the borders. The main line of defence lay along the Rhine and Danube. The division between senatorial and imperial provinces was maintained, but strict control was kept in the hands of Augustus. He ruled all the provinces that were either important or strategically significant. He had full control of the army.

Despite his formal show of a dual role, all real control rested in Augustus. Foreign embassies came to see him not the Senate, and he handled the treaties made between Rome and foreign peoples.

In Gaul there were four provinces. The original province was known as Gallia Narbonensis, while the Gaul conquered by Caesar was divided into Gallia Belgica, Gallia Lugdunensis, and Gallia Aquitania. Spain was divided into three, the old province (left to the Senate), Hispania Baetica, while the rest was divided into Lusitania, and Hispania Tarraconensis. In the East Galatia had been made a province in 26 B.C. The Upper Rhine and Danube areas became respectively the provinces of Raetia and Noricum, and in 9 B.C. the provinces of Pannonia and Dalmatia

were established in the troubled area north of Greece.

Death of Augustus. An evaluation

In A.D. 14 at the age of seventy-six, the emperor, whose frail health had so often threatened to end his career, met a peaceful end. His rule had been one of unparalleled achievement. Although himself no soldier, Augustus had established (by conquest at some points) frontiers for the empire, which were with a few minor alterations to be religiously observed as long as the empire lasted. He took the incredibly difficult step of transforming the state from its oligarchic Republican form of government to an absolutist imperial state, with remarkably little fuss, and after the proscriptions of the Triumvirate were over, without much bloodshed. In almost every field of administration Augustus set the pattern that later emperors were to follow. Even in the question of succession, his procedure, the granting of *tribunicia potestas*, set a precedent, which was used, whether the heir was the next of kin, or, as did happen not infrequently, adopted.

Literature

Finally it is necessary to examine the literature which Augustus fostered in his principate. This literature has more than ordinary historical significance, because Augustus consciously used his writers for the purpose of propaganda. The term *propaganda* should not be understood in too literal a sense. Augustus' clients (for that was what his writers in fact were) were writers of no mean stature, and when they wrote praising the Rome of Augustus, they did so from a very real conviction of the imperial destiny of Rome. None the less it is true that Virgil received back his ancestral farm owing to Augustus' protection, and that Horace, who at first fought on the Republican side, was similarly rewarded with his famous Sabine farm.

This side of Augustus' work was at first entrusted to his equestrian friend, Maecenas. He made the contacts, founded a literary circle, and tactfully suggested the writing which could serve the greater glory of Augustus' Rome.[5]

Virgil was a willing supporter. He had a genuine gratitude to Augustus for bringing peace to the Romans, and a profound admiration of the imperial destiny of Rome. In his earliest work, the *Eclogues* or *Bucolics*, he followed a pastoral theme. His characters, mainly shepherds, sang of their loves and lives, and in some at least of the *Eclogues* Virgil celebrated the peace brought to the Italian country-side by its new master. Perhaps the most famous of these writings was the fourth *Eclogue* in which Virgil sang of the coming of a Golden Age with a new-born ruler, in which war should be no longer, and nature should bear prolifically. Christian writers have taken this poem as looking forward to the return of the Messiah, and Virgil won some favour in early Christian writings as consequence.

This work he followed with the *Georgics*. He was well suited to write this poem, as he had himself been reared on a farm, and the poem was a didactic one, fulfilling two tasks: it told how one could run a well-conducted farm, and at the same time it praised the rural life. This poem chimed in well with Augustus' rather unsuccessful attempts to persuade the Romans to go back on the land.

Finally came the greatest poem of all, the *Aeneid*. In this work Virgil told how Aeneas came to Italy from Troy to found a city from which should one day come the great race of Rome. Augustus was not neglected. The goddess who guided Aeneas' steps was Venus, the patron goddess of the Julian clan. Also Aeneas was described as having an infant son Iulus, who was the mythical ancestor of the Julian family of Caesar and so Augustus. The wars with Carthage were explained by Aeneas' encounter with Dido, the queen who founded Carthage, whom Aeneas loved and left. No schoolboy has since approved that desertion. In the famous sixth book of the *Aeneid* Aeneas went down to the underworld and was vouchsafed a view of the heroes who were to lead Rome to greatness. It was then that he saw the premature shade of the luckless Marcellus, so provoking tears from Augustus himself.

Horace was a more reluctant advocate. His lyric muse was whimsical and very private, and he long refused to embark on patriotic themes. In the end, however, he yielded and sang of the peace Augustus brought Italy, and of the victories his stepsons won in the Alps. In his *Carmen Saeculare*, sung at Rome's centenary, he also sounded a patriotic note. None the less, Horace never forgot that he had once been a Republican, and one feels at times a cynical wonder on his own part at his new-found conformism.

The great prose writer of the Augustan age, Livy, seems to have owed no financial gratitude to Augustus, but to have been a wealthy man in his own right. Nevertheless, in his history of Rome, he too took the Romans back to their Trojan origins. He too told in his history the patriotic tale of the inevitable emergence of a great imperialist nation.

In his history, too, the Punic War figured prominently, as was right, in that at this time Rome finally achieved nationhood.

Tibullus in his elegies also sang of the peace brought to Rome by Augustus. The other great lyric writer Propertius rarely consented to be channelled to any such public themes, but sang of his love for his mistress Cynthia, unconcerned with imperial Rome.

Finally, the frivolous Ovid, court poet *par excellence*, was in his own way equally hard to confine. He sang of the art of love or the remedy of love; he touched on mythology in his *Fasti* and his *Metamorphoses*. Rarely did his elegant pen conform to nobler themes, and finally, we think through implication in Julia's misdemeanours, he was banished to Tomi on the Euxine, where he was inconsolable, but not more heroic.

All told, Augustus was very successful in his creation of a public image. His disreputable past was successfully buried. Both Virgil and Horace turned elegant compliments on his divine relationship, and his early opponents were successfully forgotten. Both Pompey and Antony suffered this fate.

---

[5]After his relative was found to be implicated in the 23 B.C. conspiracy Maecenas lost favour and retired from Augustus' court.

Date table

B.C.

27 Octavian renounces special powers.
    New dispensation and title of Augustus.
23 Augustus renounces consulship and
    uses *tribunicia potestas.*
20 Roman standards returned by Parthia.
17 *Ludi Saeculares* (Secular or Centenary
    Games).
15 Alpine regions conquered by Tiberius
    and Drusus.
12 Death of Agrippa.

A.D.

4   Adoption of Tiberius.
9   Disaster of Varus.
14 Death of Augustus.

Select quotations

1 Horace, *Odes* III 5, 1–12:
*We believe that Jupiter rules when we hear his
thunders in heaven; Augustus will be regarded
as a very present deity when he has added
Britain to the empire and the fierce Parthians.
Has a soldier of Crassus lived in base wedlock
with a barbarian wife and (O senate and
perverted ways!) grown old serving a father-in-
law who was our foe, obeying a Parthian King,
though himself a Marsian or Apulian, forgetting
the Sacred Shields, the name of Rome and
undying Vesta, while Jupiter and the city of
Rome are unharmed?*

2 Virgil, *Aeneid* VI, 841–853:
(Aeneas views the underworld.)
*Who would leave you unspoken, great Cato or
Cossus? Who the Gracchan family, or the two
Scipios, twin thunderbolts of war, the bane of
Libya, Fabricius powerful though poor, or you
Serranus, sowing the furrow? Where, Fabii, do
you drag a weary man? you are Fabius
Maximus, who alone will restore our state by
masterly inaction.*
*Others will show more skill to give bronze the
breath of life (so I at least believe), or will create*

*living figures from marble, will plead cases
better, will measure the movements of the sky
and the rising of the stars. You, Roman,
remember to rule the peoples (these will be your
arts) to impose the habit of peace, to spare the
conquered, and bring low the proud.*

Further reading

R. Syme, *Roman Revolution*, Oxford
    Paperbacks, 1960.
E.T. Salmon, *A History of the Roman World
    from 30 B.C. to A.D. 138*, Methuen, 1944.
M. Grant, *Roman History from Coins*,
    Cambridge University Press, 1958.
Suetonius, *The Twelve Emperors*, Penguin
    Classic.
F. Millar, and E. Segal, *Caesar Augustus,
    Seven Aspects*, Clarendon Press, Oxford,
    1984.

Topics for essays or discussion

1 It has been said that Augustus learnt from
  Caesar's mistakes. Do you think that earlier
  events did show Augustus how to achieve
  absolute power?
2 Examine the constitutional arrangements
  made in 27 B.C. What was their importance
  and why were they not finally acceptable?
3 What caused the crisis of 23 B.C.? Why was
  Augustus able to resolve it?
4 On what basis did Augustus finally establish
  his power? Would it be correct to call it a
  joint administration, shared with the
  Senate?
5 Examine the part played by (a) the senators
  (b) the equites (c) the freedmen in
  Augustus' civil service.
6 Analyse Augustus' organisation of the
  provinces. Why did he succeed where his
  predecessors failed?
7 Discuss Augustus' frontier policy. Was it
  necessary, and why did it not prove as
  successful as his other plans?

8 What part did the army play in the principate of Augustus?

9 How did Augustus settle the problem of succession? What difficulties did he encounter?

10 'Augustus took over the idea of Divine Kingship from the East but modified it to suit Roman conditions.' Discuss.

11 'With Augustus concord was brought about through violence.' Is this a fair estimate of his achievement?

12 Discuss Augustus' moral legislation. Why did it fail?

Chapter 19

Tiberius and Gaius

Sources

FOR THE RULE of Tiberius we have Tacitus' *Annals* as well as Suetonius and Dio, to which we may add the favourable account of Velleius Paterculus. Unforunately these sources, apart from Velleius Paterculus, are heavily prejudiced against the emperor. Tacitus loathed the emperor Domitian and seems to have conceived Tiberius as an emperor of the same type.

This brings us to consider how this prejudice arose. Here the character of the man played a big part. Tiberius was arrogant, like so many of the Claudian clan. He was an intellectual, and in many ways seems to have enjoyed his exile in Rhodes with his friends, the Greek philosophers and mathematicians. He was of a reserved nature, disliked ostentation and thoroughly hated the games and gladiatorial shows the common people craved. He also had a dry wit which did not make him popular. Finally, when he went to Capri to live in isolation this gave rumour-mongers free reign to make the very worst and most ill-founded accusations.

Recent research has enabled us to set the record straight and discover in him not an easy man but one of Rome's most capable emperors. Luckily Tacitus was too good an historian to twist his facts to suit his prejudices and that has made our task easier. Inscriptions have also been discovered, which show activity not disclosed by histories.

For the rule of Gaius we unfortunately do not possess Tacitus, but only Dio and the scandal-mongering Suetonius. Gaius' disastrous rule gave him full scope, so we must be careful in evaluating our sources.

The succession

When Augustus died in A.D. 14 Tiberius, who was aged 55, was in full control of the armies, which held him in well deserved respect, and he held the proconsular and tribunician powers. There was therefore no difficulty in his succession.

First, however, the funeral of Augustus was held with all due pomp. His ashes were deposited in the Mausoleum, and steps were taken for him to be deified as Julius Caesar had been before him. His will was then read out, which included gifts to the people and donatives to the army, all duly honoured, though not at once. Augustus, who on earlier occasions had tried to arrange two tiers of succession did so here also, asking not Tiberius's son Drusus but Tiberius' nephew Germanicus to be the next in line to Tiberius. This Tiberius conscientiously accepted.

One of Tiberius' aims in which he was singularly unsuccessful was to rule in genuine partnership with the Senate, something of which Augustus had only made a pretence. The Senate knew the reality of Tiberius military power and distrusted his approaches, which were not made easier by his reserved and haughty bearing. Tacitus dismissed Tiberius' attempt to consult the Senate as hypocrisy. This was unfair, but it did not work. In line with this policy Tiberius summoned the Senate and formally requested their wishes in the matter of succession. He finally accepted the role of *princeps*, but refused the title of *imperator*, although in fact none deserved it better, for he had been hailed as imperator or victorious general seven times by his troops on the field of battle. He also only took the consulship three times during his rule, and then for special purposes. When the Senate tried to name a month after him he refused, asking them drily what they would do if they had thirteen emperors!

Revolts on the frontiers suppressed

Conditions in the army were not favourable at Tiberius' accession. The recruitment of troops had grown ever harder to the end of Augustus' rule, which meant that their quality declined. At the same time it was found necessary to lengthen their period of service, and this created discontent. As a result it is not surprising that the new emperor was immediately faced with two mutinies, one in Lower Germany on the Rhine, one in Pannonia on the Danube.

Tiberius did not take the field to face either uprising. His past military career was such that he had no fear of the charge of cowardice, and he wisely held himself in reserve, sending Drusus to Pannonia, while Germanicus was already at the Rhine.

Drusus fulfilled his task with admirable firmness, aided by an eclipse of the moon, which roused the soldiers' superstition. He gained peace without making any extravagant promises.

Germanicus was less successful. He employed uncalled-for histrionics, even threatening suicide. (One unkind soldier offered him his sword.) He then promised the rebels a donative and a shortened term of service. Although he forged letters from Tiberius to give substance to his promises, the soldiers were not impressed, and he had to rifle the army chest in order to supply a donative on the spot. He persuaded the soldiers to execute their own ringleaders, which they did with enthusiasm, but to the detriment of discipline.

When Tiberius heard how his two deputies had fared, he made concessions to the troops of Pannonia, so that they should not suffer at the expense of the Rhine army. He did, however, amend the promises so that they would be within

reason. It was not an auspicious beginning for Tiberius' heir Germanicus, and the emperor must have begun already to feel those doubts of the impetuous youth which later events did nothing to dispel.

Shortly afterwards, a conspiracy by Libo was discovered. This man had hoped to take advantage of the two princes' return to Rome to assassinate both them and the emperor. When the plot was unearthed, he committed suicide.

Tiberius carries on Augustus' policies

Tiberius generally carried on the policies of Augustus. He took the formal steps to allow the Senate to elect their own new members, in line with what Augustus had planned, and he constituted the Senate as the high court, again in line with Augustus' reforms.

Like Augustus he kept to himself the minting of gold and silver, but once more he followed Augustus by minting at Lugdunum (Lyons), leaving the old mint on the Capitol to the Senate.

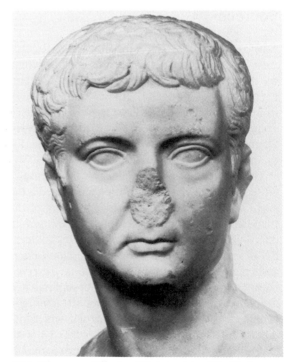

19.1 *The young Tiberius (42 B.C.–A.D. 37). He became the second Roman emperor.*

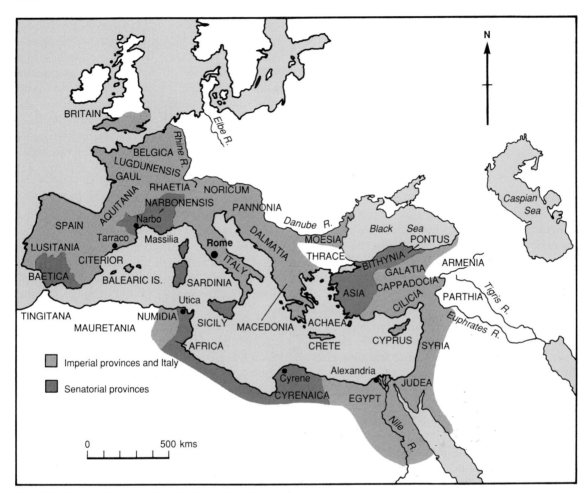

19.2 *The Roman Empire under the Julio-Claudians.*

Finally he also built up the equites, and he extended the area for their recruitment. He drew on the officer class of the army, in particular the centurions, and also on the provincials who held posts in their local government.

Germanicus is recalled and sent East

One of Tiberius' first acts was to recall Germanicus from the Rhine. Germanicus, after putting down the mutiny, had been engaging in a number of forays into Germany with doubtful success. Tiberius had too much regard for his legions to wish to lose any of them in the same way as Varus had in the past. On his return to Rome, Germanicus was consoled with a somewhat undeserved triumph and a new task was found for the young man.

In the East, Tiberius had continued Augustus' policy of converting client kingdoms into provinces. This happened in the case of Cappadocia, Commagene and Cilicia.

Germanicus was sent to see that the change to the new administration took place peacefully and to look into the ever-troublesome question of Parthia and Armenia.

All was not well in the East. Tiberius had doubts of Germanicus, not without cause, and ordered Piso, the new governor of Syria, to keep an eye on him. Unfortunately, Piso was a man without tact, who was personally a bitter enemy of the young prince. Consequently, when

Germanicus asked him to bring troops to help put Zeno on the throne of Armenia, Piso refused. The absence of Piso did not hinder Germanicus' plans; for he proceeded to carry out the annexation of Cilicia and Commagene.

After these tasks were done, he went to Egypt, breaking Augustus' regulation that no one above equestrian rank should enter the country. He opened a granary to relieve a famine there, and had statues of himself erected. Tiberius was incensed.

Germanicus was not to continue his tactless career much longer. He caught a fever, became convinced that Piso had poisoned him, and died soon after, bidding his wife Agrippina avenge him. Despite his attempts at self-justification, Piso was put on trial. He was condemned and took his own life.

The death of Germanicus was a terrible blow to Tiberius. His enemies had never believed he was sincere in giving preference to Germanicus over his son Drusus as his heir, and now ready to hand was evidence to support their suspicions.

Were the informers unleashed?

Needless to say, the *delatores* profited by his event. Tiberius did not encourage the breed. He constantly refused to allow anyone to be condemned for misconduct or disrespect in regard to himself. Yet Tiberius could not overlook the fact that the current situation with its conflict of loyalties would breed conspiracies, and it would have been the height of folly to disregard utterly the reports of the delatores. So while we cannot deny that delatores were active under Tiberius, we must insist that this was to be attributed not to malice on Tiberius' part, but to the general uncertainty in his principate, especially with regard to the succession. Amid the many misfortunes that Augustus encountered in his succession plans, he was careful always to have some possible adult successor in a strategic position. Tiberius was less successful in achieving that. Moreover his wavering between Drusus and Agrippina's children was to favour factional intrigue, even after Germanicus died.

These delatores, who were mentioned in the chapter on Augustus (p. 170), were the Roman equivalent of the Greek informers or *sycophants*. Like them they arose because of the lack of a public prosecutor. If a crime was committed against the state, a private individual could prosecute and be rewarded with some of the offender's estate. Under Roman law they received 25 per cent. The practice in both countries was a dangerous one, encouraging blackmail.

For all that, when the rule of Tiberius was carefully examined it was not proved that a reign of terror existed. This is not to say that there were no problems. Tiberius was a conscientious man and attended the senatorial court in person. The Senate was intimidated by the presence of this stern old man with his sardonic humour and tried to placate him by imposing harsh sentences. Tiberius had repeatedly to stop them condemning out of hand anyone accused of misconduct towards their emperor. Piso was condemned, but not on the charge of poisoning Germanicus, which was thrown out of court, but correctly for illegally entering his province after the end of his command. A number of people were prosecuted with good reason for misconduct in the provinces, an area where Tiberius was concerned to stop malpractice. But all of this is a very different picture from that presented by such writers as Suetonius.

Administration

Augustus had led the tax companies continue, though somewhat curbed. Tiberius left them only harbour dues, collecting other taxes through his own officials. Tiberius aimed at peace in the provinces, which meant that he spent less money guarding them. He practised a strict economy, which brought the empire as a whole to an unprecedented state of prosperity (soon dissipated by his two successors). Yet even here Rome was not grateful; for one of his economies was in public spectacles. Tiberius was confident, as a tried general, in the loyalty of his troops and made no attempt to woo the mob. They were not slow to see his essential contempt of them.

This economy was not mere miserliness. The treasury was at a low ebb on Augustus' death, after some of the gruelling campaigns in the latter part of his rule. Nor was Tiberius grasping. He consistently refused legacies, and, as time went on, repeatedly gave relief to cities smitten by fire or other disasters, in a manner imitated later by the Flavians. Nor did he allow his subordinates to use flogging to facilitate the collection of taxes.

He did not extend citizenship further in the provinces, a policy in line with his general conservatism. Actually the provinces had not yet assimilated enough of Roman ways to be very useful citizens. But he developed their system of roads, especially in Spain and Gaul, which rendered these countries more prosperous (as trade flowed more freely), easier to defend, and finally more accessible to Romanising influences. Characteristically, he did not spend money on new public buildings, but preferred to restore those which had fallen into disrepair, retaining their old names, and gaining no self-advertisement from them.

Under his rule the frontier did not extend right to the Danube. Actually the later emperors too could afford little more than outposts on that river. The real frontier was the Drave, and there too new efficient highways were constructed.

Tiberius kept a very close watch on the provinces. If he found a reliable governor, he kept him on year after year (for twenty-four years in one case, and often five to ten years).

This meant that many young aristocrats lost their chance of making a fortune, as in the old days, in the provinces. Tiberius used the same policy with his equestrian procurators, extending rule for the honest, granting no mercy to the corrupt. He encouraged local organisations in the provinces to report misconduct by their governing body, and this attitude was even less understood by his contemporaries.

The rise of Sejanus

Meanwhile problems were developing that created much uncertainty in Rome. After the death of Germanicus his widow Agrippina, convinced that he had been poisoned, openly intrigued with those opposed to Tiberius.

Here an opportunity arose for a new figure, Sejanus. His father had served with distinction under Augustus as prefect of the praetorian guard, and his son took over the post, even though it meant continuing to be an equestrian, when he could easily have gained senatorial rank. By his industry he soon made himself indispensable to the ageing emperor. This apparent modesty covered an even loftier ambition.

With the death of Germanicus, it would have been possible for Tiberius to fall back on his son, Drusus, as successor. This Tiberius would not do. He did make Drusus his heir, but only on the understanding that he held the position until the children of Germanicus and Agrippina could take over. It was not easy for Drusus, but he seems to have accepted good-naturedly enough.

This did not deter his supporters. A faction soon arose, prepared to fight for his interests, in the hope that, if successful, they would carry him with them.

For the events that follow we have to rely on inferior sources. There is a gap in Tacitus at this point and Velleius Paterculus' account ends before the fall of Sejanus. As a result some of the events of this period are not very clear.

Sejanus was steadily increasing his influence with Tiberius. The praetorian guard had been dispersed throughout Italy. Sejanus succeeded in having it brought together and put in a camp just outside Rome. This was eminently sensible, as one of its main functions was the protection of the emperor. Tiberius could hardly have foreseen the future, when it played a leading part in making and unmaking emperors. For the moment the change was advantageous to Sejanus, as he could by appointing his friends to the post of praetorian prefect, gain military support for his aspirations.

Just how far Sejanus' ambitions went is not certain. He has been accused of aiming to supplant Tiberius. This is unlikely. It is more probable that he desired to remove all rivals (and indeed nearly succeeded) so that he would become Tiberius' heir.

At first his plans worked smoothly. Drusus' wife, Livilla, was contemptuous at his lack of ambition. She became Sejanus' mistress, lured by his promise that he would make her his empress, and that her children would be the heirs. In 23 Drusus died. Ancient authorities accuse his wife of the deed.

Tiberius was overwhelmed, but led the children of Agrippina before the Senate, announcing them as his successors. Sejanus was now helped by Agrippina's stupidity. She was a silly and arrogant woman and made no attempt to conceal her dislike of Tiberius' minister.

Sejanus found little difficulty in having a number of Agrippina's supporters executed. The emperor, however, refused Sejanus' next request, that he be allowed to marry Livilla.

The successive deaths of Germanicus and Drusus, combined with his undeserved unpopularity, were too much for a man naturally not at ease with his fellow-men. He left Rome on a tour of Campania and went from there to the isle of Capri, leaving Sejanus to rule on his behalf.

In 28 Agrippina and her son Nero were guilty of indiscretion. Sejanus was now more powerful and Tiberius was weary of her rudeness. He made no objection when Sejanus sent her and her son into exile, jailing her second son not long after.

It should be noted that Tiberius' mother, Livia, died in A.D. 29 and her death removed a restraining influence on events in Rome.

Gaius, Agrippina's youngest son, was safe. He was staying with his uncle. When he was a child his mother paraded him through the camps wearing tiny military boots, as a result of which the soldiers nicknamed him Caligula. The name stayed with him, as did a certain popularity with the army.

In 31 Sejanus was made consul with Tiberius, and granted pro-consular power. He was also permitted to become engaged to Livilla. He needed only the tribunicia potestas, and began exultantly to curry favour with the nobility, seeking out the newly made senatorial families, which Tiberius had neglected.

He hoped too soon. Antonia, Germanicus' mother, had seen her daughter-in-law and grandchildren exiled one by one. She finally wrote to Tiberius warning him of Sejanus' intrigues.

Tiberius was convinced, but he had raised Sejanus too high for him to be easily crushed, especially from Capri. He did succeed by the

exercise of great restraint and cunning. A series of letters heaped new honours on Sejanus, while removing from their offices his nearest associates. Flattered but uneasy, Sejanus obeyed.

Then Macro came, bearing a letter which appointed him as head of the praetorian guard. He performed this delicate task by contacting the night watch and promising a reward. Then he handed Sejanus a long message to be read to the Senate. The letter opened with high praise for Sejanus, and the favourite read on unsuspecting. It ended harshly with an order for his arrest.

Macro arrived promptly with the night watch to give effect to the order. The mob gladly tore down the effigies of Sejanus and murdered his relatives and supporters. He did not long survive them.

Only then was Tiberius told by the divorced wife of Sejanus that Drusus had died at his and Livilla's hands through poison. Even then, although Tacitus claimed a reign of terror followed, few facts support this claim. The conspirators were executed but no wholesale proscription ensued.

The last years of Tiberius

Some writers claimed that in the last period of his life Tiberius let the affairs of state slide, but here again careful examination of the evidence refutes this view. Tiberius did stay away from Rome. He was weary of the intrigues in Rome and he felt more secure in his island retreat, with the congenial company of his philosopher friends. Scandal-mongers like Suetonius could not understand this and were convinced that he spent his time there indulging in sexual malpractices!

Yet affairs in Rome were not neglected, for he left a very efficient *praefectus urbi* (superintendent of the city), Calpurnius Piso, in charge there. This was a post instituted by Augustus for the times he was away from Rome, but Tiberius made the post permanent.

The provinces too were not neglected. He kept on the practice of leaving good governors in charge for a long time for the benefit of their subjects. One such man was Vitellius, the governor of Syria. When Zeno, the king of Armenia died, the king of Parthia tried to make trouble, but Vitellius kept a close eye on developments, allowing the rulers of Armenia and Parthia to exhaust themselves with internal quarrels. Vitellius also saw to the dismissal of Pontius Pilate, who was indeed an incompetent procurator of Jerusalem.

Finally many inscriptions from this period tell of his maintenance of roads and buildings even in the most distant provinces. Tiberius was old and weary, but he was conscientious to the end.

Death of Tiberius. An evaluation

In 37 Tiberius came back to Italy to die, with only the youthful Gaius to succeed him. It was no hopeful prospect for a man who had maintained the greatness of an empire, so ungraciously bequeathed to him by Augustus.

It is interesting to try to picture the real Tiberius. The tales of his wild dissipations on Capri seem to have been fiction. His main vice, not uncommon among military men, was a love of strong liquor, and yet even there it never seems to have impaired his efficiency. His troops loved him, for he led them well and avoided bloodshed.

Rome did not understand him. His dry austere manner put people off. He avoided great public works, which saved money but did mean less employment in the city, and he hated and cut down gladiatorial shows, a very unpopular move. Nor did the people understand an intellectual ruler. In short Tiberius was a very good man, if not an easy man to know, and Rome was lucky to have him at the time, even if it was not grateful.

The emperor Gaius

We do not possess Tacitus' account of Gaius' rule and have to fall back on the writings of Suetonius and Dio Cassius, both less reliable and over-fond of scandal.

For part of his youth Gaius had been reared by his grandmother Antonia, with four Eastern princes as playmates. Agrippa of Judaea was one of them, and they all were subsequently to enjoy his favour. From Antonia he came to admire her ancestor Mark Antony. This too was to have its effect.

On reaching adult years he was not trained in official duties, but kept for safety at Capri. The only office he held was the quaestorship.

Now, at the age of twenty-five, he was emperor. Tiberius' will was read and in it Gaius was named as his heir together with Tiberius Gemellus. (He was the son of Drusus, and Tiberius' grandson.) Gaius, however, had the backing of Macro. The Senate voted that Tiberius' wishes be disregarded, and Gaius was proclaimed sole emperor. He dutifully requested that Tiberius be deified, but easily allowed the Senate to rule against this.

Tiberius' will was kept as far as the donations to the people and to the army were concerned, indeed Gaius doubled the amount to be paid to the praetorian guard. He was hailed with enthusiasm. Tiberius' rule had not been a gay one, and they longed for the spectacles which he had discouraged.

The following year Gaius became consul with his uncle Claudius, that scholarly recluse, whose retirement was also his protection. Although Gaius did not make Tiberius Gemellus joint ruler, he bestowed some honours on him, which suggested that he thought of him as his successor.

At the same time he began a round of festivities and spectacles of all kinds, finally dedicating a temple to *divus Augustus* which Tiberius had begun, but never finished. It has been claimed that Gaius' extravagances drained the treasury. He hardly ruled long enough for that, and he probably spent less than Claudius or Nero. In particularly, Claudius' donatives to the army and early activities could only have come from a full treasury.

The merry-making was short-lived. The emperor was taken ill and almost died. Scholars are inclined nowadays to regard the attack as a nervous breakdown. Our ancient authorities claim that Gaius' subsequent conduct was that of a madman. This sounds like the sensationalism dear to Suetonius. He did have an unbridled tongue, which spared no one and made many enemies. He also had a concept of god-emperor, fostered by his Eastern princes, which was more blatant than the form practised by Augustus.

As soon as Gaius recovered, he took steps to consolidate his position. The unfortunate Gemellus was a possible danger. He was induced to take his own life. Macro was too powerful and did not disguise the fact. He and his wife suffered the same fate as Gemellus. So did Silanus, governor of Upper Germany, whose loyalty was doubted. Two commanders were now appointed over the praetorian guard.

In 38 Gaius' second sister, Drusilla, died. He was extravagant in his grief and had her deified.

In 39 Gaius staged a magnificent display, much criticised by later writers, building a bridge of boats over the Bay of Naples to welcome the newly crowned King of Parthia. One may doubt the good taste of the pageant, but it did impress the Parthian, who departed convinced of the power of the new ruler of Rome.

At the same time, Gaius resolved to revert to the Eastern policy of his hero, Antony, and at the same time honour his childhood friends. Agrippa was sent to be a client king in Judaea, while his three Thracian princes were honoured with similar appointments.

Meanwhile, the provincial armies were restless, especially on the Rhine. They tried to assert themselves early in Tiberius' reign, and a series of bad governors had improved neither their loyalty nor their discipline. Matters came to a head when Gaius learnt of a conspiracy headed by Gaetulicus, *legatus* of Upper Germany. Gaius' subsequent actions have been used to illustrate his madness, but a more cautious evaluation can see in them much sense.

He left Rome with speed, reached Upper Germany before Gaetulicus could learn of his action, and had the legatus executed. Gaius' sisters, Agrippina and Julia, were involved. They were forced to accompany Gaius to Germany and thereafter were sent into exile. The Senate was curtly informed that the conspiracy was crushed. The Senate was not gratified to learn of Gaius'

success. His conduct had already shown signs of that autocracy which later was to alienate them utterly. But they were all the more eager to dissemble their true feelings with flattering adulation.

A real expedition against Germany would have been out of the question. The state of discipline of the soldiers would have made such an undertaking foolhardy. Instead, Gaius put them under a soldier of real efficiency and loyalty, Galba, who was later briefly to wear the imperial purple. The troops were engaged, not in an invasion but in toughening-up exercises.

One deed of valour on which Gaius had set his heart was the invasion of Britain. He even made preparations for the event. But the troops were not equal to the task. It is more than likely that they even mutinied when ordered to embark to cross the Channel. He threatened the legions, and retired some of the offending officers, but he had to be content with that. It was left to Claudius to give effect to Gaius' dream.

Trouble in the East

Meanwhile trouble had been brewing in the Eastern provinces, and especially in Alexandria. This town was the seat of a huge Jewish population, whose religious feelings the emperors had taken care to respect. This had unfortunately given rise to a certain arrogance on the part of this exclusive people. The Greek population, on the other hand, had no reason to love the Roman rule. They were denied a Senate (although the Jews possessed one), they enjoyed none of the distinction that was theirs when the Grecian Ptolemies ruled, and they saw the Jews spread beyond the two quarters originally allotted to them.

Finally their bitterness could not be contained, and they forced the governor to confine the Jews to their original quarters. This was followed by a joyous looting of former Jewish possessions, and a massacre of any Jews found out of bounds.

The attacks on the Jews at this point was no accident. Augustus and Tiberius had deified their predecessors and established temples in their name, but they had not encouraged their subjects to worship them themselves as gods, as was the Eastern custom.

Gaius was the first emperor to have statues set up to himself as a god. This brought him into direct conflict with the Jews, who refused to worship any god but *Yahweh* (Jehovah) and he saw their opposition as something to be crushed relentlessly. The Greeks were no doubt aware of this changed attitude.

Worse was to follow. The Gentiles in Jamnia in Judaea set up a statue of Gaius, which the Jewish populace promptly demolished. This news, coming on the heels of the Alexandrian disturbance, left Gaius in no good frame of mind.

Gaius' verdict was that the Jews should set up a statue of himself in Jerusalem. This was unendurable to the Jews, who met Petronius their governor by mass passive resistance when he tried to carry it out. He wavered; for slaughter in cold blood was not to his taste, and the sowing of the crops was needed if a famine was to be averted.

Finally, he temporised and wrote to Gaius asking him if he was determined to carry out his plan. Luckily this intervention was not finally needed. Agrippa, Gaius' childhood friend, had already spoken to more effect, and the decision was revoked.

Gaius is assassinated

Although the stories of Gaius' madness can be discounted[1] he was developing notions of grandeur which were to be his undoing. He had fallen out with the Senate. The conspiracies were probably a central factor in destroying his trust in that order, and he began to make them a butt of his sadistic humour, turning rather to the equites for support. He also did bolster his régime with emperor-worship, in the Eastern style. The Jewish act was a challenge to this concept.

Gaius made the mistake of alienating too many people without building up a body of supporters in compensation. In pursuance of his concept of god-emperor he made the Senate do obeisance to him, which served a double purpose, as it also humiliated the proud fathers. It was a dangerous sport.

Augustus had minted gold and silver, but as a concession to senatorial tradition he had minted in Gaul (at Lugdunum) and left them the minting of bronze. Gaius consulted efficiency, but further alienated the Senate, when he brought the imperial mint back to Rome.

The Senate controlled the province of Africa, and under Tiberius had been most ineffective in its administration. In particular, they could not quell the insurrections which continually troubled it. Gaius took over portion of the province himself. Again his action was branded as arrogance, but in fact Claudius completed what Gaius began in that area.

In 40 Gaius came back to Rome, well aware that trouble was impending. One conspiracy was detected and its ring-leaders executed. The next was more successful.

Many senators were involved, as was Clemens, a prefect of the guard, and Callistus, one of Gaius' secretaries. The deed itself was carried out at the order of Chaerea, a tribune of the guards. Gaius was the first Roman emperor to be assassinated. He was not the last.

An evaluation of Gaius

Gaius' rule is interesting in that we see a further development of emperor-worship, in a somewhat extreme form. It is marked too by the emergence of the praetorian guard as a power behind the throne, both in the beginning, when Macro gave him protection, and at the end, when the same body destroyed him. He was not mad, but he was not a very sensible person. He was far too free in making enemies, and failed to see that even an autocrat cannot rule alone.

---

[1]He does seem, however, to have suffered from the family tendency to epilepsy.

Date table

A.D.

14	Accession of Tiberius.
19	Death of Germanicus.
23	Praetorian guards brought to Rome. Death of Drusus.
27	Tiberius goes to Capri.
31	Execution of Sejanus.
37	Death of Tiberius, accession of Gaius.
39	Conspiracy of Gaetulicus.
41	Assassination of Gaius.

Select quotations

1 Tacitus, *Annals* I. 11:
(Tiberius is asked to rule.)
He began to discuss in some detail the greatness of the empire and his own diffidence. Only the mind of the divine Augustus was equal to a burden of this kind. When the emperor had called on him to share his responsibilities he had learnt by experience how wearing and how dependent on fortune was the task of ruling everything. Surely in a state supported by so many outstanding men they should not offer the whole rule to one. It would be easier for a greater number to share and carry out the tasks of government. Such a speech was dignified rather than convincing.
(As usual, the narrative of Tacitus is accurate, the author's own comment tendentious.)

2 Suetonius, *Life of Tiberius*, 42:
In camp even when he was a raw recruit he was nicknamed because of his excessive love of wine 'Biberius' for Tiberius, 'Caldius' for Claudius. 'Mero' for Nero. (i.e. 'A boozer with a partiality for a hot toddy.' An amusing anecdote, and probably true.)

3 Suetonius, *Life of Gaius Caligula*, 46:
(Gaius prepares to invade Britain.)
Finally . . . he drew up his forces on the shore of the Ocean . . . and when no one knew or guessed what he was up to, he suddenly bade them to pick up sea shells and fill their helmets and pockets.

(Two explanations: one is that Suetonius misunderstood a slang term for 'to pick up one's gear'. Another is that Gaius was by this order humiliating his rebellious forces.)

Further reading

Refer again to Suetonius, *The Twelve Emperors* and to R. Graves, *I Claudius*.
Tacitus, *Annals*, I-VI. Covers the rule of Tiberius, viewed unfavourably.
Velleius Paterculus, *Compendium of Roman History*, Loeb. A favourable account of Tiberius but incomplete. Written before Sejanus' conspiracy.
J.P. Balsdon, *The Emperor Gaius*, Oxford Clarendon, 1934. A necessary corrective to the traditional account, but in his enthusiasm the author goes a little too far in vindicating the emperor.
B. Levick, *Tiberius the Politician*, Croom Helm, London, 1976.
A. Garzetti, *From Tiberius to the Antonines*, London, Methuen, 1960.

Topics for essays or discussion

1 Mommsen has declared that Tiberius was the best of the Roman emperors, Tacitus condemned him. Can you explain the disagreement?
2 Compare and contrast Tiberius' relations with the Senate and those of Augustus.
3 Analyse and explain the growth of autocracy under Tiberius. Why did he fail to prevent it?
4 'Tiberius' main achievement, under Augustus and as emperor, was to consolidate the frontiers of the Roman empire.' Discuss.
5 It has been said that Tiberius' policy was merely to carry out the plans of Augustus. Do you agree?
6 Do you consider that Tiberius' failure to solve the problem of succession made the tragedy of Gaius inevitable?
7 'The rule of a young and inexperienced emperor brought out weaknesses inherent in the principate'. Discuss.

Chapter 20

Claudius and Nero

CLAUDIUS is another emperor who has been rehabilitated by modern research. Needless to say Claudius' physical appearance (he was a cripple) gave every excuse to writers who wished to present him as a poor shambling idiot, and this is what they tended to do.

Sources

We have the usual sources, Suetonius, Dio and Tacitus for his rule, although Tacitus does not cover his accession. In addition there is Seneca's lampoon, 'The Pumpkinification', which parodied the deification of Claudius, and contributed greatly to the low opinion of him in earlier histories. Tacitus too wrote of him unfavourably, highlighting the many executions for which he was undoubtedly responsible, and presenting him as a tool of his wives and freedmen.

For once Suetonius provides a favourable counterbalance. Suetonius was himself an administrator, and he took a keen interest in Claudius' many administrative achievements. Nevertheless far the most important evidence has been that

recovered by archaeologists, which reveal an emperor of great ability and many achievements.

In a number of places, inscriptions and papyri have been found containing his edicts. A very characteristic style, somewhat erudite, a little rambling but in its final gist, down to earth and eminently sensible, shows them to be genuinely the emperor's words, not merely the products of his secretariat. Thus we are now able to assess Claudius at his real worth.

In the case of Nero we again have Tacitus, Suetonius and Dio, although we do not possess Tacitus' account of the last years of Nero, including his visit to Greece. Tacitus is by far the most reliable source, for although he was no lover of Nero he did not allow his prejudices to distort the facts. Suetonius and Dio were far more prepared to present the mass of scandalous detail that embroidered the account of Nero's rule. In general, however, it must be said that the ancients were justified in their disapproval of the unbalanced young man who ended the Julio-Claudian line of emperors.

The accession of Claudius

Our traditional account of this episode presents Claudius as a rather comic figure, but apart from the general denigration of the man, a particular factor comes into play. As we know, Tacitus did not describe it but the Greek historian Josephus, a man of Jewish nationality, did. He not unnaturally was keen to give credit to Claudius' Jewish friend, Herod Agrippa, who undoubtedly did play a part, but not as dominating a part as Josephus would have us believe. Claudius was chosen, but he was not a mere tool of his protectors and himself seized his opportunity.

When Gaius was killed the Senate briefly found itself in control again. But, just as after Caesar's assassination, they had no clear plan of action. A return to Republican government was clearly an anachronism even to them, and natural rivalries made it hard to elevate any single member of their body to the principate.

In any case they were not given long to make up their mind. They had, for the moment, the support of the urban cohorts, but not of the all-

20.1 *The coin of Claudius showing Claudius and the praetorian camp where he was hailed as emperor.*

powerful praetorian guard. The latter had taken possession of Gaius' uncle, Claudius, an unlikely figure of an emperor but for all this, a brother of Germanicus. The Julio-Claudian blood was still the essential requirement, and Claudius was hurried into the camp for his protection. There he promised the soldiers 15 000 sesterces each for their support, a dangerous precedent, but a necessary step in the circumstances,[1] and he was hailed as emperor. He then sent Herod Agrippa to inform the Senate.

The Senate blustered, but it had been deserted by the urban cohorts, and was powerless. So, making a virtue of necessity, they acknowledged the soldiers' choice, and Claudius was installed as ruler of the Roman world.

He was physically infirm, owing, as we now think, to an attack of polio. He walked in an unsteady fashion, his head shook and he stammered. This would in itself make him a ready butt for caricature, but when it was coupled with a very shrewd and efficient mind, which made short shrift of those who underestimated him, venom was added to their laughter.

Claudius' earlier years

Claudius had led an undistinguished life in the past. Augustus had not given him public office. His main recognition had been from the equestrians, who chose him as their representative on several occasions. Still, lack of distinction was probably his salvation, for his life was spared, even in the reign of Gaius.

He devoted his energies to scholarship, and he wrote a number of histories, including a work on Augustus, and two others on the Etruscans and Carthaginians respectively. These historical pursuits were no bad training for the future emperor. He also had an interest in the Roman alphabet, which he in due course reformed, at least for the duration of his rule.

This background explains much of his later policy. The recluse, not on easy terms with the Senate, nor even entirely with the equestrians, made great use of the freedman class. His unsureness of his position made him on the one hand eager to win popularity by gifts, by games, by military success, on the other suspicious of conspiracy. This kindly and considerate emperor is said to have executed thirty-five senators and two hundred or more equestrians. In fact Claudius had some justification for his fears. The fate of Gaius made it clear that he too as emperor was

---

[1] Suetonius declared that he was the first emperor to do so, but actually each emperor from Augustus down had made gifts to the troops. It was simply the culmination of a growing trend.

not immune, and in his own time there were at least three genuine conspiracies. These facts must not be forgotten.

Actually Claudius was a man of many abilities. His scholarly energy, diverted to administrative channels, produced a great enthusiasm for organisation. This resulted in a more centralised rule, and in a transfer to his sphere of powers which the Senate was so chronically unable to wield efficiently.

These features were to emerge later, but at the beginning Claudius' desire was not innovation but security.

Claudius takes command

The soldiers received their donative. Gaius' assassin Chaerea was executed, but Claudius wisely refrained from extensive reprisals. No move was made to have Gaius deified, and Claudius stated on one occasion that he had been mad. Equally, however, there was no general vilification of the emperor's predecessor. He took the names of Caesar and Augustus, as was customary, but refused the title of Imperator.

In the first year of Claudius' rule, the philosopher Seneca, being convicted of adultery with one of the sisters of Gaius, was sent into exile. This event was to have unfortunate consequences, for after the death of Claudius Seneca published a skit on his deification, labelling it the 'pumpkinification', *Apocolocyntosis*. In this work he is presented as a near imbecile, dominated by his wives and freedmen secretaries. The satire was clever, and, being reinforced by the emperor's personal appearance, it contrived to stick. Moreover, despite his earnest desire to please, Claudius succeeded in alienating both the Senate and the equites, and our main historians of the period, Tacitus and Suetonius, drew on hostile sources.

Claudius' foreign policy

His first problems concerned the foreign field. He secured part of his Eastern frontier and rewarded a friend by making Herod Agrippa the King of Judaea, which he greatly increased by the addition of neighbouring territory. Agrippa proved worthy of his trust, and no further trouble was experienced in this area until the prince's death.

Two other tasks were inherited from Gaius. Mauretania had been a client kingdom, but when trouble arose there Gaius took it over. On his death the war with the inhabitants still raged, and Claudius sent two of his generals who speedily subjugated the land. It was then divided into two provinces under imperial control.

Claudius was not ill-pleased that opportunity should be given to him of presenting the public image of a successful man in war. Gaius' abortive invasion of Britain showed the way to an enterprise dreamt of from the days of Julius Caesar. The people of Britain were rapidly absorbing Roman culture, and trade was brisk between the island and neighbouring Gaul. On the other hand Britain had been developing an aggressive nationalism, and was far too convenient a shelter for refugee princes from the Gallic province.

In 43 the invasion took place, led by Aulus Plautius in command of four legions. Vespasian, the future emperor, was one of the *legati*. Claudius himself crossed the Channel to join the advancing troops in their hour of victory. The south-eastern portion of Britain was subjugated and Plautius appointed as its first governor— under imperial control. The emperor returned to Rome, where in the following year he celebrated a triumph and named his son Britannicus in commemoration.

Britain had long been in close contact with Gaul and it quickly accepted Romanisation. It is interesting that the capital of the new province was Londinium (London), which even then found its location near the mouth of the Tamesis (Thames) favourable to its growth.

The bureaucracy

The emperors from Augustus down had used freedmen as secretaries. They had also been assisted by a council consisting mainly of senators and relatives. Claudius had no wish for such a council. He had no confidence in the Senate, even though he was most polite in his dealings with the body, and he had some fear of assassination, after the example of Gaius.

He therefore built his administration on his freedmen, but organised them in a more systematic way than had been attempted before. Four freedmen headed his bureaux and came to be exceedingly powerful. Narcissus was chief secretary (*ab epistulis*). He handled and organised all Claudius' correspondence. Pallas[2] was financial secretary (*a rationibus*), and was in charge of all the emperor's *fisci* or treasuries. The claim made by some that Claudius united the fisci into one is probably not true, but the mere fact of putting them all under the control of one department and its head would have considerable unifying effect. These two freedmen are the best known and seem to have wielded the greatest power.

In addition, there was Callistus, secretary in charge of petitions (*a libellis*), who was probably also in charge of judicial matters. He had held office under Gaius and took part in the conspiracy that led to his assassination. Finally there was Polybius, suitably named, for he was literary secretary (*a studiis*), no sinecure with so scholarly an emperor.

Relations with the Senate

Even though Claudius was no favourite of the Senate, he made an earnest endeavour to cooperate with it. In 44 he gave them Achaea and Macedonia (as senatorial provinces), adding later Lycia in the East. He attended their meetings regularly and consulted them repeatedly. Unfortunately, the love of order, apparent in the departments he organised, made him impatient of their inefficiency, and like Tiberius, he was depressed at their unwillingness to express opinions freely. We possess an extract from one of his speeches, in which he condemned them, saying that as a rule only the consul designate would speak to a motion, and he would simply repeat the consul's original proposal. The rest would say 'I agree', then depart happily, saying 'I gave my opinion'.

It is thought that he restored to the Senate the right to elect new members to its body.[3] He forbade senators to leave Rome without permission. This was probably because he feared they might gather secretly and foment a revolt.

Claudius was indefatigable in attending the law courts, an activity which the satirist lampooned. He seems, however, to have done some good work in that sphere. He made short work of informers who tried to prosecute men for affronts to the emperors, and took steps to foil accusers who prolonged cases in order to harass their victims.

The provinces

In the provinces he pursued a mid-course of expansion and caution. We have already mentioned his conquest of Britain. Corbulo invaded Germany and won a number of victories. Claudius, however, had no desire to repeat Augustus' mistake. Once Roman authority had been established, he recalled Corbulo and set the frontier, as before, on the Rhine.

The East was in urgent need of attention. Repeated disturbances in Thrace led to its annexation as an imperial province. Judaea too was turned into an imperial province on the death of Herod Agrippa, for fear that it might fall under Parthian domination. This left the ever-vexed question of Armenia and Parthia. Gaius had solved it by leaving Armenia to Parthia in return for Parthian recognition of Rome. Claudius took the other course of installing a pro-Roman prince in Armenia and fomenting trouble in Parthia. He also sent a competent general to Syria, Cassius Longinus, who disciplined the army of this province and from there kept an eye on Parthia. Claudius' policy was not finally effective, and indeed Rome never solved the Eastern question, but it did bring stability until the last years of his principate.

---

[2] It was he who brought Tiberius news of Sejanus' treachery.
[3] Gaius had given this right to the assemblies again.

He created six new provinces most of which he ruled through procurators, who were of course equestrians. They were Britain, Lycia, Thrace, Judaea, and the two provinces of Mauretania. (Britain, however, was ruled by a *legatus pro praetore* of senatorial rank.)

From Gaius he inherited the discontent of the Jews, especially in Alexandria. We possess the text of his letter to the Alexandrians on this matter. In essence he preserved the *status quo*, leaving the Jews their freedom, but at the same time warning them not to stir up trouble in the future and to end the wholesale Jewish immigration from Judaea. He adopted a generally tolerant attitude to the Jews, giving them freedom in their religion and exemption from emperor-worship. At the same time he forbade them undertaking missionary activities, especially in Italy. When they rioted in Rome in 49 he exiled the extremists. He likewise expelled the astrologers when he felt they were having a pernicious influence, and outlawed the Druids, who in Gaul and Britain were the core of national resistance, apart from their unpleasant love of human sacrifice.

Despite Claudius' lack of military experience, he enjoyed good relations with the army, which hailed him as imperator twenty-seven times. He chose good generals and gave them every support. To the soldiers he granted the legal privileges of married men, a wise concession, as they were not allowed to marry legally until they retired.

It was a good record and Claudius had some justification in celebrating Rome's secular games in 47.

He extends the franchise

In 48 he took an unpopular but necessary step. Augustus and Tiberius had followed a conservative policy in the extension of the franchise and in the allied question, the composition of the Senate. Claudius knew that senatorial opposition to change would be strong, and decided that the best way to deal with it would be to revive the old office of censor. He did so, and took on the censorship in 48–49.

He purged the Senate of some of its members and added to it new recruits from *Gallia Comata*, members of the tribe of the Aedui. We have a portion of the speech he made in support of this move. It was a wise one; for Gaul had rapidly become Romanised and the honour thus conferred helped to wean Gauls from a revival of nationalism with the support of the Druids and of neighbouring German peoples.

Public works and monetary policy

Claudius displayed incredible energy in public works. In Italy he completed two aqueducts which Gaius had begun, thus increasing Rome's water supply. He established a new port at Ostia, building huge harbour works to contain it. He dug a tunnel to drain the Pontine marshes, thus reclaiming a large area for cultivation and removing a health hazard. Nero's neglect frustrated the final success of this project which was not completed until this century.

In the provinces he built a vast network of roads extending over most of Rome's territory. He took special pleasure in completing some projects conceived by his father Drusus on the Rhine frontier, and he built innumerable roads in Gaul, aiming particularly at constructing roads across Gaul linking Italy with the Channel Coast. This fostered trade with Britain and gave easy access in the event of an uprising.

All these projects were expensive and had to be met by a vigorous monetary policy. Claudius centralised the mints by bringing the senatorial aerarium under his control. Instead of the praetors who had managed it, he appointed quaestors who were imperial appointees, paid a salary and holding office for three years. The Senate was allowed to retain the coinage of bronze but he coined the precious metals, mainly in Italy. There was a certain debasing of the currency under him. This was partly caused by the need to meet the huge expense of his public works programme, partly by the unfavourable trade balance with the East.

Luxury imports from the East had been increasing throughout the imperial period and by now were on a vast scale. Payment for these goods was made in precious metals, constituting a serious drain on the gold and silver reserve of Rome. It was left to the Flavians to bring the trade to a more balanced state.

Claudius' final years

History has cast doubt on the belief that Claudius was dominated by his wives. None the less, he did have little control over the beautiful and youthful Messalina. Her infidelities came to a head in 49 when she was accused of implication in a conspiracy and of marriage with one of the conspirators. She and her paramour were executed.

He now married Agrippina the Younger. She was his niece, a woman of immense ambition and drive. Politically the marriage had advantages. She was a Claudian and descended directly from Augustus, and the wedding removed a potential threat to the throne. Agrippina was not however content with the position she had achieved. Her ambition was to win the succession for her own son at the expense of Britannicus.

She persuaded Claudius to recall Seneca to be the youth's tutor. Next she had him adopted by Claudius, changing his name from Domitius to Claudius Nero. In 51, Burrus, with whom Agrippina was on good terms, was made prefect of the praetorian guard. Soon after Nero married Octavia, Claudius' daughter, and the emperor was persuaded to adopt him as his successor instead of Britannicus. This action was not as unnatural as has been suggested. Lineal descent in the principate was actually extremely rare, and Claudius was no oddity in considering the security of the empire above mere family ties.

In 54 Claudius died. The tale that Agrippina poisoned him with a dish of mushrooms has given spice to his end ever since, but the authority is doubtful. That the ailing emperor should have met his end at the age of 64 is not surprising, and scandal has fastened on the end of most of the emperors of Rome.

An evaluation of Claudius

Claudius was promptly deified. For all his oddities he had been popular. The Senate and his countrymen had never understood his care for the welfare of the provincials, but it was appreciated by his subjects themselves. The Eastern states had taken a pride in the authority he gave to his Eastern-born secretaries. The west could point to the honours he bestowed on Gaul and to his tireless public works. In Italy and Rome he had shown himself a generous ruler who saw that the people received their share of circuses and corn (*panem et circenses*), and he had regard for the welfare of the small man. The most valid criticism of his rule would be that his increased centralisation helped the later development of bureaucracy, but this trend was in general inevitable.

To sum it up, the foundations of the Roman empire were laid by three men, Augustus, Tiberius and Claudius, and Claudius' role was very important. This is not to say that the popular image of Claudius the clown was wrong. Claudius' clowning kept him safe in his younger years and he did not change when he became emperor. Garzetti speaks of this 'sincere and tractable person, quick to laughter and anger, a great glutton and a relentless joker, an incautious person, who talked to everyone about everything in any one's presence'.[4] Not a conventional emperor, but a very likeable one.

Nero's accession. The five good years

So Nero came to the throne, at the early age of seventeen. His youth was well protected. His mother Agrippina, his tutor, Seneca, and Burrus, the prefect of the praetorian guard, were only too pleased to rule the Roman empire on his behalf. The praetorian guard was content. It received a gift of 15 000 sesterces a man, the same as Claudius had bestowed. Nero's subjects

---

[4]*From Tiberius to the Antonines*, p. 145.

were happy to see the accession of one who could claim descent from Augustus and Germanicus.

At his inauguration his behaviour left nothing to be desired. In his speech, which was in fact written by Seneca, he was deferential to the Senate, assisted in Claudius' deification, and refused the title of Imperator. The Senate received back the right to coin gold and silver.

The first five years of his reign were a model. It is thought that these were the years Trajan meant, which he described as the best five years of the Roman principate. Seneca was no model Stoic. He owned huge estates and used his position to gain more wealth, but Burrus and he were competent administrators. Meanwhile Nero was left to enjoy his youthful pleasures. Much of the credit for this should also go to the emperors Augustus, Tiberius and Claudius, who, as we mentioned, had built up such an efficient administration that it could continue to operate very well without assistance on its own without central direction.

The death of Britannicus and Agrippina

Nevertheless there were ominous signs. Agrippina was not content to stay in the background. Her image appeared on the coins of the period, and it was she who received foreign embassies. Narcissus ceased to enjoy her favour and committed suicide, while Callistus simply vanishes from our records.

Seneca and Burrus took this ill and contrived to arouse Nero's hostility to petticoat government. As a result he dismissed Pallas, who was his mother's supporter, from his post. Agrippina flew into a rage and threatened to secure the throne for Britannicus. Her favour was fatal to the young prince, who met a mysterious end in 55, it is thought from poison. Agrippina was then forced into retirement, where she occupied herself writing her memoirs.

Meanwhile the government went on, unperturbed by these domestic disputes. Nero accepted the consulship in 55, 57 and 58, but refused to accept the office permanently. The

harbour works at Ostia were completed, and the aerarium was put under tighter control when imperial prefects were appointed to be in charge of it.

Nero was irked by his mother's domination even in retirement. In 59 he contrived to put her on a boat at Baiae, which was prepared so as to sink some time after she embarked. The indomitable woman swam ashore, and the emperor was forced to send a band to kill her openly, alleging a plot against his life.

If the Senate was shocked it gave no sign. When after a decent interval Nero came back to Rome, they voted thanks to the gods for saving his life.

Burrus dies and Seneca retires

In 62 Burrus died and this gave Nero his chance to shake off restraint. He appointed in his stead Faenius Rufus and Tigellinus to command the guard, the latter, a depraved individual, who pandered to Nero's vices. Nero was attracted by Poppaea Sabina, the wife of Otho, soon to be briefly emperor of Rome. He sent the husband abroad to be governor of Lusitania, which he governed very well, divorced Octavia[5] and married Poppaea.

Without Burrus, Seneca had no authority. He was allowed to retire to write on philosophy, while the treason trials resumed at Rome under the guidance of Tigellinus. They served a useful purpose in replenishing the coffers of Nero, which were feeling the strain of his extravagance.

Nero the artist

The Julio-Claudians had all had an interest in the arts, even the gloomy Tiberius, and it was this interest which flourished most as a result of Seneca's education. Nero was, however, the first emperor to exercise his artistic talents in public.

---

[5]She was later executed.

20.2 *Hall of Nero's Golden House.*

Nero's passionate conviction was that he was an artist. He played, he sang, he made up verse (which was not without some merit). He regarded Greece as his spiritual home. He celebrated games run on the style of the Olympic Games, and, to the scandal of the respectable, he acted on the stage at Naples.

These activities were interrupted in 64 by a terrible fire which ravaged Rome. Nero, who was away when it broke out, hastened back and organised relief operations with commendable efficiency. When, however, he took advantage of the destruction to introduce some town planning,

straightening the city's crooked streets and building for himself an enormous palace, 'The Golden House', the rumour spread quickly that the fire did not displease him, and indeed that he began it.

It was a vile calumny, and most unlikely, but Nero's popularity was waning. In order to find a scapegoat for the fire, Nero accused the Christians of starting it, and had a number executed in spectacular fashion. This, the first persecution of the Christians, helped to damn his memory in later years, but made little impression at the time.

The economy and the provinces

The fire must, however, have helped the deterioration of Rome's financial position, which was already suffering from the emperor's wastefulness and from the export of metals to the East. Nero tried to meet this by devaluing the currency as Claudius had done. He turned this act to advantage by issuing a new and elegant bronze series as a variant on copper, and by establishing a practical exchange ratio between the currency of the Roman empire and that of Greece and the East. His standardisation of the coins persisted, the bronze coins did not.

In the provinces peace was general except for two areas. Parthia had become over-confident as the ageing Claudius had relaxed his watchfulness and it put a Parthian nominee Tiridates on the Armenian throne. Nero sent Corbulo to Syria to restore order. Corbulo had first to discipline his troops, which had suffered the usual fate of soldiers living in this pleasure-loving area. Then he attacked, deposed Tiridates and put a Roman supporter in his place.

This arrangement proved only a temporary solution. When Rome's choice was unable to hold his own, Corbulo was summoned back and finally agreed that Tiridates could have the crown, providing he came to Rome and officially accepted it from Nero.

In Britain Paulinus seized the island of Mona which had been a stronghold of the Druids. Then he had to deal with the uprising of Queen Boudicca (known popularly as Boadicea), provoked by the outrageous conduct of local Roman officials. The fighting was fierce, but eventually Boudicca was defeated and committed suicide. The next governor of Britain was more tactful in his dealings with the people and peace then returned to the island.

The conspiracy of Piso

In 65 the conspiracy of Piso was discovered. One of the praetorian prefects, Faenius Rufus, was involved. He was jealous of Tigellinus' influence, and actually Nero's lack of concern for the army generally was losing him the support of the military class. The Senate too was involved. In particular, the adherents of the Stoic philosophy, which Seneca affected, had developed an opposition to the principate and desired a return to Republican rule, a desire which they were to cherish, despite oppression, for a long time after this period.

Seneca was found to be implicated and was forced to take his life and so was the poet Lucan, his nephew. Many others soon joined them, some guilty, like Faenius, others simply men whom Nero disliked or suspected. The Stoics suffered greatly in this purge, and the dilettante Petronius, author of the *Satyricon*, was made to commit suicide.

Even before the conspiracy, the Senate had viewed with indignation Nero's use of freedmen in important posts, but the conspiracy, by destroying his confidence in that body, meant that he turned to freedmen more and more.

At the same time Nero had begun increasingly to identify himself with the gods. In the coins of the period he appeared with a halo round his head, and his vanity was tickled when Tiridates came to Rome to receive his crown, and amid the most splendid pageantry hailed the emperor as Mithras (the deity of the religion of Persia).

20.3 *The bronze coin of Nero.*

Last years of Nero's rule

Nero was almost consoled, and in 66 he set out on a grand tour of the East, leaving a freedman in charge of Rome. He had great plans. He undertook to cut through the isthmus of Corinth. (The project was never completed in ancient times.) All four Greek festivals were celebrated in succession and he won nearly two thousand prizes. Amid cheers he declared Greece free.

While Nero was indulging his bent, more serious matters were occupying the army. A huge revolt broke out in Judaea, which the general Vespasian confronted, and eventually crushed. Then, when Nero arrived in the East, he summoned his general Corbulo and made him commit suicide. This was outrageous, when for so many years Corbulo had successfully handled the Parthians, always one of Rome's worst problem areas. Nero and his officers had done nothing but obstruct his efforts, on one occasion sending a general Paetus to replace him, who was captured by the Parthians, and whom Corbulo had to rescue.

The army had never favoured the Greek-loving Nero, who thought so little of them. Now they wondered who would be the next to fall under suspicion. In 68 Vindex rebelled in Gaul, with the support of Galba, the governor of Spain, and Otho, ruler of Lusitania. The rebellion was crushed by Verginius Rufus, but he too then offered to carry out the wishes of the Senate.

At this point, the praetorian guard, accepting the offer of a donative, called on Galba to be emperor. Nero found himself deserted on all sides and took his life.

Nero has suffered official condemnation, especially at the hands of Christian writers, yet his love of show, his extravagance, even his self-display, succeeded in winning him wide popular favour, and positive adulation in the East. This is probably why his death was disbelieved, and a number of pretenders arose in Eastern countries, claiming to be Nero, returning to claim his heritage.

His great fault was his neglect of wider issues in the empire, and particularly of the army. This failure to supply a central loyalty to the soldiers gave a chance for local loyalties to assert themselves, for the first time in the imperial period, a fact which threatened the continued existence of the empire itself.

The Julio-Claudian Period

It is now time to summarise the achievements of Augustus and his successors, and to show some of the characteristics of the age.

Central to it was the army. It was Augustus who refashioned Rome's armies, turning them from an offensive force, normally recruited only when the need arose, to a permanent garrison, settled along the frontiers of the empire. It was during his reign also that the Rhine-Danube frontier emerged as the main line of Roman defence and the area where most of Rome's armies were concentrated.

Obviously, the existence of huge armies, settled many kilometres from Rome, involved some danger of revolt. Augustus and his successors helped to insure against this by seeing that almost all the provinces which contained armies were under imperial control, their governors being appointed by the emperor and responsible to him. The building of roads linking the capital with the provinces ensured that if trouble did break out, forces could swiftly be despatched to quell it. Moreover, although senatorial provinces were in general left to the Senate, the imperial procurator or tax collector could keep an eye on affairs there and see that all was well.

Tiberius took one vital step in bringing the imperial bodyguard, the praetorian guard, to the outskirts of Rome, where, especially under Claudius and Nero, they came to play an exceedingly important role in making, unmaking and controlling emperors. They appointed Claudius; Burrus made and dominated Nero, and Nero finally was unmade by the same body.

The power of the emperor

Nevertheless, in this period the military could not be said to control Rome. For one thing, the actual line of the Julio-Claudians enjoyed a prestige which gave them authority. The emperor, besides his close relations with his soldiers, gained further prestige especially in the East from emperor-worship. Gaius and Nero actively encouraged the cult. The other emperors made use of it, while discouraging its more extravagant manifestations. In general, it was not so much a religion, in any mystical sense, but more an expression of patriotism. In many parts of the provinces the celebrations carried out in this way served as a meeting of the local people, where they aired grievances and arranged to send deputations to the emperor. Only with the monotheism of the Jews and later of the Christians did the rites of emperor-worship meet an obstinate stumbling-block, which the emperors dealt with more or less tactfully.

Even though Augustus set out, at least in theory, to rule jointly with the Senate, the emperor soon came to usurp more and more authority. His power of patronage, that is of giving important and lucrative jobs, was immense, and meant that no ambitious man would dare flout him. Even Augustus denied the Senate any control of the army. His successors took over increasingly the control of the finance of the state. In addition, the emperor developed his own administrative staff, which made him increasingly independent of the Senate as a source of administrators. With Claudius and Nero came the use of men who were not even from the senatorial class, which once had monopolised the running of Rome's affairs.

The civil administration

The development of the civil administration, especially under Claudius, was partly made necessary by the huge volume of business entailed by governing the provinces. The department *ab epistulis* handled correspondence, most of it from the provinces, likewise the petitions (*a libellis*). We have noted the encroachment by the emperors on the senatorial right of minting. The Senate was quite incapable of handling the business of minting enough to supply the whole empire, especially for that vast organisation, the frontier armies. It is significant too that Claudius, despite the creation of these departments, felt it necessary to alleviate the pressure on the central executive. He gave the procurators in the provinces the right to hear locally law suits connected with tax-collection. Later they came to extend their legal jurisdiction to certain other cases.

The result was inevitable. The Senate became more and more aware of the minor role to which it was being relegated. It had no alternative to offer; for there was no road back to Republican Rome, but it did become a source of stubborn if useless opposition to the emperor, punctuated by conspiracies. To these aims the Stoics lent an air of respectability, while the senators themselves looked back to a noble but highly unrealistic picture of their past, before degeneration set in with the imperial age.

The equites, as we have noted, gained an important place in the public service from Augustus. They collected taxes, helped to administer imperial provinces, controlled many public services. Augustus even used some of them in his imperial council. That body continued for a while, but ceased to be used when Tiberius retired from Rome. It was not revived by the later Julio-Claudians. Claudius was not a great favourite of the equites, and it was the freedmen who benefited particularly from his administration. Still he did expand their functions, especially at the expense of the senatorial class. The latter had not shone as administrators and Claudius not only instituted two imperial provinces with equestrian governors, but gave the equites control of overseeing the harbours (especially Ostia), the roads and the corn supply; none the less, it was under the Flavians that the equites were really to come into their own.

The state of the economy

Economically the period was one of prosperity. Roman peace allowed trade to flourish without the savage blood-lettings of earlier days, and the attendant uncertainties. In particular Gaul flourished. The armies on the Rhine were a market for their produce. Emperors, especially Claudius, enriched them with highways. The conquest of Britain added to Gaul's importance.

It is no wonder that the country flourished and began to develop many industries of its own. For a period Lugdunum (Lyons) was the site of the emperor's own mint. Its pottery came to be much in demand. Finally their wealth was so well known that Claudius could give it as one reason for allowing Gauls to be senators.

Some problems remained. The East drained the empire of its money through unbalanced trade. Rome, though the largest importer of any town, itself produced nothing, except administrators. Finally one strategic problem defied solution. Parthia was distant and too powerful to control. Yet, while it was free, Armenia was in an impossible position. Free, it was a thorn in the side of the Eastern provinces. Controlled by Rome, it was itself too exposed to Parthian attack and endlessly expensive to maintain.

Literature

In a literary sense, the age was not noteworthy. Oratory could not flourish where there was no freedom, and no new Cicero emerged. Yet, oddly enough, rhetoric, the art of empty and often highly artificial declamation, flourished, and had an influence on many other arts, including verse. This was made worse by the habit of recitals, where authors lured their friends and acquaintances with the promise of a meal, and read to them large extracts from their work. This boring practice was later mocked by Martial and Juvenal.

The work of Petronius is a refreshing counterblast to this rhetoric. His *Satyricon* is the unedifying but amusing tale of three rogues, one of them a schoolmaster, in some of the less respectable parts of an Italian city. Perhaps the best known portion is *Trimalchio's Dinner*, where the host, endowed with more money than taste, overwhelms his guests with a combination of luxury and vulgarity.

Seneca wrote as well as governed. His philosophy has been admired wherever improving if unexciting literature was in demand. He would

make a good peg on which to hang a sermon, but had little real depth. His tragedies, in which blood and rhetoric shared equally, had an influence beyond their merit when modern Europe tried to find models on which to base its own writing of plays.

Seneca is noteworthy in other respects, as being of Spanish origin, and he and his nephew, Lucan, were the first two gifts to Rome from that newly civilised province which was later even able to produce emperors. Lucan's epic, *Pharsalia*, presented the tale of Caesar.

To sum up, the age which succeeded Augustus, apart from the isolated phenomenon of Petronius, rose very little above the level of mediocrity in the field of literature.

Date table

A.D.

41	Accession of Claudius.
43	Conquest of Britain.
49	Claudius marries Agrippina.
54	Death of Claudius; Nero succeeds.
59	Murder of Agrippina.
61	Revolt of Boudicca.
62	Death of Burrus.
64	Fire at Rome.
65	Conspiracy of Piso.
68	Death of Nero.

Select quotations

1 Seneca, *Apocolocyntosis*, 5:
(Claudius arrives at Olympus.)
A message is brought to Jupiter that a man had arrived, of reasonable height, grey-haired; he seemed to be threatening something or other, for he never stopped shaking his head. His right leg trailed behind him. He was asked what country he came from, but in reply mumbled something quite unintelligible. They could not understand his language, whether it was Greek or Roman or of any well-known country.

2 Rushforth, *Latin Historical Inscriptions*, 79, lines 22 ff.:

(Claudius grants to certain Gallic tribes citizenship which they had held in fact for some time.)

As for the position of the Anauni, the Tulliasses and the Sinduni, who, according to my information, are in part attached to the Tridentini, in part not connected in any way, although I remark that this community does not have an over-firm basis for Roman citizenship, still, since they are said to have long laid claim to and enjoyed that right, and are so commingled with the Tridentini that they could not be separated from them without serious damage to a distinguished town, I allow them as a favour to retain the privilege which they thought they had, the more willingly as very many from that community are even said to be serving in my guards, some also to have received promotion, a number to be enrolled in the judiciary and to be judging cases at Rome.

3 Tacitus, *Annals*, 15, 44:

So in order to quell the rumour Nero made up charges against and inflicted the most excruciating punishments on those known to the people as Christians, and unpopular for their misdeeds. Christ, from whom they derived their name, had been sentenced by the procurator Pontius Pilate when Tiberius was emperor. The vile superstition was crushed for a while then broke out again, not only throughout Judaea, the origin of the evil, but also in the city to which all that is dreadful and shameful makes its way and takes root.

Further reading

A. Garzetti, *From Tiberius to the Antonines*, Methuen, 1974.

V.M. Scrammuzza, *The Emperor Claudius*, Harvard University Press, 1940.

J.H. Bishop, *Nero*, Robert Hale, 1964.

Topics for essays or discussion

1 Discuss the development of administration under Claudius.
2 Discuss the relationship of Claudius and Nero to the Army.
3 How did the provinces fare under Claudius and Nero?
4 Analyse the continuing opposition of the Senate to the emperors under Claudius and Nero. How do you account for it?
5 What were the main economic trends in the Roman empire under Claudius and Nero?
6 Examine the growth of emperor-worship under the principate. What were its uses and its disadvantages?
7 Comment on Claudius' more generous policy in granting citizenship to states outside Italy. Do you approve?
8 The Romans could see little merit in Claudius. Modern historians praise him highly. Account for this difference in view.
9 Compare and contrast the rule of Claudius and Nero.

Chapter 21

The Flavians

Sources

THE SOURCES for this period are uneven. They are best for A.D. 69, the year of the Four Emperors as it was called, which is covered by Tacitus' *Histories* and also by Plutarch and Suetonius. For the rest our main source is Suetonius. As we have noted, he was not always reliable, and he suffered from the general fault of biographies, not observing strict chronology in his account. There are also specialist works. Tacitus in his *Agricola* wrote about his father-in-law's work as governor of Britain under the Flavians, while Frontinus, who was governor before Agricola in that province, wrote one book on military strategems, and one on aqueducts! Josephus wrote about the Jewish War, and Pliny about the eruption of Vesuvius. We do not possess Tacitus' work on the Flavians, and although he did not like them, least of all Domitian, the loss is to be regretted.

Archaeological material is as always valuable. Buildings, coins and inscriptions fill in the gaps left by our ancient writers, and are especially useful in providing evidence of some positive aspects in the rule of the much criticised Domitian.

The year of the Four Emperors

Nero died in 68 and the following year, A.D. 69 is known as the Year of the Four Emperors. It was a time of great instability that was nearly fatal to the Roman empire. Tacitus remarked that it was then that they learnt that emperors could be made elsewhere than in Rome.

The choice of the praetorian guard, Galba, met with instant approval from the Senate. He was of old senatorial family and had had a distinguished public career. He arrived from his province in Spain, bringing with him Otho, the governor of neighbouring Lusitania (modern Portugal).

Unfortunately Galba was old, over seventy in fact, and began at once to display many of the unlovable characteristics of age, notably an incredible facility in making enemies. A donative had been promised by him to the praetorian guard. He refused to pay it. He recalled Verginius Rufus, the popular commander of the Rhine, and appointed as his successor one as old and as unpopular as himself. He reduced the corn dole. As if this were not enough, he proceeded to choose as his successor Piso, a youth of senatorial family but of no military experience, by-passing the men who had helped bring him to power.

This was too much. The legions on the Rhine hailed one of their commanders, Vitellius, as emperor, and in Rome, Otho, who had hoped for Galba's favour, and been disappointed, promised a donative to the praetorians. Galba and Piso were promptly killed and Otho found himself on a highly precarious throne.

He was hailed as emperor by the troops on the Danube and in the East, and the Danubian legions prepared to march on Italy to give him their support. Their help was too slow arriving. The army of Vitellius arrived first, crossed the Alps, and at Cremona crushed the forces of Otho, who committed suicide.

Vitellius had little to commend him. Tacitus asserts that his main characteristic was gluttony, and this for a brief space he indulged to the full, but he had few qualities of leadership. He discharged in disgrace the praetorian troops, who had supported Otho, and set a Danubian legion to work building an amphitheatre at Cremona. The insult was not forgotten.

Then the Rhine legions, plundering at will, proceeded south to Rome, where Vitellius plunged into a series of orgies, neglecting more important business. He reinstated Nero's favourites and appointed a new praetorian guard picked from his own Rhine legions.

Vespasian is hailed as emperor

Meanwhile, local rivalry had been stimulated by Vitellius' appointment, and excused by his excesses. The legions on the Danube would gladly have set up a rival, but had no candidate in any way noteworthy. Mucianus, legate of Syria, had the distinction but not the ambition. So the Eastern choice fell on Vespasian, a man of senatorial rank, though of equestrian descent. He was hailed by the legions of the Danube and of Egypt, and by his own men in Judaea.

Vespasian's predecessors had rushed to Rome and to their doom. Vespasian made no such mistake. Indeed it was full year before the capital saw him in person. An energetic young officer from the Danube, Antonius Primus, was the first to lead his troops Rome-wards. Mucianus was not far behind, but had to turn aside to quell an incursion of the Dacians.

Once again the issue was decided at Cremona, between Primus and Vitellius' officers. Mucianus and Vespasian sent messages to Antonius urging him to wait, but he ignored them. This is known as the second battle of Cremona. The legions of the Danube won, and avenged the earlier insult by pillaging most pitilessly the city where their fellows had laboured.

Vitellius in Rome took no action. His legions forced him to make some resistance, but valour without leadership availed little. Rome was taken once more, his soldiers slaughtered, and he himself killed.

Primus' rapid successes had been watched with mixed feelings by his superiors. When Mucianus reached Rome he paid scant respect

21.1 *Vespasian, Roman emperor* A.D. *69–79.*

to him and the young officer soon left to join Vespasian. Thereafter we hear no more about him. Domitian, Vespasian's youngest son, had been in Rome in a rather perilous position while it was held by Vitellius. The Eastern troops hailed him as Caesar. He was, as we shall see, an arrogant and ambitious young man, and Mucianus kept a careful eye on him also in case he got out of hand.

Mucianus then set to work to restore order in Rome. He also sent an army north to deal with insurrection on the Rhine. There a Roman-trained soldier, Civilis, had started an insurrection among the Batavians, taking advantage of the absence of the Rhine forces.

Finally discipline was renewed at Rome, the Batavian revolt crushed, and late in 70 Vespasian at last came to Rome, leaving Titus to complete the taking of Jerusalem.[1]

---

[1]With Vespasian's return Mucianus too retired to an honoured but inconspicuous position. He died not long after.

Vespasian himself was 69, but his was a vigorous old age. He was of Sabine descent, and his father had been a tax collector. He brought to the imperial purple a down-to-earth peasant commonsense which at times seemed a little incongruous, but which was of incalculable benefit to the office and the empire. His rule was not beset by the palace intrigues which proliferated under Claudius and Nero, fed by ambitious wives. His own wife had died some time ago and he quietly carried on a relationship with a freedwoman Caenis.

He was not popular with the Senate, which regarded him as an upstart. This disdain worried him little, and while he treated the Senate with respect, he gathered his own administrative body, based on the equites not the freedman class. Despite the blood-letting that began his rule, Vespasian avoided any wholesale executions. Only a handful of men were put to death under him, and they with the utmost reluctance. He did, however, when the philosophers, and in particular the Cynics, fomented dissatisfaction with his rule, banish the philosophers and astrologers from Italy.

Vespasian's first care was to set his rule on a firm basis. The Senate voted him the normal prerogatives, in particular the tribunician and proconsular powers. He took the titles of Imperator Caesar Augustus. Unlike Claudius he had no need to hesitate in accepting the military title and, lacking the Julio-Claudian blood, he was not loth to take the official titles of power. For this reason, too, he held the consulship almost continuously throughout his rule, most frequently with his son Titus as colleague.

Vespasian takes Titus as partner in his rule

Vitellius had swollen the numbers of the praetorian guard, and handed it over to the German legions. Vespasian reorganised it, reduced it to its original size, and, when Titus came back to Rome, made him the praetorian prefect. There was to be no danger, at least from that quarter. In fact, Vespasian could truly be said to have made the imperial office a partnership with

Titus. Titus was his colleague in the consulship, held tribunician and proconsular power and was constantly by his father's side. Domitian was given some regard, receiving a number of suffect consulships, but his youth and his temperament did not encourage them to give him more authority. Both the sons received the title of Caesar, and this was in future to be the title of the heir to the throne.

Meanwhile Titus completed the subjection of Jerusalem, amid vast slaughter, despite the fanatical resistance of the Jews. The Temple was razed to the ground and Titus returned to Rome. A legion was left permanently in Judaea and its commander was the real head of the region, taking precedence over the procurator.

When Titus arrived Vespasian ceremoniously closed the doors of the Temple of Janus as Augustus had done before him, to proclaim peace throughout the empire, and father and son celebrated a joint tirumph.

Vespasian and Titus reorganise the Roman empire

In 73 Vespasian and Titus held the censorship together. There was much work for them to do. In particular the Senate had been sorely depleted by civil strife, being reduced to two hundred. It was now brought up again to one thousand.

In filling the gaps Vespasian followed Claudius' example of drawing not only on the upper class of municipal Italy but on the Romanised section of the provinces. Needless to say, this confirmed the low opinion which the Senate already held of him. Many Patrician families had died out over the years, and Patricians were needed to fill certain traditional posts. Vespasian for the first time gave the honour of Patrician rank to some members of the provincial aristocracy. His nominees included Agricola, the famous governor of Britain and father-in-law of the historian Tacitus, Ulpius Traianus, the father of the emperor Trajan, and Verus, the grandfather of the emperor Marcus Aurelius. The two latter were of Spanish origin, while Agricola was from Gaul. The year 80 saw Fronto as consul, the first of African origin. For Vespasian the main function of the Senate was to supply administrators, and he increased the number of suffect consuls, so as to to have a better supply.

The equestrian lists were likewise reinforced from the provinces, and, most important for the emperor's purposes, Roman citizenship was widely extended especially in the western provinces. The whole of Spain received the Latin rights, and many towns had full citizenship conferred on them. As we shall see, this extension was to serve a useful purpose in the reorganisation of the army. Under Vespasian the distinction between the senators and equites became much less important. This was really a natural process as for some time the Senate had been continually refilled from the equestrian ranks, but of course this attitude was yet one more reason for the old guard in the Senate to dislike the emperor.

Another important change took place under Vespasian. The old Roman tradition had been to combine civil and military careers, something which was not easy for peace-loving souls like Cicero. Vespasian tended to ignore this and encourage specialisation. Nerva, who began the next line of emperors, never served in the army, nor did Pliny.

The census fulfilled one other very important purpose. It served as the basis for another most important task facing Vespasian, the reform of taxation.

Rome's finances

One aspect of Vespasian's administration to which he brought a special talent was finance. It was not for nothing that his father had been a tax-gatherer, and he earned for his line the title of the bourgeois emperors. There was need for a shrewd business head at this moment. Recent disorder, reckless donatives and the lavishness of Nero had combined to bring the finances of the empire to a very low state. On the other hand, the provinces had enjoyed a long period of peace and prosperity under the Julio-Claudians, so that when Vespasian increased, in some cases even doubled, taxation, they could well support this step, without bringing destitution to themselves.

Vespasian cancelled the tax exemptions which some cities had enjoyed but he was careful not to be oppressive. One example of this was the directive he sent out to warn the couriers of the imperial post not to burden the provincials by requisitioning horses for their purposes, thus leaving the farmers without their services.

The money thus acquired was not squandered. Vespasian had promised no inflated donative to the troops as a reward for his appointment, and he gave only what was normal. In his own court too his manner of living was frugal. As well as increasing provincial taxation, Vespasian devised other taxes to swell the imperial purse, at times with some ingenuity. To the scandal of many he even taxed public lavatories, and today the name, *la vespasienne*, applied to these utilities, still commemorates him in Paris.

One source of financial disturbance was corrected under the Flavians, namely the one-way trade with the East. From this period the Roman empire began to export goods in return for their imports and the drain on bullion was checked.

Vespasian's interest in coins went beyond the financial aspect. He followed Augustus, whom he greatly admired, in employing his coins for propaganda purposes, even using some of the same slogans. PAX (peace) was the motto on one coin, CONCORDIA (concord) on another. One coin bore a picture of the Temple of Capitoline Jupiter which he had rebuilt.

The reform of the army

One side of imperial administration needed urgent attention from the emperor, and that was the army. The years 68 and 69 had shown them their power. Luckily, the same years had shown the dangers that would result from abusing this power, and Vespasian was eminently the man to restore order among the forces. Indeed Rome had to thank him for the peace which it was to enjoy for the century that followed.

He sobered them from the outset by refusing to make an extravagant gift to win their favours. The praetorian guard was brought under control and restored to the Italian soldiery. The provincial armies needed more thought. They had shown dangerous signs of indiscipline and of regional rivalry. Vespasian cashiered four of the Rhine legions which had taken part in the revolt of Civilis.

Much of the unreliability of the legions was blamed on the low standard of recruits. The soldiers levied in Italy were being drawn from the lowest classes and were of poor quality. Under Vespasian the Romanised provinces were to play an increasing role, and in particular Spain with its newly acquired Latin status and its long tradition of valour in the field. From now on Spain was to play an important part in supplying Rome, not merely with soldiers but with its leaders, including writers and even emperors. As the field of recruitment was a wider one, it was possible to insist on a higher standard and to call on the stalwart middle class of the provincial towns. Only the praetorian guard was recruited in Italy.

The auxiliaries were also a problem. It had become more and more the practice to recruit them locally, on the Rhine, on the Danube, in the East, but the practice had obvious dangers. Vespasian changed this. He insisted that they should be sent to a different area to serve, and that the auxiliary forces of any one area should be of varied origin. The new province of Britain gave him an additional source of supply.

The frontiers

So much for the army. It remained to find out the most effective use for his forces. Vespasian carried further what had been Augustus' intention, to use the army on the frontiers rather than distributed generally throughout the empire. In particular, both the Eastern forces and the Rhine legions were strengthened at the expense of armies which were stationed in provinces within the empire. Moreover, whereas Augustus had stationed his armies in large camps, each containing a number of legions, Vespasian spread them out along the whole frontier, normally in camps of one legion, to form a continuous line of defence.

Vespasian was not happy at the state of the Eastern defences. The whole of Asia Minor was undefended, except for client kingdoms, never a satisfactory substitute. The main bulwark was the army of Syria to the south. Vespasian reconstituted the eastern portion of Asia Minor as provinces, so that now a continuous line of defences ran along the Euphrates.

The Dacian attack had shown that the Danube frontier needed attention. The legions in this area had not been based on the Danube itself but further back on the River Drave. Vespasian moved them up to the Danube.

Another weak point was the area between the Danube and Rhine frontier, roughly the region where the Black Forest now lies. A German army could easily move south at this point, by-passing the two lines of defence. The emperor undertook a campaign of conquest there and acquired the intervening territory, the *agri decumates* as they were called, so that now the frontier was continuous.

Although the imperial legions had built themselves permanent camps they were wooden constructions, vulnerable in particular to fire. Stone camps now rose in their place and elsewhere stone forts which housed auxiliary units. These extended along the whole frontier, and were the predecessors of the more famous wall of Hadrian.

The disposition of the legions was changed to meet the current needs. Spain was now left only one legion. Britain was still a problem area, so it had four legions. Eight were based on the Rhine and six on the Danube. A fleet was also stationed on the Danube.

Archaeology has added to our knowledge of Vespasian's work in the provinces, work of an eminently practical nature. A large number of milestones and bridges bearing his name are evidence of his concern to keep Rome's communications in good order. As always Rome's soldiers were its road-builders.

It is worth noting that never before him had Rome had an emperor so well acquainted with every corner of the empire, and afterwards only Hadrian could be compared to him.

In Britain a scheme of conquest was pursued under competent governors, the last being Agricola. The whole of Britain and Wales was

21.2 *The Colosseum was a brilliant essay in concrete engineering. The great arena was built A.D. 70 and A.D. 82. A third storey added in the third century gave accommodation for 80 000 spectators. The massive piers supporting the arcades were originally covered with marble.*

overrun. An incursion was made into Scotland, and even Ireland was envisaged as a possible venture. Of this, more later.

Public works under Vespasian

In Rome Vespasian countered the charges of meanness which were levelled at his head by his extensive public works. The first act of his rule had been to begin rebuilding the Temple of Capitoline Jupiter, destroyed by the followers of Vitellius. As well, he added to the imperial *fora*, which served to give facilities to trade and public business, and furthermore by their open spaces prevented the danger that the heart of Rome would be utterly choked by its many buildings.[2]

In keeping with his boast that he brought peace to Rome, he called his creation the *Forum Pacis* and build in it the *Templum Pacis*, to which he added a library. Not far away he began the amphitheatre which is still the most conspicuous

landmark of the empire in modern Rome, the Colosseum, as it is known. The building was placed in some of the ground which Nero had with more enthusiasm than discretion set aside for his vast Golden House. It gained its name from the colossal statue of Nero which Hadrian moved to its vicinity after replacing the head of Nero by that of the sun-god.

Literature

Though no devotee of the arts, Vespasian was not heedless of culture. Teachers as well as doctors were granted tax exemption by him, and he endowed a chair of rhetoric. The first professor was the famous Quintilian, who was to

---

[2]Many cities are at this very moment trying to find a solution to the overcrowding of their central portions, which leads to their decay.

have such a profound effect on the practices of education in the Europe of later times.

Apart from Quintilian, Vespasian's rule did not produce great literary talent. We could point, however, to the Jewish historian, Josephus, who fought against him and was spared by him, later to adorn his court and under his patronage to write the history of the Jewish wars. The encyclopedic Pliny the Elder was one of his functionaries, and dictated his endless books to his scribe as he was conveyed on his official business. This era also knew the youth of Plutarch and of Tacitus, who adorned a later age with their writings.

The death of Vespasian

In 79 the hard-working old emperor died and was deified. Many have laughed at his peasant ways and lack of presence, but there was little to criticise in this rule so singularly free from persecution or foolish extravagance. His effect on the later empire cannot be overestimated.

In fact our ancient traditions are not really favourable to Vespasian. His achievements in stablising the finances of the empire, in bringing discipline and security to its frontiers, even of reorganising the bureaucracy and transferring it from the hands of the freedmen to the equites were prodigious. Yet to the establishment in Rome that hardly counted against the fact that he was not one of them, and the fact that he would personally carry some of the first blocks up to start the building of the Capitoline temple, while worthy, only illustrated the point.

Moreover the genuine hostility roused by Domitian reflected on all the Flavians. Add to that the fact that Nerva, who started the new line of emperors by briefly holding the purple really was a senator, and even if Trajan was a Spaniard, he was mainly interested in fighting Rome's wars far away, leaving the day to day running of the empire to its administrators, which included the Senate. Nerva and his successors wished to justify their usurpation of power by denigrating their predecessors, and Rome's writers, led by Tacitus, were happy to oblige.

In some ways Vespasian recalls Claudius, even if in others they were so different, and both these unpretentious men built up the machinery which enabled the Romans to hold wider and longer sway than any other empire (apart from China) in history.

The accession of Titus

Titus' assumption of power created no problems. He had long been co-ruler with his father, and he simply took the usual titles and made the usual donative to the troops. He also immediately nominated Domitian as his successor, but did not associate him with his rule. He was only thirty-nine, not an old man like his father, and also there seems to have been a genuine sibling hostility between the brothers.

Yet his advent did arouse mixed feelings. He had been a young man of immense charm, and indeed had won over the childless Mucianus to favour Vespasian, despite a personal dislike of his father. Yet he had grown up at court under Claudius and Nero, enjoying to the fill all the pleasures of the day, and taking as his mistress king Agrippa's sister Berenice. He had, however, sent her away during Vespasian's rule, and when she reappeared on his accession he sent her away again, though Suetonius adds with great reluctance.

Titus' long apprenticeship served him in good stead. In his short reign of two years he continued the responsible style of government he had helped maintain with Vespasian, and won every heart.

Disasters strike

It was in many ways a calamitous two years, for it was heralded by the eruption of Vesuvius in 79, which overwhelmed Pompeii and Herculaneum, a terrible disaster, even though it has turned the two towns into a permanent folk museum for the modern world. Pliny the Elder was led on by his curiosity to investigate the eruption too closely and met his end there.

The next year there was a huge fire in Rome, in which the Temple of Capitoline Jupiter met its end once more. This in turn was followed by a plague.

These events enabled Titus to show the generosity which made him beloved, but which has led some to suggest that a protracted rule, while it might have been brilliant, could have had adverse effects on the treasury.

Titus succoured the victims of the two disasters liberally, then in 80 completed the Colosseum, celebrating its opening by games and largess on a lavish scale. He also built the Baths of Titus, and in 81 erected the Arch of Titus, on which he portrayed his conquest of Jerusalem.

Archaeologists add to our knowledge of his activities. They have established that like his father he was diligent in road-works in the provinces and that he also undertook maintenance work on the canals of Egypt.

In 81 Titus died suddenly, at the age of 42, mourned by all except his handsome but sullen brother Domitian, who had been overshadowed by him in his lifetime, and does not seem to have been on the best of terms with him.

Some have conjectured that a second Nero lay hidden in Titus, but unlike his predecessor, he was no teenager when he took power, and it is doubtful if he would have been susceptible to such degeneration. Extravagant he well might have been on occasion, and more impetuous than his father, but he would probably not have diverged so markedly from the man who had ruled beside his father for so long before.

The accession of Domitian

In 81 Domitian was hailed as emperor by the praetorian guard and then accepted by the Senate. Domitian had not been prepared for his task in the same way as Titus. He had been given no military experience under Vespasian and Titus, and no significant share in public administration. The office of suffect consul which he held at times was only of two months' duration, and was of little practical importance. There is indeed the suggestion that Vespasian did not regard him as reliable, and that Titus actively disliked him. This is confirmed to some extent by the fact that the latter did not grant him either the tribunician or proconsular power, the outward sign of inheritance, even though Titus had no children. The lack of concord between the two is probably correct, although the shortness of Titus' rule and the disasters which plagued it left him little opportunity to make thorough plans for his administration, or succession.

In a financial sense Titus' death was unwelcome. It meant that a new donative had to be given to the troops within two years of the donative given by Titus. This fact, coupled with the generosity of Titus and the disasters with which he had to cope, must have meant that the treasury was reduced to a low state on Domitian's arrival. It is significant, as Rostovtseff points out, that no attempt was made to rebuild Pompeii and Herculaneum after the eruption. There simply was not enough money to do so.

Domitian was thirty years old when he succeeded. He conducted no elaborate obsequies for his brother, except for arranging for his deification, and even that only after some months. His overriding concern was to get on with being an emperor.

Uprising by the Chatti

He was not left in peace for long. The first crisis, a military one, was welcome to him; for he had not proved himself with the soldiers, and he now had his opportunity. The occasion was an incursion made by the Chatti, a powerful tribe across the Rhine not far from the *limes*[3] which Vespasian established through the *agri decumates*.

The uprising was crushed, and Domitian took the opportunity to extend the limes northwards. The area thus taken over was protected by a

---

[3]'Boundary', used here for the border between the Rhine and the Danube.

series of roads linking it with the Gallic provinces, and it was civilised, proving a valuable addition to Rome's provinces.

A series of stone forts on the same lines as those Vespasian had built were constructed on the new frontier, but on a much more ambitious scale. The reorganisation of the Rhine frontier was to prove very successful, and enabled Domitian and his successors to reduce the number of legions there in order to strengthen the Danube.

He reduced the number of legions on the Rhine to seven, increasing the Danube force to ten. He also followed Vespasian's policy and actually made it a strict rule that no more than one legion should be housed in each fort.

Relations with the Senate

Domitian returned to Rome to celebrate a triumph and accept the title of *Germanicus*. It seems to have been at this time that he increased the annual pay of the soldiers from 225 to 300 denarii, a measure which must have imposed a strain on his treasury. It was, however, the first increase they had had since Augustus.

The Flavians were not popular with the Senate, and Domitian incurred their chief odium. This was partly because he was the last of the dynasty, and it was he whom Nerva replaced, but even more it was his lack of tact in dealing with that body. Like his predecessors he held the consulship at least in the early part of his rule. Later he seems to have disdained such a conventional office. Before he became emperor he was consul seven times, afterwards ten more, a record. Domitian also worried the Senate because he would not give the promise his predecessors normally gave on their accession, never to impose a capital sentence on a senator. This seemed ominous and in the event their fear was fully justified.

In 85 he took the title of permanent censor. Vespasian had used that magistracy in order to reform the Senate, and Domitian's act gave him a perpetual control over that body, a most unwelcome move. Domitian's abuse of the office of censor caused it to become as unpopular as the

title of dictator after Sulla. It symbolised thereafter the brow-beating of the Senate by the emperor, and later emperors carefully avoided it. Even when they revised the senatorial lists they used the censorial powers implicit in the consulship, as Augustus had done many years before.

Domitian made regular use of the senatorial committee, the *Concilium*, which Augustus had initiated, but which had since fallen into disuse, and even used a number of equites in it, a progressive reform. Yet he continued to develop his own administrative bureaux, in which he made considerable use of freedmen.

He also accepted, even encouraged, emperor-worship, being saluted by poets as *dominus et deus* (lord and god), a title which he finally used himself. This gave great offence, especially as *dominus* was the title used by slaves to their masters.

Britain under the Flavians

Military operations in Britain were continuous under the Flavians. Vespasian sent out Cerealis to govern it in 70, an able man who had been one of the commanders who put down the Batavian revolt. Cerealis subdued northern England as far north as the site of the future Hadrian's Wall, and he was also engaged in fighting in south Wales. His successor was the writer Frontinus, who completed the south Wales campaign.

In 77 Vespasian appointed Agricola. He was a notable governor in his own right, but he is even better known because his son-in-law Tacitus wrote of him in his book called *Agricola*. He put the government of Britain on a more equitable basis, outlawing plundering, and undertook a most ambitious campaign. He conquered the rest of Wales, took the island of Mona, the Druid stronghold, and extended Rome's domination yet further north to the line where the Antonine Wall was later built. Finally in 84 in one glorious battle he defeated the Scottish forces and made plans to invade Ireland, but this was the end, for Domitian recalled him to Rome. The recall was not unusual; for he had already held the governorship for two terms, but he was advised to retire from public life. Actually

Agricola's policy in Britain was not the most sensible; for both the Scottish and Irish ventures would be hazardous and of doubtful profit.

Trouble on the Danube and the Rhine

Meanwhile trouble was arising on the Danube. A new prince of the Dacians, Decebalus, roused national aspirations and led an army across the Danube, defeating the army sent against him. This frontier had been somewhat neglected by Vespasian in his concern for the west and for the Euphrates. It had insufficient troops and was not guarded along its whole length.

Domitian went to the front and was at first successful. Subsequently he sent Fuscus on a punitive expedition into Dacia itself, where he was defeated and killed. A second expedition was more successful, but Domitian was not able to benefit from this victory; for just then, encouraged by the emperor's preoccupation, Saturninus, the governor of Upper Germany, began a revolt, seizing the soldiers' savings chest, both to finance his venture and to ensure their loyalty.

Domitian set out at once to deal with Saturninus, bidding Trajan, the future emperor, to join him from Spain. Before he arrived the uprising had been crushed by Norbanus, the general of the Lower Rhine army.

Before Domitian left the Danube area he came to terms with Decebalus, and granted him an annual subsidy to guard the frontier. This was no heroic solution, but it was a practical one. The neighbouring tribes, the Marcomanni, Quadi and Sarmatae, were in a great state of unrest, and Decebalus did provide some guarantee against their inroads during the following years.

Norbanus had tried to prevent a resulting flood of executions by destroying all Saturninus' papers. He was only partly successful. Domitian was horrified that a conspiracy could be formed, and was only made less secure by his inability to find the actual names of those involved. From this time dates the renewed activity of the informers, which was so bitterly criticised by the writers of the next period.

An evaluation of Domitian

It has been suggested that Domitian's treason trials served a further purpose. The increased pay he awarded his army and the campaigns he had to wage must have begun to eat into his financial resources. By confiscating the property of the condemned, Domitian did in fact gain a new source of income. To suggest that this caused the trials is, however, too much. It is typical of the campaign of vilification directed at the Flavians and especially at Domitian. As in the case of Claudius, inscriptional evidence has helped modern historians to gain a more balanced view.

Domitian had undoubtedly a most unfortunate personality. He was arrogant and rigid in his beliefs and could not stand opposition. Yet these faults had their compensations. In the provinces his insistence on obedience had good results. Even Suetonius admits grudgingly that the government in them had never been fairer. Like Vespasian he was insistent that the imperial post did not impose a burden on the people they travelled through and he was diligent in road works. Incidentally he converted the military posts of Upper and Lower Germany into provinces.

He was also interested in culture. He built up the libraries and was on good terms with the writer Quintilian, whom he paid a salary. His unyielding views had some comical if inconvenient aspects. He insisted that the toga be worn to the theatre, though that clumsy and hot garment had long been abandoned for everyday use. Even Horace said that the toga was only used to be buried in, and that was in the time of Augustus.

In Rome the philosophers were incurring unpopularity. The Stoics had always been somewhat critical of the emperors, especially if they became too absolute, but a related sect, the Cynics, went further, and made a general attack on the whole idea of imperial rule. They had worried Vespasian, and Domitian had no hesitation in expelling them from Rome, together with the astrologers, with whom they were associated in the public mind.

Domitian continued his family's concern with

public works. He completed the Colosseum,[4] the Baths of Titus and the Arch of Titus, all still incomplete at his brother's death, and rebuilt magnificently the Temple of Capitoline Jupiter, which had been for a second time destroyed in the fire which swept Rome under Titus. He also erected a fine temple to the deified Vespasian.

As we have noted, the state's finances were at a low ebb in his time, owing to the disasters under Titus and the double donative caused by Titus' early death. Most of Domitian's work was finishing what had been started by his predecessors, but he consoled himself by putting his own name on the works he completed, another action condemned by his critics.

However, the activities of the informers and the suspicions of Domitian were soon to recoil on the emperor himself. He had no near relative to command the praetorian guard and therefore restored the dual leadership of that body, with frequent changes. He had no sons and had not named a successor.

Finally, when he ordered his cousin, Clemens, a man generally regarded as harmless, to be executed, following him with Glabrio, an ex-consul, fear of conspiracy produced the dreaded reality. The commanders of the guard and his own wife, who feared to be a victim, planned the deed, and in 96 Domitian fell at the hands of a butler. The Senate in exultation condemned his memory, annulled his acts and had his images destroyed.

An evaluation of the Flavians

The Flavians were not loved by the Senate, and consequently were ill-spoken of by the historians, who were either senators themselves, like Tacitus, or in the case of the Greek writers, enjoyed senatorial patronage.

In addition, the emperors who followed could themselves be regarded as upstarts, especially when one considers the provincial birth of most of them. They were not unaware of this fact, and endeavoured to counter it by contrasting the benefits of their rule with the undesirability of those who came before them.

Yet in fact Trajan and Hadrian were logical successors of the Flavians. Like them they were military men more closely connected with the army than with the ruling class of Rome. From the Flavians too they inherited that preoccupation with the frontiers of the empire, a concern which was soon proved so necessary.

With the Flavians there was a general replacement of freedmen by equestrians in the important administrative posts near the emperor. Even Domitian, who made some use of freedmen, pursued the same general policy, and the succeeding emperors followed their example.

Finally the period was marked by the increased enrolment of the more Romanised provincials both in the citizen ranks and in the Senate. Spain, in particular, benefited and, as we have noted, two of the new emperors, Trajan and Marcus Aurelius, came from Spanish families which had been advanced by the Flavians.

So, despite Tacitus, who hated Domitian and in consequence vilified Tiberius as the emperor on whom Domitian modelled himself, we must be cautious in accepting the verdict of ancient historians. Whatever the Flavians lacked in aristocratic manners or tact, they brought Rome back from the brink of anarchy, and enabled it to continue mistress of the Mediterranean world through many later trials.

Pompeii and Herculaneum

The eruption of Vesuvius in 79 buried two cities, Pompeii to the south-east and the smaller Herculaneum to the south-west of the mountain. Pompeii was covered by volcanic ash to the depth of about seven metres, but Herculaneum, which was closer, suffered a worse fate. It was overwhelmed by lava to a depth of nearly twenty metres. Yet it was Herculaneum that was first discovered.

It lay beneath the Italian city of Resina and in 1709 a peasant digging a well came on blocks of

---

[4]He added one row of seats and a building to house the gladiators.

21.3 *Aerial view of Herculaneum.*

marble. The Austrians were then in control of that part of Italy and Prince Elbeuf heard of the underground marble. He wanted to build a villa in nearby Portici and continued excavations. A complete theatre was disclosed surmounted by a bronze horse and chariot. It was also found that the town was Herculaneum. No matter. The villa was built from the marble and the horse thrown aside. Work was then abandoned. These years were made particularly unpredictable by the political instability of Italy.

The Spaniards under Charles III were next to hold Naples. Charles III heard of the finds and had excavations continue and used the villa of Portici as the first museum of Herculaneum. Yet he too was basically a treasure-hunter. The

bronze horse was melted down to make a statue of him and his queen. Now a new site was found and excavated near Naples. It was some years before it was found that it was Pompeii.

So it went on, while Italy was tossed in wars. Successive rulers were interested or neglectful. Salvation finally came when Garibaldi united Italy in the Risorgimento. He first put the writer Alexandre Dumas in charge of Pompeii, which roused an uproar, then made a more careful choice—an archaeologist of great ability, Fiorelli.

Fiorelli began his work in 1861 and he is the father of Pompeii as we know it. He excavated and restored with care, even replanting the gardens of the houses, carefully documenting his work as he went, so that at last Pompeii appeared

21.4 *A bakery in Pompeii.*

as it once was, of immense value to the historian and a delight to the tourist.

Herculaneum could not be opened up as easily, being so solidly buried, and a series of tunnels had to be used to reveal it. Yet the lava had in compensation preserved even more completely, not crushing in the roofs as in Pompeii.

In 1980 a severe earthquake shook Pompeii, damaging buildings, so now only a small part is safe to visit. Also industrial smog is destroying the wall-paintings that are one of Pompeii's glories. Money is needed in abundance to save the city and Italy lacks that money.

Then in 1982 an expedition financed by the National Geographic made an interesting discovery at Herculaneum. Whereas many bodies were found at Pompeii, few were unearthed in Herculaneum, and it was thought they had escaped. Then excavating the beach area, in modern times set back from the sea, a sea wall was found and over a hundred bodies crouched behind it in a pathetic attempt to escape from the volcano.

It would be most rewarding to read a book on Pompeii. I suggest you begin with a book that has good illustrations. It gives a vivid picture of a bustling, commercial city, many of the industries in the hands of Greek freedmen. It is thought that possibly Petronius' novel, the *Satyricon*, was set in Pompeii. Herculaneum was a less active city, but the villas of the aristocrats overlooking the sea, are a revelation.

The city of Ostia

It is convenient here to discuss the town of Ostia, the other important site showing life in Roman Italy.

In Republican times Rome had no nearby harbour. There was no natural harbour near the mouth of the Tiber, an area also made difficult by the Fucine marshes. The corn supply, so necessary for the city as it grew, was brought to the harbour of Puteoli, near Neapolis (Naples), many kilometres from Rome and requiring a difficult and expensive journey for the supply to be transported to the city.

The emperor Claudius saw that Rome needed a more convenient harbour and he developed the little town of Ostia, which lay at the mouth of the Tiber. He drained the marshes, built a large artificial harbour and set above it a four-storied lighthouse, modelled on Pharos, the world's first lighthouse, which was in Alexandria. He built an aqueduct to the town, constructed granaries and a fire-station to guard against the hazard of fire, just as prevalent then as in modern cities. It was an ambitious project and, although he saw Ostia in use, the work was not complete when he died.

Domitian, that much maligned emperor, was the next to do important work there, as we know now from archaeology, not of course from ancient historians. He added a number of buildings and took the important step of having them raised above flood level, another danger in such a low-lying area by a large river.

In 62 there was a violent storm which created havoc to the ships in Claudius' harbour. It was too large and exposed for final safety, and Trajan took the necessary step of adding an hexagonal inner harbour to provide extra protection. The harbour Puteoli had continued to be used, but by Trajan's time Ostia supplanted it almost completely.

When the Roman empire fell Ostia became a ruin and for a long time was only a source of lime-stone blocks to be used directly by builders, or burnt in their kilns to make cement.

With the Renaisssance some antiquarian interest in Ostia developed but serious work on the site did not begin until 1855 conducted by Visconti authorised by Pope Pius IX, at which time an Ostian Museum was also established. However, the most important work began in this century, in 1907 and especially in 1912 when Guido Calza took over the work. He excavated Ostia and published his discoveries, using all modern techniques until his death in 1946, and we owe to him the full development and restoration of the town.

Ostia also shows a Roman town of the early empire, but as it did not have as tragic an end, it is without its inhabitants. It is of special interest too because, whereas Pompeii was a town of houses and shops, Ostia was a city of apartment houses. They were justly called *insulae* as they were huge blocks, often four stories high, and were like islands with streets on all four sides. Another point of interest is that Ostia recorded its local events on certain public buildings, a public calendar as it were or *Fasti*. As Ostia was so linked with Rome they provide some interesting details of Rome's history where they survive, notably for the reign of Trajan.

Thus between Pompeii, Herculaneum and Ostia we have a vivid visual record of the life of the ancient Romans to supplement the accounts of its writers.

Date table

A.D.

69	The year of the Four Emperors. Vespasian's accession.
71	Judaea finally conquered and Temple of Janus closed.
79	Death of Vespasian and accession of Titus. Eruption of Vesuvius.
80	Fire in Rome.
81	Death of Titus, accession of Domitian.
83	Campaign in Germany.
85	Domitian becomes life censor. Agricola recalled. Dacian revolt.
89	Revolt of Saturninus.
96	Assassination of Domitian.

Select quotations

1 Pliny, *Letters*, VI, 16, 16:
(Eruption of Vesuvius.)
The houses shook with repeated huge tremors and seemed as if they were moving from their foundations and waving this way and that. In the open air the falling pumice, even though it was light and hollow, caused anxiety. After weighing the dangers, it seemed best to go out of doors. With him (Pliny the Elder) it was a case of opposing arguments, with others of opposing fears. They put pillows on their heads, tied with

bandages. That afforded protection against falling objects. It was now day-time elsewhere, while there it was night, darker and thicker than any night. . . . My uncle, lying down on a heap of linen, repeatedly asked for cold water which he drank. Then flames, and the smell of sulphur, heralding flames, turned others in flight and woke him. He rose, supported by two slaves, and at once fell back dead.

2 Tacitus, *Agricola*, 41:
(Agricola returns to Rome after his governorship of Britain.)
Repeatedly during those days he was accused and acquitted before Domitian in his absence. The reason for his peril was no misdeed, no wrong which any one had suffered, but an emperor who hated virtue, the man's own glory, and, the worst kind of foe, men who praised him. And the subsequent condition of the state was such that Agricola could not be ignored. So many armies lost in Moesia, Dacia, Germany and Pannonia through the rashness or cowardice of their leaders. . . . So when loss succeeded loss and every year was marked by death and disaster, the popular voice called for Agricola as general.
(It is now thought that Tacitus rather overestimated his father-in-law, but he never forgave Domitian for the treatment accorded him.)

Further reading

A. Garzetti, *From Tiberius to the Antonines*, Methuen, 1970.

M. Brion, *Pompeii and Herculaneum*, Elek Books, London, 1960.

M. Grants, *The Art and Life of Pompeii and Herculaneum*, Newsweek, New York, 1979.

R. Meiggs, *Roman Ostia*, Oxford Clarendon, 1973.

Suetonius, *The Twelve Emperors*.

Tacitus, *Agricola*, Penguin Classics.

Juvenal, Martial and Petronius for the life of the period.

Topics for essays or discussion

1 Show how the Flavians restored order to the empire after the anarchy of 69. Are there signs of renewed trouble under Domitian?

2 How did Vespasian try to give prestige to a new dynasty? Did he succeed?

3 It has been claimed that Vespasian took Augustus as his model. Show what basis if any the assertion has.

4 Compare and contrast Vespasian's provincial policy with that of Claudius.

5 'Vespasian needed all his down-to-earth shrewdness to make good the wastefulness of his predecessor.' Discuss.

6 It has been said that Vespasian tried to cooperate with the Senate, whereas Domitian openly flouted it. Account for the change.

7 Was Tacitus justified in his vehement hatred of Domitian?

8 Analyse the growth in importance of the equites under the Flavians.

9 Do you consider that Titus, if he had lived, might have become a second Nero?

10 Analyse the Flavians' relations with the army. Do you consider that they succeeded in this field? If so, why?

Chapter 22

Nerva, Trajan and Hadrian

Sources

FOR THIS PERIOD our main sources are Dio Cassius. Unfortunately only the eleventh century summary of this writer, and *The Augustan History*, a fourth century work of unknown authorship, which began with the life of Hadrian survive. To this should be added Pliny, who lived and wrote in Trajan's time and gives an invaluable insight into many aspects of his rule, not least when he was Trajan's governor in Bithynia-Pontus. There is also Trajan's Column, illustrating the Dacian Campaign, a tantalising monument, like some comic strip without the captions, which raises as many questions as it answers. Fortunately archaeology has been invaluable, as there is an abundance of inscriptions and papyri from the second century.

Unfortunately our sources are as prejudiced against Hadrian as they are adulatory of Trajan. In particular, Dio Cassius was a senator and the Senate was very hostile to the emperor, as both as the beginning and end of his rule there were conspiracies against him and senators were executed. His homosexuality, which has affected

some modern writers, should not have been a concern to an age which accepted such behaviour. He was, however, a devotee of culture, especially of Greek culture, and that would not please the traditional Roman, and he was both finicky in matters of detail and, especially towards the end, prone to suspicion, traits that would not endear him to his associates.

The accession of Nerva

The line of rulers that follow are commonly known as the 'good emperors'. The title was not undeserved, although the endeavour to enhance their prestige through belittling the Flavians was not commendable.

Upon the assassination of Domitian the praetorian prefects and the group which had planned the deed promptly chose a senator, Nerva, to be the next emperor, and the Senate welcomed the choice with acclamation. Nerva was over sixty. He had held no military command, but he had been the only colleague Vespasian had taken in the consulship apart from Titus. He had been on good terms with Nero and was generally popular. He also had no family. Finally, and this was probably very important, on his mother's side he was distantly related to the Julio-Claudians.

The Senate then proceeded to damn the memory of Domitian. A number of informers were dealt with, and there was even briefly an ugly riot, but this was settled.

Nerva was a kindly man. After giving the donative to the troops he refused any further execution of men prominent in Domitian's time. Those exiled by the last emperor were recalled.

In 97 Nerva was appointed consul. He made Trajan the commander on the Lower Rhine.

In Rome he completed the Forum which Domitian had been building. Naturally it would not be called after that emperor. It came to be called the *Forum Transitorium* ('passage-way forum'). In addition, a scheme was set up to distribute land to the needy, a necessary move, as economically Italy had been degenerating steadily towards the end of the first century.

Meanwhile, all was not well. The treasury had met the donative. The increased pay to the army was proving a heavy burden, and the land scheme was an additional strain. More serious was the gradual realisation by the guards that the hand at the helm was not a strong one. The praetorians had not been happy at Domitian's assassination, for he was popular with them. They now took direct action, burst into the palace and demanded that those responsible be executed. Nerva was powerless. Petronius, who had been a commander of the praetorians and had taken part in the conspiracy, was killed, and others met the same fate.

This mutiny was an ominous sign. Nerva knew his limitations and feared that chaos might return at any moment. He had no children of his own; so it was both natural and necessary for him to adopt a successor. He chose Trajan, the commander on the Lower Rhine. His action quelled any further unrest and he enjoyed peace for the brief space remaining to him, dying three months after.

This was Nerva. He might, like the Forum, sometimes called after him, be dubbed the passage-way emperor. He did not achieve much that was positive, but he did enable a safe transition from the Flavians to the orderly and prosperous period that ensued.

Trajan

Trajan was the most restless emperor Rome had yet possessed. He barely saw the capital. The reason for this could have been that he had no natural attachment to Rome, being of Spanish origin, and that he never ceased to regard himself as a general first and an emperor second.

Primary sources are meagre for his rule. Neither Tacitus nor Suetonius wrote about this period, and Pliny the Younger's address to the emperor, which does deal with this time, is too monotonously eulogistic to be reliable. His letters are of more value.

Trajan's cousin Hadrian, the next emperor, brought him the news of his elevation, but he took it calmly. He made no haste to return to Rome. He gave orders for the deification of Nerva in his absence and sent for the commander of the praetorian guard and his accomplices, who

22.1 *Trajan, Roman emperor* A.D. *98–117.*

had mutinied against Nerva. They were promptly executed.

His next thought was to assure the frontiers. He left two good governors on the Rhine, Servianus and Licinius Sura, both Spanish, and made some raids over the Danube. Only then did he come back to Rome, in 99.

Trajan is welcomed in Rome

The Senate was eager to welcome Trajan and he fulfilled every expectation. He entered Rome on foot, made the customary declaration that no senator would suffer capital punishment under him, and was assiduous in attendance at the Senate. He and his wife established an unostentatious lifestyle, and made themselves approachable on all occasions. He also took steps to assure Rome's corn supply, always a touchy point. Yet for all the affability his rule was still basically an autocracy, and apart from the welcome absence of informers, was not in its essentials so very different from the rule of Domitian.

One interest that Trajan shared with the populace was the spectacle. He at once saw to the enlargement of the Circus Maximus, and he put on a number of large gladiatorial displays. In 100 Pliny, then elected as *consul suffectus*, delivered his *Panegyric*, extolling the virtues and achievements of the emperor.

The Dacian Wars

In 101 Trajan prepared to invade Dacia. His reasons were not hard to see. The ruler of Dacia, Decebalus, was very capable. Domitian had paid him a subsidy to keep the peace in his area, and he took his opportunity. He unified and fortified Dacia, and made a series of alliances with neighbouring peoples. Meanwhile Rome was in a low financial position. Trajan had made the customary gift to the people, but he had to pay the donative to the troops in instalments. Their increased pay was still a problem, and the subsidy to Dacia was an extra burden.

Trajan was not provoked to war, but for him it made sense. He was an excellent general and here was a chance to use his talents to the profit of Rome. He assembled an army of about 80 000 legionaries, and as usual the same number of auxiliaries. The Danube fleet was also there, and the praetorian cohorts, led by Claudius Livianus who was their commander during most of Trajan's rule. Hadrian came with him but with no specific command.

We do not possess a detailed literary account of Trajan's campaigns in Dacia. He did commemorate them in a narrative frieze which went in spiral form up Trajan's Column, but although scholars have tried to interpret them, pictures unadorned with inscriptional comment are very hard to decipher.

He does seem to have invaded from Upper Moesia, and advanced slowly, consolidating his advance by building roads and establishing garrisons as he went. He did not, however, manage to get beyond the Iron Gate that year.

In 102 he attacked the Iron Gate, while his general Quietus took a force and encircled Decebalus, taking him from the rear. Decebalus asked for peace, which was granted on condition that Dacia accept the status of a client state. Trajan then withdrew, but left garrisons and built an excellent bridge over the Danube.

Decebalus was not content. As soon as the Romans left he began to reorganise his resources and in 105 he attacked the adjoining Roman provinces. Trajan returned.

Trajan left Rome in June, as we find recorded in the Fasti of Ostia, but proceeded with his usual caution. He spent that year and the beginning of 106 making preparations.

When he did advance he met little real opposition. The capital was taken and Decebalus fled. He was pursued and committed suicide. Dacia was made a province and Trajan returned to Rome to celebrate a magnificent triumph.

Trajan celebrates peace with public building

Dacia was a rich prize and its wealth came principally from its gold mines. Trajan soon had them working once more, bringing him and his country renewed prosperity. As for the Danube frontier, Trajan's expedition was effective, bringing fifty years of peace. Dacian gold finally enabled him to reward his troops generously, and to continue putting on gladiatorial shows of which he was so fond.

The next seven years Trajan spent in Rome and they were busy ones, continuing the work of his predecessors and developing his own.

Nerva had made loans at a low rate of interest in order to enable men to buy land in Italy. The interest paid by these people he had used to finance the upbringing of free-born Italian children, a form of child endowment in short. This scheme Trajan continued and amplified.

His building activities were diverse, including a number of aqueducts, temples, baths and arches, but he is most famous for his Forum. Trajan's Forum, continued by the *Basilica Ulpia* (named after his family), ends the line of imperial *fora* and is the most spectacular of them. In the centre of the Forum stood Trajan's Column, offered by the Senate but paid from the spoils of the Dacian Wars, which bore a pictorial representation of the Wars upon it. Trajan's

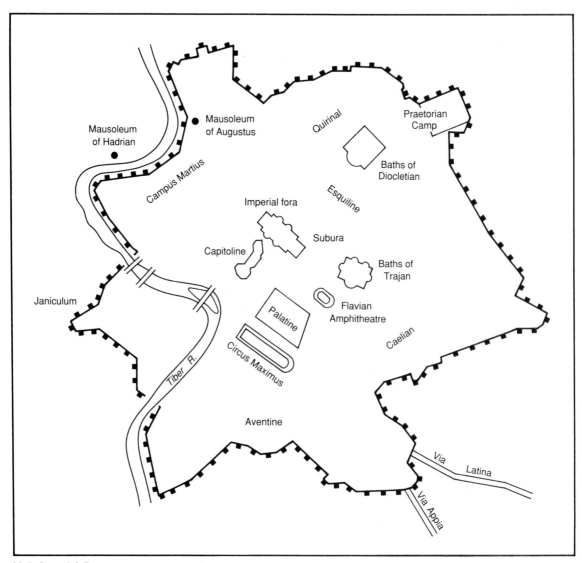

22.2 Imperial Rome.

market was set around the Column, while the Basilica Ulpia, which was roofed in bronze contained two libraries, one Latin, one Greek. According to the *Fasti Ostienses* they were dedicated in 113.

As would be expected, Trajan was also industrious in road-works. Under him the via Appia was almost entirely remade, while mile-stones bearing his name testify to his work in the provinces. Spain received special attention, while Gaul, which already had good roads, needed less.

In the East he built a number of roads feeding his new bridge over the Danube.

Trajan's administration

Trajan, like his predecessors, had a senatorial *concilium*, which was headed by a Spaniard, Licinius Sura. In his administration he made a point of departing from the Flavian policy in certain obvious matters. As part of his general

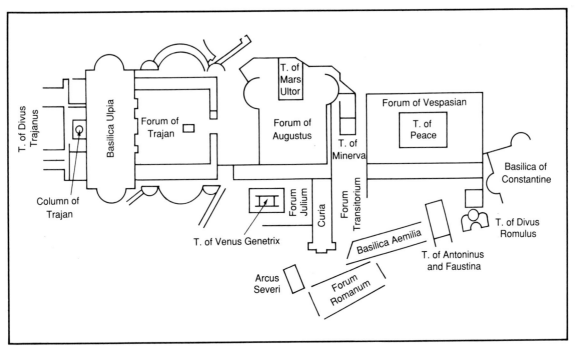

22.3 The Imperial Fora.

conciliatory attitude to the Senate, he only accepted six consulships. He also did not take the office of censor with its implied control of Senate membership.

In other respects he actually followed his predecessors quite closely.[1] Like them he used equestrians in administrative posts, going even further in this matter than they had. They had replaced the tax farmers (publicani) more and more by their own officials. This process Trajan completed. When Trajan became emperor, he found Domitian's appointees governing the provinces. Many of them continued in their posts.

Again, for all his friendliness towards the Senate, he did not leave it untouched. Himself a provincial he raised the proportion of provincial senators to forty per cent. Whereas Spain and Gaul had been called on in earlier years to provide recruits, he turned rather to the Eastern provinces. He was a practical man. The new senators were called on to help the depressed state of Italy, and had to invest one-third of their capital in Italian land.

One institution which he founded has met with criticism. A number of municipal towns and indeed whole provinces had been inefficient or over-ambitious and had become embarrassed financially. To curb this tendency he sent out inspectors who looked into the affairs of these centres, and if necessary gave advice. That would seem to be a very practical idea, but as a result local governments hesitated to take any action on their own initiative and this helped the inevitable growth of a top-heavy over-centralised bureaucracy.

One of the inspectors was Pliny the Younger, who was sent to Bithynia. We still have his correspondence with Trajan covering this period, carefully preserved, needless to say, by Pliny, who was a great social snob. Among these letters

---

[1] Trajan followed Flavian policy in favouring the provinces as recruiting grounds for the legions. Indeed, by now Italy supplied little except the members of the praetorian guard. Parker, *The Roman Legions*, brings evidence against the theory earlier held that Vespasian actually stopped the recruitment of the legions in Italy.

is the famous exchange concerning Christians, who were causing embarrassment by refusing to take part in emperor-worship. Trajan's instructions were a model of good sense, counselling firmness, while avoiding as far as possible provoking any confrontation with this difficult section of society.

Trajan's last years

Trajan's military prowess, which was his claim to glory, was also his weakness. He had fought Dacia, which was embarrassing Rome. In was inevitable that he should finally attack Parthia.

In 113 Parthia deposed the king of Armenia and installed a king of its own choice. Trajan set out at once. The new Armenian ruler tried to be conciliatory, but in vain. Armenia was made a province, and Trajan then went on to seize a number of Parthian dependencies. In 116 he went over the Tigris River and seized the Parthian district on the other side, calling it the province of Assyria.

These were mighty achievements, but they overtaxed the resources of the empire and the ageing emperor. Trajan had depleted the frontiers of soldiers for his expedition and as a result revolts broke out over a wide area, extending as far as Britain. The revolts were crushed, with success and also brutality, but the effort was too much. Trajan had a stroke and died, as he would have wished, in the field.

Trajan is a somewhat controversial figure. There is no doubt of his ability, especially as a soldier, and his Dacian wars helped restore the Roman finances when they urgently needed relief. On the other hand, he did go too far in his conquests, and Hadrian's subsequent action in withdrawing to earlier frontiers was necessary. Some say that none the less his military achievements were important, in that they restored the prestige of Rome's arms, and ensured peace for the following period. Others hold that his capture of Dacia and the crushing of Parthia (which never entirely recovered from his invasion) removed two useful buffer states, which might have helped to keep back the advancing barbarians. Both claims are probably correct.

Hadrian is acclaimed by the army as Trajan's successor

The man who was to succeed Trajan was his cousin, born in the same Spanish colony, Italica. He was orphaned at the age of ten and left to the guardianship of Attianus and Trajan. It was Attianus who first took on the task, and he brought the lad to Rome where he studied and conceived the love of Greece and of its culture which was to dominate his later life.

At the age of seventeen he was summoned by Trajan, then one of Domitian's generals. Trajan's wife Plotina had no children and conceived a great fondness for the youth, whose interests she furthered. In 100 she arranged his marriage to Sabina, a grandniece of Trajan.

Trajan was now emperor, and he took Hadrian with him in his campaigns, where he seems to have acquitted himself well. By the time of the

22.4 *Hadrian, Roman emperor* A.D. *117–38.*

fatal Eastern campaign he had served a consulship and was governor of Syria. When Trajan died he was proclaimed emperor by his legions, and it was stated that Trajan had appointed him his heir. He was aged forty-two. The Senate in due course ratified the succession. It had really no option in the matter.

The appointment caused some gossip and ill feeling. It was asked why Trajan had not given Hadrian the customary tribunician and proconsular powers, as a sign of adoption. Some suggested that the inheritance was the doing not of Trajan but Plotina. However, the hardy old warrior had been at no time willing to recognise his limitations, as the Parthian campaigns themselves proved, and he was not the first or the last man to put off arranging for matters attending on his own death.

On the other side, although Nerva had set the example of adoption, which was to become characteristic of the emperors of this period, there were many, particularly among the generals, who had served Trajan with ability and loyalty, who failed to see what qualities in the young man justified the choice. In short, jealousy fanned rumour when there was no clear adoption or blood link to quell it.

Hadrian restores order in the provinces

Hadrian found that his immediate task was no easy one. There were revolts on every side, and he felt a lack of support from some of Trajan's leading generals. One of the most important of them, Quietus the Moor, he passed over in dealing with the Eastern revolts, sending instead Turbo, who was devoted to him. He saw that one problem was that the frontiers were stretched beyond endurance, and he immediately fell back on the Euphrates, leaving Armenia in its old state of a client kingdom, and giving up new acquisitions such as Assyria.

The army was favourable to him, as he was a tried soldier (and throughout his reign he kept this popularity with them), but, leaving nothing to chance, he gave them double the normal donative.

Like Trajan before him, but with more urgent reason, he was in no hurry to go to Rome and accept his nomination as emperor. It was eleven months before he arrived. Turbo crushed the rebels, taking terrible toll of the Jews of Alexandria who had been some of the most fanatic. He put the key post of Syria in the hands of Severus, whose great-grandson was to be the future emperor Marcus Aurelius.

Even before he arrived at the capital trouble broke out. It was announced that there had been a plot against the new emperor headed by four of Trajan's leading men, including Quietus. The Senate, urged on by Hadrian's former guardian Attianus (then one of the prefects of the praetorian guard), had the four men seized and executed.

Hadrian put Turbo in charge of the still troubled northern region and now at length hastened home. He professed great distress at the executions. Whether he had really known about them we are not certain, and doubtless never will be. He made Attianus retire from his post as praetorian prefect, together with his colleagues, but he heaped honours on the old man in recognition of his many services.

Past history had shown the importance of choosing loyal men for the head of the guard, and Hadrian recalled Turbo to be one of the prefects. Hadrian was a puzzling man. After appointing Turbo, a very wise choice, he named as the man's colleague, of all things, one of his literary friends.

Hadrian's relationship with the Senate

Hadrian had come to Rome under a cloud, and he did his best to dispel it. He promised the Senate that no senator would in future be condemned except by his fellows, a promise he kept. He gave largess to the people and celebrated splendid games, in Trajan's honour. He had ordered the dead emperor to be deified as soon as he had succeeded him, and before his own return. He was consul at the time of his return, but he never held another consulship. This was also intended to win favour with the Senate.

Reforms

In addition, he cancelled all outstanding debts to the imperial treasury, and impressed his generosity on the people by having the records burnt publicly. This could have served a double purpose. It did win favour. It also enabled Hadrian to make a clean sweep of the debts which inefficient collection had allowed to mount for years in unproductive piles. Having made these gestures to the citizens of Rome, he felt free to organize his administration to suit his plans.

On the events of Hadrian's life, the order in which he carried out his reforms, even the itinerary of his innumerable tours of the provinces, we are ill informed. It is true that the *Historia Augusta* begins with his rule, but it is too scrappy to be entirely satisfactory and there is argument concerning many events in Hadrian's reign.

It will be best to discuss some reforms which must have been instituted then, although they were worked out more fully later. The system of lending money to farmers, and using the interest paid for child endowment he continued. Indeed he helped the underprivileged throughout his life, enacting some very humane laws regarding the treatment of slaves.

He likewise continued his predecessors' policy of using equestrians not freedmen at the head of his administrative posts. He was, as said before, deeply concerned with efficient organisation. He further developed the bureaucracy, which was a gain for the time being. When, however, the impetus to efficiency died down under later emperors the body developed a stranglehold on the empire.

He helped enhance the prestige of the equites in a number of ways. One post which he gave to an equestrian (and which was extremely important because of his many absences from the capital) was that of prefect of the city.

Like Trajan he used the imperial council Augustus had developed, giving it a more formal status and adding to its tasks by making it a legal court of appeal. He also included equestrians in the council, including the praetorian prefect Turbo. It was under Hadrian that the praetorian prefect shared in the imperial courts and gained a real judicial function. Some of them in later times were to be famous jurists!

Hadrian's tours of the provinces

He may already have begun planning some of the buildings which he later erected, but of that we cannot be certain. In any case he cannot have proceeded very far with any of his plans, for the empire was still restless, and in 121 he set out to tour the western provinces, including Britain. This was to be the only time he visited the western half of the empire. Later it was always the East, including his beloved Greece, that engaged his attention.

First he inspected Gaul and the Rhineland. Under him the army ceased to be an attacking force and returned to its normal imperial role of guarding the frontiers, but this made him all the more determined that discipline should be maintained at the highest level of efficiency.

He went over the armies meticulously, and set an example by himself taking part in their military exercises and route marches.

Next year he crossed to Britain, where a fierce revolt had been crushed. There he saw the building of that line of defence which was called Hadrian's Wall and divided northern Britain from the Scots.

The old idea of this wall as a protective barrier like a city wall has been somewhat discounted. It would not have been very effective in that sense. It did, however, delimit the frontier. The road which ran behind it gave the legions easy access to any danger point along its length, and commercially it served to enforce the customs barrier which even then made trade assist state finances.

The extent to which Hadrian generally created artificial walls along the empire's frontiers has probably been exaggerated. As we have seen, much of that work was done by the Flavians, not least by Domitian. Historians eager to denigrate that unpopular figure would not have hesitated to give some of his achievements to Hadrian.

While still in the west, he was distressed to learn of the death of his adoptive mother Plotina. He also was informed that the Parthian king had led an uprising and set off to confront him. The Parthians at once agreed to a settlement and left the emperor free to inspect his Eastern provinces.

Asia Minor first engaged his attention. He visited many of its cities, bestowing public works on them with a liberal hand. Aqueducts, baths and temples were the usual gift. Earlier emperors had tended to centralise the minting of coins. He reversed the trend, granting minting privileges to ten Eastern cities. It was on this visit that he met the beautiful youth Antinous who was to be his favourite until his death nine years later.

In 128 he went to Africa, reorganised the Roman farming estates, which were in a run-down condition, and inspected the troops. We have by a providential chance the actual text of part of his exhortations to this army.

Next year he at last felt free to visit his spiritual home, Greece. Here too he bestowed public

works, but for Athens itself that was not enough. He prepared designs for a completely new suburb to lie to the east of the old Athens. It was to be called Hadrianopolis after him, as was the custom, and to include a huge temple to Olympian Zeus. The temple itself was not a new project. It had been started by a former ruler of Athens and long abandoned. Hadrian regarded himself as a gifted architect. He saw to the drafting of the initial plans, then returned to Asia Minor.

This time he went to Judaea, and made a fatal mistake which was to cost Rome dear. He inspected the site of Jerusalem, razed to the ground by Titus, and determined that a new city should rise on its ruins. It was to be called Aelia Capitolina, thus commemorating his family name, in association with Capitoline Jupiter. On the site of the Jewish temple to *Yahweh* (Jehovah) a new temple to Capitoline Jupiter

22.5 *A section of Hadrian's Wall today.*

should arise, where Hadrian too was to be revered. He obviously had no concept of the fanaticism which this practical scheme would arouse in the Jews; for in 130, having drawn up the plans, he departed to visit Egypt. There he was horrified by the depressed state of the Egyptian peasants, to whom he gave a measure of taxation relief. He toured the country, visiting some of its more memorable cities. It was then that Antinous was drowned in the Nile. The emperor was overwhelmed with grief. He had the youth deified, built a whole city near the place of his death, called after him Antinoopolis. Temples rose in many towns in his honour, also innumerable statues, many of which still survive.

Administrative reforms

In 132 Hadrian at last returned to Rome. At this point it will be convenient to examine his administrative reforms, and his building programme in the city, even though the actual date of many of these events is far from certain.

As noted earlier, Hadrian enhanced the position of the equites. Senators had for some time enjoyed an honorary title, *vir clarissimus* (most illustrious personage), abbreviated as *V.C.* To his leading equestrian officials, such as the heads of departments and members of his council, Hadrian granted a corresponding title, *vir eminentissimus* (most eminent personage), abbreviated as *V.E.* He also paid his departmental heads a high salary. The salary distinctions have quite a modern ring. Hadrian's department heads received the top salary, 200 000 sesterces, the procurators of the imperial provinces were paid at the next level, 100 000, while the procurators who worked for them were on the third range, 60 000. Incidentally he added a new head of department, head of libraries, which was appropriately given to Suetonius. The distinction between equestrian and senator became less rigid under him, although not as the result of any formal enactment, and it grew easier to move from one class to the other.

The publicani had lost their task of collecting taxes, which was entrusted to government officials under the procurators. Hadrian set up a special taxation department, concerned particularly with the collection of the inheritance tax.

His imperial council was also a court of law. To one member of it, Julian, was given the task of preparing a permanent praetorian edict. The praetor each year had issued his edict stating the regulations under which he would administer justice. Although the edict could theoretically be altered, human nature ensured that, as praetor copied praetor, it became fairly fixed. This was not enough for Hadrian. Moreover he had set up four judicial divisions of Italy with travelling judges to tour them, a very useful provision. But the multiplication of the judiciary made a standard law even more necessary. Julian prepared this edict, which was to serve as part of the basis for the later code of Justinian. Hadrian's judicial division of Italy was cancelled in response to the protests of the Senate (but revived by Antoninus Pius). The edict remained.

The army and the provinces

Just as the division between the equites and the Senate became blurred, so in the provincial armies the distinction between provincial and citizen, between the auxiliary forces and the legions diminished. Provincials gained the right to reach officer rank in their forces. At the same time the Flavian principle of sending soldiers to areas away from their own country was abandoned. Not only were the armies recruited locally, but they came to be called after their own area, 'the Army of Germany', 'the Army of Africa', thus emphasising their national character. Such a move enhanced the soldiers' pride in their own corps, but had the obvious danger of developing again that separatism which had been so nearly fatal in 68. Both auxiliaries and legions now served as guards on the frontiers. As there were no major wars under him, Hadrian was very concerned to keep his armies efficient by supervising their training, and he paid much attention to this in his tours. His discipline was stern but not harsh and he set an example by giving himself no more comfort than his troops, who were always devoted to him.

Hadrian took a great interest in developing

urban life in the provinces, and under him it reached its peak. The cities he founded in his tours helped the process. In addition, he encouraged existing towns to take a pride in local affairs. That was done in two ways. Many municipia demanded and were granted by him the right to be called colonies. This title conferred no extra privileges. It did, however, enhance the prestige of the town and was valued enormously. Finally he set up a division in the granting of Latin rights between the Greater and the Lesser. In towns which enjoyed the Lesser Latin Rights, the magistrates were given Roman citizenship. In those which belonged to the other class, the whole local council received that privi-

lege. Thus he encouraged local participation in public life.

Hadrian's public building. The Jews revolt

Hadrian brought to Rome his passion for building. Many older temples and public buildings he restored. Near the Colosseum he built a temple to Venus and Rome, the largest of any of the Roman temples. He also rebuilt the Pantheon of Agrippa which had been completely destroyed in 80. It had, and still has the largest dome in the world (it is larger even than that of

22.6 The Pantheon.

St. Peter's), and was constructed with no
supporting columns. By a lucky fate it was used
later as a Christian Church. This, and its subsequent use as a public monument, have meant
that it is now the best-preserved ancient
building.

Hadrian was not long left in peace. In 132 the
rebellion in Palestine came to a head, under the
leadership of Bar Kokhba. Two letters written
by him have been found among the Dead Sea
Scrolls. Like all Jewish revolts this one was
ferocious and required the utmost severity to
crush it. The governor of Britain, Severus (great-
grandfather of the future emperor Marcus Aurelius), was sent to deal with the war and it is said
that more than half a million were killed before
order was restored. After this, Aelia Capitolina
was built and remains the basis of modern
Jerusalem.

Death of Hadrian

Hadrian had gone East to assist in the Jewish
war. In 134 he came back to Rome. He was
already suffering from the disease that was to end
his life four years later.

He now shunned society and in Tibur built
himself a villa where he spent the rest of his life.
It was, like most of Hadrian's creations, gigantic,
and was in some sort a museum of his travels.
In it he recreated the Lyceum and Academy of
Athens, the valley at Tempe in Thessaly. Even
a model of Hades figured in it.

These were Hadrian's distractions. His most
pressing problem was his approaching death.
Over the Tiber he built himself a huge mausoleum in imitation of that of Augustus. It still
survives as the Castle of Saint Angelo.

Determined to avoid the ambiguity which
began his reign, he proceeded to choose a
successor. His first choice was unfortunate.
Lucius Commodus Verus was not young and was
a libertine. He died soon after. Next Hadrian
chose a Roman senator, known later as Antoninus Pius. He was of Gallic ancestry (his family
came from Nemausus or Nîmes) and of great
wealth. Like Augustus, Hadrian ensured two
generations of emperors. He made Antoninus,

22.7 *This part of Hadrian's Villa at Tibur (modern
Tivoli) is known as the Canopus. The great sprawling
villa was built between A.D. 125 and A.D. 135. The villa
contained libraries, small baths, great baths, marine
theatre, stadium, swimming pools, Philosophers' Hall,
courtyards and colonnades.*

who had sons, adopt Marcus Annius (Marcus
Aurelius as he was known later), a nephew of
Antoninus, and Aelius Verus, the son of the man
he had first selected. He arranged also that
Marcus should marry Antoninus' daughter
Annia.

In 138 Hadrian died. Despite his many
achievements he had never known how to make
himself generally popular, and his conduct
towards the end had earned him the hatred of
the Senate. When, however, that body tried to
treat him as they had treated the dead Domitian,

Antoninus stood firm. He buried Hadrian with all solemnity in the mausoleum and made the Senate proclaim his deification.

Literature

We have already noted Martial (*c*.40–102)· who actually did most of his writing under the Flavians but continued into the reigns of Nerva and Trajan. He was another Spanish product, having been born in Bilbilis. Pliny the Younger was one of his patrons and helped Martial to return to his beloved Spain in 98. Martial was one of the greatest epigrammatists of all time and has influenced many modern practitioners of the art. From our point of view he is valuable for the picture he gave of the Rome of his time, the picture of a man with no great moral values, ready to flatter whenever it might benefit him, but with a keen eye for detail of all kind, and for the absurdities of his fellow-men.

Juvenal also gave a detailed picture of Roman life, but in many ways he was a complete contrast to Martial. We know almost nothing of his life, except that he was born at Aquinum, was a teacher when young, and died some time after 127. In his first *Satire* Juvenal promised to attack only the dead, but that suited him well. He loathed particularly the Rome of his youth and bitterly attacked the Flavian age. Humour he lacked completely, and a dose of Martial is a wise corrective to his wholesale abuse.

In *Satire* One he explained his reasons for writing, making his famous statement that when a man sees the corruption of Rome 'it is difficult not to write satire'. In *Satire* Three he attacked those consummate flatterers the Greeks: 'you may praise a rich man too, but he will be believed!' In *Satire* Six, the most celebrated, he dealt with the other object of his hatred, women.

A prose writer, Pliny the Younger (*c*.61–113) completes our picture of Rome at this time. He was a nephew of Pliny the Elder, and was adopted by him. His *Panegyric of Trajan* is one of our few accounts of that emperor, but it is too full of flattery to be of much historical value. By contrast he is most useful for his letters.

Thanks to Pliny, Juvenal and Martial we have an excellent picture of the daily life of the Silver Age, as this period is often known. The only other period where we are as lucky is the late Republic where we possess Cicero's letters.

The historians Tacitus and Suetonius

Tacitus (*c*.55–*c*.117) also wrote at this time. We know little of the life of this greatest of Roman historians, not even where he was born. He did, however, marry Agricola's daughter, and conceived a great admiration for the man, and a corresponding hatred of Domitian, who failed to appreciate him.

He published his *Agricola* just after Trajan became emperor, following it with the *Histories*, which covered the period from Nero's death till that of Domitian. The part we possess ends with Vespasian's accession. At the very end of his life he brought out the *Annals*, which began at Augustus' death and ended with that of Nero. The whole of Caligula's life and portion of that of Claudius and Nero are missing.

Tacitus wrote his history from the viewpoint of senatorial aristocrat, who regarded the imperial period as fundamentally corrupt, contrasting it with the sturdy virtues of an imaginary Republican Rome. He also had a particular detestation of Domitian, and in consequence of Tiberius, whom he regarded as similar in character.

He was a writer of great power, epigrammatic, with a poetic vividness of vocabulary. The corruption of Rome unleashed in him a satiric vehemence closely akin to that of Juvenal, though on a loftier plane. On the other hand, he was limited by his prejudices. The intrigues of Rome preoccupied him. He was unaware of many wide issues, and especially of the administration of the provinces, where he could have found a far more cheerful picture. Yet, granted his prejudices and limitations, Tacitus was a conscientious historian. He would recount the deeds even of Tiberius with some exactness, though the interpretation he put on these deeds was highly coloured.

By contrast Suetonius (*c*.75–160) was somewhat of a gossipmonger. He had been encouraged by Pliny the Younger. Hadrian gave him a public office then dismissed him. Perhaps this affected Suetonius' outlook; for when he came to write his *Lives of the Caesars* he recounted the vilest scandal with utter enjoyment and little attempt to assess the reliability of his information. Suetonius is useful in providing facts, but when, as in the life of Caligula, we do not possess Tacitus to help sort fact from fiction, we realise his deficiencies. He wrote the biographies of Julius Caesar and of the eleven emperors, up to and including Domitian.

There would be no great point in resuming our examination of the social life of the period. Most of the trends of the Flavian era continued, and some of the main changes have been noted in the accounts of individual emperors. The student would, however, derive great benefit from reading some of Juvenal, Martial and Pliny for a picture of the time, written when it was happening.

The province of Britain under Hadrian

It would be of more value to give an account of one of the Roman provinces at this point, namely Britain. The province developed considerably under Hadrian, which makes this a suitable time to present such an account.

The initial conquest of Britain by Claudius did not proceed far beyond the south-eastern section of the island. There Romanisation had begun even before the invasion, through the trade which developed between it and Gaul.

Britain like Gaul was Celtic, with similar institutions to that country, and the conquerors followed a plan of assimilation differing little from their practice on the other side of the Channel. As in Gaul, they were concerned to win over the leading families and persuade them, particularly the younger generation, to become educated as Romans. They were then the starting point for wider assimilation.

Now the basis of Roman civilisation was urban life, and Britain was not a country of cities. The people were basically tribal, and their main meeting-place the market, where not only commerce but tribal business and religious rites

were carried on. The market was a possible centre from which a town could grow.

In addition, a settlement inevitably developed round the Roman camps, as traders arrived to supply them with goods and set up shop nearby.

The first serious attempt to build a town was made at Colchester, then known as Camulodunum, seven years after the conquest. The nucleus in this case was a colony to provide for veterans, but it was envisaged as a mixed community. The local market had served as a centre for Druidism, but this religion, which involved human sacrifice, was banned here as in Gaul. Instead a temple was built to Claudius and the cult of emperor-worship encouraged.

Meanwhile reaction had begun to build up. The new ways did not immediately appeal and the conquerors were not always tactful. The culmination was the revolt of Boudicca of the Iceni, during which Camulodunum went up in flames. After this Londinium and Verulamium were burnt to the ground.

The revolt was crushed and wiser administrators sent out. Then the process of assimilation went on. The traders went further north, the camps multiplied and the roads were built.

By the time of Agricola's governorship the Romans were beginning to succeed, and his expansionist policy brought with it a rapid increase in Romanisation. Camulodunum was rebuilt.

Hadrian's rule began with a serious revolt, but his wall helped further progress. It gave added security to the province, and, as on the Rhine-Danube frontier, towns grew up along the frontier, centring on the forts.

New towns were growing up on every side. They were surrounded by walls, for Britain was not very secure, and the inhabitants needed to be protected not only from tribesmen as yet uncivilised but from brigands. The usual public buildings arose, a temple for emperor-worship, triumphal arches, theatres, sometimes baths.

Although many such towns developed from military settlements, the Romans welcomed the opportunity of turning the market towns of the Britons themselves into cities if they desired, and a number of them were so converted. At the

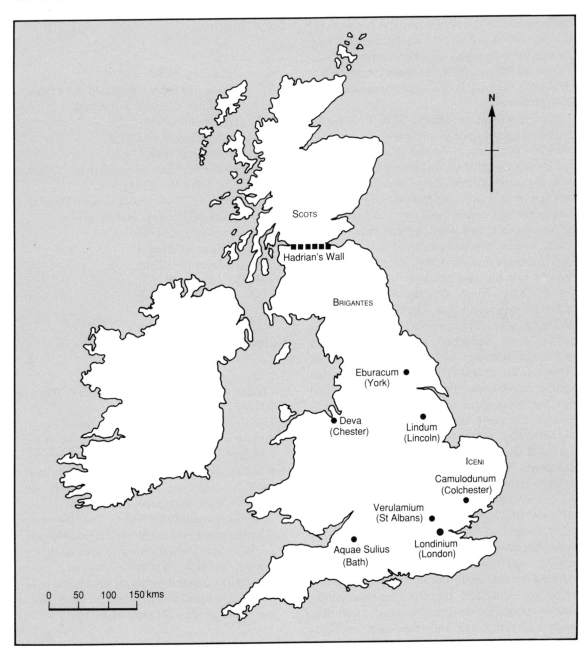

22.8 *Roman Britain.*

same time many of the people felt no need to take up city life. The noble continued to inhabit his farm, though, as elsewhere in the empire, he modified it as time went on to conform to the type of the Roman villa, or country house. A bath-house would be added to the building, a dining-room, and finally, supreme sign of sophistication, a courtyard. Villas were to become extremely widespread later, in the fourth century.

The waters of Bath had even then been found to have curative powers and the town of Aquae

Sulis arose with the largest mineral baths in the western section of Europe. Londinium, too, soon showed the advantages of its incomparable site. It grew steadily and by the fourth century was to become the capital of the province instead of Camulodunum.

As in the other provinces, so in Britain, the Roman citizens, partly composed of veterans from the army, partly of the aristocracy which had earned the privilege by holding a magistracy, were expected to run their community. They supplied priests for emperor-worship, contributed to erecting public buildings, collected taxes. Britain did not, however, develop that feverish rivalry which elsewhere produced such a crop of fine buildings in provincial centres, while it brought ruin on their builders.

It has been claimed that the famed tin mines of Britain were one reason why Claudius invaded the island. If so, his hopes were not realised. Tin mining never developed to any great extent under the Romans, who obtained what they needed from Spain. This is not to say that mining had no importance. Lead was mined, and was the main export in this category. It was found in the north and west areas, still industrially important today. Copper was also found in the north-west, while iron, which was abundant, was mined in the south.

Wine arrived with the Romans, as did olive oil, but the natives even then showed a fondness for beer, which had the additional advantage of being cheap.

So Britain developed on the fringes of the empire, untouched by many of the crises suffered by the lands nearer Rome, but never quite free of anxiety regarding its own neighbours. After Hadrian the Antonine wall was erected further north but abandoned by Caracalla. Land enemies were at that time joined by foes from the sea, in particular the Saxons, and a fleet was set up to guard against them. Finally, towards the end of the fourth century Rome found it had too many problems of its own to guard outlying areas, and gradually the legions were withdrawn from the province, leaving it to relapse into barbarism.

Date table

A.D.

96	Accession of Nerva.
98	Death of Nerva; succeeded by Trajan, Tacitus' *Agricola* published.
*c.*102	Death of Martial.
102	First conquest of Dacia.
105–6	Second war with Dacia.
113	Trajan marches against Parthia. Death of Pliny the Younger.
117	Death of Trajan; accession of Hadrian.
*c.*119	Death of Tacitus; Suetonius' *Lives* appear.
122	Hadrian in Britain.
129	Hadrian in Athens.
131–35	Jewish revolt.
138	Death of Hadrian.

Select quotations

1 Pliny, *Letters*, X, 97:
(Trajan writes about the Christians to Pliny in Bithynia.)
My dear Pliny, you acted as you should in hearing the cases of those brought to you as Christians, for it is impossible to draw up a procedure to cover every contingency. They are not to be sought out. If any are brought to you and their guilt established, they must be punished, provided that such as deny they are Christians and prove it by offering sacrifice to our gods, even though their past conduct is suspect, should be forgiven as repentant. Anonymous accusations are on no account to be accepted. That would set a vile precedent and is not in accord with the spirit of the age.

2 Dessau, *I.L.S.*, 2487:
(Part of Hadrian's address to the African army, found on a column at Lambaesis.)
Ramparts which others spend many days building you completed in one. You have built a wall which would be quite adequate for winter quarters, taking hardly longer than to build a rampart of turf. . . . The wall you have built consisted of large heavy stones of all shapes and sizes, which you could not bring and fit, unless

they were matched very carefully. . . . When this was over, back you went at full speed to the camp, and, collecting your rations and arms, set out at once after the cavalry. . . . I compliment my legate, Catullinus, on choosing exercises so like real war for training you, and for giving you such thorough practice. I congratulate you most heartily.

3 *Historia Augusta, Hadrian, 25:*
(Poem composed by Hadrian on his soul.)
Winsome, fickle soul of mine, guest and comrade of my body, where now will you go away, poor naked creature, still and pale, and not make jokes as once you did?

Further reading

A. Garzetti, *From Tiberius to the Antonines*, Methuen, 1974.

S. Perowne, *Hadrian*, Croom Helm, 1960.

I.A. Richmond, *Roman Britain, Pelican History of England*, vol. 1, Penguin.

R. Meiggs, *Roman Ostia*, Oxford Clarendon, 1973.

Topics for essays or discussion

1 The line of emperors introduced by Nerva was highly praised by the ancients, who contrasted them with the Flavians. Do you agree?

2 Analyse the advantages and disadvantages of Trajan's military policy. Was he right to abandon the limits imposed by Augustus?

3 Do you think that the foreign origin of Trajan and Hadrian affected their policies? If so, how?

4 Nerva and the emperors who followed him solved the problem of succession by adoption. Was this a new idea? Was it a success?

5 Discuss the relations of Trajan and Hadrian with the Senate *or* the equites. What administrative changes did they bring about, involving these classes?

6 'Trajan came to the frontiers as a conqueror, Hadrian as an inspector.' How would you explain this? Was Hadrian's policy wise?

7 What contribution did Hadrian make to the development of the provinces? Discuss this with particular reference to their urbanisation and the encouragement of civic pride.

8 'Despite all his achievements Hadrian was not really popular.' Do you agree?

9 Discuss the importance of Tacitus as an historian. What were his virtues and limitations? Compare his treatment of Tiberius with that of Suetonius.

10 How did the Romans bring civilisation to Britain? How far were they successful? Did this province present any peculiar problems?

Chapter 23

Antoninus Pius and Marcus Aurelius

Sources

THIS PERIOD is not the worst recorded we have to deal with. True, we do not have the great historians at our disposal, and the *Historia Augusta* together with Dio Cassius, available only in summary form for these years, are poor substitutes.

To compensate, the legal activities of Antoninus and Marcus, and they were both indefatigable in this area, are recorded in Justinian's *Digest* when he quotes from earlier periods on legal matters, including this time. Inscriptions again are most useful as a record of the emperors' work in the provinces, and we have an abundance of second century inscriptions.

Finally, there are a number of writers, who although not historians, give us a picture of the life of the day. The notable Greek writer, Lucian, who wrote satires to which such authors as Swift are indebted, condemned the vices of his age. The orator Aristides does give us some historical facts in his speeches, although they have to be treated with the caution always necessitated with orators, especially when like

Aristides they flatter. Fronto was a lawyer of Numidian origin who worked under Trajan and was appointed by Antoninus to be a tutor to Marcus Aurelius. His correspondence to and from Antoninus Pius and Marcus Aurelius are a revelation of the simplicity of lives of these men but are of no mighty historical significance. Finally we have the *Meditations* of Marcus Aurelius, which deal with his reflections on the Stoic philosophy he practised, but are little concerned to discuss historical events.

Antoninus Pius' accession is welcomed

When Antoninus succeeded Hadrian as emperor in 138 he had already enjoyed a full and successful life. At the age of fifty-one he was probably the richest man in Rome, had been a consul, governor of Asia and a member of the imperial council.[1]

Being himself a senator, he was a welcome appointment in the eyes of the Senate, and he continued to be on the best of terms with it throughout his rule. On his accession he made the expected promise not to impose capital punishment on any senator, and he was careful to accept only two more consulships. He made the gift to the people and donative to the troops normal for an incoming emperor. Indeed he gave nine donatives in all to the soldiers during his rule. As we noted earlier, he was also firm with the Senate and insisted that Hadrian be deified.

There is no question that the equability of his temperament assured him a general popularity. He was as well a skilled and experienced lawyer, a useful qualification for his post. Those were his assets. On the other side, he had no military experience, and no wish to gain any. Also his easy-going nature had the disadvantage that he was lacking in drive and initiative.

He took a cynical view of Hadrian's extensive tours of the empire, and intimated that by forgoing them he was saving the state consider-

---

[1]His family came from Narbonese Gaul, but he himself was born and reared at Lanuvium in Latium.

able expense. In the whole of his long rule he only left Rome once, for a short visit to the East.

To compensate for this lack of travel he was a very hard worker and wrote innumerable letters to all parts of the empire. He kept the imperial post at a peak of efficiency, so his letters arrived and did give him a necessary close contact with his subjects. In private life he had simple tastes. He loved hunting and fishing, spent much time on his country estates, and had no extravagances.

Towards his subjects he showed the generosity expected of an emperor. He continued to give child endowment, made grants to senators who were in want, and presented many games to entertain the populace. He showed equal liberality to the demands of provincials, helping them in public works and in particular granting taxation relief when they were struck by an earthquake, or some other public calamity.

Building projects and administration

On the other hand, he had no desire to compete with Hadrian in ambitious building projects of his own. He was mainly concerned to complete those begun by his predecessor and to see to the maintenance of roads and other public utilities. One building of his does survive to remind us of him. When his wife Faustina died, he built a temple dedicated to her on the Sacred Way near the Forum. After his death it was renamed the temple of Antoninus and Faustina. It was used as a church in Christian times, which has meant that it is quite well preserved. He also built a temple to Deified Hadrian.

The Circus Maximus collapsed with a great loss of life and had to be rebuilt, and a fire and a flood in Rome also meant rebuilding. He also did turn his farm on the *via Aurelia* into a fine villa. Milestones bearing his name are evidence of his maintenance work in every part of the empire.

His administration was not noted for new departures. He was conscientious in supervising the administration of justice, and under him the *Institutiones* of Gaius were composed. This was a legal text-book, a fore-runner of that series of

attempts to codify Roman law which culminated in Justinian's *Code* and *Digest*. He showed tolerance to Christians, and would not allow them to be persecuted for their faith. He tended to leave governors in their provinces for long periods, even up to eighteen years, when they proved competent.

It was the same with his praetorian prefects, one of whom, Gavius Maximus, served him for twenty years.

Basically he was a frugal emperor, and that was just as well. During his rule there were worrying signs of economic exhaustion throughout the empire. The coinage generally showed this, as the denarius lost weight and was adulterated.

The frontiers

Superficially, his rule was marked by peace on the frontiers, but there were many minor disturbances, and the lack of positive activity on his part must have helped to encourage the barbarians in the feeling that they could challenge the might of Rome. This bore fruit in the next reign. There was an uprising in Britain soon after he came to power, as a result of which the governor built a new wall on the northern frontier, the Antonine wall, 120 kilometres beyond Hadrian's wall, and accordingly shorter. Likewise the frontier defences at the limes between the Rhine and Danube were moved up above the Neckar valley and consequently shortened. Otherwise Antoninus followed the policy of Trajan and Hadrian.

Antoninus had one other important responsibility, to assure the succession. Hadrian had chosen the actual successors, Marcus Aurelius and Verus, and Antoninus saw that his wishes were honoured. The young men were given the normal public offices so they would have experience, Marcus Aurelius taking precedence, both because Hadrian had given him special consideration, and because he was ten years older.

In 145 the emperor married Marcus Aurelius to his daughter. The following year he gave him tribunician and proconsular powers, and made him joint ruler with himself. In 160 Marcus Aurelius and Verus held the consulship together.

The following year Antoninus died, regretted by all, and was duly deified. He left an empire at peace, and a full treasury. His laxness probably did lower the discipline of the armies, and so make them less able to meet the troubled times that followed. On the other hand, there is some need for caution here. The plague which played such a large part in the disasters of the next few years could not be set at his door, and without it even his defects might well have had no evil consequences.

Marcus Aurelius succeeds

Marcus Aurelius, who was of Spanish origin and a nephew of Antoninus Pius, had been brought up under the eye of Hadrian. He was well aware of the youth's talents, and inspired him with his own love of learning and of Greek culture. Marcus Aurelius had a very full education and became a convinced Stoic, being influenced particularly by the rhetorician Fronto. His beliefs sustained him in all the terrible events of his rule.

Perhaps his most obvious characteristic was an immense conscientiousness. He was co-ruler with Verus, and, although the latter was a frivolous young man, not well suited to his office, he gave him a full share in the rule as long as he lived. In point of fact Marcus Aurelius' sense of duty was excessive.

At the time of his death Antoninus designated him alone as his successor, and the Senate hailed him as emperor. Even Vespasian had only taken Titus as a junior partner. Marcus Aurelius insisted on making Verus an Augustus, in short a full co-ruler, an unnecessary and basically a foolish step.

Troubles were not long in starting. No sooner had the troops received their donatives and Antoninus Pius been deified than Rome itself was subjected to a flood, and uprisings occurred in the provinces. There was a revolt in Britain, some German tribes crossed the Rhine, and the King of Parthia attacked Armenia. The main threat was from Parthia, and in 162 Verus was sent with an army to meet it. Whether his own love of peace or a fear of seeming to push himself forward stopped Marcus from taking over this task is uncertain. In any case, he claimed later that he had thoroughly worked out the details of the campaign with his colleague.

Verus lived up to his earlier reputation. He used his visit to the East merely as an excuse for a life of dissipation, and left all the fighting to his generals. Luckily they were able men. Statius Priscus and Avidius Cassius brought discipline to the forces on the Eastern frontier and drove the enemy from Syria and Armenia. Armenia was then made, as before, a protectorate. This was not a satisfactory solution, but no better one had been found.

At the start of the war Avidius Cassius had been governor of Syria, the key province for the defence of the East. He was now given an over-riding command over the whole of the East.

So far all had gone well but now disaster struck. A terrible plague attacked Verus' forces, and he brought back to Italy an army already depleted by the disease and still being ravaged by it. None the less, he and Marcus Aurelius celebrated a triumph in honour of the victory.

Any hope that the disease would run its course and leave them in peace was vain. It spread to Italy and throughout the empire. In some parts a third of the whole population died, and the troops on the frontiers were weakened to danger point.

In addition the loss of manpower meant that there were not enough left to work the fields and a disastrous famine was added to their woes.

A new threat on the Danube

As we saw, the tribes in the north had already been restless, and these new events gave added encouragement. The weakest point of Rome's defences was the Danube, which had not been furnished with a regular line of frontier forts as had the Rhine. A wholesale invasion ensued, led by the tribes known as the Marcomanni and the Quadi. They overran the Danube frontiers and soon had reached as far as Italy itself.

This time Marcus Aurelius had no hesitation. The wars in Parthia had depleted the treasury.

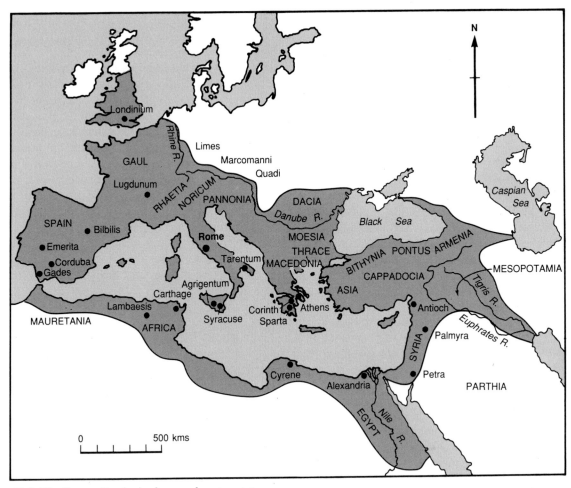

23.1 *The Roman Empire in the second century* A.D.

He sold the imperial art collection to raise the needed money.

The plague had decimated the population, but he enlisted all available men, including slaves and gladiators. He also adopted a new procedure that was to become the norm in the later empire. One problem of having the army stationed in camps along the frontier was that they were by their nature immobile and not easy to move to deal with a specific threat.

Marcus now enlisted a special mobile force, whose function was to meet this need. They were to be trouble-shooters, to go swiftly to meet a threat where it occurred and to reinforce any forces that might be in the area.

Marcus was now ready and he set out with Verus, making it his first task to sweep out the forces which had invaded Italy. His prompt action was effective. He was asked to grant a truce, which he did, and returned immediately to Rome. Verus died of apoplexy on the journey. The death of his colleague (in 169) was a relief to Marcus. The young man had been little but a burden, and even though the problems continued unabated, he could at least devote himself to them undistracted.

The respite was a welcome one, for the plague continued unabated, and the celebrated doctor from Pergamum, Galen, whose medical writings were to dominate the science for a very long time, was sent for by Marcus Aurelius, to see if he could help. We know this from the writings of Galen himself.

Marcus Aurelius' last campaigns

Few details are known of the last campaign of Marcus Aurelius and the column he built to commemorate it does not help greatly. It suffered from the same problem as Trajan's Column that pictures with no text are not very informative. As well it seems that the builders of this column were not very concerned with exact chronology. At least we are pretty sure now that the column does cover the period from 172 to 175.

The Danube was still unsettled, and in addition the Chatti (Domitian's old enemies) crossed the border on the Rhine. Marcus Aurelius went back and one by one defeated the enemy countries. During this war Marcus Aurelius suffered a personal loss when his old tutor Fronto, at the time governor of Upper Moesia and Dacia, was killed.

In 175 Marcus named his son Commodus as his successor, and in the same year his generalissimo Avidius Cassius led an uprising. It was probably no coincidence. Ambition seems to have spurred the man on and he may well have hoped that Marcus would follow the procedure of earlier emperors and adopt as heir a successful general, namely him. Marcus prepared to march against him but Cassius' own troops forestalled him, killing the rebellious general and sending his head as proof of their action.

Marcus had him buried and burnt all his correspondence as Pompey had done many years ago, to prevent a blood purge. He did, however, punish the ringleaders, including the cities of Alexandria and Antioch. He then made a tour of the East to ensure its loyalty. At this time he suffered a further loss in the death of his wife.

He also took a step entirely necessary at the time, but to be of considerable significance later. The plague had depopulated whole areas of the empire, and he brought Germans to settle in the empty spaces near the Danube, in Gaul, even in Italy.

The last years of Marcus Aurelius

He now had little to look forward to. He had distracted his mind from his cares by writing his *Meditations*, which, significantly, contained nothing of his public life. It was time to set his affairs in order. He returned to Rome and completed the formalities necessary to make his son Commodus his heir. While there, he began the column that his son finished, which in imitation of Trajan set out the details of the Marcomannic Wars.

One last effort remained. In 178 there was a fresh outbreak on the Danube. He set out, accompanied by Commodus, and defeated the enemy. Before he could return home he fell ill, perhaps of the plague, and died, as he had for so long lived, in exile.

The 'good emperors'

The period which began with Nerva and came to a sad end with Marcus Aurelius was a fortunate one for the Roman empire.[2] Actually, although this was not acknowledged at the time, these emperors were much indebted to the Flavian emperors. Their shrewd business sense had put the affairs of state on a sounder basis, checking the headlong inflation which threatened the end of the Julio-Claudian dynasty, building up a well-organised bureaucracy, and consolidating the frontiers.

Unfortunately, Domitian, the last of the Flavians, had brought disrepute on the whole line. In addition, as equestrians, these emperors had distrusted the Senate, thus ensuring its hostility, and as often happens, did not even succeed in winning the loyalty of their own class.

The emperors who succeeded them were actually even further from the traditional concept of emperor, being provincial in origin (except for Nerva). This made them anxious to gain accept-

---

[2]You will note that strictly the Antonine line ended with Commodus, but the inglorious rule of that youth formed little more than a post-script. It had more affinity with the period of anarchy that followed than with the preceding time.

ance at the expense of their predecessors. They succeeded for a number of reasons. They took care to conciliate the Senate, which was initially flattered that Nerva was a senator. Then, too, the use of adoption instead of direct family inheritance gave the Senate the illusion that Rome was still ruled by the leading man (the princeps), the ideal originally cherished by them and fostered by Augustus. Their action of replacing freedmen by equites in the bureaucracy also conciliated the latter class.

The era was then one of general harmony. The emperors were conscientious, and their administration efficient. Trajan's conquests gave a great stimulus to Rome's economy, and the building programmes undertaken by him and by Hadrian helped to enhance the national pride of the citizens.

The provinces too had little cause for dissatisfaction. Their wants received ample attention, especially from Hadrian. They also had the satisfaction of seeing many of their leading citizens accepted into the Senate, and so joining the ruling body of the empire.

It was a paternalistic age, with child endowment and state-supported education. There was also a high degree of city development throughout the whole empire.

There were some features which were ominous for the future. Now that the camps on the frontiers were becoming more permanent and were increasingly locally recruited, they were coming to be more and more self-sufficient. With the slowness of ancient communications, they tended to promote local industry to meet their needs both in Gaul and in the Rhineland itself. Thus the economic centre of the empire shifted northward, and not only south Italy as before, but the whole of Italy became less important.

Eastern religions continued to be popular in the empire and two new cults won widespread acceptance. From Persia came Mithraism, the worship of the sun-god Mithras. This religion, with its baptism in the blood of a bull, the high place it gave to courage, and its doctrine of comradeship made it especially popular among the soldiers. As the upper classes did not esteem it, we do not possess literature on this religion as practised by the Romans, but we have found

a number of shrines, many in caves dedicated to the god.

The other religion was that of Asclepius, the Greek god of medicine. This comfortable age was one where health was of supreme value, and sanitariums, run by the priests of the god, sprang up on every side.

Literature

Meanwhile, the renewed confidence of the age, coupled with the emperors' encouragement of the arts, brought about a new literary flowering, which is also regarded as part of the Silver Age.

Apuleius, a man of African origin, wrote a book called the *Metamorphoses* or the *Golden Ass*, which, like the work of Petronius, is one of the ancestors of the novel as we know it. This story of the adventures of a man turned into an ass is imbued with Apuleius' own devotion to the Eastern religion of Isis.

The letters of the Younger Pliny, while revealing a man of no outstanding qualities (Pliny was in many ways a very ordinary, somewhat snobbish lover of respectability), do give a good picture of the age, and his correspondence with Trajan has a special interest.

It is not surprising that an age dominated by Hadrian, the Greek lover, should see a revival of Greek writing. The following are the most noteworthy.

Lucian was imbued with the spirit of mockery which was one aspect of this age. He made fun in his satires of quack doctors, philosophers and tellers of travellers' tales. Arrian, who was given Roman citizenship by Hadrian, wrote his history of Alexander, which is our best source for the life of the Greek conqueror. Appian wrote about the civil wars which ended the republic. His work is not of a high order, but where, as in the case of the Gracchi, other material is scanty, he has importance.

Pausanias wrote a travel-book describing the public buildings of Greece, which has been of great value to both historians and archaeologists. Plutarch, whose name occurs so constantly in any history of Greece or Rome, also lived during this era.

Galen wrote his medical encyclopedia, which was to be authoritative until the development of medicine in modern times.

Finally, one cannot omit the *Meditations* of Marcus Aurelius, composed in Greek also, which are interesting as a revelation of the emperor's character, even though they are not of concern for the historian.

The Spanish provinces

Having completed our discussion of the Antonine emperors it is appropriate to speak of the Spanish provinces, for it was under these emperors, especially the great Spanish emperors, Trajan and Hadrian, that they reached their greatest development. We have dealt with them in the course of our history at numerous points, but here we can give an overall examination, having special regard for what we learn from archaeology.

Of the colonies of Spain, the earliest seems to have been Tartessus, a city of fabulous wealth in the south of Spain near Cadiz. It derived its wealth from trade and its mines, and it seems possible that it was Etruscan, but we cannot be sure, for Tartessus has not yet been unearthed. All we know is that in 520 B.C. it was destroyed by the Phoenicians, who themselves founded colonies, of which Cadiz was the most famous, in the south of Spain. The Phoenicians also were interested in the mineral wealth of Spain, and rich treasures have been unearthed from their sepulchres.

The Greeks, the Iberians and the Celtiberians

The Greeks also were not idle and founded a number of colonies along the east coast of Spain. The most important of these was Emporion (Ampurias), the Greek word for a market place, a very appropriate name. It had a long history going on into Roman times. It was founded by Massilia (Marseilles). The work of excavating the site was done by Amalgro, who found that it was surrounded by Cyclopean walls, probably to defend it against the Carthaginians. It was an important trade centre and contained a fine temple to Zeus Serapis, an interesting mixture of Greek and Egyptian mythology. This temple was of Roman date, and in fact when the Romans invaded Spain they were welcomed by Emporion. Cato took it as his base, and when he exploited the local mines shipped back to Rome over 11 000 kilograms of silver and over 600 kilograms of gold. It is no wonder that Rome welcomed its new acquisition. Then Julius Caesar founded a Roman Emporiae, as he renamed it, giving it an ampitheatre and a palaestra, so that its prosperity continued.

The native inhabitants of Spain were called Iberians by the Romans. They were small peasants, courageous but not wealthy, and they did produce some fine sculptures. An excellent example of their culture is Ullastret, not far from Emporion, which was excavated by Oliva. It was defended by massive walls and towers, and seems to have traded with Emporion. The Iberian language was not Indo-European. It has been deciphered, but we cannot interpret it.

The Celts filtered down into Spain and intermarried with the Iberians in the north-west and in Lusitania (Portugal). This mixed race was known to the Romans as the Celtiberians, and they much admired them for their courage and fighting ability. We know of them best from the Celtiberian War, which began in 153 B.C. and ended with the destruction of the Celtiberian stronghold, Numantia.

It was a German archaeologist Schultan who came in 1905 and not only excavated the town of Numantia itself, a collection of thatch-roofed houses with a population of about 3000, but a series of camps built by the Romans who attacked the city. It was a bloody struggle and a whole series of camps were unearthed. The end of the siege was led by Scipio, and Schultan found Scipio's seven camps and the wall he built around Numantia, about five metres high and four metres thick. The camps themselves were impressive, as a normal camp covered ten hectares. Scipio's main camp was kept smaller and only covered seven and a half hectares. The camps were all surrounded by stone walls, about four metres thick. The general's quarters or praetorium was built of stone, while the troops' barracks had a stone foundation, adobe walls and were roofed by boughs. They show to what an extent the Romans had developed the art of warfare.

Roman Spain

Peace did not really come until the end of the Civil War in Rome, but under Augustus Spain was organised in typical Rome provincial style. Colonies were set up to house the veterans of the armies and act as centres of Romanisation.

The most famous of these was founded by Agrippa for his retired soldiers, his *emeriti*, and called appropriately Augusta Emerita (Mérida). It became the capital of Lusitania, and one of the largest cities in the Roman Empire. It has yielded up a huge number of buildings and other public works, including three aqueducts, a

23.2 *The aqueduct at Segovia in Spain. It is about 800 metres long with 128 arches and nearly 30 metres high.*

23.3 *The bridge at Alcantara over the Tagus River. It was built by Trajan in* A.D. *106.*

circus, an ampitheatre, and a very luxurious theatre. The theatre seems to belong to Hadrian's time, which is not surprising.

It was excavated by a Spaniard, Melida, who had dug at Numantia after Schulten. He excavated the town itself, but probably the highpoint of his work was the unearthing of the beautiful theatre with its colored marble and fine stage building.

Spain under the Antonines

The period of Trajan and Hadrian was the highpoint for Spain, and this was helped by the fact that at that time their mines were at their most productive. We have already mentioned their road-building, and as well there were countless other public works. These included the huge aqueduct which supplied Tarraco (Tarragona), the capital of Hither Spain, and in the west the bridge at Alcántara over the Tagus River, the best known of all Trajan's bridges.

Of the towns of this era Italica is outstanding. It was founded by Scipio for his veterans and both Trajan and Hadrian were born there. It had many famous excavators, including the Duke of Wellington, but unfortunately no systematic control, so the excavation was not scientific. None the less the results are impressive. It had about 10 000 inhabitants, and boasted a theatre, the fourth largest amphitheatre of the Roman Empire, which could seat 30 000, and two public baths. Italica was a port and was famous for its salt fish.

The provinces of Gaul

Archaeology has also added to our knowledge of Gaul in Roman times. From Rome's earliest days their people feared the Celts, and even more so when they even captured Rome. Hence Caesar's conquests, whatever his motives, were not regarded by the Romans as simply imperial expansion, but the removal of a dreaded foe. None the less, once conquered Gaul followed the normal process of Romanisation, and in the end was regarded as one of its most civilised dependencies.

The French have taken a keen interest in their past. The emperor Napoleon III organised a systematic excavation of the places connected with Caesar's campaigns, and then wrote a book about them. He had his German archaeologist Stoffel excavate Gergovia (Puy-de- Dôme) where Vercingetorix, the leader of Gallic resistance, actually defeated Caesar. The French took Vercingetorix to their hearts and built a statue of him at Alesia, where he was finally defeated and killed.

Gaul under Augustus

In Gaul as in Spain it was Augustus who put the provinces on a firm basis and as in Spain the process of Romanisation spread from the colonies founded there.

An early colony was Arelate Sextanorum (Arles) near Massilia (Marseilles), a colony founded for the veterans of the Sixth Legion. It contains a huge amphitheatre and a theatre. The amphitheatre was used as a fort in the Middle Ages and as result is in excellent condition. Not far off huge tunnels were found buried underground, where wheat was stored ready to be sent on to Rome.

Narbo Martius (Narbonne), the capital of the Gallic province Gallia Narbonensis, (Provence)

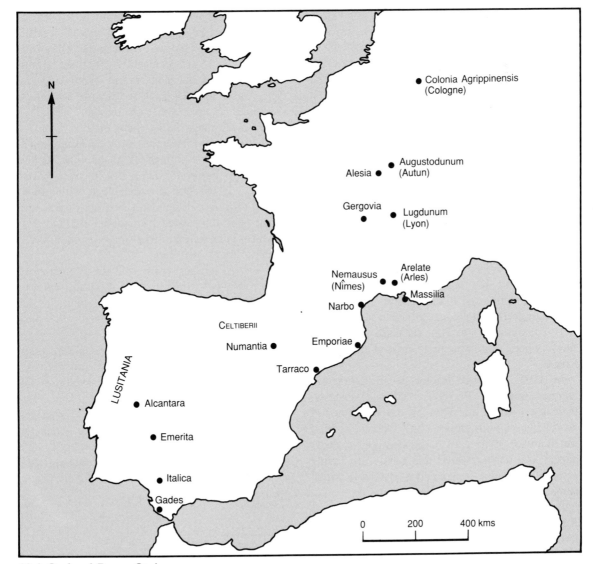

23.4 *Gaul and Roman Spain.*

from which an ampitheatre and some other buildings survive, is interesting in that Caesar settled the veterans of his famous Tenth Legion there.

A very famous colony was Lugdunum (Lyon), founded on Augustus' orders, to be the capital of the central province of Gaul, Gallia Lugdunensis. It contained a large forum which has been excavated, and not far from it was the palace where Claudius was born.

Lugdunum inevitably had its amphitheatre, a theatre which received its last and finest form under that lover of culture Hadrian. It also had a roofed music hall or odeon. In 177 the amphitheatre saw the terrible martyrdom of the Christians which marred the rule of Marcus Aurelius, however excellent a ruler he was in most ways. On the site of the amphitheatre was also found a bronze inscription, which bore the text of the speech Claudius made when he first admitted Gallic citizens to be senators. Lugdunum also contained a number of fine villas, evidence of its prosperity, and was watered by four aqueducts.

Not far off in Provence was Nemausus (Nîmes), a very well-known Roman foundation. It contained baths for the treatment of the sick, a facility of which Gaul had a number, and was surrounded by well constructed city walls. In the town was the elegant Maison Carrée of Nîmes, originally devoted to the worship of Augustus and Rome, that is a centre of emperor-worship, but preserved for our enjoyment because it continued to be used in later times, at one time as a church. The aqueduct which waters Nîmes is also famous, as the Pont du Gard remains to show where the aqueduct crossed the Gard River.

In 1907 the Abbé Sautel began excavating another town in Provence, Vasio (Vaison-la-Romaine), which like Pompeii has a number of lovely houses with gardens and frescos, so that McKendrick justly calls it the Pompeii of Provence.[3] The abbé restored this town with loving care. It also had a theatre and a basilica in which some shops have likewise been restored.

In the territory of the tribe of the Aedui is Augustodunum (Autun), founded by Augustus, famous for its university, the leading one in ancient Gaul, and for its vineyards. Unfortun-ately the university has not been discovered, only its amphitheatre.

The Villas and industries of Gaul

If France is still dominated by its farming lobby the rural interest began early, for in Roman Gaul literally hundreds of villas, which were basically the gentry's combined pleasure and farm-houses, have been found.

One of the most famous is at Chirargon near Martres-Toulosanes. The villa covered three hectares and its whole land sixteen. It really was sumptuous. It was originally built in the age of Augustus but kept being added to and reached its final and most glorious form under Antoninus Pius. It was made of marble, contained a bath block and summer houses and overlooked the River Garonne. Nearby were the farm buildings, including houses to accommodate about a hundred families, barns, sheds etc.

About thirty kilometres away at Montmaurin was the biggest and finest of all the villas. It had almost two hundred rooms and it covered four hectares. It too had a baths block with green-veined marble columns and summer-houses and it was centrally heated from under the floors. It was of a later date and the house as we know it dates to about A.D. 350.

It is then not surprising that the French word for a town, *ville*, derives from the Latin *villa*, as the *villa* with its surrounding workers' houses really was a town, and a number of villas have come down to our time as towns.

McKendrick mentions a famous collection made by Esperandieu of the arts and crafts of Gaul[4], which gives us a vivid impression of the activities of the inhabitants of Roman Gaul. The main industries were pottery (the red-glazed Arretine ware the Romans used), for which the principal centres were La Graufesenque, and Lezoux, glass-ware, for which Colonia Agrippinensis (Cologne) was renowned, and inevitably wine.

---

[3]P. McKendrick, *Roman France*, p. 105.
[4]*Ibid*, p. 106.

In antiquity the wine industry flourished especially on the Rhône, and Hermitage and Burgundy wines, which we still drink, go back to Roman times. Ausonius also spoke of the wine of Moselle! It is interesting in many ways then to see how many of the characteristics of France as we know it go back to very ancient times.

Date table

A.D.

138	Accession of Antoninus.
161	Death of Antoninus. Accession of M. Aurelius and Verus.
163–5	Parthian War, followed by plague.
167	Marcomanni revolt.
169	Death of Verus.
180	Death of M. Aurelius.

Select quotations

1 Marcus Aurelius, *Meditations*, I, 8:
(A description given by Marcus of Antoninus Pius.)
He was not given to bathing at all hours, or to heedless, extravagant building; he was not fussy about his food, or the quality and colour of his garments, or the appearance of his slaves. His clothes were supplied from his country estate down in Lorium, and most other things from Lanuvium. . . . He was in no way rude, overbearing or rough; as the saying is 'he never got into a lather about anything'. He thought everything out step by step, at leisure, without fuss, in an orderly, purposeful, methodical way. You could apply to him the remark made about Socrates that he could either give up or enjoy things which most could not resist and tended to indulge to excess.

2 Correspondence of M. Cornelius Fronto (Naber, p. 230):

(A letter from Antoninus to Fronto)
Greetings to my teacher!
I have just received your letter, which I will enjoy shortly, for at present duties hang over me which I cannot escape. Meanwhile I will give you the news you wish, briefly as I am indeed busy, that my little daughter is better and is running around the bedroom. (Antoninus then goes on to say that he is trying to take a more relaxed approach to his duties, as Fronto recommended.) But, I beg you, what is it you say at the end of your letter about your hand giving you pain? If the good gods grant my wish your pain will not have continued.
Farewell, best and most loving teacher.

Further reading

A. Garzetti, *From Tiberius to the Antonines*, Methuen, 1974.
Marcus Aurelius, *Meditations*, Penguin Classic.
Historia Augusta, Loeb.
P. McKendrick, *The Iberian Stones Speak*, Funk & Wagnalls, New York, 1969.
P. McKendrick, *Roman France*, G. Bell & Sons, London, 1971.

Topics for essays or discussion

1 Louis XV is reported to have said 'After me the flood', and his inaction did help cause the French Revolution. Could the same be said of Antoninus?
2 'The second century A.D. saw the rise of the welfare state concept in the Roman Empire'. Is this true, and if so, what were the consequences?
3 Why was the reign of Marcus Aurelius so disastrous? Was he in any way responsible? What reasons would you give for this return of chaos?
4 Compare and contrast the frontier problems faced by Vespasian and Marcus Aurelius.

Chapter 24

The Severi to Dioctetian

Sources

FOR THIS and the following chapter the main ancient sources are still Dio Cassius and the *Historia Augusta*, to which must be added the evidence of archaeology and inscriptions. However, this is not all. The spread of Christianity throughout the empire meant that there were a flood of religious pamphlets. They mainly dealt with religious matters, but they yield a modicum of historical information if carefully sifted. This gargantuan task was undertaken by the best modern historian of the period, A.H.M. Jones in his work, *The Late Roman Empire*. As in the earlier chapters we can also gain valuable information from legal writings as the *Digest*.

Commodus ushers in a period of anarchy

Commodus was a sad appendage to the series of able emperors that succeeded the Flavians. The last of the Antonines ushered in the anarchy which lasted for most of the third century.

Marcus Aurelius had abandoned the principle of adoption, being the first emperor who had a son to succeed him since Vespasian. Commodus was nineteen when his father died and his only serious interest was in gladiatorial shows, where he delighted the populace by participating in person.

He made peace on the Danube, in itself possibly not an unwise move, then returned to Rome, where he gave himself up to riotous living, while his favourites were allowed to govern. Unfortunately the youth was capricious, and as soon as he grew weary of his minister, he had him executed and replaced. When this became apparent, a conspiracy was formed, and he was killed.

The ensuing events followed much the same course as those which came after Nero's assassination. The Senate appointed as emperor a member of their body, Pertinax, already over eighty years old. He tried to restore order and financial solvency, but amid his economies made the mistake of giving no donative to the praetorian guard. They promptly assassinated him, and brought shame on the imperial post by putting it up for auction. The senator Julian, whose riches gave him this prize, was not to enjoy it for long.

Septimius Severus

The people were outraged and the provincial armies took action. The Syrian legions acclaimed their commander Niger as emperor, Britain did the same for Albinus, while on the Danube Septimius Severus was the nominee. Severus was of African origin. He was a capable and energetic commander, but as well had studied philosophy. He was forty-seven. His qualities made him a good choice for emperor, and he took immediate steps to secure the position. He divided his rivals by appointing Albinus as his Caesar and accordingly his heir, then marched east, where he met Niger, who was defeated and killed.

Albinus was not deceived by Severus' offer and began mobilising troops. Severus heard of this and set off with all speed, meeting him in Gaul. Albinus was defeated and committed suicide.

Severus executed huge numbers of the supporters of Niger and Albinus and confiscated their estates. The towns of Byzantium and Lugdunum, which had declared for them, were ruthlessly sacked. As some senators had given Albinus support, he included them in his purge. This may have contributed to his antisenatorial policy in subsequent years. His confiscations brought in vast quantities of booty for which he created a second imperial treasury, the *res privata*, distinct from the fiscus. This helped to complicate imperial finances in later ages.

The praetorian guard had always been a threat to the emperor whom it was supposed to protect. Severus dismissed it and installed in its place a force drawn from his own Danubian legions. The army had given him power, and it was rewarded. The pay of the soldiers was raised to five hundred denarii. This was not as generous as it might seem, for inflation was making their pay of less value, but it did represent a genuine increase. His confiscations helped to finance it, and he himself further devalued the denarius, which was now only half silver.

The number of legions was increased to thirty-three, and he changed the nature of their highest appointments. Perhaps partly from an anti-senatorial bias, but even more for practical reasons, he ceased to give them to senators, but to equites, many of whom rose from the ranks, via the post of centurion. He removed one anomaly by legalising marriages made by soldiers on active service. Such unions had long existed in practice, but the legislation made it easier for the men to provide for their wives and children.

The administration

The emperors before him had wooed the Senate. Severus did not use it to bolster his régime. He did, however, try to give himself prestige by encouraging emperor-worship, and he claimed descent from Marcus Aurelius. He took prompt action to nominate Caracalla, his elder son, as his successor, so that this question should not cause intrigue.

He did not trust the Senate, but he tried to assure himself of its support by filling the vacancies in its ranks from the East and from Africa, the areas with which he was associated. Even then he avoided as far as possible making them governors of provinces, preferring equestrians. As far as administration went, he followed Hadrian in giving increased prestige to the Imperial Council. This body was composed partly of senators, partly of equites, and included many lawyers. The emperor's deputy on the council was the praetorian prefect. This official was becoming continually more important, having control of the corn supply, and of all the forces in Italy. Severus first appointed to this post Plautianus, an ambitious and dangerous man, who came to wield great power until the emperor grew suspicious and had him killed. His successor was a renowned legal man, Ulpian.

A distinction was developing between two groups in society, and the justice granted them. The *honestiores*, who included all the army and all civilians of any rank, could be punished only by exile, whereas the unprivileged commoners, the *humiliores*, could be sent to a living death, working in the mines.

The provinces

The provinces of Syria and Britain, where Severus had encountered opposition, he divided into two provinces each, and created an additional province in Africa. The child endowment which Commodus had cancelled, he revived, and he undertook many public works. A number of these were in the provinces of Africa and the East, but in Rome there survives the arch of Septimius Severus at the end of the Forum, more noted for its size than its elegance.

Severus worked hard and successfully to consolidate his control of the empire, but it was natural for him to seek military renown as well. At the very beginning of his rule he had been about to attack Parthia for supporting Niger, but Albinus' preparations diverted him. In 197 he returned to that task and made it surrender the area of Mesopotamia, which had been briefly a province under Trajan. He returned to Rome in 199 after completing this mission but in 208 set out on the more difficult project of subduing

Scotland. The Scots and his failing health combined to defeat him, and in 211 he died in Britain on his way home, asking Caracalla as his last wish to share the rule with his brother Geta.

Caracalla and the end of the Severi

Caracalla had his father's military ability, but there is no evidence that he shared his cultural interests. In any case he had little time to develop them. He remained but a brief time in Rome. There the first question was which of the two brothers would survive, for they hated each other. Caracalla succeeded in murdering Geta first. After this savage deed, he assured the loyalty of his soldiers by raising their pay to 750 denarii.

Again, he was partly countering inflation, and again his action made the downward trend worse. To secure money, he deflated the currency once more. He also doubled the inheritance tax paid by Roman citizens, and in order to spread his net wider, made every free member of the empire a Roman citizen. Although his motives were dubious, his extension of citizenship was a significant step, completing a process that had been initiated in the earliest days of Rome.

While still in Rome he began the Baths of Caracalla which remain in the capital as our memorial of him. He did not await their completion. In 213 he set off to the East to attack Parthia and in 217 during the campaign was assassinated by his praetorian prefect, Macrinus.

Macrinus tried to seize power, but the army had always a certain loyalty to an imperial line, once established. Severus' sister-in-law made use of this loyalty to plant on the throne Elagabalus, one of her grandsons, who had been a priest of the sun god Elagabal. This strange young man brought his god to Rome, where he made worship an excuse for riotous living. The real ruler was his grandmother Maesa. When her puppet became too outrageous she had him removed, and replaced by her other grandson Alexander Severus.

This poor child (he was only fourteen) was guided by Maesa, and on her death by his own mother Mamaea, but though his rule was conscientious he was obviously unfitted to cope with any military crisis. The rulers of Parthia, who had held power for nearly five hundred years, were in a state of decline, and the attacks of Severus and Caracalla sealed their doom. In 227 a new Persian dynasty seized power, strongly nationalist in character, backed by a nationalist religious revival. The eastern nations, which had been Parthia for so long, now became Persia again. One cult which developed at this time, Manichaeism, spread to Africa, and St Augustine professed that belief before his conversion to Christianity.

The new dynasty was not long in trying out its strength against Rome. Alexander went east to meet their armies and fought an indecisive battle. From there he was called to the Rhine to face an invasion. The youth tried to buy off the Germans, but the army was outraged. They mutinied and killed him.

In this way ended the line of the Severi, who had for a short while stemmed the growing disruption of the empire. For the next fifty years the army took over. The history of this period contains their struggles against the Persians in the East, the Goths, Huns and Vandals on the Danube, and the Germans in the west. They created a series of emperors, mostly uncouth soldiers from their own ranks, who seldom lasted more than a few years, and as a rule met violent ends. Some few had more success, and began the process of reintegration which Diocletian was to complete after the storm was over.

The second ruler of the new Persian dynasty was Shapur I, its greatest king. He readily defeated the troops sent against him and spread Persian rule widely over the Middle East. Then in 253 Valerianus became emperor, and ruled with his son Gallienus. Shapur captured Valerianus when he led a force against him, but the son had better success. Despairing of holding a unified empire, he allowed a pretender, Postumus, to hold down the western provinces. Similarly, a Roman army, together with the ruler of an oasis town Palmyra, met Shapur, defeated him soundly and drove him out of Asia Minor, not to return. When the king of Palmyra (which Septimius Severus had brought to a high pitch of prosperity) died, his queen, Zenobia, ruled in his place. Thus Gallienus held the empire by allowing virtual secession of the west to Postumus, of the East to Zenobia. In 268 he was assassinated.

Aurelian

Two years later another strong ruler emerged, Aurelian. He gave up Dacia, which was stretching the frontiers too far, but in compensation he reunited the empire, sacking Palmyra (Zenobia was brought to Rome and married to a senator), and conquering the west again.

A massive inflation had been taking place. It had begun with the Severi, and by the time of Gallienus copper coinage had disappeared, while silver coins were only five per cent silver. Stability was only preserved by giving the soldiers much of their pay in kind. In short, the money economy was collapsing.

As if this were not enough, a huge plague swept over the empire under Gallienus, and broke out again several times later. This forced emperors to let German tribes settle in the areas thus emptied of people. These new settlers tilled the soil and provided recruits for the army. In this way the army grew more barbaric, but gained in strength. At the same time Gallienus and Valerianus began again to develop a crack division of troops to meet a particular crisis, as distinct from the ordinary frontier troops. Diocletian and Constantine developed this idea fully. It was Marcus Aurelius who first thought of this idea.

Diocletian restores order to the empire

It was in 285 that Diocletian became emperor and ended the era of chaos. He was from Dalmatia in the Danube area and was aged about forty. Fortunately for Rome he was a most able man, and a superb organiser.

He saw at once that the threats facing Rome could not be met by one man alone and appointed a fellow general and friend Maximian to rule and subdue the west. Next year Maximian was given the title of Augustus.

A pretender, Carausius, did arise, who gained control of Britain, but for the time being he was left in peace. Diocletian brought order on the Danube and in the East, and Armenia was forced to accept the position of a client kingdom once more.

By 293 Diocletian realised that if he was to control the whole of the empire he needed more assistance. Accordingly two Caesars were created to assist the two *Augusti*, Galerius in the east, Constantius in the west. Each was married to a daughter of their Augustus to cement the alliance, and the new rulers were given their tasks. To Galerius was assigned the Danubian area, while Diocletian attended to the Eastern frontier; Constantius was given the western section, including the rebellious Britain.

Constantius soon proved his value. Carausius was assassinated in 293, and three years later Constantius had reconquered the island. After this he drove the Germans back across the Rhine. Galerius had similar success with the Goths, who were expelled from the empire, and the frontier along the Danube was strengthened against renewed attack. Next Galerius went to meet the Persians, who had invaded Armenia. At first he was defeated, but then recovered, drove them back, and even restored to the Roman empire the province of Mesopotamia which Trajan and later Septimius Severus had briefly held.

There were now four emperors, and four courts. Diocletian, like the Severi, used emperor-worship to enhance the prestige of the rulers, and lent it a more Eastern aspect. He gave himself the title of Jovius (i.e., belonging to Jupiter) and Maximian of Herculius (belonging to Hercules). The emperors wore purple and many jewels, as well as carrying the diadem and sceptre, in short the apparel which royalty was to inherit in Europe from the Middle Ages on.

Access to the emperor became more difficult, and the Eastern habit of prostrating oneself in their presence was adopted.[1]

This ceremonial helped give dignity to the imperial position, but it would have been useless without competent government. As was noted earlier Diocletian was a superb organiser.

Diocletian's reforms

Basic to much of Diocletian's work was his financial reform. Inflation had made money virtually useless, and this fact he recognised. For a long time armies and governors had requisitioned food and other supplies, and this was now their main source of livelihood. Diocletian, with the help of his deputies, conducted a vast census of the empire, and assessed it on the basis of population for the poll tax, and of cultivated land for a land tax. The latter was subsequently given a fixed relation to the poll tax, so that there could be one unit of taxation.

The praetorian prefect, an official whose power was constantly increasing, had control of the levying of supplies. The new form of taxation was simply an extension of that levy, and he virtually became the treasurer, and now even issued a budget.

He would assess how much corn, leather, wine, wool and other commodities would be needed in the coming year, then divide the amount, on the basis of the census, among the provinces. The ones who suffered were the farmers and the local councils. The farmers did pay a high proportion of the tax. They were required to go back to their farms for the taking of the census, and this was used as an excuse for keeping them there later, even to making their farms hereditary, whether they wished it or not. The farmer became tied to the soil. Thus the basis of serfdom in the Middle Ages was laid.

The local councils were compelled to collect the taxes, and had to make up any deficiencies. For a long time local patriotism had led them to spend profusely on public buildings, and public shows in their district. Inevitably this weighed on them and made men reluctant to take on the function. Their taxation responsibility was the

last straw. Diocletian and his successors had to fight as hard to keep men on local councils, as to keep the peasant on the land.

Nevertheless, Diocletian did not allow the inflation to continue without a struggle. He did issue new coinage of better quality. His silver and copper coins were not a success, but his gold coin, the *aureus*, was more popular and showed the way for Constantine to make gold coinage the basis of a revived money economy. At the same time he tried to fix prices, and issued many edicts with this end in view. Here he was leading a lost cause. Black market operators sprang up at once, and made his laws a dead letter as soon as they appeared.

The new taxation meant a great increase in the administrative work of the provincial governors who had to see to the collection within their provinces. Diocletian also insisted that they take a more personal part in local legal cases. A governor simply could not handle all this work for a province of the old type. Diocletian solved this problem by increasing them to about one hundred, twice their former number, so that they were half the size they had been. Italy too was divided into provinces.

This huge number of provinces urgently required organisation, so they were divided into twelve dioceses under civil officials known as vicars. They were in turn responsible to the four praetorian prefects of the emperors. The vicars helped in supervising taxation. They were also supposed to hear appeals in law suits, but the tendency to carry appeals to the highest court possible, which was the praetorian prefect, meant that they were normally by-passed, and the post did not become very important.

The governors were tending to lose their military function, and under Diocletian civil and military careers grew more and more distinct. Late in his rule he began to appoint separate military leaders, *duces*, who at times were put under a senior leader, a *comes*, fore-runners of

---

[1]As a result of the autocratic nature of the emperor, the term 'dominate' is used to describe the manner of rule Diocletian fostered, as contrasted with the 'principate', which was the ideal advocated by Augustus.

the dukes and counts of the Middle Ages. The army was practically doubled under his rule, a process accelerated by the fact that there were four emperors each with an army. In all there were about seventy legions.

The number of court officials was similarly increased, both by Diocletian's reorganisation and by the fact that there were four courts (even if two were of lesser status, and doubtless less elaborate). No longer were the courts settled in one place. They had to be mobile, following the emperors in their wanderings, and they were given the appropriate title of *comitatus* (the accompanying band). The same title of comitatus was given to a crack division of the army, mainly cavalry, which was kept to meet an emergency attack as distinct from the *limitanei* or frontier troops.

Thus Diocletian brought order back to the harassed empire. By subdividing control and winning the loyalty of his colleagues he pushed back the barbarians. System and peace were re-established within the borders. The price paid was the enormous increase, both in the army, and, even more burdensome, in the bureaucratic body. Finally this burden was to prove too much, but for the moment the gains were worth the disadvantages.

It is not surprising that an emperor whose concepts were generally on a grand scale should also engage on ambitious public buildings. This he did, and he built many memorials of his reign in the eastern part of the empire, which was under his direct control. In Rome itself he built a new Senate House, but he is best remembered for the huge Baths of Diocletian which have been well preserved. Portion of them was made into a church by Michelangelo, and the baths now serve as a museum.

Persecution of the Christians. Diocletian retires

Towards the end of Diocletian's rule the persecution of Christians was renewed, a fact for which Diocletian's deputy Galerius is blamed, probably with justice. In 299 an edict was issued against them, but it was not until 303 that any

24.1 *The Catacombs where the early Christians buried their dead and sometimes sought refuge from persecution. As the burial places were dug out under inhabited areas, the Christians had to meet strict building code specifications to prevent cave-ins.*

action was taken. Some churches were destroyed and the clergy forced to sacrifice to the pagan gods. Even so the persecution was not carried out with any enthusiasm except in Galerius' domain, and in the west Constantius gave only token support.

In 305 Diocletian, who had been very ill, determined to retire. He forced a reluctant Maximian to do likewise, and made Constantius and Galerius Augusti, with Maximinus and Severus as their Caesars. This remarkable man then retired to the palace he had built himself in the East and cultivated his vegetable garden with the same devotion once given to an empire.

The African provinces

It is appropriate that we should end this chapter, which tells of the African emperors by examining the provinces of Africa. Once more it should be noted that Africa has been dealt with in the course of this history, but it is now worth examining it as a whole, with special consideration to what we learn from archaeology.

During the Republican period Africa played a very important role, when we think of Carthage and the Punic Wars, of the Jugurthine War, of the battle of Thapsus, of Antony and Cleopatra, of the battle of Actium, and finally of Augustus' special settlement of Egypt as his special domain.

By contrast Africa figured very little in the Imperial age, and it is significant that in the whole of that period one legion alone, the Third Augustan at Lambaesis, together with a cohort stationed for the governor at Carthage, were enough to keep peace in Africa.

In the east of North Africa we had Egypt and the Greeks, notably at Alexandria and Cyrene. To the west, there was a native population of Numidians, the Roman rulers and the Roman settlers, especially the colonies of the veterans. A very strong Punic influence still persisted, so that the language was used in the later years of the empire and even Punic titles were often used for magistrates' titles.

Although Egypt was the main source of wheat for Rome in this area the other African provinces also played a considerable role, for North Africa was much more fertile than it now is, the change being partly due to a climatic change and partly to the depredations of man. Another most significant export was olive oil, that staple item for the peoples of Italy, for the olive grew abundantly in that country. The final, most infamous export was of wild beasts for the games. Here Rome had an insatiable appetite, and in the mosaics in North Africa we have scenes showing the snaring of animals for this purpose.

The first important city we come to travelling west is Lepcis Magna, the birthplace of Septimius Severus. It was of Phoenician origin, and it is not hard to see why it was founded. North Africa had few natural harbours and Lepcis Magna had one. It was a very prosperous town, boasting the largest amphitheatre in North Africa, two-thirds the size of the Colosseum. It also had a theatre, built in the time of Augustus by Annobal Rufus, a man whose Punic connections are obvious.

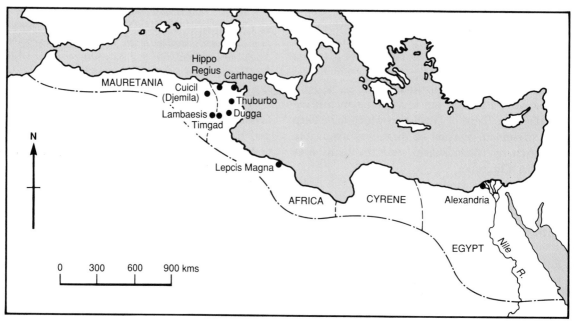

24.2 *Roman North Africa.*

24.3 *The ruins of the wealthy Roman town of Lepcis Magna.*

The same man built the very fine market-place of the town. It was a busy place, for Lepcis Magna was the port for one of the caravan trains from the south, and it was famous for its anchovy sauce as well as olive oil. Some very fine baths dated to the day of Hadrian.

Further west lies Thugga (Dugga) a little town somewhat inland. It was of Phoenician origin but then was made a Roman colony. It was not an important town, but that very fact has meant that its remains are in good condition. The main public building in Thugga was its Capitolium, to Jupiter, Juno and Minerva, but it had also a market-place and a theatre.

Not far from Thugga but a little nearer the coast lies Thuburbo. This town is like a number we have discussed—native and Punic origin, then turned into a Roman colony, with a Capitolium and, a special feature, a number of fine mosaics found on the floors of its houses.

Our next two finds are of a different type, Lambaesis, home to Africa's solitary legion, and Timgad, the home of this legion's veterans. Of the quarters of the legion only the forecourt of its main hall remains, but it is quite an imposing building. More remains of Timgad. This colony was built specifically for the legion by Trajan and it was very different from the other haphazard and rather charming towns we have considered. Like the Roman camps it was built on grid fashion, and walled. It had its Capitolium and its theatre, which looked upon the most imposing remains, the triumphal arch, set in the middle of the western wall, but now standing alone.

North of Lambaesis and Timgad lay another very important town, Cuicil (Djemila). It had had a local origin then a Punic influence, and was made a colony for veterans by Nerva. It is one of the largest cities of Roman Africa and contained many fine buildings. A road led from it direct to Lambaesis, and it was at the cross-roads of a number of trade-routes. In its forum was a triumphal arch to Caracalla and Septimius

Severus. It contained a cloth-market and its finest building was a temple to Septimius Severus, containing a bust of Septimius and his wife. His bust survives.

Cuicil was a very prosperous town. It had two theatres, and a very fine market building erected by Cosinius, with seventeen shops in it and an area for official weights housed in an office.

Hippo Regius (Annaba) was not a Roman colony. It was a port, almost certainly established by the Phoenicians, and later one of the capitals of Numidia. It was an important centre for the export of wheat and olive oil and also of wild beasts for the games. A mosaic in one of its houses portrayed the capture of beasts for this purpose. For us Hippo is probably best known because St. Augustine was its bishop and it was there that he wrote his book *The City of God*. He died there in A.D. 430, when the city was being besieged by the Vandals.

Although Roman Africa was not very active historically, it is interesting in the history of Christianity. As we noted, St. Augustine lived there, and so did Tertullian, who wrote many scholarly works on Christianity, which were to have a profound effect on the development of the Catholic Church. He lived in Carthage a little later than Apuleius, who also lived there. So too did St. Cyprian, another major figure in the early years of Christianity, not for scholarly writings but for his sermons and letters, noted for their charm and readableness. So, if we consider them and Apuleius and Fronto, north Africa did play a very significant role in the intellectual life of the later Roman empire.

Date table

A.D.
180–92   Commodus.
193–211   Septimius Severus.
211–17   Caracalla.
218–22   Elagabalus.

227   Sassanid Dynasty gains power in Persia.
222–35   Alexander Severus. End of Severan line.
235   Period of chaos. Maximinus made emperor.
238   Gordian III.
244   Philip the Arab.
249   Decius.
253–68   Gallienus. (Valerian 253–259.)
268   Claudius Gothicus.
270   Aurelian.
275   Tacitus.
276   Probus.
282   Carus.
285   Accession of Diocletian.
293   Diocletian sets up tetrarchy.
303   Persecution of Christians resumes.
305   Abdication of Diocletian and Maximian.

(The dates and names of the emperors in the period of chaos are given for the sake of formal completeness only. Few of them have significance.)

Select quotations

1 *Historia Augusta*, 19:
(Description of Septimius Severus.)
He was so simply attired that even his tunic had barely a trace of purple in it and he flung a shaggy cloak over his shoulders. He was a very moderate eater, fond of the beans which were the diet of his countrymen. He indulged in wine on occasion, but frequently ate no meat. He was a big man, good-looking, with a long beard and curly white hair. He had a commanding presence and a pleasant voice, but never lost his African accent, even in old age. He was very popular after he died, as then feelings of envy had subsided and fear of his cruelty.

2 *Select Papyri*, Loeb, I. 133:
(Letter from a schoolboy to his father in the early third century.)

Greetings to my worthy father from Thonis. First of all I pray daily that you and all the family keep well. Now look, this is my fifth letter I am writing to you, and you have only written once and not told me how you were, nor have you come to visit me. You promised to come, but you didn't do so, to see whether the teacher is looking after me properly or not. And he himself asks me nearly every day, 'Isn't he coming yet?' And I simply say 'Yes'. So hurry up and come, so he may teach me as he is anxious to do. . . . Look after yourself, father, and may you and my brothers long prosper, as I pray you will. Remember our pigeons.

Further reading

Refer again to *Historia Augusta*.

A.H.M. Jones, *Constantine and the Conversion of Europe*, English University Press, 1961.

Gibbon: *Decline and Fall* I, 4–13.

A.H.M. Jones, *The Later Roman Empire*, Blackwell, 1964, vol I, chaps. 1–2. Despite the portentous size of the work, 4 vols. in all, it gives a very clear account in the first volume of the events of this period.

M. Wheeler and R. Wood, *Roman Africa in Colour*, Thames & Hudson, London 1966.

Topics for essays or discussion

1 'With the Severi, rule by the army became a reality.' Is this a fair judgment?
2 Why did chaos overtake the Roman Empire in the third century? Why was there not an absolute breakdown and how was order restored?
3 'Divide and rule.' Diocletian could be said to have given a new interpretation to this maxim. Explain.
4 The term 'dominate' is often used to describe Diocletian's manner of rule, contrasted with the 'principate' of Augustus. Would you consider that the term could be applied to any emperors from an earlier period?
5 Analyse the breakdown of the money economy in the third century. How did Diocletian cope with the problem?
6 Discuss the provinces under Diocletian.
7 'Diocletian ushered in the society of the Middle Ages.' Is this a true statement?
8 Discuss the growth of bureaucracy under Diocletian. What were its advantages and disadvantages?
9 How did Diocletian succeed in making the army once more the servant of the empire, not its master?
10 Compare and contrast the achievements of Augustus and Diocletian.

Chapter 25

Constantine and his successors

Sources

FOR THIS FINAL PERIOD our main sources remain Dio Cassius and the *Historia Augusta*, but there are some other interesting writers to consider. For one, the Emperor Julian, so disliked by the Christians, with whom he equally did not feel in sympathy, was one of our literate emperors, and some of his writings, somewhat satiric in character, have been preserved, giving us an interesting insight into one of our characters.

The main new force to appear at this period is of course Christianity, and there are some writers from the Christian ranks who make an interesting contribution. One is of course St. Augustine himself, particularly his *Confessions* and his letters. There is also a chronicler of the Church, Eusebius, who wrote an *Ecclesiastical History*.

The death of Diocletian

After the retirement of Diocletian and Maximian, it seemed at first that Galerius held supreme control of the empire. The two Caesars were personally devoted to him, and he even had Constantine, Constantius' son, at his court, to serve if necessary as a guarantee of the good conduct of his father. There were, however, other factors present, which were eventually to prove fatal to him. In particular, Maximian had retired with the utmost reluctance, and both he and his son Maxentius were indignant that the latter had not been made a Caesar (even though it would have been a most unsuitable appointment).

The balance began to swing rapidly. Trouble arose in Britain, and Constantius went over to deal with it. He requested that Constantine be sent to help him. Permission was reluctantly given, and Constantine set off post-haste before Galerius could change his mind. When his father died in Britain during the same year (306), the troops hailed Constantine as Augustus. Galerius with ill grace granted him the title of Caesar, making Severus the Augustus in Constantius' place.

Maxentius had now been passed over a second time. Both he and his father revolted and marched on Rome. Severus was killed in the ensuing struggle, and it seemed as if chaos was about to return, especially as Maximian and Maxentius fell out and made separate claims to power. Galerius saved the immediate situation by calling together the rivals and forcing them to agree to a new proposal. Galerius and a fellow-general of his were to be Augusti and Constantine and Daia Caesars.

The agreement was only temporary. Maximian tried to stir up trouble in Constantine's territory, and met his end in suspicious circumstances. Constantine came into the open and claimed imperial power for himself under the protection of the God of the Sun (Sol). In particular he refused to recognise Maxentius, who had gained control of Italy.

The persecution of Christians was continuing, but it was an omen of the coming change when in 311 Galerius ordered it to stop. He died in the same year.

The Battle of the Milvian Bridge

In 312 Constantine gathered his forces and invaded Italy, taking the Christian cross as his emblem. He met Maxentius outside Rome in the battle of the Milvian Bridge. Maxentius was defeated and killed, and Constantine entered Rome in triumph. The Arch of Constantine commemorates these events.

Constantine's first act was to abolish the praetorian guard which had made and unmade so many emperors, and have their barracks destroyed. He was left with two other duly appointed rulers of the empire, Daia in the East, Licinius on the Danube. This state of affairs he tolerated, at least for the time being.

Constantine's victory had been a triumph for Christianity, although it would be a mistake to think that the emperor immediately abandoned paganism. Rather, he made the best of both worlds with a certain illogicality, but for the benefit of peace within the empire. He did however give Christianity progressively more favourable treatment, and insisted that both Daia and Licinius cease persecuting the religion.

The rise of the Donatist and Arian heresies

Constantine's patience was rewarded in 313 when Daia attacked Licinius. Daia was defeated and killed. This left only Licinius, a man with whom Constantine had no sympathy.

In the next few years problems arose to distract the two rulers from their rivalry. In Africa and in the East controversy arose in the Christian Church. They had one common

25.1 *The arch of Constantine, erected in* A.D. *312.*

feature. In both places the group of Christians who had held firm under persecution were indignant when their weaker brethren, who came back to the Church when persecution stopped, were given positions of importance within it.

In Africa the rebellious group was the Donatists. Constantine called the disputants together in 313 and tried to make them reach agreement. His efforts failed, but set a precedent, in that the bishops recognised his right to summon them and adjudicate in their quarrels, in short recognised him as having authority over them.

In the East Arius led the Arian sect. It also looked harshly on those who had not resisted persecution, but as well Arius preached that Christ was not of one substance with the Father, but only like him. Licinius had less patience than Constantine, and less sympathy with the whole religion. When their quarrel grew bitterer he finally dismissed Christians from civilian office and from his army. As well, he declared that they should only hold meetings in the open air.

25.2 *Constantine, Roman emperor* A.D. *307–37.*

Constantine defeats his last rival

In 324 the truce between the two emperors ended. The Goths crossed the Danube. Constantine went to meet them. Licinius accused him of trespassing on his territory, and soon there was open conflict. Licinius was defeated, captured and subsequently executed. Constantine was now sole ruler of the Roman empire.

With his new position he inherited the Arian problem. In 325 he called the first ecumenical council of his bishops to discuss the issue. The opposition to Arius was led by the Bishop of Alexandria. The meeting did not settle the dispute, but it did result in the drawing up of the articles of faith of Christianity and marked its recognition as the official faith of the empire. Arius was excommunicated.

Almost Constantine's last act was to call in 335 another conference of the still warring bishops. He forced them to readmit Arius to the Church, but the latter died before the decision could be carried out.

Constantinople

Even when Constantine was not yet head of the whole empire, he had begun granting privileges to the Church, recognising the courts of the bishops, and declaring Sunday a general holiday. He now gave back such of their property as had been confiscated and made large gifts to them. This set the fashion, and it became popular to leave property to the Church, which as a result increased greatly its material possessions.

Christianity inevitably also became more socially acceptable. Membership had been mainly confined to the lower classes, but it now spread to the middle and upper groups of society.

Constantine celebrated his victory over Licinius by building a new capital on the site of Byzantium, named, as was the usual fashion, after himself, Constantinople. It took five years to build, and the many churches he constructed made it a memorial to Christianity as well as to Constantine.

Constantine organises his army and court

In his organisation of the army he developed further many of Diocletian's ideas. Military and civil careers were made almost entirely separate, and the frontier armies were put under the control of the duces whom Diocletian had instituted.

He enlarged the cavalry force which Diocletian had attached to his court, and gave them the title of *comitatenses*. They received the privileges enjoyed formerly by the praetorian guard, which he had disbanded, and served to meet any onslaught on a particular section of the frontier. German troops he held in high regard, and, to the indignation of the conservative, many of their officers were advanced to high positions.

In his civil administration Constantine also followed in Diocletian's footsteps. His court comitatus had to be mobile too, in order to keep with the emperor, but he did grant members of this court, the comites, many privileges to compensate. Unlike the soldier emperors that succeeded the Antonines, Constantine had no prejudice against the senatorial class, and indeed many of them rose to high office in his service. The praetorian prefects held their powerful position. They were now the final court of appeal in law. No case could be taken beyond them, even to the emperor.

One new post, the *magister equitum*, was created. He corresponded roughly to secretary of state, and had varied duties. He was in charge of the *agentes in rebus*. These men were the imperial couriers, who carried the emperor's commands to the most distant parts of the empire.[1]

Finance and taxes

Diocletian had minted a gold coinage, the aureus. Constantine did likewise, entitling his coin the *solidus*. He was able to mint on a more extensive scale than Diocletian, as melted down pagan statues made a welcome addition to his supply of precious metals. It is a sad reflection on the inflation of money which never ceases that one descendant of the *solidus*, which takes its name from it, is the French *sou* or half-penny.

Nevertheless, although the new issue was in time to bring about a return to a money economy, this change did not take place till the next century, the fifth. For the moment, taxation and most business transactions continued to be carried on in kind. The middle class still bore the brunt of the collection of taxes. As a result Constantine issued edicts on the lines of those Diocletian proclaimed, preventing men from deserting municipal duties. Peasants too continued to be tied to the soil, and it was found necessary to make a similar restriction on craftsmen, who were in this period organised in guilds. They too were forbidden to leave their trade, and both land-ownership and trade were made hereditary.

Constantine dies

Towards the end of his life Constantine became less active and lived in semi-retirement at Constantinople. The main business of the empire he left to his sons, who were given the rank of Caesars. The three who survived him were called with true royal egotism Constantine, Constantius and Constans.

In 337 he died after a brief illness, being baptised on his death-bed by the bishop Eusebius.

On the death of Constantine the rule passed to Constans, Constantius and Constantine, with the approval of the army, which always tended to favour a continuing dynasty. The triple rule did not last. Not long after, Constantine attacked Constans and was killed. Ten years later Constans was assassinated, and Constantius II was left alone. He put down the dissident elements, but soon felt the need of a helper. He therefore chose a relative of Constantine, Julian, then aged only twenty-four, but already showing ability as a soldier.

---

[1]The view that these men became a kind of secret police is discounted by Jones (vol. 2, p. 581), although he admits that Constantius II used them for such a purpose.

Julian succeeds as emperor

Julian immediately proved his worth by driving the barbarians out of Gaul. He then proceeded to clear up taxation in that country, which was a highly corrupt state. Unfortunately he proved too popular for Constantius, who grew suspicious and began to intrigue against him. Julian's troops supported him, and when the rift failed to heal, he reluctantly marched against Rome. He did not, however, have to meet his former benefactor in battle; for he died before Julian arrived.

Julian the Apostate, as he is known, ruled only briefly, but the efficiency he had already shown helped to bring some solvency to the empire. He pruned the bureaucracy, which was swelling out of all proportion, and practised various economies. In particular, the public post, originally intended to provide conveyance for those travelling on the emperor's business, was being used by more and more officials, and becoming a financial burden on the state. It was cut back drastically.

Julian had been a pagan (though in secret) before his accession, and he was a great admirer of Greek culture. On becoming emperor he proclaimed general religious toleration. This was especially welcome to the army, which had been slow in accepting Christianity. Church privileges were cancelled and heresies were no longer persecuted. They flourished accordingly.

A troubled period follows Julian's death

In 363 Julian set out to meet a threat from Persia, was wounded and died in the same year. One effect of his reign was that a halt was called to the persecution of pagans for thirty years.

With Julian ended the line of Constantine and power returned to the army. By 364 they had selected Valentinian, who in turn chose Valens as his fellow-Augustus. They were both Christians, and though not cultured, they were conscientious men. Like the military emperors before them, they tended to favour the military class in administration at the expense of the Senate.

Valentinian was concerned at the cost of litigation. It had become increasingly common to appeal to higher courts and this, coupled with the complexity of Roman law, was putting justice out of the reach of the ordinary man. He set up the office of *defensor*, who, as in the case of the public solicitor or the chamber magistrate in our own day, gave legal aid to the poor.

In 375 Valentinian died, to be succeeded by his youthful son Gratian. He was spared a very troubled period. In the following year the Huns descended from the north. The Goths fled before them and sought sanctuary. At first Valens granted this and enlisted a large number in his army, but then he became afraid they might be disloyal, and treacherously massacred many of them. The rest joined an army of Goths that was coming south, and swiftly took revenge. They met Valens and defeated him with great slaughter, the emperor himself being among the dead.

Gratian was now alone, and appointed Theodosius as Augustus in the East. He made peace with the Goths, many of whom settled near the Danube, but Gratian was unable to control his troops. He was assassinated in 384, leaving Theodosius as sole emperor.

Theodosius was a less tolerant man than his predecessors. He reopened the attack on the Arians, and once more began persecuting the pagans. In his time St. Augustine was bishop of Hippo and corresponded with him. He had a general of ability, Stilicho.

The end of the Roman empire

When Theodosius died in 395, he left the empire to his sons Arcadius in the East, Honorius in the West. Honorius was only ten years old, and even Arcadius was not more than eighteen. Although the army's loyalty for an imperial line averted immediate disaster, it put the youths very much at the mercy of their elders. In the West that meant the army, and especially Stilicho; in the East the court and its intriguing palace officials.

It was soon apparent that no love was lost between the two halves of the empire, and that

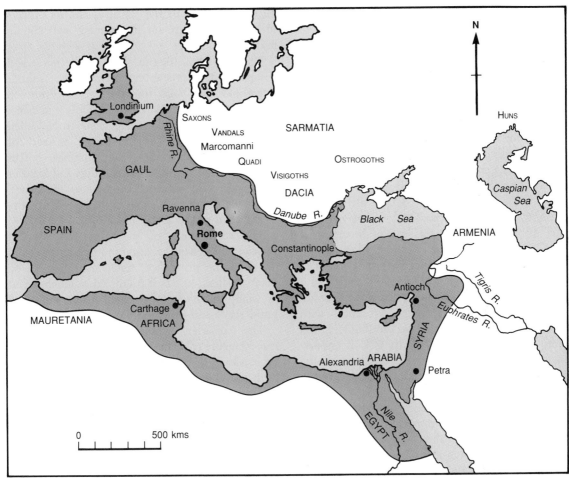

25.3 *The Roman empire in the fourth century* A.D.

Stilicho was the object of jealousy and suspicion. Alaric of the Visigoths saw in this his opportunity and led his army south. Stilicho tried to oppose him, but was repeatedly stopped from a decisive engagement. In the end Alaric was actually given a place in the army of the East. He fell out with his masters, marched on Italy, and was repelled. Then the Vandals invaded Gaul. Once more Alaric's services were in demand. This was followed by a further reaction. Stilicho was accused in 408 of plotting with Alaric and was executed. The army, which had not approved of the favour shown to the Gothic troops, rose and massacred many of them.

Alaric finally grew weary of the Romans, marched on Rome, and when negotiations failed entered and sacked it in 410. He died in the same year.

After this, Rome fell under the control of many soldier rulers of diverse barbarian culture, while the tradition of the Roman empire was preserved in the Byzantine culture of the East. Justinian (527–65), with the help of his general Belisarius, did briefly seize back some of the western possessions, including Rome itself, but the recovery was transient. More important was Justinian's final codification of Roman law. In 629 the Saracens swarmed over most of the Byzantine empire, so that even in the East the temporal power of the empire was eclipsed. But that concerns a student of the Middle Ages, and is another story.

Roman society in the fourth century

In the fourth century the Senate had ceased to have even nominal power. The body which counted for most in the counsels of the emperor was the *consistory*, which grew from the imperial council of the earlier empire, and more generally his court or *comitatus*. State decisions were very much subject then (as indeed they always tend to be) to pressure groups. The army played little part in power politics; for, except in crises, it tended to mind its own business, even though it had always to be treated with respect. The Church also was then too much occupied with internal strife, and in particular with the heresies which never ceased to plague it, to speak with a united voice. This left the big landholders (and there the Senate made up for its lack of importance as an actual governing body) and the bureaucracy itself, which this period had bred in such huge numbers.

Roman law, though excellent in principle, was beyond the small man's purse. In particular, the growing habit of appealing to the highest court possible on any occasion meant that the rich litigant had everything on his side.

The bureaucracy, which Diocletian did so much to organise, achieved something of what he planned, and helped to keep the empire working in troubled times. It was, however, a body of limited imagination. At the lower end it was unadventurous, and the clerk, like so many people in the late Roman empire, tended to become hereditary. On the higher levels appointments were made too much through influence and patronage, and were rotated too frequently (in order to grant more people favours) for efficient men to be selected, or for anybody, once selected, to come to know his job.

The army

The army was largely exempt from this criticism. That body had not lost its fine traditions, despite all the pressures of the century, and its officers low and high were on the average well chosen and competent.

The division begun by Diocletian, and completed by Constantine between the frontier army and the crack imperial force, continued under Constantine's successors. Only the name changed. The imperial force came to be called the *palatini* or palatinate corps, instead of *comitatenses*. Later too, the palatinate forces often served at points of the frontier, and frontier forces were on occasion brought to the court. Then the distinction came to be one of quality rather than of the actual place of service.

The recruitment of the army was part of Diocletian's general taxation in kind, and worked on the same principles. Each area supplied so many soldiers, just as it produced so much wheat or wine, and likewise so much forced labour to build roads and other public works.

The barbarian communities came to play an ever bigger role in the army at this time, especially in the frontier forces or *limitanei*. They even came to be used as independent troops under their own chiefs, being called federate forces. Alaric was a famous example of such a chief.

The Church

The Church, once Constantine gave it official recognition, developed its own organisation under its bishops, following in some sort the organisation of the Roman Empire. Among the bishops themselves there was at first no undisputed hierarchy. They could and did meet and discuss policy under the emperor. The bishop of Rome began very early to claim seniority on the score of the city's connection with Peter, but this claim was not universally recognised. Carthage exercised despotic rule in Africa, Alexandria in Egypt, and further east, Constantinople laid its own claims.

The clergy were recruited from the free citizens. Slaves and serfs were not as a rule accepted. The military rarely joined their ranks. In the fourth century a new institution arose within the Church, the monastery. It did not, however, become really widespread until the next century.

Meanwhile paganism lived on, especially among the peasants (and some conservative aristocrats). They were generally tolerated, at least until Theodosius, and so too were the Jews, who lived as a race apart, rarely engaging in public life, civil or military.

Education

Education continued to flourish. It was needed; for bureaucracy requires literacy. The lower schools provided the clerks, the schools or rhetoric the higher officials. The higher education (but not the elementary schools) was encouraged and subsidised by the state, as it had been, off and on, ever since the Flavian emperors, but particularly under their successors. Whereas Greek and Latin had been taught in the early empire, in this later period East and West began to split. Law, it is true, continued to be the province of Latin everywhere in the fourth century, but in most matters the West now learnt and used Latin, having only the elements of Greek, while the East used Greek and made less and less use of Latin.

Nevertheless, the schools and the university towns kept up the tradition of Classical culture, and even after the West fell, the Byzantine Empire preserved the Greek Classics for modern times.

Why did the Roman Empire fall?

The final question, which is regularly asked, is why the Roman Empire fell. This question seems an impertinence when we consider that the empire lasted longer than any other before or since except China. Still, some answer must be given. On this there is disagreement. Rostovtseff gave some importance to the drifting apart of city and country, and to the breakdown of communications, with the development of local industry, on the Rhine and on the Danube. Jones, more recently, doubts if trade was ever general enough to be a vital factor.

There was some decline in the middle classes. Again Jones suggests that this should not be exaggerated, and in particular that they did not suffer as much economically as some have supposed. Still, they did suffer loss, and in particular were drained off to supply the ranks of the new bureaucracy and the clery.

More important, and here authorities old and new seem to agree, the frontiers were simply too long to be defended efficiently, and with the passage of time the strain was felt increasingly. The terrible plagues that swept the empire under Marcus Aurelius had lost their force by Diocletian, and the diminution of manpower was made up by natural processes, and by letting in barbarian tribes. The Rhine-Danube frontier in particular was too long to man and, as well, with primitive methods of manufacture and transport, too difficult to supply and feed.

Moreover, the burden of supply the army, the ever increasing bureaucracy, the beautiful but unproductive cities, all this fell on the peasants. They were taxed heavily, often too heavily, so that they tended to desert the less fertile lands which would not produce enough to feed them and the tax collectors.

Then, and this was really the central problem, on this organisation, stretched as it was to breaking point, a new strain was imposed. With the fourth century came increased pressure on the frontiers, partly from the Goths, partly from the Huns, who, even before they attacked the empire themselves, drove the Goths before them, so that they in turn crossed the imperial frontiers. The additional burden of this new threat to security was too much for Rome. It resulted first in the partitioning of the empire, so that the rulers could each cope with the sector assigned to them. Finally, when even subdivision was not enough, it led to the abandonment of the Western half and the withdrawal to the Eastern sector which was smaller, easier to defend, and less threatened by the main invading forces. So the Roman empire, which had brought unity and peace to the Mediterranean world for so many centuries, finally abandoned its task.

Date table

A.D.
312   Battle of Milvian Bridge. Accession of Constantine.
324   Constantine rules alone. Begins to build Constantinople. (Finished 330.)
325   Council of Nicaea.
337   Death of Constantine.
361–63 Julian the Apostate.
364   Accession of Valentinian and Valens.
379–95 Theodosius rules, at first in partnership, then alone.
386   Augustine converted to Christianity.
410   Goths under Alaric sack Rome.

Select quotations

1 *Works of the Emperor Julian* (Loeb), I. 4: Hymn to King Helios (i.e. to the Sun-God). *I think that what I am about to say concerns all 'who draw breath and walk upon the earth', who partake of existence, of soul and of reason, and not least of them all myself. For I am a disciple of King Helios. At home I have more precise proofs of this fact. But I am permitted to say, without contravening what is holy, that ever since I as a child an immense longing for the god's rays pervaded my soul, and from boyhood I was so completely orientated towards his heavenly light that I not only yearned to gaze intently on him alone, but even when I encountered a clear and cloudless night I thought of nothing else, but drank in the beauty of the sky.*

2 St Augustine, *Select Letters* (Loeb), No. 11: (Letter to Eusebius written in A.D. 396.) *Not to mention other things, what could be more outrageous, may I ask, than what has now occurred? A young man is taken to task by his bishop for beating his mother like a madman again and again, and not even sparing the frame that brought him into the world on the days when our harsh laws themselves spare the most wicked criminals (i.e. at Easter). The fellow threatens his mother that he will go over to the Donatists and murder the woman whom he is accustomed to thrash with a ferocity beyond belief.*

Further reading

St Augustine, *Select Letters*, Loeb.
Eusebius, *The History of the Church*, Penguin Classics.
A.H.M. Jones, *The Later Roman Empire I*, chapters, 3–6. Also I, chapters 11 ff. for an account of the society and administration of the period.
W.C. Wright, *Works of the Emperor Julian*, Loeb.

Topics for essays or discussion

1 'Constantine reaped where Diocletian sowed.' Do you agree?
2 Analyse the growth of divided rule in the Roman Empire. When did it begin and what were the results?
3 In the fourth century, we are told, the empire was controlled by pressure groups. Was this a new phenomenon? Make a comparison with some earlier period.
4 With Constantine Christianity ceased to be an oppressed religion. What problems did it then encounter, and how did it deal with them?
5 Why did the centre of the empire move eastwards in the fourth century? To what extent did this fact cause the break between East and West?
6 To what factors do you attribute the collapse of the Roman Empire?
7 What economic problems confronted the later Roman Empire? To what extent did they solve them?
8 Which contributed most to the empire's stability in imperial times, its army or its bureaucracy?

Index

Notes